DOWN, UP, AND OVER

"Dwight Hopkins's powerful and thoughtful study illustrates how black faith has been the heart of the black community and instrumental in the construction of black history. Hopkins's work is detailed yet accessible, designed for scholars as well as students of both African American theology and social history."

> — **Manning Marable,** Director of the Institute for Research in African-American Studies, Columbia University

"Dwight Hopkins has written a major contribution to the continued development of black liberation theology. He shows that it has no future independent of the resources of its slave past."

> — **James H. Cone,** Briggs Distinguished Professor of Theology, Union Theological Seminary, New York City

"*Down, Up, and Over* is as rich a resource for biblical scholars and preachers as it is for theologians. It is powerful testimony to how African American slaves reconfigured the biblical faith, which the slave master and slave apologist intended as a tool of oppression, into a theology of resistance and liberation."

> — **Brian K. Blount,** Associate Professor of New Testament, Princeton Theological Seminary

Also by Dwight N. Hopkins

Introducing Black Theology of Liberation (1999)

Black Faith and Public Talk:
Essays in Honor of James H. Cone's Black Theology and Black Power
(1999, editor)

Liberation Theologies, Post-Modernity, and the Americas
(1997, co-editor)

Changing Conversations:
Religious Reflection and Cultural Analysis
(1996, co-editor)

Shoes That Fit Our Feet:
Sources for a Constructive Black Theology
(1993)

Cut Loose Your Stammering Tongue:
Black Theology in the Slave Narratives
(1991, co-editor)

We Are One Voice:
Essays on Black Theology in South Africa and the U.S.A.
(1989, co-editor)

Black Theology in the U.S.A. and South Africa:
Politics, Culture, and Liberation
(1989)

DOWN, UP, AND OVER

Slave Religion and Black Theology

DWIGHT N. HOPKINS

Fortress Press
Minneapolis

*For the 100 million Africans
of faith stolen in the European slave trade
and dragged to the Americas;
and for the future generations of black folk of faith
who will co-constitute a New Self
and a New Common Wealth*

DOWN, UP, AND OVER
Slave Religion and Black Theology

Cover art: *The Shout,* 1988, oil on masonite, 36" x 24" © Jonathan Green, Naples, Florida; collection of Martin Luther Polite, Esq. Used by permission.
Author photo: University of Chicago
Cover design: Beth Wright
Interior design: Peregrine Graphics Services

Scripture quotations from the New Revised Standard Version Bible are copyright © 1989 by the Division of Christian Education of the National Council of the Churches of Christ in the USA and are used by permission.

Library of Congress Cataloging-in-Publication Data
Hopkins, Dwight N.
    Down, up, and over: slave religion and Black theology / Dwight N. Hopkins.
        p. cm.
    Includes bibliographical references and index.
    ISBN 978-0-8006-2723-2 (alk. paper)
        1. Black theology. I. Title.

BT82.7 .H663 2000
230'.089'96073—dc21

99-54737

The paper used in this publication meets the minimum requirements of American National Standard for Information Sciences—Permanence of Paper for Printed Library Materials, ANSI Z329.48-1984.

Manufactured in the U.S.A.   AF 1-2723
   12   11   10   09   08   2   3   4   5   6   7   8   9   10

CONTENTS

Preface vii
Acknowledgments xi
Introduction 1

PART ONE
Historical Black Theology:
Religious Formation of Race in American Culture 11

CHAPTER 1. *Two Faces of Protestantism*
and American Culture 13
    Two Arrivals 13
    Slavery in American Culture 19
    Cultural and Religious Justifications 26
    Conclusion 37
    Notes 42

CHAPTER 2. *From Sunup to Sundown—*
Slavemasters Constitute the African American Self 51
    Black Labor for White Profit 53
    Networks of Discipline, Control, and Reclassification 66
    Architecture of Slavery Churches 83
    Conclusion 93
    Notes 95

CHAPTER 3. *From Sundown to Sunup:*
The African American Co-Constitutes the Black Self 107
    West African Religions: A Background 109
    Seizing Sacred Domains 116
    A Divine Right to Resist 128
    Creating a Syncretized Religion 135
    Conclusion 145
    Notes 147

PART TWO
Constructive Black Theology: The Spirit of Liberation. 155

CHAPTER 4. *God—The Spirit of Total Liberation for Us.* 157
    The Acts of God—Ethics—What Does God Do?. 158
    The Being of God—Ontology—Who Is God? 162
    Knowledge of God—Epistemology—
      How Does God Reveal?. 166
    The Attributes of God 171
    Notes 190

CHAPTER 5. *Jesus—The Spirit of Total Liberation with Us* 193
    The Goal of Liberation with Us. 194
    The Road to the Goal 200
    Fruit of the Journey 215
    Notes 235

CHAPTER 6. *Human Purpose—*
The Spirit of Total Liberation in Us. 237
    Created to Be Free 239
    Communalism. 251
    Micro-Resistance and Self-Creation 254
    Racial Cultural Identity. 262
    Language 266
    Spiritual Inspiration 270
    Conclusion 274
    Notes 275

Bibliography 279
Index 289

PREFACE

Constructive Theology
and the Co-Constitution of the Self

BLACK THEOLOGY is critical reflection upon the practice with and faith in a Spirit of liberation found in the black church (that is, following Jesus Christ) and the entire black community (that is, following the broader Spirit for liberation). One of the foundations of this liberation practice and faith are the lives of enslaved African Americans during the period from 1619 to 1865.

Using the context of Protestantism and North American culture during that period, this book constructs a black theology of liberation drawing on the religious experiences of enslaved African Americans. I argue that the development of constructive theology accompanies the constitution of the human person in conformity with God's wishes and designs for liberation. In particular black faith and witness— as paramount paradigms and perceptive prisms of human existence— are circumscribed by and created through particular expressions on diverse levels. Such polyvalent situations as well as African American belief structures and hope practices blossom from the rich, creative soil of enslaved black folk's religious encounters with God.

In a word, black theology results from reflection on the Spirit's will of liberation revealed in various expressions of black folk's faith and practice within the context of Protestantism, American culture, and slave religion. At the same time, black theology is concerned with the Spirit's will of liberation in the co-constitution of the new liberated black self. A faith and practice of liberation create a new self. And divine liberation brings about this faith, practice, and self. Black theology reflects on this dynamic process. And necessarily so, because the faith and practice of the slavery epoch inform this process, one has to engage the particular knowledge that saturates the practical discourse of slavery, Protestantism, and American culture. How is this knowledge formed and how does it act in relation to institutions?

What do these discursive practices, which act as a backdrop, have to do with constructing a black theology of liberation?

This book breaks into two parts. Such a division represents a discontinuity in form in order to serve the overall continuity of the book's substance. The separation of parts enhances the thematic uniformity of constructive theology and self co-constitution. Part 1 analyzes Protestantism and American culture theologically as a total way of life that develops religious racial formations, as conditions that made possible the origin of a specific religious reflection in America; these are the conditions that make possible a constructive black theology of liberation for today. Part 2 entails three doctrines of constructive black theology as gleaned from its very foundation; biblical interpretation and religious experiences of enslaved African Americans are cornerstones for contemporary faith statements on God, Jesus, and human purpose.

Furthermore, the construction of a black theology of liberation and the co-constitution of the self evolve from two intertwined concerns and overlapping trajectories—methods of constituting the self and disciplines of creativity. Methods of the self entail knowing one's self and taking care of one's self. Disciplines of creativity involve macrostructures (political economy), micronuances (everyday and ordinary life), language dimensions, and racial cultural identity formation. In fact, disciplines of creativity are another way of knowing and practicing methods of the self.

The question this book asks is: What is the relationship between the slave religion of Protestantism and American culture, on the one hand, and a constructive theological statement about black faith, practice, and self for liberation, on the other? I argue that a black theology of liberation originates from a faith, practice, and the co-constitution of the new self with the divine purpose of liberation toward a full spiritual and material humanity. Such a conscious understanding and practice of our faith evolve from the struggle for liberation and the practice of freedom. This process of constitution and effort toward the goal appear in disciplines of creativity and methods of the self.

The line of argument of the book divides into two parts. Part 1 investigates theologically the religious racial formation of African Americans and Euro-Americans. Chapter 1 dissects two religious arrivals: whites from Europe (1620) and blacks from Africa (1619). Both peoples brought with them a view of God and God's relation with humanity. But the difference in conception, faith, and practice determined the course of black religion and black theology, in particular, until today. Chapter 2 reveals how white Christians tried to recreate African Americans into oppressed and subservient beings by establishing white power as a normative and natural gift from God. Chapter 3 presents the countertheological voice and texts of enslaved blacks who fought to create themselves with the Spirit of liberation.

With Part 1 as a theological backdrop, Part 2 constructs an explicit black theology. It pursues the Spirit of liberation as it functions with the black poor and the oppressed: in Chapter 4, the Spirit of liberation *for* us (i.e., God), Chapter 5, the Spirit of liberation *with* us (i.e., Jesus), and Chapter 6, the Spirit of liberation *in* us (i.e., human purpose).

To achieve full humanity, spiritually and materially, as the Spirit has ordained us to do, we must speak about theology originating out of human-divine complexities and out of multilayered manifestations. This book is one such statement.

ACKNOWLEDGMENTS

I would like to thank the Louisville Institute for the Study of Protestantism and American Culture (now the Louisville Institute), and, in particular, the Institute's executive director, Jim Lewis, for a yearlong grant to conduct research for this project. Thanks are also in order for the ongoing support and patience of Michael West and David Lott (a former editor) of Fortress Press.

The following archival sites were invaluable for my research: the Boston Public Library Rare Books section, Harvard University's Widener Library, the University of Miami Library, the Cornell University Library Slavery Collection, the University of North Carolina (Chapel Hill) Library Southern Historical Collection, the John B. Cade Library of Southern University (Baton Rouge), Louisiana State University's Hill Memorial Library, the College of Charleston (South Carolina) Special Collection, the Ohio Historical Society Archives (Columbus, Ohio), the Library of Congress, and the National Archives.

Many of the initial ideas were debated vigorously in the BT Forum with colleagues Will Coleman, George C. L. Cummings, and James A. Noel. James H. Cone continued to be a strong intellectual supporter and challenging critic throughout this project.

On the topic of black theology and slave religion, I gave sermons and held discussions at Allen Temple Baptist Church (Oakland, California, J. Alfred Smith, Sr., senior pastor) and Trinity United Church of Christ (Chicago, Illinois, Jeremiah A. Wright, Jr., senior pastor).

I also presented lectures and engaged in conversations at the following: Wake Forest University (thanks to my colleague Alton Pollard III); the TransAtlantic Passages conference sponsored by the Collegium for African American Research in Tenerife, Canary Islands; the annual meeting of the Institute for Black Catholic Studies in New Orleans (thanks to my colleague Jamie T. Phelps, O.P. for the invitation to give the keynote address); Santa Clara University in Santa Clara, California (thanks to my former students who took my classes on slave theology and black theology; and special thanks to my former colleague, Steve Privett); Occidental College, Los Angeles (thanks to my friend and colleague, Donna Maeda, for the invitation); the

University of South Africa (Pretoria, South Africa); and the Research Institute on Christianity in South Africa, University of Cape Town, South Africa (due to the gracious support of John De Gruchy). There were other occasions as well.

Many, many thanks to my father, Robert R. Hopkins, Sr. (born in 1907), for our many discussions on the theological, cultural, and political history of slavery, informed by his memories of his parents' and grandparents' stories. He remains an insightful, humorous working-class intellectual.

The University of Chicago, the Divinity School continues to be a supportive and rigorous intellectual context. Thanks to Catherine Brekus and the students who took our slave history and theology course. Thanks to W. Clark Gilpin, dean, who extended an invitation to give a public lecture on this topic before I became a faculty member. And thanks for the invigorating debates over and affirmations of my lecture at the conference on Theology and Cultural Analysis and Criticism; my colleague Kathryn Tanner (who co-hosted this conference at the Divinity School) encouraged my project.

My wife, Linda E. Thomas, offered and gave her valuable time, intellectual energy, editorial expertise, and unending support through the many hours of writing and rewriting this book. She has been a balm in Gilead in my ongoing journey to be faithful to my vocation.

INTRODUCTION

Down, Up, and Over: Constructing Black Theology

I am no mathematician, no biologist, neither grammarian, but when it comes to handling the Bible I knocks down verbs, break up prepositions and jumps over adjectives. Now I tell you something—I am a God-sent man. . . . The children of Israel was four hundred years under bondage and God looked down and seen the suffering of the striving Israelites and brought them out of bondage.

Rev. Reed, ex-slave[1]

IN THE DOMINATING surroundings of Protestantism and American culture, the above quote from Rev. Reed speaks elements of a constructive black theology. Such a liberating encounter with God manifests in diverse ways: the belief in a God-human freedom relation- ship vivified by symbolic and signified language, made joyful by a reallocation of political power and wealth, emboldened by the creative cultural identity of society's least, and enfleshed in micropowers syncretized from multilayered practices of the poor in their ordinary ways of living.

In other words, it is on the linguistic, political-economic, cultural, and micro-everyday levels that the divine-human co-constitution of the self takes place during the struggle for liberation and the practice of freedom. This process results in the realization of a full spiritual and material humanity. Through the life and death religious examples of African American chattel, therefore, universal meanings about the final quest for full spiritual and material humanity flourish.

As it offers elements suggestive of a constructive black theology of liberation, Rev. Reed's faith claim indicates the necessity of self-constitution inspired and accompanied by a divine liberation presence. The biblical God of liberation (the ground for constructive theology today) is the same God who gave voice to Rev. Reed (the ground for self-constitution).

1

Disciplines of Creativity

In his faith statement, Rev. Reed speaks of three areas of study: mathematics, biology, and grammar. But these areas actually include a total of four disciplines: political economy, everyday ordinary living, racial cultural identity, and language. The four disciplines symbolize the structures of the status quo of Protestantism and American culture, the dominant sociocultural ethos during the slavery period in North America.

As symbols, the four disciplines represent the status quo's definition of what is normative in the sight of God. Because of the oppressive function of these disciplines as normative, they place Rev. Reed, an ex-slave who stands for the oppressed majority at the bottom of society, on the margins. Therefore, he is restricted from accessing the "legitimate" interpretive power of these disciplines. Indeed, if he were able to draw on the full resources of these disciplines and deploy them from the perspective and interests of poor and working people, such a move would allow him to enhance his faith in and practice of liberation toward the co-constitution of the self with the Spirit of liberation.

The supposedly objective scientific bodies of knowledge, mathematics, biology, and grammar (the basis of the four disciplines of creativity) serve as tools or technologies of re-creation power when used by the dominating culture. They act and attempt to recreate or transform stolen West Africans (with their own indigenous religions) into subservient African American Christians.[2]

In the re-creation dynamic, mathematics becomes a discipline that adds up to the poor always losing within the larger arena of political economy. Biology implies the possibility of natural, genetic superiority in the micromechanism of life. Micromechanism concerns the everyday aspects of life—the ordinary, daily way of being—not completely covered by the political state apparatus or capitalist economy of macropolitical economy. These micromechanisms of re-creation power are seen, perpetrated, and justified as natural, determined by genetics and by nature. Put differently, the everyday interactions of white superiority over black subordination are seen as natural.

The use of biology by the status quo of Protestantism and American culture suggests the possibility of natural, genetic superiority of white racial culture. In other words, the status quo utilizes a racial cultural identity (the ability to name oneself) to define blacks as being at the bottom of society. Therefore, the overwhelming majority of blacks are seen as a problem for civil and enlightened (read "white") society and inimical to the common good. To be black in the United States of America is to be, by nature and biology, a problem and a threat to the common good of whites, especially those with power.

In the process of re-creation of the free African self into obedient African American Christians, language creates a story and reality in the image of those with immoral privilege. The latter comprises the ruling sectors of society with power, networks, media, wealth, resources, and force that establish the parameters of linguistic discourses and the "proper" interpretations of these discourses.

Yet these four disciplines of creativity—macropolitical economy, micro everyday ordinary life, racial cultural identity, and language—are contested bodies of knowledge and pliable material systems. Hence they exhibit potential transformative spaces of maneuver and counter-hegemonic acts of liberation for the majority (that is, the bottom of society, working and poor people, the least in society, the marginalized, the brokenhearted, and the oppressed). In the four disciplines of creativity, we discover sites of struggle and contestation. On the one hand, the demonic forces of white superiority and its claims to normativity attempt to subjugate the practical discourse of black life; white knowledge and institutions suppress African American oppressed people. In these same disciplines, on the other hand, we encounter the revelation of divine liberation for the construction of faith, practice, and self for black liberation.

Politics and wealth, micropower mechanisms, language, and racial cultural identity are not neutral. Though proclaimed as objective, scientific bodies of knowledge, they reek of power—a power to sustain the differentiation between the haves and the have-nots.

Turn Toward the Spirit of Liberation

The place of the Bible in Rev. Reed's narrative indicates how sacred scriptures act as a hinge in his theological understanding of the God-human interaction. He first claims to lack a formal grasp of mathematics, biology, and grammar, three bodies of knowledge that can be developed into four disciplines of creativity. Because he concedes his lack of knowledge of these disciplines, he shuns any attempt to claim them for his own, at least not as he sees them being presented to him. He is definitely not that ("I am no"). But when he turns to the Bible, his handling of reality, his ability to be unleashed and be proactive, is enhanced immeasurably. For him, the good news message discovered in the Bible, and presumably the positive impact of that message in his own life, serves as the rock-like foundation upon which every other issue rests.

Despite the specific manner of deploying disciplines of creativity and the oppressive usages of formal discourses by others with power or prestige (that is, mathematics, biology, and grammar), Rev. Reed's own sense of theological identity derives from his inspired ability to handle the Bible. That he handles the Bible suggests he feels at home in this medium of practical knowledge and reenacted story. Moreover, "at home" is not a stationary or sedentary reality for Rev. Reed. On the contrary, it involves a degree of fluidity; that is what he indicates with the phrase "when it comes." The point is to underscore the supreme confidence he has in relation to his pedagogical task with and energetic faith in the Bible. Again, the "I am no . . . , but" initiates his turn away from established unfamiliar disciplines and toward the power of the Spirit of liberation.

Rev. Reed assumes the interpretive and practical right to claim the Bible as his own. The juncture of the "but" of handling the Bible is the hinge between the four disciplines, on the one hand, and the three action verbs (knock down, break up, and jump over) on the other; this is where God's gift of freedom to be his own adjudicator of meaning and his own black theologian of liberation is revealed to him. To speak more symbolically, this biblical juncture offers a rupture, a decision point at which African Americans become either objects of Euro-American Christian formal and dominating mechanisms of being in the world or astute and creative handlers of disciplines of creativity inspired by the Spirit of liberation.

This is what Rev. Reed's options present: should he submit to the interpretative and oppressive force of the mainstream (found before the "but") or should he follow the empowering call of the liberating Bible (found immediately after the "but")? Should he bow to the ruling sector's control over and usage of disciplines of creativity or should he seize these same areas of contestation and work with the Spirit of liberation to co-constitute a new self and new social relations among humankind? How can macropolitical economy, micro ordinary daily life, language, and racial cultural mechanisms of power be utilized with the Spirit of liberation to co-constitute the new self of full spiritual and material humanity for the poor and the oppressed and, at the same time, build a new Common Wealth for all peoples?

The liberating Spirit in the Bible empowers Rev. Reed to perform his own revolutionary textual deconstruction and reconstruction.

With the Bible, he can now knock down the verbs employed by oppressive sectors of society. Whatever their configuration, whether passive or active, auxiliary or main, the freedom Spirit helps Reed become undaunted by mainstream verbiage or mainstream talk. Similarly, he can break up prepositions, the clauses from the oppressor which serve as conditional instances clarifying further the oppression of poor folk. And with the liberation biblical hermeneutic, he can jump over adjectives, the derogatory descriptors people outside the mainstream have suffered from for years.

However, "down, up, and over" is not merely a negative, reactive deconstructive move. Deconstruction is only a small moment in the more important and strategic vocational response of heeding the Spirit of liberation's call to use verbs, prepositions, and adjectives constructively. The poor and working people, the marginalized, and those at the bottom of society need to knock down, break up, and jump over macropolitical economy, micro everyday and ordinary lifestyles, language, and racial cultural identity mechanisms of power (that is, the disciplines of creativity) in two respects. First, they must defend their humanity against the oppressive sectors of society's use of these disciplines in their schemes of oppression. And second, they must craft a radical new way of harnessing these creative disciplines to co-constitute with the Spirit a new liberated self and new social relations for the oppressed.

From a God-human relation perspective, the first half of the above quote points to all dominating theologies as they manifest in particular disciplines of power. And then the Bible enters and disrupts the norm of domination and acts as a theological hinge that swings or turns us to Rev. Reed's theological initiative and his black theology. As a God-sent person, he can disrupt oppressive norms: the norm of poverty (resulting from political economic forces), "standard" English (by reconfiguring it with knocks, breaks, and jumps), micromechanisms of discrimination (operating on a daily basis), and restricted racial cultural identity formations (the maintenance of Euro-American superiority).

The disciplines of creativity can either be used to shut out and punish the oppressed in society or become the means by which the oppressed can employ those disciplines as forms of creativity. Because God looks down, sees the suffering, and brings out from bondage the striving of the oppressed, the latter do not labor in vain. In fact, Rev. Reed's theological anthropological identity emerges from his faith, biblical interpretation, and personal witness that the Spirit of liberation works with him and all the oppressed to co-constitute a new self for the poor and a new social arrangement. This dynamic of struggling for liberation and practicing freedom seeks to realize a full spiritual and material humanity and a new Common Wealth for all.

Purpose of the Book

This text examines the following research question and presents the resulting theological argument. What is the relation between the slave religion of Protestantism and American culture, on the one hand, and a theological statement about black faith, practice, and self for liberation, on the other? In the context of Protestantism and American culture, a constructive black theology of spiritual and material liberation is informed by those fragments of liberation theology found in slave religious experiences. Because enslaved blacks and the majority of blacks today operate at the bottom of American society, a black theology of liberation working in their interests will also add to the universal emancipation of all oppressed people.

The normative dimensions of liberation in the Bible and the normative tradition of liberation within African American faith traditions seek to emancipate the universal poor and marginalized. Such a freedom operates on the inside spiritual realm against debilitating emotions and on the outside structural levels against institutional oppression. Through the struggle for liberation internally and externally, black theology of liberation adds to the formation of a new human being and new systems of human interaction for all. In sum, I argue for a black theology of liberation based on the Spirit of liberation and the poor co-constituting a new self and a new Common Wealth.

In the examination of the overarching research question, the source of slave religion and the role of the Bible in those religious experiences disclose at least four areas of contestation between the oppressor's attempt to recreate the oppressed into a subservient human being and the oppressed's countermoves to co-constitute a new free self with the Spirit. Enslaved blacks fought for their right to be full spiritual and material human beings on the linguistic, racial cultural identity, micro everyday lifestyles, and macropolitical economic levels. Consequently, black theology's source of slave religion presented part of the methodological foci around which the Spirit of liberation manifested itself. When the Spirit revealed liberation at these foci, enslaved black folk were able to know who they were and take care of themselves. They displayed a faith and witness of methods of the self (such as knowledge and care) along with the Spirit. In this sense methods of the self are another way of expressing disciplines of creativity.

Moreover, when the poor and working folk, in black theology, co-constitute the self with the Spirit via disciplines of creativity, they engage in the struggle for liberation and the practice of freedom. The struggle for liberation and the practice of freedom engaged at the foci of macro, micro, language, and culture involve real people with real pain. Material systemic pain takes place for victims of class exploitation, white supremacy, patriarchal privilege, and homophobic attacks. Spiritual emotional pain takes place with the demons of blind anger, low self-esteem, revenge, and paralyzing fear. Thus the struggle for liberation and the practice of freedom culminate in a full spiritual and material humanity, defining the substance of a new self and new Common Wealth.

The research question and subsequent claim presuppose a theoretical framework to the argument. In this schema, the Spirit of liberation reveals herself or himself as God, Jesus, and a human-divine interaction. Hence, a Christian black theology of liberation works at the junctures of theology (God), Christology (Jesus), and theological anthropology (human purpose). This revelation is incarnated, embedded, and embodied among human beings. Slave religion appears as one of five crucial sources of revelation.[3]

The conceptual framework (bodies of knowledge) or intellectual scaffolding (accumulated human experiences) through which the sources of the poor express themselves are language (for example, symbols, metaphors, signs, codes, words, sentences, and paragraphs), racial cultural identity (such as the right of self-identity; and love of the black and African self), politics and wealth (state power and economics), and micropower mechanisms (such as rituals, space, time, pleasure, the body, geography, etc.)

Within the framework, the norm and telos are tightly interwoven. The norm that glues the sources of revelation together asserts that the Spirit calls and works with the black poor to empower them for the struggle for liberation and the practice of freedom and for everyone's full spiritual and material humanity. Wherever moments of this process occur, there one finds the Spirit. Here the norm pursues self-critical and critical ways of being in the world among the oppressed. It suggests a critical and self-critical yardstick among the poor and toward the oppressor. The telos or ultimate vision seeks a new society on earth where all individuals achieve the fullness of their spiritual and material humanity for the benefit of the community.

Therefore, the norm and telos are one. The norm is the deployment of the telos as adjudicator in the now. And the telos is the highest realization of the norm in the future.

Theological Presuppositions

In the beginning of creation, according to the Bible, the Spirit gave resources to all of humanity. But the sin of hubris or of acquiring more than the necessities of life led some human beings to hoard and monopolize resources for themselves. This perspective and practice has culminated in extreme asymmetrical hierarchies in the United States, where the ruling sectors maintain private monopolization of wealth and resources by treating people as objects for accumulating profit.

In addition, the profit-driven mode, the usage of others for one's own desires, appears in a linguistic form that contradicts the original intent of the language. That is, God created humanity through the breath of language. This sound of breathing from the Spirit into human beings poured forth a liberating language. Human beings today express that liberating language in diverse tongues. But, in the United States, certain groups with power define what is "standard" English. And those from the oppressed who imitate and master this discourse succeed in life. Still, the overwhelming majority of black folk retain their own ways of speaking and, thereby, are kept outside of opportunities. In the reality of differences, there is nothing inherently beautiful or correct about white English spoken by the powerful in the United States. Standard English is normative because the ones who have the authority to define it have defined their talk as normal or standard talk.

Similarly, God grants the beauty of racial cultural identity to the black poor. But "whiteness"—Euro-American phenotype—reigns as the supreme norm. And even on the ordinary everyday ways of life (such as mannerism, pleasure, organization of space and time, etc.), the powerful have imposed upon the oppressed their micro ways of being in the world in direct contradiction to how the Spirit's grace affirms all human micro expressions.

Theologically, the Spirit acts in creation. Small sectors of society hoard and redefine the Spirit's creation, and now the poor are called by the Spirit of liberation to seek a new creation: the co-constitution of the self and a new Common Wealth. The struggle for liberation and the practice for freedom by the black poor and other oppressed people serve the long-term interests of the common human good. This good comprises political economy (common ownership and distribution of wealth and resources), language (equal aesthetic appreciation), racial cultural identity (pleasure through a recognition of difference), and micropower (freedom of being oneself in community in ordinary everyday life).

A dynamic and vibrant process of configuring and creating and reconfiguring and re-creation is at the foundation of these theological presuppositions. God configures all reality for all of humanity. But the privileged reconfigure this divinely given creative text through monopolization and white supremacy. With the Spirit of liberation, the poor reconfigure the sinful text of the privileged into a new text for all humanity in accord with divine original intent. The operating motivation of the Spirit of liberation is for all people to be the Spirit's fully created humanity effected in the dynamic and vibrant process of the poor co-constituting its new self.

With this theological backdrop, black theology is doing passionate reason and rational compassion, in the public sphere; it is doing what the Spirit of liberation has called the African American church and other faith communities to say and do in the world of human brokenness and human possibilities. Its vocation is to question whether or not the church and other faith communities are practicing and preaching what they are called to do and say: to be with and fight for the least in the black community (who are the majority there) and all of the oppressed (who are the majority in the world).

Simultaneously, those of privilege become part of the majority by carrying out the Spirit's summons and joining the oppressed. All races, classes, genders, and sexual orientations have options. The goal is to live in a prophetic fashion, as much as humanly possible, what the Spirit has brought into the world. The newness that was brought into history, that is being brought in the present, and that will be brought into future history is a new heaven and new earth. Black theology grows out of this prophetic hope and sacred struggle to be in the world, to help transform and heal this broken world. The attempt to practice this newness is liberation towards a full humanity, spiritually and materially.

The task of black theology is to affirm, assert, and advocate for the positive theological initiative of poor and working people. And, where necessary, it knocks down, breaks up, and jumps over any demonic theologies that prevent the African American church and the African American people from working with the Spirit. Therefore, the construction of a black theology of liberation for the church and other faith communities requires relying primarily on sources deriving from the African American community. Black folk need "shoes that fit our feet." At the same time, when we explore the depths and particularity of each of these sources (we focus in this book on the first source of slave religion), we need to knock down, break up, and jump over negative obstacles. But this down, up, and over dynamic is a by-product of our larger vocation to develop a positive statement on God's relation to the poor and the co-constitution of the full spiritual and material humanity—that is, the new self and the new Common Wealth.

NOTES

1. Fisk University Social Science Institute, *Unwritten History of Slavery* (Nashville, Tenn.: Fisk University Social Science Institute, 1945), 20. Hereinafter, this work will be cited by title alone.

2. For an excellent and finely nuanced collection of essays regarding the constitution of bodies of knowledge, see Ellen Messer-Davidow et al., eds., *Knowledges: Historical and Critical Studies in Disciplinarity* (Charlottesville: University Press of Virginia, 1993).

3. In my *Shoes That Fit Our Feet: Sources for a Constructive Black Theology* (Maryknoll, N.Y.: Orbis Books, 1993), I argue for five primary sources of the black poor as witnesses of liberation revelation—slave religion, black women, politics, folk culture, and social analysis and social vision.

PART 1

Historical Black Theology: Religious Formation of Race in American Culture

In part 1, we examine Protestantism and American culture as a necessary context for the development of a constructive black theology of liberation (in Part 2). The witness to and faith in God arise out of material reality. However, such a revisiting of history is not merely a look back but a theological examination of two fundamental planks undergirding the creation of any theology in the United States—the mood and feeling of white Christianity and of black Christianity. The historical and theological backdrop is a look at faith and God-talk inherent in the definition of American identity and outlook, a question of contextualized meaning. In fact, within the context of Protestantism and American culture, we find an ongoing struggle to discern and craft the meaning of Christian beliefs and an American way of life, as well as the pervasive dynamic of religious racial formations.

Consequently, Chapter 1 investigates the arrivals of the Pilgrims in 1620 and the Jamestown, enslaved Africans in 1619, both as religious formative markers. Chapter 2 reveals the Christian slavemasters' attempt to create Africans into a new submissive phenomenon. And Chapter 3 offers the theological ways in which African Americans co-constituted themselves with divine purpose.

CHAPTER 1

Two Faces of Protestantism and American Culture

In ye name of God, Amen . . . , having undertaken, for ye glorie of God, and advancement of ye Christian faith, and honour of our king & countrie, a voyage to plant ye first colonie . . . , doe by these presents solemnly & mutually in ye presence of God, and of one another, covenant and combine our selves together into a civill body politick.

The Mayflower Compact, November, 1620[1]

The oppression and the maltreatment of the hapless descendant of Africa is not merely an ugly excrescence upon American religion . . .; no, it is a part and parcel of it, a cardinal principle, a sine qua non, a cherished defended keystone, a corner-stone of American faith.

Samuel Riggold Ward, fugitive slave[2]

Two Arrivals

THEY CAME in two different ships—the Mayflower and a Dutch man-of-war.[3] One hopeful group of believers grasped consciously the ecstasy of the historical moment. As they triumphantly sailed into the dark waters of Massachusetts Bay, they thanked God for fulfilling a providential arrival into the new Jerusalem. For them, it was the beginning of a new heaven and a new earth, filled with all the possibilities and imagery of a land of milk and honey. This group looked back at the religious persecution and suppression of religious freedom endured in England. These were the Christians whose plans to reform the Church of England were dashed when James I (1603–1625) and Charles I (1625–1649) turned belligerently against the progress of the English Protestant Reformation. Escaping the religious and social consequences of an antagonistic monarchy, they fled across the Atlantic.[4]

But now, in this "New World," these religious pioneers would exercise their liberty to worship God, free from "popish" authority

13

and the administrative impurities of the English church. Here, they would honor God by deploying their political power to dominate the abundant resources offered by verdant land and by refining the principle of economic profit reward for hard work performed. Here, too, they would conjure a new language encoded with religious signs justifying their covenantal relation to the divine and undergirding their venture into the length and breadth of the wooded landscape before their eyes. They would wield their power in the daily exigencies of time, space, pleasure, architecture, and family relations. And they would position all non-whites as subordinate to European identity. God had granted them the vision, the power, and the superiority in political economy, language, microrelations, and racial cultural identity. These were the Pilgrims anchoring off the New England shores on Plymouth Rock in November, 1620. No one captures better the theological dimensions of this winter arrival than Governor William Bradford of Plymouth:

> Being thus arived in a good harbor and brought safe to land, they fell upon their knees & blessed ye God of heaven, who had brought them over ye vast & furious ocean, and delivered them from all ye periles & miseries thereof, againe to set their feete on ye firme and stable earth, their proper elemente. . . .[5]

White foam rode the black sea waves into the shallower inland waters of Cape Cod Bay. The Pilgrims crowded the deck of their ship and gave homage to God for the realization of divine prophecy. They were God's chosen people. And this November arrival would mark the theological and historical folklore to which every succeeding generation of white Americans would claim mythological allegiance. To be an American would eventually denote heirs of the old (European) country, with its political wealth, micropowers, racial cultural identity, language, and Christian religion. Anyone else would be a dissimilar Other.

The Mayflower halted at the shore, pilgrim immigrants stepped on black water and claimed ownership of this earth as their Canaan. The captain and minister gave praise to God from whom all blessings flow; the ultimate blessing was the bestowal upon God's special people of a New England—one whose lands were as virgin as the Pilgrim's religion was pure. Indeed this sense of a people, a Puritanism—pureness of superior theology, intellect, wealth, micropowers, racial culture, language—accompanied intentionally these 1620 arrivals as they proclaimed their ownership of all within their sight. And this self-perceived, religious white superiority derived primarily from a vocational sense of divine mission: to discover, possess, and rule over all lands and peoples created to be subdued by white images of and emissaries from God in heaven.[6]

In effect, the Puritans sailed not to break with old Europe, but to bring about the logic and fullest extent of a hegemonic Protestantism and cultural civilization. That is why they named their colonial settlements New Haven, New Canaan, New Netherlands, New York, and Cambridge. Unfortunately, these bold pioneers brought the same view of blacks as demonic, evil, inferior, and sinful that their European mother churches had propagated in instinct, language, and symbol.[7] The seeds of religious freedom, congregational democracy, and covenantal metaphor would grow to mean a rationalization for the development of a system of white skin privileges. And later, an American would be known as a Christian (primarily Protestant) of European tradition, a loyal patriot of the Stars and Stripes, a disciple of capitalist ownership, and fundamentally, of course, white.[8] Thus the Pilgrims set in motion a theology—a conscious religious justification—laden with signs of ordained racial hierarchy. A white American by definition enjoyed God's grace. Often, whiteness would mean divinity. A black person, consequently, represented the ultimate presence of darkness, the denial of American privileges, the signifier of the near-demonic.[9] After depositing the Pilgrims onto a firm land of religious freedom, the ship which had brought a load of white passengers fleeing from theological persecution departed towards a darker type of cargo. As one historian recounts: "The Mayflower carried the Pilgrim Fathers to religious liberty in America and went on its next trip for a load of slaves."[10]

The first European Pilgrims cast their eyes over the vast tree-filled horizon. Some gave silent prayer for those who had died en route. Others examined new species of vegetation and plant life. Couples embraced with hearts joined in plans to raise families. Still others savored the import of this historic time; a time engendering feelings of infinite power. All had been survivors of perilous adventure. What unified them was a knowledge of arrogant possibilities suited for the rugged pioneering required of strangers on novel and uncharted shores. All of human history had served as prologue to and preparation for the birth of a new creation, the phenomenon known as white Americans. Granting a divine grace of manifest destiny, God worked in history to plow the ground for God's favored (white) "little ones." Governor Winthrop (a later governor of the "holy commonwealth" of the Massachusetts Bay Colony) penned the essence of puritan theology:

> Thus stands the cause between God and us: we are entered into cov-
> enant with Him for this work; we have taken out a commission, the
> Lord hath given us leave to draw our own articles. . . .
>
> We shall find that the God of Israel is among us. . . . For we must
> consider that we shall be as a city upon a hill, the eyes of all people
> are upon us.[11]

Pilgrims crafted a way of life, a sacred culture, saturated with specific codes of conduct and expectations. No other communities would perceive themselves as the recipients of an exclusive divine commission which situated their racial group on a hill above all others. No other group would have the opportunity to foster social patterns which imaged their phenotype as aesthetically normative. No other Americans would (or could) act with impunity while hoarding resources. No other race could openly name something and then claim it as universal reality. Pilgrims acted as if God had given them the invincibility to walk the earth without repercussions resulting from treading on the backs of the Other. And to their children, they would pass on a tradition of relegating blacks to a secondary status—a heritage of assumed superiority and presupposed correctness. They would socialize Christian generation after generation in this manner. Despite notable future exceptions who betrayed their racial class (e.g., John Brown[12]), a theological glue intertwined with white power and identity; thus an intransigent system was born. The Pilgrims' arrival, an ambiguous and simultaneous thrust toward universal freedom and racial superiority, signified one foundational strand of Protestantism and American culture.

A year earlier, in 1619,[13] and unknown to the pathbreaking Pilgrims, another ship had entered the white waters of Jamestown, Virginia, established by English settlers in 1607. Enduring a fierce storm, this vessel held the first group of Africans forced to come to the future thirteen colonies. Like the Pilgrims, they too were a group of believers whose entire theological worldview was now shaken. They must have wondered how their traditional High God with a pantheon of intermediary divinities and ancestors could have brought such suffering and enslavement upon them and their unborn. Unlike the Pilgrims who came with Christian hopes of conquering, this first group of twenty Africans must have felt their faith riddled with dread, confusion, and horror at the sight of white men with guns and whips.

Perhaps the personal experience of Olaudah Equiano, captured off the West African coast during the European slave trade but later freed, speaks to the gut feelings of these 1619 Africans. Forced onto a slave ship, Equiano spoke to the other bound Africans:

> I asked them if we were not to be eaten by those white men with horrible looks, red faces, and long hair. . . . I would have jumped over the side; but I could not; and, besides, the crew used to watch us very closely . . . lest we should leap into the water: and I have seen some of these poor African prisoners most severely cut for attempting to do so, and hourly whipped for not eating. . . . I feared I should be put to death, the white people looked and acted, as I thought, in so savage a manner.[14]

Though slavery was not established legally in the colonies until a few years later, it is clear that this August 1619 arrival of seventeen African men and three African women marked a violent involuntary presence of black bodies in the colonies. Entering the Chesapeake Bay, the ship on which they traveled was a Dutch man-of-war controlled by pirates and thieves. Originally this initial group of twenty blacks had been stolen from Africa by Spanish subjects and doomed to the Caribbean. But the Spanish slave ship was intercepted and captured by Captain Jope and Pilot Marmaduke of the Dutch man-of-war, who bartered Antony, Isabella, Pedro, and the other seventeen abducted Africans for food to the leaders of Sir John Rolfe's Jamestown settlement.[15] Rolfe, a Virginia tobacco planter, wrote: "About the last of August came in a dutch man of warre that sold us twenty Negars."[16] Thus a foundational representation of black bodies as commodities for white use and exchange value became reality in the New World.

But one has to remember that these were not atheists conducting business transactions over ebony skins. The government of the Jamestown colony was a religious settlement, Anglican in tradition.[17] Indeed, "it seems that [the imprisoned Africans] had been purchased from their Dutch captors by the [Jamestown] colonial government itself. Acting as middleman, the government then distributed them among the private settlers."[18] This first interaction and domination of blacks by whites on North American soil would plague an ensuing white Christian theology. Henceforth, the image of God would reside in the corporate white privilege to expect and demand black compliance and silence. Much later, one former slave remembered and confirmed the existence of such a Christianity:

[Slaves] didn't go to the church building; the [white] preacher came and preached to them in their quarters. He'd just say, "Serve your masters. Don't steal your master's turkey. Don't steal your master's chickens. Don't steal your master's hogs. Don't steal your master's meat. Do whatsomever your master tells you to do." Same old thing all the time.[19]

The institutionalization of religious slavery in America grew out of the primordial act of a white Christian government "acting as middleman" in the commodification of black skin subservience and profit (that is, the bartering process) and then distributing imprisoned blacks (who held their own theological worldview) among white Christian "private settlers." This Jamestown arrival is also a plumb line in the establishment of Protestantism and American culture.

Neither the noble freedom implied in the "we" of the covenantal language of New England Puritanism, nor the Anglican theology of Jamestown included Africans. In fact, no African accompanied the Pilgrims (1620) or the Virginia colonialists (1607) upon their arrivals to the New World. This should not be surprising since the Christian settlers who arrived in the New World came out of a European slave trading culture with roots reaching back to the 1440s.[20] From that time on, white Europeans arrogantly perceived their churches, nations, and peoples as more developed and the center of the world. Conversely they labeled black Africans as pagan (in religion), heathen (in civilization), and savage (by nature). For instance, Richard Sibbes (later founder of Protestant missionary thinking and Master of St. Catherine's College in Cambridge, England) preached a sermon reflecting both the fifteenth-century European outlook on Africa as well as the subsequent missionary outreach to foreign lands:

Now, God in preparation for the most part civiliseth people, and then Christianiseth them. . . . For the Spirit of God will not be effectual in a rude, wild and barbarous soul. . . . Therefore, they must be brought to civility . . . to cast them down; and then they are brought to Christianity thereupon. Therefore they take a good course that labour to break them from their natural rudeness and fierceness.[21]

Historian George M. Fredrickson situates the root of racial inequality—the apparent need for white Christian culture to foster a casting down and breaking up of black people—in the European Renaissance and Reformation: "There were two crucial distinctions which allowed Europeans of the Renaissance and Reformation period to divide the human race into superior and inferior categories. One was between Christian and heathen and the other between 'civil' and 'savage.'"[22] Thus a theological attitude of racial difference was brought from the European continent to colonial America. And "heathen" and "savage" Africans, stacked like sardines in a can, were relocated across the Atlantic by Christian and civilized slave boats named Brotherhood, John the Baptist, Justice, Integrity, Gift of God, Liberty, Mary, Hope, and Jesus.

Slavery in American Culture

Just as the founding Protestant families of America seeded the religious soil with racial hierarchy, so too did they encode American culture with laws governing racial distinctions. In a sense, slave laws served as a negative affirmative action whereby an increasing number of the white community could enjoy the opportunity of access to power by virtue of a white-black caste system. Though the first twenty Africans did not suffer a legal slave status, in fact they bore the badge of difference. They were worse off than white indentured servants, who did not suffer from the viewpoint and practice of juxtaposing black and the demonic brought from Europe. Nor was violence developed into an intense art form of abduction and transport for poor whites as it was for Africans. Admittedly, some blacks were officially termed "indentured" and some were made free eventually. However, in practice, various forms of slavery existed as racial difference, de facto (without legal sanction for several years) and de jure (with statutory support for the majority of the time), from 1619 to 1865.[23]

As the years progressed, the schism between European colonialists with property and their indentured (white) servants, on the one hand, and the Africans forced to Jamestown, on the other hand, became codified in legislative acts. By 1630, customary practices of discriminating against blacks culminated in the first prohibition against white and black relationships. In the Virginia colony, on "'September 17th, 1630,' Hugh Davis, a white servant, was publicly flogged 'before an assembly of Negroes and others,' for defiling himself with a Negro woman. It was required that he should confess as much on the following sabbath."[24] Indentured white servant Davis was guilty of an unnatural act—joining white flesh with less-than-human, black flesh. Moreover, such a perverted practice was not simply a private affair; an example had to be made to the public conscience. Curiously enough, the historical record emphasizes that his violent punishment, implemented by a Christian government, took place before "Negroes," indicating a specific sign to Africans which signified black animality. Obviously, it would be unnatural for (black) animals to copulate with (white) humans, even if the whites were only indentured servants. And we must not lose sight of the fact that this display of confession before the public gaze occurred on the Christian holy day, marking some connection between Christianity and the prohibition of a white man's sexual relation with a black woman.

Indeed, the required confession on Sunday implied that a white servant had committed a sin against Christianity and God and needed to repent. Theologically, black sexual flesh, particularly black women's, embodied the demonic, thus the sinful nature of a white human crossing the taboo zone and daring to enter the devil's handmaiden. Instead of Sunday worship entailing an embracing of racial differences and diverse cultures in God's one house, white Protestantism used the house of worship as public space for furthering racial separation on theological grounds. More than likely, on the following Sunday, this sinner prayed to God for forgiveness: "Forgive me Lord, for I have sinned. I have defiled myself inside a black woman's flesh: an ultimate representation of communing with the devil."

Basically, white colonialists engineered a type of religion and life which justified a total domination of Africans in America. The paradoxical nature of Protestantism and American culture persisted with the presence of black people. The freedom of religious worship and the freedom to live life to its fullest were simultaneously held out as available to whites and as unnatural and sinful for African Americans. Consequently, difference became normative in statute, policy, and polity.

On January 6, 1639, the Virginia "Christian" General Assembly passed a law requiring all men, except "Negroes," to bear arms or be subject to a fine imposed by "the Governor and Council."[25] At this point, whites did not deny their religious privilege of bearing arms to blacks for fear of the latter organizing an insurrection. Blacks numbered only twenty-two in 1624 and three hundred in 1648. Instead, blacks were denied the right to share in the benefits of a religious government because white Christians, as a group, perceived blacks, as a group, as uncivilized and not fit to own guns. We could infer that Africans in these religious colonies were caricatured as bearers of heathen unpredictability, animalistic volatility, and intellectual inferiority.

By 1640, indefinite servitude had become a way of life for blacks who broke colonial laws. John Punch, a Negro, attempted an escape with two white servants. The latter had four years added to their work obligations. But the court ordered Punch to "serve his master or his assigns for the time of his natural Life here or elsewhere."[26] In contrast to blacks, whites without property were never codified into a perpetual slave class.

Although various communities in Virginia had already established slavery, this racial institution became law for the entire Virginia colony in 1661, thereby solidifying chattel within American culture.[27] The following year on December 14th, a law regulated the biological determination of free and slave. Even when a white male co-conceived a child with a black female, the offspring would follow forever the status of the mother.[28] Maryland gave legal recognition to the existence of slavery in 1664; the Carolinas colony (founded in 1663) sanctioned chattel relations less than ten years after its origin; and Georgia brought in slaves (1750) within twenty years of its colonization. The refinement of black slavery penetrated all spheres of cultural life. Colonial statutes prohibited free assembly, the use of firearms, the beating of drums or the blowing of horns, the purchase of liquor, intermarriage, property ownership, political rights, rights to education, use of African languages, the assembly of more than three slaves after working hours, and proscribed Africans from raising "their hands against whites even in self-defense."[29]

At a much later date, former slave Henry Bibb described the refined and systematic legal censers of states considered moderate in culture:

> The laws of Kentucky, my native State, with Maryland and Virginia, which are said to be the mildest slave states in the Union, noted for their humanity, Christianity and democracy, declare that "Any slave, for rambling in the night, or riding horseback without leave, or running away, may be punished by whipping, cropping and branding in the cheek."

Continuing his story, Bibb describes the dismembering of blacks' bodies as public items of display in Christian and democratic slave states.

> "Any slave convicted of petty larceny, murder, or wilfully burning of dwelling houses, may be sentenced to have his right hand cut off; to be hanged in the usual manner, or the head severed from the body, the body divided into four quarters, and head and quarters stuck up in the most public place in the county, where such act was committed."[30]

Nowhere does the exhibition of irony (in Protestantism) and hypocrisy (in American culture) reveal itself more than in the legal proscription against freedom after religious conversion. Theologically,

Protestantism preached Christianity as liberation from persecution and freedom to construct a new covenantal community. And American culture prided itself for creating a genuine democracy. Yet, when slaves entered the "body of Christ" through baptism, they gained confirmation of their status as chattel, not a new life. In 1667, the Virginia legislature wrote: "the conferring of baptisme doth not alter the condition of the person as to his bondage or freedome."[31] Moreover, prior to the British government's official decree (1729) stating that baptism did not grant earthly freedom, every southern colony and two northern settlements already had established similar laws.[32]

The northern colonies accompanied their southern brethren in implementing Christian laws systematizing black slavery. Within ten years after the birth of the Massachusetts Bay colony, African slaves appeared. Five years after the founding of Harvard, the Massachusetts colony legalized slavery in 1641; Connecticut followed suit in 1650. Rhode Island (a Baptist community fleeing from Puritan persecution) simply ratified the reality of slavery in 1652. Black slavery became law in New Hampshire in 1714. "Although New England's Negroes were often termed 'servants,' they were in most instances slaves, the former term being preferred by Puritan masters."[33] Even before the English acquired ownership of the New Netherlands (which then included New Jersey) in 1664, the Dutch had institutionalized chattel relationships. For instance, starting in 1709, a slave auction market prospered on Wall Street. Similarly, in 1681 and 1682, when Quaker William Penn received the territory that would become Pennsylvania and Delaware, he simply accepted the ongoing practice of slavery as a way of life beneficial to white Christians.

Eventually, in the midst of revolutionary and anticolonial consensus against Britain, northern antislavery sentiment grew to such an extent that New England colonies and (post-1776) states gradually abolished black chattel. Vermont ended slavery in 1777; Massachusetts and Pennsylvania in 1780; New Hampshire, Rhode Island, and Connecticut all in 1784. The legislators of New York passed emancipation laws in 1799 which, in some cases, did not take full effect until 1851.[34] Finally, New Jersey legally emancipated its bondsmen and -women in 1804, transforming them from the realm of chattel commodification of black skins into the democratic rank of free labor for capital usage. However, in fact, "New Jersey's slaves were not entirely free until the Thirteenth Amendment in 1865."[35] But the official legislative ending of slavery on some state levels did not knock down the building blocks of Protestantism and American culture, the contradictory ethos of religious freedom and civil democracy for whites at the expense of African Americans. Indeed, the events of 1776 and 1787 indicated the contrary.

With the successful American Revolution (1776), the push toward cultural freedom and democratic Christian principles on the one hand and the pull toward human exploitation of fellow humans on the other became enshrined in one of the most historic documents of America, the United States Constitution. At the 1787 Constitutional Convention, white men with property

> wrote both the institution and the benefits of slavery into [their] Constitution. . . . In the document the black population was included in the determination of Congressional representation, based on a formula which allowed enslaved people to be counted as three-fifths of a person. The Constitution also guaranteed the right of slaveowners to track down black fugitives across state lines and have them delivered back into captivity. It promised the use of federal armed forces in any struggle against insurrection.[36]

Northern states did help enslaved blacks to terminate their chattel circumstances in their own region of the new nation, signifying a measure of revolutionary and humane Christian impulses; but the north conceded far more to the pro-slavery federal powers. By law and custom, the national government obligated the return of fugitive slaves to their original slavemasters. And northern states, soaked in their own patriotic jingoism of revolutionary independence, agreed to conspire against any black seeking liberty in the "free" states of the north. Not only was this complicity merely an act brought about by voting in a law, it was also a military commitment to defend American religious culture against any insurrectionary attempts on the part of enslaved black Christians who sought their own "life, liberty, and the pursuit of happiness." Apparently the federal government perceived no contradiction in a religiously democratic government employing deadly violence against poor African Americans pursuing democracy and religion to achieve American citizenship. Pro-slavery sentiment in the north persisted long after the Constitutional Convention and the formal abolition of northern slavery.[37]

Indeed, until the resolution of the Civil War in 1865 and despite the legal ceasing of international slavery in 1807, hoards of stolen Africans (so-called *Saltbacks*) were crammed into both European and American vessels on their way to North America and the Caribbean. Around 1855, the following interview took place in New York with a captain imprisoned for illegal trading in Africans:

"New York," says Captain Smith, "is the chief port in the world for the slave trade. . . . Neither in Cuba nor in the Brazils is it carried on so extensively. Ships that convey slaves to the West Indies and South America are fitted out from the United States. Now and then one sails from Philadelphia; more from Baltimore; but most of all from New York. This is our headquarters."[38]

The official banning of international trade in black skins suffered due to weak national enforcement; the profit motive gave way to a low priority toward African American life. "The importation of black cargoes from Africa and the West Indies [averaging five thousand black contraband per year] proved hard to stamp out. The profits were high, and the risks were reduced because of the federal government's failure to vigorously search out the offenders."[39] As a result, the accumulation of capital by American propertied white families persisted. Captain Smith was asked a question concerning the percentage of profit yielded in the illegal trade:

"Are the profits of the trade very large?"
"My brig cost 13,000 dollars to fit her out completely. My last cargo to Cuba was worth 220,000 dollars."[40]

Black unpaid, slave labor built America from the beginning of the seventeenth to the end of the nineteenth centuries. In the process, white Christians with capital attained the ranks of millionaires. The slave trade

formed the very basis of the economic life of New England; about it revolved, and on it depended, most of her other industries. The vast sugar, molasses, and rum trades, shipbuilding, the distilleries, a great many of the fisheries, the employment of artisans and seamen, even agriculture—all were dependent upon the slave traffic.[41]

Not only New England clans, but also wealthy families throughout the colonies and then the entire United States accumulated funds, resources, and capital as a consequence of unpaid African American work. Along with the slave trade, profits soared for the cotton industry; twenty-five years before the Civil War, southern cotton fields "were producing three-fourths of the world's supply."[42] The military might and legal power of the national government intentionally held African Americans down in order that a small group of affluent white Christian families could control permanently American wealth.

The collusion of capitalist interests, a democratic federal government, and a racial Christian environment deepened further the incongruities of Protestant liberties and American cultural inequalities.

At its core, American religious culture nurtured a system granting white skin power over black skin. In their joint autobiography, ex-bondspersons William and Ellen Craft cited an official legislative policy during the antebellum days:

> If any slave, who shall be out of the house or plantation where such slave shall live, or shall be usually employed or without some white person in company with such slave shall refuse to submit to undergo the examination of any white person, (let him be ever so drunk or crazy), it shall be lawful for such white person to pursue, apprehend, and moderately correct such slave; and if such slave shall assault and strike such white person, such slave may be lawfully killed.[43]

The first half of the law underscores the complete restrictions imposed on blacks; that is, they could only occupy safe spaces defined by supervising whites—houses, plantations, or monitored movements. By law, whites held the privilege of stopping any African American who might have appeared suspicious or a potential law-breaker. Even if the white was "drunk or crazy," the policy suggested that a mentally inferior or intellectually mediocre white was still superior to and arbitrator over a black. Moreover, this type of white, or any other, could correct a black worker and, encountering self-defense on the part of the black, could kill the slave by law.

Note too the language: "any white person", "ever so drunk or crazy," "pursue, apprehend, and moderately correct such slave," "slave may be lawfully killed." "Any white person" stipulates adults and children; "drunk or crazy" makes the point that absolutely anyone with white skin, regardless if they were insane or disabled by whiskey, could make decisions about black workers' movements. "Pursue," "apprehend," and "moderately correct" imply white obligation to name blacks as animals or infantile children to be moderately corrected. Finally, "lawfully killed" suggests that, at all costs and by any means necessary, enslaved African Americans had to be taught that the price of resisting the image of whites as absolute, unquestioned authority was disposal of a black life. Such oppressive texts communicated a certain way of talking about the status of white and black people both in the popular culture and in the more formal jargon. The thoroughness of white power suggests that white men had a God complex.

Similarly, Mississippi's, as well as other southern states', laws stated that "every negro or mulatto found in the state, not able to show himself entitled to freedom, may be sold as a slave."[44] For instance in Alabama, the following notice was recorded in *The Mobile Com. Register and Patriot* newspaper of August 28, 1830. The white courts and police had apprehended a black man who had asserted his freedom.

> To the Jail of Mobile County, on the 9th inst. by B. B. Breeding, Esqr., a Justice of the Peace in and for Mobile County, a negro man who calls himself Levi Stanly. He is about 27 years old, about 6 feet in height, a fine thick wellset fellow and of dark complexion. He says he came from the Eastern shore of Maryland and professes to be a free man. His owner is requested to come forward prove property.[45]

This newspaper advertisement states that the man "professes to be a free man"—capturing the voice of a free black. But immediately the next sentence dismisses this claim and automatically calls for the "slave's" owner. The silent space between these two sentences thunders loud with the codes of white cultural assumptions. The white reader/spectator of this narrative naturally interprets the loud, empty space as an example of a black who cannot account satisfactorily for his existence, who is obviously a lawbreaker and chattel, and must have a master.

In other words, African Americans were presumed to be slaves and guilty until proven to the contrary. Such laws engendered a cultural social relationship in America where whites, on the psychological level, took for granted and by force of habit privileges for white skin. Deep within the consciousness and, one could conclude, the subconscious of white Christian America, layers of rational and irrational thought patterns began to take on a life of their own. With such oppositional perspectives branded deep within the white cultural psyche, European Americans, when encountering a black, began to expect, on instinct, criminal activity, evil intentions, immediate compliance, or an inferior being.

Cultural and Religious Justifications

Leaders in the national culture and Christian denominations fashioned religious and intellectual justifications for both enchained and free blacks. White Christian clergy and cultured intellectuals deployed all means to serve their pro-slavery ideology and theology. Beginning with the Christian presidents of the early United States, we immediately discover the persistent ambiguity of leadership: a claim to present a New World religious and secular democracy in the modern period while promoting the involuntary servant nature of black life.

Presidents Washington, Jefferson, Madison, Monroe, and Jackson were all slaveholders. Hero of the War of 1812, Andrew Jackson "saw the profitability of the slave-labor system as evidence of its moral integrity."[46] Thirteen of the first fifteen presidents were Southerners who held blacks as private chattel or Northerners who supported black legal subordination. And Benjamin Franklin, though not a president, kept black "servants" until 1750.[47]

Thomas Jefferson, the powerful and artistic hand behind the Declaration of Independence, immortalized the words "That all men are created equal; that they are endowed by their Creator with certain inalienable rights; that among these are life, liberty, and the pursuit of happiness." Here he bases this statement on religious principles and the scientific movement of nature. Both rationales, for Jefferson, are made manifest in the just and free relations in human culture. But the recurring "Mr. Hyde" side of Jefferson surfaces when he comments on how nature has damned African Americans' black color in contrast to whites':

> And is this difference of no importance? Is it not the foundation of a greater or less share of beauty in the two races? Are not the fine mixtures of red and white, the expressions of every passion by greater or less suffusions of colour in the one, preferable to that eternal monotony, which reigns in the countenances, that immoveable veil of black which covers all the emotion of the other race? Add to these, flowing hair, a more elegant symmetry of form. . . .

Owner of over two hundred slaves and the biological father of some, Jefferson is reading the slave body as an aesthetic text and arguing for and concretizing a national consensus that devalued black chattels' beauty in order to further entrench the primacy of white skin ("the fine mixtures of red and white"). One could suggest that his declaration that God had created "all men equal" implied white cultural beauty as the norm and that blackness fell short of this white aesthetic. And the founding father's founding document not only named black-white value but also determined who, in the space of the new nation, could pursue life, liberty, and happiness. Could this national leader have included black workers in American culture and faith when he indicated the "preference of the orangutan for the black woman"?[48] It is hard to believe that this great statesman would ever accept blacks as humans and Americans if he believed they copulated with monkeys.

Jefferson links, though in a qualified manner, racial beauty and the African American intellect as negative justification for not liberating blacks: "The unfortunate difference of color and perhaps of faculty," he wrote, "is a powerful obstacle to emancipation of these people."[49] All persons enjoy inalienable rights, but black folk's inherent, God-given rights were tarred by their ("perhaps") inferior intelligence. The formative planks of the new American nation—born with self-perceived divine ordained freedom and superior culture—contained a hesitation, if not denial, regarding black workers' aspiration. A collective white reading of the African American body produced a structural equation in American imagination, values, and life. Ignorance and ugliness equaled blacks.

Moving beyond artistic judgments, other national leaders advanced arguments concerning black people's need for guardianship as a blessing of their survival. In 1840, Secretary of State John C. Calhoun firmly asserted that liberation of the "negro or African race . . . would be, indeed, to them a curse instead of a blessing." His views imply a religious opinion, because a curse suggests a divine punishment, a type of condemnation to an absolute state of evil. In contrast, freedom for the white non-chattel population was a blessing or gift from God. Furthermore, Secretary of State Calhoun continues: "The African is incapable of self-care and sinks into lunacy under the burden of freedom. It is mercy to him to give him the guardianship and protection from mental death."[50] This voice from the federal government connects the inability of black people to control and think for themselves with intellectual life. Therefore, if whites gave them freedom, they would fall into a realm of insanity.

Calhoun believes the horizon of manumission could not provide blacks the possibility of gradual rising to eventual self-care, even under white protection. His dogmatic reasoning failed to consider any angle of interpretation granting black capability. His entire language revolves around dualistic antagonistic negatives—"curse," "incapable," "sinks," "burden," and "death"—reflecting a systematic worldview of polar opposites within a racial hierarchy. The Secretary of State feeds the national population with subliminal signs full of metaphorical meanings about black freedom. If slaves achieved equal civil status, they would, perhaps, run wild as lunatics, force the state to care for their basic needs, or become intellectual zombies. Calhoun, therefore, exposes and reinforces the crass linguistic structures of racial conversation and negative approaches to black people's particularity.

The sixteenth head of state, Abraham Lincoln, likewise suffered from the contradiction between the principles of "all men are created equal" and the American cultural patterns maintaining harmful racial difference. Initially Lincoln did not desire the abolition or the continuation of slavery; he wanted to avoid a fratricidal war between the north and south. If necessary, he wanted to save the union with chattel intact and without resorting to bloodshed. At one point he was pro-Colonization—the effort of the American Colonization Society to export (particularly free) blacks to Africa. Though the Civil War began in 1860 and seven southern states had already seceded before his inauguration, he did not feel forced to sign the Emancipation Proclamation until 1863. And, finally, Lincoln suggested compensation for the defeated Confederacy for its loss profits once African Americans obtained their freedom.[51]

The popular notion of Lincoln the Great Emancipator has served to obscure the depths and complexity of race, morality, and culture in the status of black people in America. Lincoln's leadership role in religious America and cultural convictions cause pause because of the essential emphasis placed on him as the major, if not determining, touchstone for white America's favorable conscience toward enslaved black and free people. He symbolizes the best and perhaps the ultimate in what is good in the nation's tradition. However, despite the standard re-creation of the chain of events and the surface representation of historical, social, and racial relations at the defining moment of the Civil War transforming blacks from a chattel status to a manumitted reality, Lincoln the president stands as a premier paradox.

He embodied the lack of the national will to prioritize blacks on par with all Americans, an act requiring consistent interpretation of equality for all in the biblical text. And he lacked the intention to reframe the basic documents of the republic, an act that would have required reconstructing the exclusive (racial) nature inherent in the Declaration of Independence and the U.S. Constitution. To say he signed the Emancipation Proclamation as a friend of the Negro, and thus to place him at the apex of favorable white leadership toward enslaved African Americans, is to further continue the false mythology of white consciousness that stretches back to the religious arrival and formative claims of the Plymouth Rock Pilgrims. (The latter claimed a city on a hill for their new covenant. But the "we" in their God-human covenant excluded Africans, African Americans, and American Indians.) The point is to name and reconstruct the reality of the Lincoln act, which reflected the pervasive concerns of white Americans to preserve their union. The mythology of Lincoln radically contrasts and contradicts black workers' theological perspective, which favored divine intent of universal freedom embedded in American culture (shown in Chapter 3 and following).

Just as national political leaders used the weight of their elected offices to present and signify justifications to the broader culture, so too did church leadership leverage the strength of their Christian pulpits and religious positions to present theological rationales for slavery and black subservience. Leading British clergy helped to set the tone for their English colonies by affirming the necessity of Christianizing slaves in order to make blacks more obedient. Dean George Berkeley urged religious conversion for this purpose in his position: "It would be of Advantage to [the colonial slavemasters'] Affairs, to have Slaves who should obey in all Things their Masters according to the Flesh. . . The Gospel Liberty consists with temporal Servitude; and that their Slaves would only become better Slaves by being Christians." This theological conviction emphasizes the voice of the slavemaster: the protection of his property and profits. It calms the master's fears and qualms regarding the religious implications of freedom propagated in the Bible. First, Dean Berkeley has to acknowledge the essence of the gospel as humanity achieving its full potential. He has to affirm this truth because it resonates with the colonial masters' self-declared faith and reading of Scriptures, the latter being a cultural and ideological underpinning for the original British settlers in the New World. But, second, he narrows access to God-ordained liberty to whites only. Specifically, he employs an interpretation in which the good news of Jesus Christ ("Gospel Liberty") accompanies ("consists with") physical bondage. According to Berkeley, the Hebrew and the Christian scriptures never intended to alter the status quo of earthly human relations.

However, if Christianity does bring the convert some type of newness or radical change or movement from the old to the new (an identifying and distinguishing mark of the Christian religion), how could black workers' acceptance of "Gospel Liberty" make a difference in their lives? A bishop of London and contemporary of Dean Berkeley resolved this perplexing dilemma with his epistle to the British colonies, "To the Masters and Mistresses of Families in the English Plantations Abroad." The Anglican bishop accepts the transformative presupposition of conversion but with a difference for blacks. His letter reads in part:

Christianity, and the embracing of the Gospel, does not make the least Alteration in Civil Property, or in any of the Duties which belong to Civil Relations. . . . The Freedom which Christianity gives, is a Freedom from the Bondage of Sin and Satan, and from the Dominion of Mens Lusts and Passions and inordinate Desires.[52]

Instead of defeating the physical, earthly, and visible structures and instruments of bondage entrapping the enslaved, the gospel causes a revolution in power relations on only the metaphysical and individual level. Here a theology of polar kingdoms is advocated. White colonial men rule supreme in civil matters, a realm where God enters only in order to support the masters' systemic supremacy and freedom. In the matters of (narrowly defined) personal sin, Christ rules over and defeats the manifestations of unbridled (slave) lusts and passions, a realm where God grants movement from the old self to the new spiritual being. The nagging question of freedom in the Bible in contrast to slavery in the colonies resolves itself by allowing a universal freedom—earthly for the white master and heavenly for the black worker.

A major Puritan thinker and prominent Boston pastor, Cotton Mather accepted the divine ordination of African American chattel. His theological attitude derived from connecting enslaved blacks in the colonies to the worst offspring in the Old Testament. He believed that blacks were the "miserable children of Adam and Noah." Out of one Bible and one historical human family arose two diametrically opposed races, black and white. Therefore to African Americans, he exhorted: "[Be] Patient and Content with such a Condition as God has ordered for [you]." By ordering the bondspeople into slavery, in Mather's theology, God helped to bring fear and trembling to the blacks as they (symbolically speaking) stood before the divine throne.

But Mather knew it would be both difficult to teach Christian principles to black workers and have masters take his efforts seriously. Regarding this formidable task of converting African Americans, he wrote: "Indeed their Stupidity is a Discouragement. It may seem, unto as little purpose, to Teach, as to wash an Æthiopian." But this "stupidity" presented itself as a challenge to the white Christian teacher and not a deterrent. And Mather sought to build on this ignorance so that the black person might be uplifted in knowledge of religious things. Cotton Mather synthesized his unique Protestant theology over against African Americans—their condemnation by divine intent, stigmatization by a wretched biblical lineage, and subordination by natural imbecility.[53]

Building on Cotton Mather's theological perspectives, which called for the religious instruction and care of Negro slaves, George White-field initiated the New England Great Awakening with subsequent implications for massive conversions of blacks to Christianity throughout the colonies. In the fall of 1740, Whitefield undertook a six-week, whirlwind religious revival in New England. His theological goal, which he achieved, was to awaken the dead preaching and pray-ing among Puritan clergy and churches of New England. He preached repentance and redemption from sin and salvation in a new life. All could allow Christ in their hearts. Stressing the priesthood of all believers, such evangelical zeal held strong spiritual egalitarian and democratic tendencies.

Indeed, in his pamphlet to southern colonial planters, he ques-tioned whether or not they felt their children "are any way better by Nature than the poor Negroes? No, in no wise. Blacks are just as much, and no more, conceived and born in Sin, as White Men are. Both . . . are naturally capable of the same [religious] improvement."[54]

However, though hinting at the possibility of spiritual and physi-cal equality, such evangelical enthusiasm succumbed to the domi-nant Protestant religious culture. In practice, Whitefield pursued the opposite course. He agreed that the colonies could not succeed with-out unpaid black slave labor and he could not alter that reality. The institution of white supremacy, in his convictions, was valid by law. Accordingly, Whitefield purchased a South Carolina plantation and roughly seventy-five enslaved black workers. The status of chattel, he reasoned, served to enhance the black person's conversion to Christ.

Likewise, George Fox, founder of the Quakers, preached a form of white-black, master-slave equality. Surpassing Whitefield, he harangued plantation owners to manumit their chattel eventually. In his proclamations, he urged white owners to "not slight them, . . . the Blacks . . . in that Christ dyed for all." And if slaves served whites, in Fox's judgment, the blacks should be manumitted at an appointed date. Fox continued his theological opinion by calling on masters "to let [slaves] go free after a considerable Term of Years, if they have served [whites] faithfully." But Fox's thrust toward a correct biblical interpretation of universal liberation, especially for those in bondage, and his accent on all humanity enjoying an inner divine light suffered from his qualifying clause (e.g., "if they have served faithfully")—a symbol of his openness to self-contradiction. The ultimate authority for abolishing slavery, for Fox, still remained in the perception of the

master's insight, not in black workers' inner light of love and freedom. His qualifying clause rendered authority to white human beings
and contradicted the universal inner light.

While arguing for the prospects of a set future manumission, Fox
simultaneously preached and accepted the slave system as "an institution that could be rationalized by the ancient dualisms of body and
soul,"[55] the physical and the metaphysical. His hesitation at immediate freedom, his granting the master the ultimate verdict over the
timetable, and his inconsistent religious teachings represented one of
the clearest instances of the push-pull phenomenon in Protestant theology. Here he draws on ancient European traditions as well as a European thought form which could rationally understand such dualisms.

Both north and south, a chorus of less prominent church leaders
echoed the pro-slavery arguments in Protestant theology. In their
autobiography, fugitive ex-slaves William and Ellen Craft document
the prevailing religious instructions given to white Christians, particularly in the north. The Rev. Dr. Gardiner Spring, a New York
Presbyterian minister, stated "if by one prayer he could liberate every
slave in the world he would not dare to offer it." Professor in the
Theological College of Andover, Massachusetts, Rev. Dr. Moses Stuart, taught that "many Southern slaveholders are true Christians."
Boston orthodox preacher Rev. W. M. Rogers declared, "When the
slave asks me to stand between him and his master, what does he
ask? He asks me to murder a nation's life; and I will not do it, because
I have a conscience,—because there is a God."

Episcopal pastor Rev. Dr. Taylor of New Haven, Connecticut, ref-
erencing his Christian and patriotic duty to return "fugitive slaves"
to their lawful masters, proclaimed, "Have I not shown you it is lawful to deliver up, in compliance with the laws, fugitive slaves, for the
high, the great, the momentous interests of those [Southern] States?"
Rt. Rev. Bishop Hopkins of Vermont offered his biblical interpretation, "It was warranted by the Old Testament. . . . What effect had the
Gospel in doing away with slavery? None whatever." And a Rev. William Crowell of Maine preached a Thanksgiving sermon in which he
exhorted his parishioners not to support fugitives because it would
bring further suffering on the millions of blacks still in chains.[56]

A Rev. Dr. Davidson of New Brunswick, New Jersey, presented a
theology of a recognized hierarchy of evils. In his view, slavery was
"an evil, but Disunion [of the United States] would retail a thousand
evils. One is a partial, and local evil, the other would be a universal,
and national disaster."[57] This starting point argues that Protestant

justice for enslaved blacks (that is, the correction of a small evil) subordinates itself beneath the demand to preserve the unity of the cultural way of life for slavemasters and other white citizens of the union (to avoid a catastrophic evil). To contradict the substance of the Christian religious and national social patterns threatened the expendability of black existence. In other words, Rev. Dr. Davidson confirmed a national message of a perpetual secondary status and an afterthought approach to black people.

A New York City clergyman, Rev. Dr. Krebs, added a voice for keeping blacks out of his region of the country when he preached: "Can we afford to have the refugee slave population of the South poured in upon us? . . . . and is the North prepared to welcome them en masse?"[58] Rev. Krebs hints at a bifocal religious lens differentiating between European immigrants' continued arrival from the old country and black workers' desire, as American residents, to experience the full terrain of their own country. He apparently concluded such a distinction by applying to only one group the biblical warrant of shelter for the homeless and the stranger. To African Americans, Krebs clouds their longings for shelter with pictures of hordes of blacks flooding white neighborhoods. A biblical interpretation of two sets of rules rationalized whites' sacred northern space. Similarly, Rev. Krebs would perceive an affinity with those from the old country because they would resonate, from his perspective, with American culture. Black residents in his own country, however, were not part of the definition of American values, lifestyles, and religion. Such inconsistent usage of the Scriptures and an exclusionary understanding of U.S. culture comprised one strand of white clergy's theology.

With some exceptions, Protestant ministers assumed one of three theological positions regarding white supremacy and black slavery. Fugitive Samuel Riggold Ward indicated two stances in these observations:

> Northern pulpit orators defend slavery from the Bible, the Old Testament and the New. . . . It is so of the most learned, most distinguished of them, of all denominations. . . . Another class of them maintain the most studious silence concerning it. . . . They neither hold nor treat slavery as sinful; and when pressed, declare that "some sins are not to be preached against."[59]

The first theological position honestly and openly stood for principles, founded on public and identifiable sources of debate. In Protestant teachings about slavery, this belief boldly offered a biblical perspective to undergird its defense of the chattel system. The second religious conviction appeared at first not to support African American bondage, but, in this case, silence meant consent. The "studious silence" of some northern clergy indicated their conscious attempt to shield pro-slavery perspectives while offering a public silence that might give the impression of a pro-justice stance. Arising out of a slave culture, this latter trend in Protestant theology developed a negative duplicity when confronted with the Christian treatment of blacks. Those who held this position remained silent when the time came for them to oppose the Christianity of the slavemasters. "Studious silence" eventually became the hallmark of liberalism.

Excluding the rare exceptions who fought against slavery based on religious grounds, a third theological option in Protestant thought was advanced in a pamphlet entitled "On the Duties of Christians Owning Slaves," by Calvin H. Wiley, a Presbyterian minister. After calmly and carefully waxing eloquent about general Christian principles, Wiley cuts to the heart of the matter: Should masters "liberate slaves" as a Christian imperative? His religious instructions counseled: "'Shall I liberate my slaves, or continue to hold them in bondage.' This question each owner must answer for himself. . . . It will be his imperative duty to determine, if possible, what is best for him and his servants."[60]

Wiley's pamphlet presents the centrist position assumed by Protestant clergy. It is neither a viewpoint of defense nor of silence. It speaks to the issue but shifts the burden to the Christian conscience of slaveholders. Resuming his instructions, however, Wiley unveils his pro-slavery religious posture when he writes: "Authority was ordained of God—and all authority must have the power of enforcing its lawful commands, otherwise it is not power at all." And he asserts: Just as children are subject to parental rule and discipline, likewise are slaves to their masters. By connecting the master's authority to God and giving the decisive decision of manumission to the owner, the centrist theological doctrine (a contorted linguistic gymnastics) supported the cultural lifestyle and profit accumulation shared by the overwhelming majority of slaveholders.

Religious denominations reflected similar theological claims, given the apologetic worldview of national leaders who provided vision to American culture and church spokespersons who educated Protestant believers. As national denominations, no Protestant churches vigorously opposed slavery. National religious organizations were racked with at least three major internal agendas: to be (a) champions of pro-slavery causes, (b) advocates for excommunicating slaveholders from a denomination, and (c) minority voices for slavery's abolition. Even the latter two positions did not always and automatically mean their groups called for the universal and immediate death of the chattel system. Assuming conviction (b), a Christian could vote to expel a slaveholding member without standing for the freeing of chattel outside of the denomination. This person could simply want no slavemaster as neighbor in the body of believers. And the defender of the abolition preference (c) could argue for denominational membership based on freeing only those slaves who belonged to members of his or her denominational members, still avoiding the issue of universal liberation of black people.

Again the question of murky ambivalence versus forthright justice or support for black slavery versus Christian freedom determined the character of American Protestantism, this time on the organizational level. Even denominations that passed resolutions did not exhibit the commitment or willpower to enforce them. Slaveholder membership and pro-slavery sentiment simply coexisted with revolutionary Christian positions. This state of affairs defined Protestant churches from the beginning of the seventeenth century until the 1860s.

The Presbyterian church underwent its first major split over doctrinal issues in 1837. And both the resulting Old and New School groups included slaveholders in their memberships. By 1861, the second major realignment occurred, this time around pro- and anti-slavery theological beliefs. In other words, not until 1861 did the Presbyterian denomination rid itself of those owners of black people. The latter white Christians separated and formed their own Presbyterian organization. Much earlier, the Methodist church strongly had attacked slavery in 1780 as "contrary to the laws of God, man, nature, and hurtful to society." But this and future declarations were ignored by the Methodist membership. Finally in 1844, the religious group split into the Methodist Church North and South. Yet at the 1860 northern General Conference, sympathizers of black racial subordination defeated every resolution to expel slaveholding members.

The Southern Baptist Convention originated in 1845 in order to solidify those Baptists who believed theologically in white supremacy. The remaining northern Baptists differed theologically with their southern brethren on the grounds that it was against the faith to have slavemasters as denominational members. However, the northerners did not take the next step and argue for the universal abolition of slavery for all of God's people, inside and outside of the denomination. The northern Baptists opposed the admission of slaveholders into their group—a major theological difference from true Christian desire to witness for the universal freedom for the black enslaved. Not to take the Lord's Supper with a southern Baptist was one thing, but to mobilize the northern Baptists to break the social relations of white-black chattel was another. For the northern Baptists to be for the exclusion of the master did not automatically mean they were for breaking slavery's chains. The southerners were openly embracing the evil of racism, while the northerners fell short of a consistent Christian way of life.

The Disciples of Christ supported slavery as late as 1853. And the Congregational churches, which had slaveowners and non-slaveowners in its denominations, could not assume a strong anti-slavery posture. Therefore they remained deadlocked and compromised theologically. In the south, slaveholders dominated the Episcopalian church. As a national group, it steered clear of the controversial issue by allowing its pro-slavery members (north and south) to speak out, tolerating what some saw as a necessary evil. However, it did contain a few prominent anti-slavery spokespersons such as John Jay.

The Quakers suffered internally from a dual theological attitude toward slavery and African Americans. Until 1797 the Quakers had spoken for the rights of blacks, as long as they did not join their religious organization. After 1803, a lull ensued in the Quaker egalitarian religious impulse and anti-slavery activity. The 1805 Philadelphia meeting decided to end all meetings for blacks, "as Friends upon weighty deliberation, were united in the belief that the service of them [blacks] was over, and they have now several places for worship of their own." And a strong pro-Colonization representation permeated the group for some time, urging the deportation of free blacks to Africa.[61] Still, a small group of Quakers, along with a scattered few heroic individual persons and local churches from other denominations, persisted in perceiving slavery as the epitome of sin theologically.[62]

Conclusion

During the slavery era, Protestantism and American culture were torn apart by polar opposites—a push toward divinely inspired human fellowship and a pull toward self-centered avarice. The Pilgrims' arrival initiated this dilemma with a theology, a language, and way of life that positioned them as "a city on a hill" above all others.

Such a potentially harmless faith claim could have marked the beginning of the Puritan religious witness to serve those voices locked out from God's earthly resources. Instead, the 1620 Plymouth Rock and 1607 Jamestown pioneers from Europe employed an ambiguous but deadly approach toward the Other, those who differed from European convictions, culture, and conscience. A fundamental plank in American faith and lifestyle positioned white and black as extreme opposites. Thus a subservient African American existence in Christian America challenged the possibility of revitalizing and enriching the collective faith and national identity.

A litany of perplexing dichotomies and contradictory metaphors permeated colonial and pre-Civil War North America: white versus black, earthly freedom versus heavenly freedom, democracy versus civil restrictions, equality versus racial hierarchy, theologically ordained privilege versus divinely backed subordination, mind versus body, civilized versus heathen, and intellect versus emotion. Systemically, symbolically, and linguistically a framework of lethal contradiction characterized Protestantism and American culture.

Spiritually, instead of white Christians extending the love and justice of the Bible to those other than themselves, whiteness came to signify the in-group and blackness the Outsider. An inviting spirituality of embracing difference would have relished the resources and contributions offered by the diversity and plurality in the total human family. But Plymouth Rock and Jamestown colonies narrowed the mainstream, so that Africans and African Americans bore the weight of permanent marginal status. It is as if the "founding Christian fathers" created a "white us against black them" demonic genie who has not been placed back in its bottle. Such a warped biblically based spirituality skewed the mood and decayed the development of the universal national health and well-being. Only by overcoming a narrowly defined ethnocentric spirituality can the beneficent winds of the collective breathe new life into an overall community afflicted by stunted faith and lethargic witnessing.

American slavery days institutionalized a political economy featuring black bodies as commodities for white use and profit. The Puritan claim over abundant natural and human resources in the New World left broken bodies as an attendant side effect. The new earth of America acquired by adventurers from Europe yielded opportunity for European Americans. Immigrants built a republic on the efforts of unpaid African and African American labor. This foundational discrepancy between reapers of fruit and the workers in God's vineyards damaged at the root all potential for a communal sharing in a divinely created ecology and economy. Africans and African Americans literally constructed colonial and post-colonial America from the ground up. White Protestant families made millions, reaped from a monopolization of affluence and an exclusive grip on political offices. Government and industry stood on the side of Christian whites, especially those with wealth. And such concentrated power kept blacks in their subordinate place. Yet the nation would turn in on itself because those with riches required the Other to labor to create more wealth and, then, to purchase the commodities produced by wealth as the only way to create more profit for the wealthy. But the physical and emotional proficiency of the laborers to produce efficiently and their shrinking purchasing ability would decline over the long term, thus endangering the national product for all. To correct this overall sinful political economic disequilibrium and engender the success of the whole—success defined as each individual and community having the necessities of life—will depend on equalizing the collective say over economic and political power. In a word, it will require a new Common Wealth.

Anthropologically during slavery, European Americans argued that their biological characteristics were superior and more pleasing to the eye aesthetically—thereby claiming whiteness as the image of God. On the other hand, blacks suffered a caricature of a kinship to the orangutan, ensnared by childlike emotions and sexual passions, and repelled by things of the intellect. It seemed as if, by nature, two types of human beings existed. If natural genetic structures produced higher attributes in one race, then logically that group should command the heights of leadership and have control over the naturally inferior race. Drawing on its inherent inclinations, the latter community should serve the former. Blacks should not only labor for the greater group but also provide sports, laughter, and sexual entertainment for naturally superior people. But this biologically determined argument failed not only from logic and scientific experiment, but also from the negative effects of blocking the full contributions of all human capabilities to the national treasury. A nation's success results from all sectors attaining full human potential.

Culturally, colonial and pre-Civil War America systematized a way of life privileging white skin over black. In time, it became a force of habit, an instinctual reflex for white Christians. Dominant social patterns were infused with accepted, normal, and expected human interactions. In other words, American fabric and identity encouraged whites to accept adventure and lack of limits to their domain. But blacks were expected to cast their sights on circumscribed realities and goals, mainly in the realm of service to and entertainment for others at the expense of themselves.

Culturally, this meant regularizing a worldview, a perception and understanding of the cosmos, in which European Americans took for granted their having the final word on reality or having some major part in a decision-making process. They facilitated their control and expertise by defining the universal nature of cultural codes and criteria to suit, primarily, their capabilities. However, the parts of a national culture (for example, mutual nature-human interaction and transformation, nuclear and extended family ties, exchange of goods, and shared perception of the common well-being) arise out of balance and harmony between, and respect for, particularities and recognition of common threads. Privileging hierarchy and undemocratic control decays culture. Promoting balance, harmony, and respect in public spaces serves as vitamins and fresh air for a healthy organism, such as national culture.

In terms of language in American culture, a way of talking about race relations developed that conveyed a symbolic representation of unequal social patterns. A structural discourse included both signs about racial reality and methods of communicating these significations. Biblical images and metaphors took on negative meanings when associated with African Americans (e.g., "dark," "curse," etc.). Indeed black life imaged a theory of negativity: colonial and postcolonial North America began to talk about the abnormal status of blacks in order to verify, by contrast, the normalcy of white reality. Consequently the naming of blackness brought a sense of reference for white identity. Talk about enslaved African Americans implied the power politics of negative naming.

Furthermore, symbolic representation included a systematic ordering of recognizable language codes. For the master, this suggested the distinction between an uppity Negro and an obedient chattel. For the African American, forgetting black-white codes could be a matter of life and death. Still, the memorization of sign vehicles embodying crucial survival pointers was merely the starting point for blacks. For black folk, decoding these signs was not the end, but the beginning process. In addition to categorizing and codifying race relation statements and definitions, the African American had to navigate the diverse contexts in which a certain code might arise. In other words, a sign in and of itself meant one thing; but positioned in various contexts (e.g., different black-white situations), the substance for which that sign stood assumed multi-layered meanings.

Black workers had to read verbal and body texts with intense purpose. These language and flesh signs were vital since a so-called standard English had been established in early America that, under the guise of objectively expressing correct methods of communication, separated the blacks who would inch toward full life from those who would not. Perhaps certain free blacks and house Negro slaves were most astute in reading the signs of the times. The most successful ones were those who adopted so-called standard English. (In reality, "standard" English was simply one of many regional dialects that the master had the resources and naming power to claim as universally standard.) What was needed was a national language—based on metaphors, symbols, codes, grammar, and communication methods that privileged democracy and the equality of all dialects in English. A change in language would have enhanced the reality of race relations in American culture.

The theology of Protestantism covered a range of arguments and justifications. Some raised the curse of Ham in Genesis chapter nine to justify slavery; they saw African Americans as the embodiment of those condemned forever to be hewers of wood and drawers of water. In contrast, Pilgrims, Anglicans, and subsequent religious groups began to accept covenantal faith creeds. Some preached this in doctrines. Others simply witnessed in the world as if they occupied a special space of God's grace. Theologically, nowhere did the dominant religious denominations develop a theory or practice that allowed for black workers to possess an authentic, intellectual interpretation of the Bible and Protestantism.

Some denominations claimed that Jesus never spoke out against slavery directly. Others taught that Jesus allowed for two allegiances, one to Caesar (or the civil slavery authority) and one to God (the invisible spiritual authority). With a split between the mind and body, the earthly and heavenly kingdoms, and the power of divine church institutions in holy matters and of human plantation organization in secular affairs, masters accepted slave conversion into the body of Christ. Now plantation owners could cite how the lordship of Christ paralleled their lordship over the plantation. Christ brought a universal liberation for all, in the spiritual realm for the slave and in the earthly realm for the master.

Protestant denominations built themselves theologically on soft foundations regarding slavery. No religious group could take a stand for democracy, freedom, justice, and compassion for blacks in bondage because the denominations were captured in or paralyzed by the ideology of pro-chattel Christians. No denomination could place another Christian slave supporter outside of the entire body of Christ as an actual representative of the Anti-Christ. While the conservatives stood up on theological principles of white supremacy, their liberal members kept silent or claimed overall unity at the expense of black bondage. Part of the fundamental problem of "white" Protestantism was its inability to discard an exclusionary fiber from its theological heritage. A more true Protestant theology indigenous to America would have to grow out of the witness and intellectual religious contributions of African American communities of faith physically positioned on the margins of the mainstream.

A black theology could combine with the ever present remnant of faithful witnesses to Scripture signified by the John Browns of pre-Civil War America. Similarly every denomination had a few white anti-slavery proponents who aided the black leaders of the Underground Railroad and other liberation vehicles. From the mainline Protestant churches, some minute groups of Christians drew theological lines of demarcation and formed anti-slavery splinter groups— the Wesleyan Methodists, the American Free Baptist Mission Society, the Free Presbyterians, the Franckean Evangelical Lutheran Synod, the Indiana Yearly Meeting of Anti-Slavery Friends, and the Progressive Friends. Out of the margins and remnant of the center, the two faces of Protestantism and American culture may well become a unified theology and social patterns of democracy, justice, and liberation for all Americans. Through the complete freedom of society's least, we attain the ultimate goal of full spiritual and material humanity for all.

NOTES

1. From Sydney E. Ahlstrom, *A Religious History of the American People,* vol. 1 (Garden City, N.Y.: Image Books, 1975), 183–84.

2. Quoted from an excerpt of his *Autobiography of a Fugitive Negro: His Anti-slavery Labours in the United States, Canada, and England* (London: John Snow, 1855); found in *The Anti-Slavery Advocate,* January 1856, 326, at Boston Public Library Rare Books section.

3. For an overview of Pilgrim and other European Christian arrivals to the New World, see Williston Walker, *A History of the Christian Church,* 3d ed. (New York: Charles Scribner's Sons, 1970), 412 and 432–36.

4. See Ahlstrom, *A Religious History of the American People,* 134–35; and Walker, *A History of the Christian Church,* 402–19.

5. Ahlstrom, *A Religious History of the American People,* 183.

6. This white Protestant vocational journey did not differ substantively from a similar momentous, white Roman Catholic act in 1492. In the early 1490s, Pope Alexander VI commissioned King Ferdinand and Queen Isabella of Spain along with Christopher Columbus in the same manner concerning the latter's European discovery of the New World: " . . . out of the fullness of our apostolic power, by the authority of Almighty God conferred upon us in blessed Peter and of the vicarship of Jesus Christ, which we hold on earth, do by tenor of these presents, should any of said islands have been found by your envoys and captains, give, grant, and assign to you and your heirs and successors . . . forever, together with all their dominions, cities, camps, places, and villages, and all rights, jurisdictions, and appurtenances, all islands and mainlands found." Then the pope went on to use God as a justification of European Christian violence against others: "Let no one therefore, infringe, or with rash boldness contravene, this our recommendation. . . . Should anyone presume to attempt this, be it known to him that he will incur the wrath of Almighty God and of the blessed apostles Peter and Paul." For the full text of this papal bull, see H. S. Commanger, ed., *Documents of American History to 1898,* vol. 1 (New York: Appleton-Century-Crofts, 1968), 2–3.

7. See Winthrop D. Jordan, *White Over Black: American Attitudes Toward the Negro, 1550–1812* (New York: W.W. Norton, 1977), 4–30, for British attitudes toward blacks and Africans in Europe prior to 1607. Also reference Audrey Smedley, *Race in North America: Origin and Evolution of a Worldview* (Boulder, Colo.: Westview Press, 1993).

8. Historian Forrest G. Wood writes: "The idea of individual ownership of land appeared in New England as early as 1623, when Governor William Bradford of Plymouth, after a plan for communal property ownership had failed, divided the land among individual households." See his *The Arrogance of Faith: Christianity and Race in America from the Colonial Era to the Twentieth Century* (New York: Alfred A. Knopf, 1990), 233.

9. For the treatment of blackness and evil in contrast to whiteness and purity, see Joseph R. Washington, *Anti-Blackness in English Religion* (New York: Mellen Press, 1984); Edward K. Trefz's three-part series in volumes VII and VIII of *The Boston Public Quarterly,* "Satan as the Prince of Evil: The Preaching of New England Puritans," (January 1955), 3–22; (April 1956), 71–84; (July 1956), 148–59; and Adolphe Didron, *Christian Iconography: The History of Christian Art in the Middle Ages,* 2 vols. (New York: Frederick Unger, 1965). In Didron's vol. 2, see "Iconography of Devils," 109–52, and in volume 1, 467.

10. Emma Julia Scott, "The Underground Railroad" in *The Underground Railroad in Illinois,* vol. III, Box 75, page 3, Ohio Historical Society Archives, Columbus, Ohio, Wilbur H. Siebert, Collection 116. Hereinafter these archives will be cited as "Siebert Papers."

11. Ahlstrom, *A Religious History of the American People,* 195.

12. Documentation on the role and religious views of the white patriot John Brown as he waged armed struggle to free black slaves can be found in the Siebert Papers.

13. Cyprian Davis, O.S.B. (a black Benedictine monk) describes an earlier arrival of blacks to the Americas. According to Davis, these blacks were brought to the New World by European Roman Catholics. See his *The History of Black Catholics in the United States* (New York: Crossroad, 1990).

14. Found in *Africa Remembered: Narratives by West Africans from the Era of the Slave Trade*, ed. Philip D. Curtin (Madison: University of Wisconsin Press, 1968), 92–94. For another insightful and graphic personal experience of being captured in Africa and sold into the European slave trade, see the autobiography of Venture Smith in *Five Black Lives*, introduction by Arna Bontemps (Middletown, Conn.: Wesleyan University Press, 1971).

A similar response to a first sighting of white people was expressed by a Mr. Johnson, an African captured near the Gambian River. He offered the following testimony. "First white man I ever saw was Capt. Boss, of Newport, R.I., and I tot he was de devil. . . . [Another African] tole me he was a man, but I could not believe it." (John W. Blassingame, ed., *Slave Testimony: Two Centuries of Letters, Speeches, Interviews, and Autobiographies* (Baton Rouge: Louisiana State University Press, 1977), 125.

15. See Lerone Bennett, Jr., *Before the Mayflower: A History of the Negro in America, 1619–1964* (Baltimore, Md.: Penguin Books, 1973), 29–30; and Vincent Harding, *There Is a River: The Black Struggle for Freedom in America* (New York: Harcourt Brace Jovanovich, 1981), 27.

16. Quoted in Donald R. Wright, *African Americans in the Colonial Era: From African Origins Through the American Revolution* (Arlington Heights, Ill.: Harlan Davidson, 1990), 19.

17. See Walker, *A History of the Christian Church,* 431–32.

18. See Benjamin Quarles, *The Negro in the Making of America* (London: Collier Books, 1969), 33.

19. Found in B. A. Botkin, ed., *Lay My Burden Down: A Folk History of Slavery* (Chicago: University of Chicago Press, 1945), 25.

20. Historian James Pope-Hennessy writes: "[H]istorians have generally agreed upon the year 1441 as that in which the modern slave trade was, so to speak, officially declared open. In that year ten Africans from the northern Guinea Coast were shipped to Portugal as a gift to Prince Henry the Navigator." See his *Sins of the Fathers: A Study of the Atlantic Slave Trade 1441–1807* (London: Cassell Publishers, 1967), 8.

21. See John S. Pobee, *Toward an African Theology* (Nashville, Tenn.: Abingdon, 1979), 54–60.

22. See Fredrickson's *White Supremacy: A Comparative Study in American and South African History* (Oxford: Oxford University Press, 1982), 7–8.

23. See George W. Williams, *A History of the Negro Race in America, 1619–1880* (New York: Arno Press, 1968), 123. Indeed the first twenty Africans brought to Jamestown in 1619 "were almost certainly slaves kidnapped from the Spanish. . . . When, as was sometimes the case, a black was free, or an indentured servant, qualifying adjectives were added, as in the case of John Philip, a 'free Christian Negro,' probably a sailor just passing through Virginia in 1624"; see Robert McColley, *Slavery in Jeffersonian Virginia* (Urbana: University of Illinois Press, 1973), x–xi.

24. Williams, *A History of the Negro Race in America*, 121.

25. Williams, *A History of the Negro Race in America*, 121–22.

26. Quarles, *The Negro in the Making of America*, 35; and Jordan, *White Over Black*, 44.

27. Jordan, *White Over Black* , 44.

28. Williams, *A History of the Negro Race in America*, 123; Also see former slave William Grimes (in *Five Black Lives*, 62) whose father was one of the "most wealthy planters in Virginia" but whose mother was a slave. Consequently, his status was chattel because "[i]n all the Slave States the children follow the condition of their mother."

29. Harding, *There Is a River,* 27; Quarles, *The Negro in the Making of America,* 72 and 41.

30. Henry Bibb, *Narrative of the Life and Adventures of Henry Bibb, An American Slave, Written by Himself* (1850; reprint, Philadelphia, Pa.: Historic Publications, n.d.), 35.

31. See August Meier and Elliott Rudwick, *From Plantation to Ghetto* (New York: Hill and Wang, 1970), 41; Quarles, *The Negro in the Making of America*, 36; and David Brion Davis, *The Problem of Slavery in Western Culture* (Ithaca, N.Y.: Cornell University Press, 1970), 210.

32. Jordan, *White Over Black*, 181 and 92–93.

33. See Quarles, *The Negro in the Making of America,* 36–37; William Z. Foster, *The Negro People in American History* (New York: International Publishers, 1970), 37; and Meier and Rudwick, *From Plantation to Ghetto,* 44. For a more personal account of slave laws, see ex-slave James Mars's story in *Five Black Lives*, 38.

34. Refer to Nell Irvin Painter, *Sojourner Truth: A Life, A Symbol* (New York: W.W. Norton, 1997), 23.

35. See pages 18–19 of "The Liberty Almanac" for 1851, found in the Cornell University Slavery Collection. For the actual ending of slavery in New York and New Jersey, see Graham Russell Hodges, ed., *Black Itinerants of the Gospel: The Narratives of John Jea and George White* (Madison, Wis.: Madison House, 1993), 3.

36. See Harding, *There Is a River*, 46.

As late as 1846, the southern states stood confident in the federal government's absolute commitment to maintain slavery violently. "Says the Editor of the Marysville (Tenn.) *Intelligencer,* in an article on the character and condition of the slave population:

[The north and the south] 'have also agreed with each other that through the agency of the Federal Government, they will protect each of the States against invasion, and . . . against domestic violence. Thus the entire power of the General Government is pledged to crush the slave should he refuse to obey his master."

Quoted in "Slavery and the Slaveholder's Religion; As Opposed to Christianity" by Samuel Brooke, Cincinnati, 1846, 14–15; found in *May Anti-Slavery Pamphlets 40,* Cornell University Slavery Collection.

37. In the early to mid-1840s, former slave James L. Smith confirmed the rabid pro-slavery feelings in the north. See his autobiography in *Five Black Lives,* 185 and 193. Likewise review the text of the 1850 federal Fugitive Slave Bill in William Still's *The Underground Railroad: A Record of Facts, Authentic Narratives. Letters, Etc., Narrating the Hardships, Hair-breadth Escapes and Death Struggles of the Slaves in their Efforts for Freedom As Related by Themselves and Others, or Witnessed by the Author; Together with Sketches of Some of the Largest Stockholders, and Most Liberal Aiders and Advisers, of the Road* (1872; reprint, Chicago: Johnson Publishing Company, 1970), 355–60.

38. Quoted in *The Anti-Slavery Advocate,* London, January 1855, 235. Also see "Seizure of a Slaver" in *The Anti-Slavery Advocate,* London, May 1856. Both are found in the Boston Public Library Rare Books section.

Fugitive John Brown, residing in London in 1855, confirmed the regular replenishing of "Saltbacks" to Georgia slave plantations: "It is supposed that there are no slaves imported into the south from Africa. I am quite sure that the reverse is the case. There was a planter lived on an estate adjoining my old master Stevens. . . . That man had, to my knowledge, five hundred of them, all fresh from Africa, and I know that new ones were constantly brought in. We call them 'Saltbacks.'" See an excerpt from *Slave Life in Georgia: A Narrative of the Life, Sufferings, and Escape of John Brown, a Fugitive Slave, Now in England,* ed. L. A. Chamerovzow, Secretary of the British and Foreign Anti-Slavery Society, London, 1855; found in *The Anti-Slavery Advocate,* London, April 1855, 257.

For a detailed account of how a British ship stops and boards an American vessel smuggling African cargo in September 1857, see *The Anti-Slavery Advocate,* March 1858, 116–17.

39. Ibid.

40. Regarding the continued illegal smuggling of Africans and their mode of transport, Captain Smith responded in his interview below:

"How do you pack [the Africans on the boat] at night?"

"They lie down upon the deck, on their sides, body to body. There would not be room enough for all to lie on their backs."

(See *The Anti-Slavery Advocate,* January 1855, 235, found in the Boston Public Library Rare Books section).

Also compare Quarles, *The Negro in the Making of America,* 63–64; James L. Smith in *Five Black Lives,* 193; and Bennett, *Before the Mayflower,* 47.

The sandwiching of Africans en route, in addition to the entire slave trading process, decimated the numbers stolen from the Continent. Lord Palmerston (of the 1844 British House of Lords) made this point: "that of the three Negroes seized in the interior of Africa, to be sent into slavery, but one reaches his destination, the two others died in the course of the operations of the slave trade. Whatever may be the number landed, therefore, we must triple it to obtain the true number of human beings." See "Preliminary Report: Touching the Condition and Management of Emancipated Refugees; Made to the Secretary of War, by the American Freedmen's Inquiry Commission, June 30, 1863," found in the Slavery section at the National Archives, Washington, D.C., file 3280, 1863, microfilm roll 199, p. 37.

The voices of dead African ancestors cry out for a conversation with those European and European American Christian slave cultures that were responsible for founding Protestantism with freedom for one group and subordination for another. Coming to terms with such a foundational dichotomy, its growth, and current manifestations will be one way of strengthening the positive aspects of Christianity while attending to the empowering parts of its culture.

Regarding the violation of the 1808 end of the international European slave trade, other texts documenting the continuation of the Europeans' importing of Africans as slaves are: W. E. B. Du Bois, *The Suppression of the African Slave Trade to the United States of America, 1638–1870* (New York: Longmans, Green, and Co., 1896); John C. Rives, *The Congressional Globe: The Official Proceedings of Congress, U.S. 35th Congress. 1st Sess.*, (Washington: Rives, 1858), 1362; and John J. Labor, ed., *Cyclopaedia Political Science, Political Economy, and of the Political History of the United States*, vol. 3 (Chicago: Melbert B. Cary, 1884), 732ff.

41. Quarles, *The Negro in the Making of America* , 63.

42. Quarles, *The Negro in the Making of America*, 63; and Bennett, *Before the Mayflower*, 45.

43. William and Ellen Craft, *Running a Thousand Miles for Freedom; or the Escape of William and Ellen Craft from Slavery* (1860; reprint, Salem, N.H.: Ayer Company, 1991), 14–15.

44. Quoted in Charles H. Nichols, *Many Thousand Gone: The Ex-slaves' Account of Their Bondage and Freedom* (Leiden, Netherlands: E. J. Brill, 1963), 22.

45. Taken from the Library of Congress, Manuscript Division, Slave Narrative Project, Box A891.

46. See Wood, *The Arrogance of Faith*, 41.

47. See Wood, *The Arrogance of Faith,* 333; and "Facts for the People of the Free States" found in the *May Anti-Slavery Pamphlets 40* (n.d., n.p.) at Cornell University's Slavery Collection. The Ben Franklin reference comes from Davis, *The Problem of Slavery in Western Culture*, 191.

48. Jefferson's full quote privileges white physiognomy over blacks: "And to these, flowing hair, a more elegant symmetry of form, their own judgment

in favor of the whites, declared by their preference of them, as uniformly as is the preference of the orangutan for the black woman over those of his own species." From his "Notes on Virginia" in Kenneth J. Zanca, ed., *American Catholics and Slavery: 1789–1866* (Lanham, Md.: University Press of America, 1994), 50.

49. The latter quote comes from Leslie Howard Owens, *This Species of Property: Slave Life and Culture in the Old South* (Oxford: Oxford University Press, 1977), 9, and the former from Jordan, *White Over Black,* 458.

50. Quoted in Owens, *This Species of Property,* 3.

51. See Nichols, *Many Thousand Gone,* 182.

52. Both quotes from Dean Berkeley and the Anglican bishop are found in Jordan, *White Over Black,* 191. One of the most concentrated efforts by the British mother country clergy was the Society for the Propagation of the Gospel in Foreign Lands (SPG, the official arm of the Church of England), established in 1701 to convert to Christianity slaves and American Indians. Since its inception, the SPG missionaries sent to the colonies affirmed only temporal and not physical freedom for slaves. Their thesis was that the gospel made blacks better slaves. See Davis' exposition of the SPG, *The Problem of Slavery in Western Culture,* 212ff.

53. See Wood, *The Arrogance of Faith,* 256–57; Wright, *African Americans in the Colonial Era,* 75; and Jordan, *White Over Black,* 187.

54. Quoted in Jordan, *White Over Black,* 214. Also see Davis, *The Problem of Slavery in Western Culture,* 148 and Wood, *The Arrogance of Faith,* 122 and 127.

55. Quoted in Wood, *The Arrogance of Faith,* 77. The quote on eventually liberating slaves is found in Jordan, *White Over Black,* 194.

56. Craft, *Running a Thousand Miles for Freedom,* 94–96.

57. Ibid. See also *The Anti-Slavery Watchman,* no. 1 (November 1853): 24–25; found at the Cornell University Slavery Collection.

58. From *The Anti-Slavery Watchman* no. 1 (November 1853): 24–25.

59. Excerpts from Samuel Riggold Ward's *Autobiography of a Fugitive Negro: His Anti-slavery Labours in the United States, Canada, and England* (London: John Snow, 1855), found in *The Anti- Slavery Advocate,* January 1855, 326, located at the Boston Public Library Rare Books section.

60. His pamphlet is found in the University of North Carolina at Chapel Hill, Southern Historical Collection. The date is around the early 1850s. Hereafter, references to these archives will be given as UNC Southern Historical Collection.

61. Notes on Quakers are from: Jordan, *White Over Black,* 195, 401, and 419–22; Davis, *The Problem of Slavery in Western Culture,* chap. 10; and the *National Anti-Slavery Standard,* New York, August 13, 1840, 38, found in the Widener Library, Harvard University. Hereinafter, references will be noted as Widener Library, Harvard.

Commenting on the Quakers' ambiguous theological discourse, author Alama Jagsch wrote: "[W]ith all their anti-slavery professions, the Quakers in New England, as a religious sect, were not much more friendly than others to the immediate emancipation of the slaves. Quaker meeting houses, except in a few instances, were closed against anti-slavery lecturers, and members who became too zealous in the cause were often labored with as those who had strayed from the true path and, in extreme cases, were disowned."

See Jagsch's *The Underground Railroad in Connecticut*, the Siebert Papers, Box 70, n.p.

Regarding Congregational churches, see *The Anti-Slavery Advocate*, London, January 1853, 1, found at the Boston Public Library Rare Books section; for the Disciples of Christ, see the same publication for November 1853, 105; for the Episcopalians, see Wood, *The Arrogance of Faith*, 140 and 276–77, Jordan, *White Over Black*, 206–12, and James Gillespie Birney, *The American Churches: The Bulwarks of American Slavery* (1842; reprint, New York: Arno Press and The New York Times, 1969), 39–40; for the Baptists, Methodists, and Presbyterians, see Wood, *The Arrogance of Faith*, chap. 8, and Brooke, "Slavery and the Slaveholder's Religion; As Opposed to Christianity," 64. For other Presbyterian references, see *The Anti-Slavery Advocate*, London, February 1854, 129 (The Boston Public Library Rare Books section); Brooke, "Slavery and the Slaveholder's Religion; As Opposed to Christianity," 41–42; and James Gillespie Birney, *The American Churches*, 29–34. For other Methodist references, see Margaret Washington Creel, *A Peculiar People: Slave Religion and Community-Culture among the Gullahs* (New York: New York University Press, 1988), 141; and Birney, *The American Churches*, 13–22.

62. For the role of individual Quakers in assisting the abolition of slavery, see the "Narrative of William W. Brown" in *Five Slave Narratives*, ed. William Loren Katz (New York: Arno Press, 1968), 102; Wood, *The Arrogance of Faith*, 281; and a letter from Avis Cox Woodard, who migrated to Indiana, to her mother, Miriam Bishop Cox, of Wansboro, N.C., dated September 20, 1832, found in the UNC Southern Historical Collection. For other anti-slavery religious activities, see the *National Anti-Slavery Standard*, June 1842, 6, at Widener Library, Harvard.

For examples of individual white churches fighting against slavery, see a December 6, 1892 letter to W. H. Siebert (of Ohio State University) from an unidentified correspondent (of Sardinia, Ohio) describing the history of the Underground Railroad and the participation of Presbyterians, Quakers, and Wesleyan Methodists in Ohio's Brown County, Pleasant Township, and Sandusky between 1835 and 1856. Note that black settlements of former slaves in these counties and towns would help runaways get to these white churches; it was safer for runaways to hide out at white churches than stay in black communities. (Found in the Siebert Papers, Box 69, Collection 116.)

The paramount white antislavery Christian was John Brown. Brown freed slaves in Missouri and Kansas and was on a third armed exhibition to Harpers Ferry, Virginia before being betrayed; see the Siebert Papers, and Gwen Everett, *John Brown: One Man Against Slavery* (New York: Rizzoli International Publications, 1993).

CHAPTER 2

From Sunup to Sundown: Slavemasters Constitute the African American Self

Servants be obedient to your masters according to the flesh, with fear and trembling, in singleness of your heart, as unto Christ.

Ephesians 6:5

Q. Who gave you a master and a mistress?
A. God gave them to me.
Q. Who says that you must obey them?
A. God says that I must.

Slave Catechism

Sometimes we'd work from sun up to sun down, stopping only a little while for lunch and then right back to work.[1]

Ex-slave Jennie Burns

IN THE TIME and space from sunup to sundown white Protestant slave owners took the initiative to fashion former Africans into physically enslaved, spiritually stunted, and culturally subordinated African Americans. White Christians with power sought to recreate black bodies into "civilized," human, and Christian labor commodities. Moreover, Protestantism attempted to remake the African American subject into a reference point, a blackness of evil and dirtiness, whereby whiteness could assume superior aesthetics, an angelic cleanliness conveying sacred substance. Writing in his autobiography, former slave John Jea, born in southern Nigeria in 1773, asserted:

> Our labour was extremely hard, being obliged to work in the summer from about two o'clock in the morning, till about ten or eleven o'clock at night, and in the winter from four in the morning, till ten at night. The horses usually rested about five hours in the day, while we were at work; thus did the beasts enjoy greater privileges than we did.[2]

Essentially, the intentional deployment of all the power and language of Euro-American Christianity and culture—its political-economic structures, its everyday micropower mechanisms, its spiritual definitions, its grammatical style, and its textured racial cultural way of living—served to create a unifying definition of what it meant to be white in the New World.[3] For the initial and successive waves of English, Italian, French, German, and other Christians from Europe, bonding into "whiteness" occurred at the expense of a fabricated "blackness." As European Christians arrived, they gradually dropped self-descriptions based on their specific countries of origin, and simply became "white."[4] The forging of this new Christian culture of white only occurred through the forced invention of black people, looked upon as ugly and given the status of less-than-human work animals. Theologically, from this perspective, God created white skins to have the privilege of defining and exercising the power of the final word over black people. Within the context of Protestantism and American culture, African Americans became lesser religious beings created by white power.

Still, in this normative movement of creation privilege and arrogant power on the part of Euro-Americans, a few white Christians, even in the south, raised voices of dissent against the equation of bondage and Christianity. For instance, one ex-slave from Tennessee reported: "Our mistress had a brother who didn't believe in slavery. He used to tell his sister [that he] didn't see how she could be a Christian and own slaves. He wouldn't own a slave. He was a good Christian. Old lady was a member of the church, but was as mean as you please."[5] This specific bondperson employed an intuitive and empirical theology that knew the irreconcilable contradiction between bad and good Christians. The female slave owner professed Christianity, but only her brother was a "good Christian" based on the enslaved black person's rules and criteria of which white person held or did not hold African Americans in slavery.

Indeed, in Protestantism and American culture, the prevailing voice was this paradox, from the African Americans' perception, of whites who were both Christians and slave owners, both believers in Christ and maintainers of black labor. Consequently, the slave-owning communities created an entire slavery framework as part of their Christian faith, worldview, and lifestyle. Lecturing his assembled group of African Americans, one upstanding Christian master, through his justifying words, heralded the new order:

> You must not think hard of me for telling you the truth about your-
> selves and the Whites. The great God above has made you for the
> benefit of the Whiteman, who is your law maker and law giver. . . . You
> must understand you are just the same as the ox, horse, or mule,
> made for the use of the Whiteman and for no other purpose. . . . If you
> don't do what is right by me, why, my duty is to kill you. . . . That is
> the law that you must go by.[6]

Fundamentally, from sunup to sundown, masters took the holy
time and sacred space to assume a God-like initiative of making and
regularizing blacks into chattel. Slave owners fostered the construction of the African Americans as objects by inventing technologies of
re-creation power—*a black labor complex for white profit, a network of discipline, control and reclassification*, and *a multidimensional architecture of slavery churches for blacks*. This is the foundation for establishing white reality as the norm, like God.

Black Labor for White Profit

Enslaved African Americans built the United States of America so
that whites could accumulate wealth and privilege, go into professions, make decisions, enjoy the pleasure of thinking, maintain a
reference point for white self-worth, and have more leisure time to
develop their version of Protestantism and normative American culture. The adventures of a white Christian community in the early
1800s substantiates this claim. After leaving South Carolina, settling
in Tennessee, and building a Presbyterian church, these intrepid pioneers began to reflect on the languishing souls of enslaved blacks who
had come with them and labored without reward for the white settlers' comfort:

> To our shame we have to confess that the education of these people
> had been criminally neglected. A great number of them had been
> companions and nurses of our infantile years. They had been doomed
> to hard labor in order to procure means to secure our education and
> let us live in ease, and yet we had not taken that pains and trouble
> which we ought to have done in training them and teaching them a
> proper knowledge of that God who made them.[7]

After establishing the hegemony of whites in this Christian fron-
tier community, the free people now turn to the welfare, spiritual but
not physical, of their ebony chattel. Christian shame over black subordination comes only when white power is firmly entrenched. Theological instruction ensues, in other words, as an afterthought. But

prior to this Protestant concern, unpaid black humanity had cleared the wilderness, constructed the homes, grown the crops, shepherded the livestock, nursed white babies, made clothes for masters, and built the physical world that the slavemaster enjoyed. While blacks were becoming lowly workers, whites were becoming educated, partakers of leisure, groomers of their offspring with codes of domineering postures, definers of Christianity, and monopolizers of wealth. With these planks in place, then and only then did "shame" and "criminally neglected" Christian duties come to mind. Protestantism and American culture, for the colonial and antebellum white religious communities, meant establishing normative techniques of being in the world and mainstream religious beliefs of ritual justifications upon the free labor of black backs.

And African American chattel knew that they were bred to work for slave owners. Former Texas slave John Bates, illiterate but not unlearned, interpreted the foundation of racial social interactions during slavery: "Dat white man wus jes as mean as a dog to us. We would often be made to work all day fum fore erclock in de mornin till half the night wid half nuff to eat." The closest analogy Mr. Bates could fathom was the state of the livestock on the plantation. Resuming his ethical and cultural critique, "Dey seem to treat de slaves bout lack de would treat de mules and horses."[8]

Black abolitionist David Walker offered a similar insight. Walker, gifted with a sharp theological eye and a non-stuttering tongue, wrote from his Boston office in 1829 that whites were dragging blacks around in chains and handcuffs to new states and territories "to work [white peoples'] mines and farms, to enrich them and their children." Furthermore, these Christian masters, in Walker's opinion, believed firmly that African Americans "were made by our Creator to be an inheritance to them and their children for ever."[9] Slave labor resulted from divinely created intention. Likewise, a faith in racial superiority, that blacks should serve Euro-Americans and their progeny, became part of white people's common sense vocabulary.

The creation and domination of the African American particularity assumed various levels—justifications with God (theological), descriptive classifications (linguistic), governmental sanctions (political), defining identity (cultural), and ensuring micromechanisms of control (non-political and non-economic power). The re-creation of Africans into capital and the slaves' economic value and profit generation saturated the different but interrelated dynamics of creation and domination. To exist in the United States as a black person came to signify being capital—that is, some white person's private property and wealth. Along with mules and horses and other such livestock, African Americans were employed to yield wealth. For instance, owners of blacks listed the latter at banks in order to have their accumulated capital assessed and, therefore, to leverage black bodies for increased bank loans. The Louisiana records of an antebellum financial institution reflect this.

> Banque des Citoyens de La Louisiane. Certificat D'Estimation
>   Assermente. Nom Du Proprietaire. Felix Dejrau.
> Magasins, Granges, &c., . . . 500.
> Chevaux et Mulets, . . . 200.
> Boeufs, . . . 100. . . .
> Esclaves—Hommes, One . . . 1000.
>   Femmes, One . . . 800.[10]

In the ledgers of this Citizens Bank of Louisiana, we find horses and cattle enumerated alongside male and female slaves. No differentiation is made to depict the humanity of African Americans in contrast to the animality of four-footed creatures, because the normative status of blacks was potential originators of wealth. For the owners of ebony flesh, it appeared natural and by design to situate the black object in a spiritual and corporeal grouping of subordinated total otherness from white citizens. (Indeed, the proper name of this bank should have been "White Citizens Bank.") Black workers were the objects of pure investment for continued capital accumulation.

BLACK LABOR DIVISIONS FOR WHITE PRIVILEGE

To maximize the squeezing of profit out of African American capital, plantation owners designed an organization of labor for the complete maintenance of white citizens' welfare. Job descriptions varied. Some black servants acted as universal or handyman chattel. Ex-chattel Cornelia recalled how her father in Kentucky "was a yardman, houseman, plowman, gardener, blacksmith, carpenter, keysmith, and anything else they chose him to be." Others were assigned more limited but useful functions. One servant opened fences all day for his master who, "when he left home on his horse . . . wouldn't get down till he got back home." And Julia Henderson remembers how her mother "toted" the slave mistress's dress on the way to Christian worship: "Walking to church, on account of de trail, dey make her walk behin' and tote dat old long dress."[11]

A small sector was trained to be skilled workers. Jobs included woodcrafters such as sawyers, coopers, and carpenters; leatherworkers such as tanners and shoemakers; clothmakers such as tailors, weavers, and spinners; and building-trades persons such as painters, bricklayers, and plasterers.[12]

And an even smaller group made up the sector of black labor called Negro drivers who lorded over a section of the black field hands. These African American drivers were given permission by plantation owners to punish their fellow slaves; at the same time, drivers engaged in producing crops for the slavery system. Recalling his former slavery days in Louisiana, Solomon Northup explained the role of the drivers. "The drivers are black, who, in addition to the performance of their equal share of work, are compelled to do the whippings of their several gangs." The notion of being compelled indicated the ambiguous and precarious function of the Negro driver within the chattel strategy. Ex-driver Aus Davis confirms the duality of his dilemma: on the one hand, being circumscribed by the master's wicked intentions, and on the other, harboring compassionate impulses. "I would rather have worked myself then [sic] to have been forced to punish the poor slaves," asserted Davis. "but if I failed to do so my master would punish both of us severely." Usually a white man acted as overseer over a group of Negro drivers, thus amplifying the wedged dilemma of the African American drivers.[13]

In other words, the slavery organization developed a stratum of black handpicked labor leaders (that is, the Negro drivers) whose job entailed speaking for the owners and interpreting the latter's wishes to the remainder of the slaves, primarily through the threat and the actual usage of the whip. Negro drivers were given permission to be spokespersons for what black people should do in the larger schema of American culture's systematic crusade to constitute African Americans into profit creators. Below we explore how owners gave meaning to black life and death and joy and punishment in the ritualization of work by building up and showcasing a group of blacks who had become "successful"—by creating the house Negro caste as a "carrot" approach in the invention of African American slave workers. With the particular instance of the Negro drivers, we encounter how the structures of slavery gave meaning to black labor by fabricating African American leaders licensed to wield instruments of maiming and death. The physical harm and killing of black bodies indicated the "stick" approach. Whites created a black buffer zone between themselves and the masses of African American workers.

Moreover, apart from the sectors of the Negro driver, handyman, and skilled workers, the overwhelming institutionalization of slave labor was symbolized by the classic roles of field and house chattel. Ex-slave Bell McMillan of Texas "was a house servant, she always carried mail from one rich family to another. She would carry it in a pouch on her back." McMillan saved owners money by making unnecessary a hired mail carrier. Instead, black hands, uncompensated labor, delivered the correspondence and facilitated the networks of white communication and information relationships that strengthened further the evil bondage of black bodies. On another plantation, Ned Lacy would bring in the wood and water, wash dishes, and run errands. One former chattel in Tennessee recounts how she waved peafowl feathers over tables to prevent the presence of flies on white faces and food. Likewise, she had to stand guard over her master during his nap time to prevent flies from landing on his body.

In Georgia, Addie Vinson did the same: "I had to stan' 'hind Old Miss' cheer and fan her wid a turkey-feather fan to keep de flies off." Susan Castle, also from Georgia, acted as a party attendant whenever her owner held her frequent grand social gatherings. Consequently, "de slaves what was house servants," she testifies, "didn't have no time off" except during late Sunday evenings. Tom Hawkins slept in a trundle bed below and adjacent to his mistress. He remained on twenty-four hour call, subject to the violent whacks of his mistress's "long stick." He kept the fire burning in her room "winter and summer"; and in the night, this white woman would awaken him with a firm blow as a signifying alarm to light her pipe. According to Mr. Hawkins, she "smoked dat pipe a po'ful lot."[14]

Perhaps one of the more distinguishing characteristics differentiating the creation of blacks into house slaves rather than field hands was the owners allowing the house servants to physically touch the skin of the class of whites. Callie Hopkins of Texas recalls bitterly her task as her mistress's groomer—a job requiring, literally, nurturing a white woman from foot to head. "I didn't like being bossed around, washing ole Mistress feet, rubbing her toes, bathing her legs, picking lice out of her hair, and hundreds of other similar duties."

On the larger plantations, these "other similar duties" entailed a panorama of refined tasks. Ellen Claibourn described the intricate structure and organic web of black household laborers at the residence of a more wealthy master. "De cook cooked, and the washer, she didn't iron no clothes. De ironer did that. De housemaid cleaned up, and nurse tended the chilrun. Then they was butlers and coachman." Systemic racial and social differences ensured that the master's family would not have to perform any work except for thinking and receiving the benefits, monetary and otherwise, enabled by black workers. Inside the physical arrangement of the Big House, chattel owners manufactured a subservient stratum of people whose sole purpose was to, in turn, create an earthly heaven free from the stress and dirt of the world on the other side of the threshold of the slave-master's house. Relative to their servants, white masters occupied a safe sacred space. And blacks secured the authority of the plantation owners in that familial culture.

Often, house slaves were compelled to stretch out their black bodies on top of their owners' white flesh to preserve the life-heat in white bodies. When plantation owner John Calhoun was absent, states ex-chattel Mary Calhoun, "Mistress would make me sleep at her feet on cold nights to keep her feet warm."[15] As a footwarming commodity on the mistress's body, Mary Calhoun the slave surrenders some of her heat, energy, and (perhaps) spirituality in a ritual analogous to a blood transfusion. The warm constituents of the black person's life were being poured out into (if not sucked out by) the coldness of the Euro-American owner.

Symbolically, at minimum, chattel relations were hierarchical configurations where whites could only be warm at the expense of blacks suffering the loss of their life-heat. Put differently, while the African American acted as a heat generator, an implement to warm Euro-American flesh, the slave's back was exposed to the cold. Black chattel was heating that part of the white mistress which, once rejuvenated or brought back to life, would be employed to walk over the very same black woman who kept white feet heated and alive. Thus values and instincts of sacrifice, self-emptying, and long-suffering for one's neighbor assumed an inside-outside dynamic in the racial blueprint of American culture: these noble qualities of mutual concern for one's neighbor denoted honorable ethical codes of behavior inside of the Euro-American group. But the same behaviors performed by blacks for whites worked against blacks by reinforcing the caste and class stratification of the owners' superiority over enslaved African Americans. For blacks, outside of white privilege, the giving of the self for fellow humanity translated into an ethos and expectation of serving whites.

Those less fortunate African Americans who did not experience the "privileges" of house servants were bred as field hands—outdoor workers. They plowed, hoed, seeded, reaped, tilled, harvested, and performed any type of instructions outside of the Big House. Though slaves who were house servants often suffered lack of self-defined leisure time, the field servants were most brutally deprived of determining their time, space, and humanity. At its core, the phrase "sunup to sundown" images the field slave, the overwhelming majority. Sister Kelly, remembering her antebellum bondage, asserts:

> I have plowed many a field, honey. Sometime, we was in the field time it was daylight, and sometime even before day broke; we would work there all day, then we had to shell corn at night when it was too dark to bend yo' back any longer in the field. Everybody had to shell a bushel of corn most every night, after we had come in from the field.[16]

White power pre-ordained black existence into fixed sections of labor to sustain the life, leisure, and luxury of the plantation owners. The identity of an African American became linked inextricably to forced servanthood.

INTERNAL ATTITUDES OF SELF-DISDAIN

The slavemasters' premeditated invention of black labor divisions for white privilege furnished the external brute power and dehumanizing regulations in the creation of the slave work force. At the same time, however, a significant number of blacks accepted and interiorized plantation attitudes and norms. This provided, within the chattel community, the internal conditions that facilitated a smoother and easier maintenance of racial hierarchy throughout the larger society. Specifically, the arrogance of many house servants exposed this fact. Antagonistic black attitudinal friction amplified ossified racial codes and practices in labor divisions.

The house slaves, enjoying privileged access to the master's residence, lived in close proximity to the normative portrayals of refined American culture (and white interpretations of Christianity). And just as little children "play house" in reference to their parent's affairs, so too did many house servants, like juveniles, imitate their owners' clothing, speech, and mannerisms. Frederick Douglass offered this literal and metaphorical account: "The delicately-formed colored maid rustled in the scarcely-worn silk of her young mistress, while the servant men were equally well attired from the overflowing wardrobe of their young masters." House servants, outfitted in the hand-me-downs of white wardrobes, established the dress codes and rules for fashionable and acceptable apparel in the black community. Words would not have to be expressed to describe the caste differential between house and field hands. The visible spectacle and silent pecking order of clothing became a communication method with its own signs and codes and meaning. Even in matters of fashion, house Negroes were empowered with a sense of dress that leveraged their status in the African American community.

When they did speak, house servants talked like the master to signify their renunciation of African American culture and acceptance of the power and perks of the dominating culture. Imitative language, like the efforts of a parrot, signified the demeaning process of nihilism and co-optation on the part of many house workers. Through altered language, these black servants were making public witness to their adoption of the white master's English, and its constituents of foreign grammar, syntax, and vocabulary. But what came with that discourse was not simply a language. An entire superstructure of talking "correctly," regurgitating so-called "standard English," embracing a way of life, adopting a belief system, acquiescing to European tradition, and championing the slavemaster's mannerisms accompanied verbal expression. In fact, the carefully groomed mannerisms of these servants displayed a certain degree of buffoonery. As long as white skin defined European/Euro-American culture and Protestantism as constituting a human being and an American, and as long as house workers accepted the white power of naming normalcy, then many house servants appeared to be black animals parading and disguising themselves as thinking and decision-making homo sapiens.

To enjoy closeness to the plantation owners (in the proud words of a former house servant, "Yes, I was a house slave; I slept under the stairway in the closet"), these African Americans relinquished the multilayered complexity of a rich black culture and identity. Furthermore and as a consequence, imitation in clothing, speech, and mannerisms set them apart from most of the workers. Frederick Douglass resumed his observations: "These servants constituted a sort of black aristocracy. . . so that in dress, as well as in form and feature, in manner and speech, in tastes and habits, the distance between these favored few and the sorrow and hunger-smitten multitudes of the quarter and the field was immense."[17]

The black aristocracy's imitation dynamic of dress, talk, and habit was the fruit of intentional training on the masters' part. Training of the house slave, like the pedagogy of imitation, assumed several faces and purposes. They were trained to be "stars." House Negroes became the extraordinary event out of mundane, black subservient life.

Underscoring the natural glamor role of house labor, ex-slave Austin Steward wrote in his autobiography: "House servants were, of course, 'the stars' of the party; all eyes were turned upon them." They modeled a theatrical entertainment of hope, in a sense, because they concretized certain possibilities and partial imaginations of what black living could be like by living "high on the hog." This latter folk wisdom phrase implied both a symbolic and literal meaning in slave talk in the quarters. Symbolically, the house Negro illustrated what the field Negro was not and could never be—an occupier, relatively speaking, of a higher tier within the strictured gradations of the white community's slave labor system. Literally, house labor had access to better cuts of pork, which the white owners ate from the parts higher up on swine.

In addition, whites trained house slaves as betrayers of any independent thinking or liberation activities initiated in the slave quarters. Resuming his analysis, Steward penned the following:

> Many of them are the most despicable tale-bearers and mischief makers, who will, for the sake of the favor of his master or mistress, frequently betray his fellow slave . . . and for these acts of perfidy, and sometimes downright falsehood, he is often rewarded by his master, who knows it is for his interest to keep such ones about him. . . . Hence it is that insurrections and stampedes are so generally detected.[18]

Basically, house servants were trained to mirror what it meant to be a responsible Negro and to act as a buffer zone between the Big House and the slave dwellings. The net effect kept field hands' energies and emotions of fear, hatred, jealousy, and awe away from the power centers of the white owners and fixated on the black aristocracy within the African American community.

Finally, attitudes of self-disdain in black chattel labor occurred when house blacks, who were usually lighter in color, exhibited the superiority of their near-white skins. "I think they treated the house slaves a little better than they did the others," commented one ex-slave. And resuming by juxtaposing these privileges with color: "Some of them was bright and some was brown skin." By treating house slaves better and establishing aesthetic meanings of flesh, masters engendered intra-racial hostility among African Americans. This induced feeling of color superiority is remembered clearly by former chattel Lula Washington: "One thing 'bout de mulatto niggers, wuz dey thought dey wuz better than de black niggers. I guess it wuz 'cause dy wuz half white. Dere wuz a bad feelin' 'tween the mulatto slaves an de black ones."[19]

Taught to imitate, trained as leaders, and bred for color arrogance, certain house Negroes and those like-minded field slaves digested and embodied the most negative images and practices of internal self-disdain. Self-hatred, coupled with strict job definitions, slowed down rebellious visioning and insurrectionary moves on the part of black workers. Henry Bibb concluded in his autobiography: "This is one of the principal causes of the slaves being divided among themselves, and without which they could not be held in bondage one year, and perhaps not half that time."[20] Thus whites sought to fabricate and maintain a pacific and malleable labor corps with the creation of a black buffer zone.

THE BLACK FAMILY

The structures and atmosphere of Protestantism and American culture created the black family as part of a productive work force under slavery from sunup to sundown. Therefore, in addition to fostering slave work divisions for white privilege and internal attitudes of self-disdain, the purposeful destabilization of the African American family was a third component of black labor for white profit. In order to build the United States for plantation owners and their followers, the African American family had to be created and controlled in numerous ways.

The slavery institution created the African American family through mechanisms of power suitable for breeding livestock. The ultimate prerogative for birthing the black family was held by the slave owner (and other white men of the plantation system). Consequently, by procreation, the masters literally created the slave family. An unnamed former, female chattel remembers:

> Dr. Gale [her master] had about 24 up here in Tennessee, but I reckon he had thousands in Mississippi, and lots of them was his children. They [his children] had to work just like we did and they had to call him marster too; and the overseer would take them down and whip them just like the others.[21]

The master's privilege of siring existed not for the building of an African American community—with attendant siblings, parents, extended relatives, and emotional and spiritual bonds. The white master impregnated enslaved black women to create a larger workforce, often as a spinoff from expended male lust. Furthermore, sexual intercourse proved a cheaper means than purchasing blacks on the slave market.

Perhaps to avoid the existence of half-white children on their premises or the wrath of their wives, or out of a sincere feeling regarding the immorality of white and black races copulating, some masters established and employed two new categories for black men and women—stud and breeder, respectively. The side effect, not the intentional motive, of the stud's and breeder's jobs was the African American family. Their resulting offspring endured a precarious existence, subject to immediate sale on the open capitalist market and, perhaps, never living with their breeder-stud parents on the same plantation. Former Georgia slave William Ward recalled: "Dey uster take women away fum dere husbands an' put wid some other man to breed jes' like dey would do cattle." And just as prize bulls carried out a daily routine of fathering offspring, so too did black men function as basic sperm donors. Ward resumes his observations: "Dey always kept a man penned up an' dey used im' like a stud hoss."[22]

Christian masters were notorious for creating and fracturing the black family through planned reproduction. Even Sundays provided them with the opportunity and time to contemplate the labor productivity of breeders and studs. An unnamed female freedwoman remembered how her master would have her dress for church and walk ahead of him in order for him to imagine her body producing a larger slave work force. She claimed: "They would dress us up after we ask them if we could go and they would have me walk off from them and they would look at me, and I'd hear them saying, 'She's got a fine shape; she'll make a good breeder." The master's gaze upon the displayed black woman's body measured the contours of her hips and breasts as they all walked to worship Jesus Christ.[23]

With the breeder-stud configuration, masters acted crassly without ceremony. In contrast, many of the white owners offered the semblance of a wedding authorization and marriage ritual (though legally enslaved blacks could not be married and thus the marriage was non-binding) to enact the African American family as black labor for white profit.

Thus within the trappings of marriage, the slave owner entered the sanctity of black nuptial unions and further actualized his God complex. Instead of an African traditional religious spirituality, or Christianity, or some combination of both consecrating the marriages of black people, masters chose and ordained who could perform the ritual of "until death do you part." Freedman Stephen Jordon commented on his previous owner: "When he thought one of his men needed a wife or one of his women needed a husband he would choose them and put them together." The issue was the sacredness of selection in the making of the African American family. In the holiness of the choice dynamic, not only was the prerogative of blacks embracing one another based on love denied, but the master routinized the time periods of matrimonial mating. "He would never," resumed Jordon, "allow the men to be single after they were eighteen, nor the women after they were fifteen."[24] For the plantation owners, women, because of the attractiveness of their reproductive capacities, attained their womanhood and hence marriageable ages when they reached their childbearing levels—from eleven to fifteen years.

In his remembrances, Mr. Jordon expresses the master's power to define the slave family according to his imagination and preference: "whenever he thought" and "he would choose." However, in certain particulars, enslaved African Americans would take initiative within the restrictions of the owners' delineation of the black family and seek union with a loved one. Still, even in these cases, ultimacy in naming and finality in describing rested in the master's hands. First the different owners of the bondswoman and -man would have to give consent to the slaves' request. Then, if a wedding ceremony was held (such as the blacks jumping over a broom, carrying a glass of water over their heads, or marrying with a lamp), it took place in the authored space of the master, e.g., in the Big House. Various accounts rendered by former slaves from Mississippi, Alabama, and Tennessee substantiate how whites ensured jurisdiction over black marriage by forcing signifying rituals to occur in the Big House. Hence the thinking, choice, and spacial arrangements governing the formation of the African American family as profitable laborers remained in the whites' purview.[25]

Even when masters granted marriage privileges, they made it quite clear that matrimony denoted more work, not less. An ex-chattel recounted how an "Old Mistiss" in Tennessee would force the "newly weds" to "get up and tell them that married life was too good for them; and tell them to get up and get out and go to work." This former slave then offered her theological interpretation, foundational statement, and imponderable conclusion on the fundamentals of God's relation to evil: "I know God didn't like that, and if he forgives the white folks for that, then I don't know what to think."[26]

Moreover, the plantation system insured the further humiliation and instability of the black family as a primary component of black labor for white profit by: forbidding a healthy environment of a safe familial context for children, discarding the African American elderly, effecting the permeating slave fear of separation, and denying the sacred rite of funerals.

Harriet Jacobs, in her autobiography, detailed one slave mistress's rabid enmity toward slave parents' relation with their own children. The mistress became enraged when a black woman suggested the possibility of having children with a black man. "'I will have you peeled and pickled, my lady,' said she, 'if I ever hear you mention that subject again. Do you suppose that I will have you tending my children with the children of that nigger?'" African American natural instincts of parenting carried less weight than a feather for many white women. And this black woman who requested permission to have children was recognized as a mechanical tool to work and care for others or as a surrogate mother for white babies.[27]

Likewise the elderly suffered immorally after rendering a black life of free unpaid labor for white life within the plantation system. At least three tactics were employed to discard the living ancestors in slave quarters. Broken down and burned out old black workers were either given a shack out in the forest in which to be alone and die, left to die on their sick beds, or sold on the auction blocks for a nominal fee. Moses Grandy testified in his autobiography how "aged and worn-out slaves" were commonly "sent to live in a lonely log-hut in the woods."[28]

Perhaps second only to the horror of whipping was the omnipresent terror of familial separation. This demonic act could occur at any moment. One boy slave in Missouri accidentally cut his thumb and, while in the process of being attended to by his mother, was taken away by a Negro buyer. He subsequently "remembered his mother by the scar on his hand." In other instances, black family separation resulted from the whims of white men and women. A Mississippi Valley slave owner named Thompson lost one slave to a Negro slave trader in a horse race. This former chattel (named Mr. Davis) later remembered: "I left behind my father, mother, and two sisters." And in a similar account rendered by another ex-slave: "My old master had the reputation of being a very humane and Christian man, but he thought nothing of selling my poor old father, and dear aged mother . . . to different persons."[29]

Finally, having served the chattel way of life from birth, through precarious family contexts and separations, blacks who died were often forbidden the proper burial ceremonies, a slight that was devastating both for African American Christians and those believers of African indigenous religions. In both particularities, the soul and its journey would be troubled due to the forced insufficient and improper attention on the part of family and community.[30] But from the master's and mistress's perspective, a dead black had fulfilled its primary role in the political economy of plantation social relations. An inability to labor meant insignificance.

Networks of Discipline, Control, and Reclassification

The re-creation of the African American as object during sunup to sundown, in addition to the system of black labor for white profit,[31] entailed intricate and deliberate networks of discipline, control, and reclassification. To sustain a permanent work force in a suppliant and subservient mode, the chattel system had to chastise, rein in, and arrange black life into a wounded and fearful mass. Effective racial structures were put into play for this metamorphosis. The corporeal nature of African American existence endured this three-pronged approach to concede to Euro-American meaning and truth for a black working class.

DISCIPLINE

A white culture of disciplining the black body arose from legal and biblical interpretation and foundations. By legal statute, South Carolina owners had to castrate any enslaved African American who sought freedom by running away. If the master did not perform this civic duty of white Americans, then the slave owner was subject to loss of the black property. Similarly, the northern state of New Jersey standardized its "gelding law" (that is, castration) in 1706. On a parallel track, Euro-American clergy stood in solidarity with politicians by ensuring the sanctity of violently removing a black man's reproductive organs. Some Baptists and Anglicans rendered the following theological justifications:

> We apprehend, the Master Acting according to the Law of your Province, in gelding his slave, hath not committed any crime, to give any member to break communion with him in the church; because we see by Scripture, that 'tis lawful to buy them. (Gen. 17:13, 23, 27). And if lawful to buy them 'tis lawful to keep them in order, and under government; and for self-preservation, punish them to prevent further mischief that may ensue by their running away and rebelling against their master, Exodus 21:20, 21.[32]

The Genesis chapter, founded on God's beginning of all creation in goodness, and the Exodus chapter, noted for a primary theme of liberation of slaves from torture and forced labor, became linguistic contortions for dismembering the black male sexual organ. As early as the colonial days—the end of the 1600s and the beginning of the 1700s—white sectors of economic and political powers laid a foundational pattern and institutionalized an attitude of suspicion toward African American men's bodies by intentionally maiming them. And white clergy, ordained by their exegesis of God's word, blessed this religious ceremony of violence theologically with a liturgy of biblical claims: God gave power to destroy the black sexual body as punishment for deeds done and as precaution against future crimes.

Branding, another form of black bodily mutilation, was a more common discipline. Like cattle or sheep, African American workers were either tied or held down while the master had hot irons imprinted into their flesh. This claiming of the black body through forced desecration often took place at a very young age. Recalling the experience of this painful ordeal, a former slave stated: "When I was about 8 or 10 years old, my master burnt on my breast, with oil of vitriol, the letters W. L." Other enslaved African Americans suffered branding identification techniques as forms of punishment for failing to fulfill the work expectations and quota for a day.

In this instance, branding meant "cutting gashes into their skin."[33] Branding denoted exact ownership; the white master's name or initials could be seen clearly on the flesh of the ebony body. A public display of permanent marking for which master owned which slave, branding served as an immediate badge distinguishing the racial, class, and caste dynamics in Protestantism and American culture. Perhaps the most damaging effect of the accepted procedure was the psychological boost in ego given to the white populace—the maturing conscious and subconscious belief in the necessity of tearing apart the black body with impunity. Fundamentally, branding was a sign in the public theater that offered the black body to be read as text for whites' meaning of ownership and slaves' compliance with an imposed truth.

The environment of acceptability and the ethos of expecting the disciplining of the black body manifested further in the refined torture techniques perfected after numerous applications. One master dragged a live cat with claws extended over the prone body of an accused slave. "The cat sunk his nails into the flesh, and tore off pieces of the skin with his teeth." Then the master applied the cat, not from the prostrate accused slave's shoulders down, but from the waist up. In another instance, Lilburn and Isham Lewis, two nephews of Thomas Jefferson, slowly chopped up the body of a live slave as a lesson to deter other chattel from running away. In a deliberate manner, one of the nephews hacked off the feet, paused to lecture the other slaves in attendance, continued by chopping off the legs below the knees, cast these into a ferocious fire, and proceeded slowly with intermittent lectures while the victim howled in pain, with finally nothing remaining except the bodiless head, which was likewise tossed in the flames.[34]

However to standardize the refined torture mechanisms, a comprehensive profit-making industry and visionary repressive expertise arose signifying the role disciplining the black body played in furthering technology and experimentation in American culture. The more whites with power experimented on the black body, the more technological innovations occurred. One innovative owner created a gradation of stocks, one on top of another. When he accumulated enough guilty chattel, he placed them in the stocks above each other. "They would all be required to take a large dose of medicine and filth down upon each other." Old Mack Williams, another owner, developed chains that he placed around black necks as fatal punishment; he would have the slaves picked up by the chains, thrown into a river, and drowned. And in the words of a former slave: "My marster had a barrel with nails drove in it that he would put you in when he couldn't think of nothin' else mean to do." With the slave secure in the torture barrel, the owner would push it down a hill.

The most established industries of pain devised various forms of "the runaway's irons." After fleeing and being captured, whipped for four days and left for four days in the stocks, a former chattel named Lewis suffered the following:

> Early the next morning Lewis was taken out of his prison, and led by two men to the blacksmith's shop, to receive "the runaway's irons." An iron ring, weighing fourteen pounds, was welded on his ankle; and to that was fastened one end of a heavy log-chain, the other end of which was brought up and passed twice around his waist, where it was secured by a lock. A collar was then put around his neck, from which an iron horn extended on each side nearly to the point of the shoulder.[35]

Likewise fugitive John Brown recited the detailed features of the circles of iron, padlocks, rods, and bells strapped around his chin, forehead, and neck. "I wore the bells and horns, day and night, for three months," he wrote. "At night I could not lie down to rest, because the horns prevented my stretching myself, or even curling up."[36]

A group of entrepreneurs—complying with the wishes of plantation owners, the policies of politicians, and the theological blessings of religious leaders—sat down to envision the most efficient way to wrap iron around the necks, heads, waists, and limbs of black men and women in America. Measurements had to be taken. Bodies had to be fitted and refitted for precision. Poundage had to be calculated to ensure optimum weight and pain, short of death. Controlling the labor force through appropriately sized torture devices must have necessitated trial and error experimentation. Consequently, a mindset unaffected by the breaking of black bones and skin engendered a worldview where pain for African Americans was deemed in their best interests and, of course, in the interests of national security. Blacksmiths and related businessmen reaped profits while African American chattel agonized in disfigurement, and the white nation felt safe.

Of the disparate manifestations of disciplining the black body and refashioning the African American object, whipping ranked highest in regularity and familiarity. Indeed, the most daily brutality inflicted upon enchained chattel during the construction of the black personality under slavery—the foundational space where Protestantism and American culture established their democratic etiquette of subduing the black body—was realized by the whip. The intricate fascination with how to distort, contort, and cut up the African American physical reality was regularized with precision and frequency.

There were at least four types of standard whips crafted specifically for blacks: the holed paddle, which could make blisters to be subsequently filled with pepper; the ox whip, which suggested a capability of confining any slave, even one endowed with ox-like strength; the bullwhip, used interchangeably on both African Americans and bulls; and the Negro whip, exclusively designed for punishment. Fugitive William W. Brown, in his autobiography, described the meticulous genius of the latter implement: "The handle was about three feet long, with the butt-end filled with lead, and the lash six or seven feet in length, made of cowhide, with platted wire on the end of it."[37]

The four types of whips could be employed by choosing one of five styles of whipping positions—the buck, the log, the stake, the tree, and the stocks. The stocks especially signified the institutionalized violence condoned and regulated by the state. Roy Refield, ex-slave, conveyed this account: "When I would go there with my young marster I would see 'em whipin' the slaves. You see they had stocks there. . . . Your marster or mistress would send you to the courthouse with a note and they would put you in them stocks and beat you, then they would give you a note and send you back."[38]

Legalized structural torture unfolded within the building housing justice and law and order. As a result when African American chattel conjured up definitions of white justice and its manifold meanings, they imaged the courthouse as a place where hired whips stripped off flesh and bones and released puddles of black blood onto the floor. In one sense, justice, in the tradition of American culture, became ethical memories and moral expectations of blacks wailing and screaming in pain within a courthouse designated as the determinator of right and wrong for all of society.

After choosing from a delicious menu of whipping implements and manners of discipline, slavery owners could select various standard daily times set aside for whippings. Jefferson F. Henry recalled how his fellow slaves were whipped regularly "in the mornin's 'fore they went to wuk," while William McWhorter recalled sessions occurring "'fore dey et supper." Easter Brown remembered that "Mondays and Tuesdays wuz set aside for the whippin's"; and one unnamed ex-slave testified that "every Thursday was when you got your beating."[39]

The interwoven dimensions of whippings (implements, genres, and appointments) should not obscure the sane reasons held by owners as well as the intentional usage of Christianity as moral justification. One ever present and overarching rationale, though not always enunciated, was the plantation masters' struggle to beat pride out of chattel, to make them fearful of whites, and to exorcise any evil thoughts of running away. Former slave Nath Perkins of Texas related how his master violently chastised the slaves not because they had become unruly but because "the master want the slaves to fear him and never to rise up against him."

Furthermore, owners and their representatives employed the whip to maintain an obvious white superiority over black inferiority in the racial caste pecking order of American culture. Some beat enslaved African Americans as a public text of instruction to other chattel. Others sought to increase the work capacity and output of their private human property. Still others, submitting to bodily lust, victimized black women through power domination with the whip and sexual exploitation. In other instances, punishment served to correct or prevent blacks from learning to read or write (expressions of intellectual proficiency), while many owners simply performed the torture of beating just for fun.

Punishment for impudence, however, was the slippery policy and ambiguous term utilized to draw a quick whip on black bodies. It plagued African American chattel mainly because it relied on the momentary mood, inconsistent intuitions, and sporadic spontaneity of the person holding the whip, all nurtured under an inherently evil system justified by the master's theology. Frederick Douglass retells and represents, in his autobiography, the fickle disposition of the impudence charge.

> This crime [of impudence] could be committed by a slave in a hundred different ways, and dependent much upon the temper and caprice of the overseer. . . . He could create the offense whenever it pleased him. A look, a word, a gesture, accidental or intentional, never failed to be taken as impudence when he was in the right mood for such an offense.[40]

Whipping as a form of disciplining the black body—thus refashioning it during the sunup to sundown period—drew its inspiration and justification from the strength of Christianity. As a Christian in good standing, a white person assumed a high moral ground by flogging African American slaves. A Mrs. Flint, for instance, lacked the physical stamina to administer the whip upon her chattel. However, her Christian spite and hatred enabled her to act as voyeur of others assigned to injure black workers: "her nerves were so strong, that she could sit in her easy chair and see a woman whipped, till the blood trickled from every stroke of the lash."

The lashing of African Americans, moreover, attempted to beat out the black person's initiative in experiencing, hence defining, their own relationship with God. If chattel assumed authority in the realm of religious definition and freedom, this could, from the slave system's perspective, threaten the caste social rearrangement; both the accepted automatic privileges of white skin and the normal assigned role of black workers. A former slave confirmed the following: "When they got a little happy [during worship], the overseer would come and whip them. I have known him to whip a woman with 400 lashes because she said she was happy. This was to scare religion out of them, because he thought he wouldn't be able to get anything out of them if they were religious."

A fear that blacks might encounter the message of the gospel independent of the slave owners' interpretation led slave owners to a warped embracing and practice of Christianity; white theology preferred the damnation of the black if that state of humanity ("to scare religion out of them") would ensure white rule and black compliance.

The former slave resumed this testimony about the overseer: "He said he would rather see them stealing and swearing and whoring than be religious. Such things are common."[41] The good news of an empowering Holy Spirit, in this instance, proved to be a stumbling block for white cultural purposes. Therefore, if teaching blacks to be Protestants failed to serve the authority of white culture, then human chattel were whipped into stealing, swearing, and whoring.

Religious justification of slave whipping was enmeshed in a sinister net of white power forces. Often the church "class leader was the town constable—a man who bought and sold slaves, who whipped his brethren and sisters of the church at the public whipping post, in jail or out of jail." Here a white follower of Jesus Christ, in slavemaster Protestantism, acted as an official arm of the state (as town constable), a thriving capitalist entrepreneur (by buying and selling black flesh), and surrogate torturer (by lashing blacks dropped off at the jail by their masters). The solid foundation of this intricate intrigue rested on a moral imperative driven by monetary accumulation, for this class leader "was to perform that Christian office [of whipping] any where for fifty cents."[42]

Like a sculptor crafting a refined piece of art work, those who disciplined the black body used a variety of techniques, approaches, and creativities: from Christian castration, to branding, to the use of cultivated torture implements, to a selection of whipping options. And it was the slavemasters' belief in Jesus Christ that helped to empower and urge on the calculated and systematic dismembering of African American flesh.

CONTROL

The further re-creation of the African American person from sunup to sundown in Protestantism and American culture not only demanded discipline, but also control of black bondspersons. Slavemasters sought control of their (a) food, clothing, and shelter, and (b) repetitive rituals (daily and weekend routines). To assume the power of an omnipotent, omniscient, and omnipresent creator who controlled black life, white Christians had to determine what went into, on, and around the black body as well as regulate and define meaning for the intervals of time in black lives.

Food concerns yielded control of exact measurements of edible intake by blacks and their methods of consumption. Masters evolved a precise weight of food per African American family (woman, man, and child) and systematized the distribution of provisions. Exactly how much victuals would a black person need per set interval to transform her or him into a controllable work unit for white profit and pleasure? Control by food, in a word, narrowly averted the threshold of starvation for the enslaved so she or he could labor another day for the white master class.

Moreover, masters and mistresses claimed supremacy in determining the nature of vitamins, minerals, and energy a black body required to adequately maintain proper functioning. To regulate food was to regulate the very biology of the enslaved African American. This mechanism supervising the black body literally governed the blood, flesh, and oxygen of the chattel, for the black worker did not have possession of her or his physical self to initiate a healthy or poor diet. Access and avenues to choice of balanced nourishment remained closed, further signifying the power of growing a healthy internal body residing in thoughts and desires of Euro-Americans in slave society. The priorities of this system employed food manipulation for institutionalized white supremacy and systematic accumulation of wealth. Food became a weapon for diminishing the self of the black chattel (through forced dependency) while exalting the self-perception of the plantation owners (through white privileges). Thus, what went into a body was more than mere food, but a symbolic reflection and stratified ranking, on various levels, of the healthiness of an organism (e.g., the body) and the configuration of peoples in broader social engagement (e.g., race-ownership relations). An unhealthy human body mirrored an unhealthy social body.

African American accounts of what edibles they were allowed verify the fact that they were controlled by food rationing calculated by whites. Frederick Douglass relates the dimensions of monthly allowance: "eight pounds of pickled pork, or its equivalent in fish. The pork was often tainted, and the fish were of the poorest quality. With their pork or fish, they had given them one bushel of Indian meal, unbolted, of which quite fifteen percent was more fit for pigs than for men." This menu, Douglass concludes, had to suffice for a full-grown slave toiling from morning until night every day of the month except Sunday.[43] Similarly, former chattel Milton Hammond described weekly rationing that, distributed every Saturday night, consisted of three pounds of bacon (or fatback), one peck of meat, and one quart of syrup—this for an entire family's seven-day subsistence. Other plantation owners tossed in small quantities of cornmeal.

In many instances rationed offerings became slimmer choices. Various former slaves described how even their meager rations were reduced. Eli Coleman recalled eating only meat and bread and, sometimes, only bread and water as staples. A Mrs. Sutton recalled having only sour milk. In the same vein, another freed slave "mostly" had buttermilk and corn bread. And Lue Boman used to avoid starvation by trailing behind her master's children and picking "up the crumbs that would fall from their hands."[44]

While white plantation owners' children savored a fuller menu selection, enough not to be bothered about crumbs and other leftovers, offspring of enslaved blacks were treated like pig litters. The practical implications of Christianity and the saner logic of raising well-fed future workers bypassed the interpretive skills of white slave owners. One would think that Christians would perceive children as the spiritual heirs of a society's values and traditions, both transcendent qualities of a community transferred to each generation. Likewise, one would think that black children, as future labor units yielding wealth and value to whites, would have been given adequate nutrients early in order to ensure their longevity. On the contrary, African American youngsters were treated no better than animals on the plantation. One ex-slave recounts:

> Sometimes there would be as many as ten and fifteen [children] for each to look after. Around noon they were fed from a trough which was about ten or fifteen feet in length. Pot liquor by the buckets was thrown in the trough until they were filled. The children with spoons in their hands would then line up on each side. No sooner was the signal given than they began eating like a lot of pigs.

The smaller ones, driven by hunger, would often "jump in with their feet." Former slave accounts of feeding children overflow with metaphors about and comparisons with livestock. In some cases, children and animals actually ate together. When Annie L. Burton remembered her childhood feeding times from a bowl, she reminisced, "This bowl served for about fifteen children, and often the dogs and the ducks and the peafowl had a dip in it."[45]

The dispersal of clothing, likewise, deepened the control apparatus in the reconstitution of the black person. The re-concoction of the content—that is, the redefined African and African American as enslaved private property—was accompanied by a reconstructed form—that is, the low-quality clothing tailored for a subhuman humanity. Clothing was a sign stating that what one saw (black people in shoddy attire) was not fully human, but people of another world, a species of castaways and ragamuffins. And certain clothing had codes that gave meaning and definition to African Americans whenever whites encountered this ill-clad dark humanity. The coded meaning signified white affirmed superiority and black confirmed infantility. Clothing, furthermore, acted as a form of rhetoric: a persuasive use of clothing as language speaking to both the master and the slave using the words of presence and absence. To the master, the slave wardrobe spoke volumes about and defined a shadow of real human substance, thus contrasting the black absence of worth with the white presence of value.

"The yearly allowance of clothing," in the words of an ex-slave, "was not more ample than the supply of food." For summer, two shirts and a pair of trousers of the same coarse material were allotted along with one pair of stockings and ill-fitting rough shoes. Other former chattel described the addition of a coat in the winter or every other year and a wool hat every two or three years. Children, female and male, wore nothing but a shirt consisting of a sack with the head and arm openings cut in place. Children did not wear underwear; and sometimes adults were not rationed any, winter or summer. Many who survived slavery recalled never having shoes. "Why, honey," in the words of Emma Hurley, "I never had no shoes 'til after freedom come. I've walked on snow many a time barefooted with my feet so cold my toes wuz stickin' straight up with no feelin' in 'em."[46]

Christian plantation owners forced black people into small confines as residential places, often called nigger quarters or slave shacks. The lack of space offered no sense of movement linked to "home." The open space of the field, in contrast, became the primary sense of home and movement due to the amount of time spent there by black workers and if one connects dwelling place and mobility space with home. To control African Americans, their living quarters were intentionally crafted narrowly in space, implying: (a) a submission to a totality and expansiveness of the masters' all-seeing presence, in contrast to the black person's real home being in the open air fields lacking borders where blacks could name and identify as their own; and (b) no privacy for parents or individual family members. Small confines suggest a communal living like rabbits—whose being and purpose equaled the generation of offspring and production value for the market.

Usually, slave quarters lacked floors, bed frames, bedding furniture, windows (unless the master granted permission to cut a hole in the side of the shack), adequate arrangements for cooking (if any were provided), and durable chimneys and ceilings. Often, smoke from fireplaces stayed in the shack instead of exiting out of the chimney. And decrepit ceilings offered African Americans the unwanted luxury of watching stars at night as they lay sprawled on floors or on makeshift beds of dry grass. Five or six children had to sleep in one bed. In certain situations, a long house was partitioned off like mule stalls, contrived so that a black worker could squeeze in, go to sleep, and squeeze out in the morning.[47]

The clearest instances of control through housing construction can be surmised by juxtaposing the Big House (of whites) to the nigger quarters (of blacks). Freed chattel Rev. Green describes the following: "The houses that the slaves lived in were all built in a row, away from the big house. Just at the head of the street, between the cabins and the big house, stood the overseer's house. There was some forty or fifty of these two-room cabins facing each other across an open space for a street."[48] This landscaping of racial-caste division of labor denotes a geography of hierarchy, authority, and gazing. The polar opposites (master versus slaves) are depicted in a linear fashion with the Big House and the nigger quarters situated at top-bottom extremes. Government over slave labor and hired help is displayed with the Big House residing at the top of the chain of command. And a scrutinizing eye is seen peering both from the overseer's house (into the terrain of the slave shacks) and from the plantation owner (into the domain of those charged to oversee and be overseen).

To reinforce the gaze as a mechanism of power and control, the Big House was positioned at the commanding heights of the plantation owner's blueprint of space. On the Walton plantation, former slave Rhodus Walton recalled, the Big House stood "on an elevation near the center. The majestic colonial home with its massive columns was seen for miles around and from its central location the master was able to view his entire estate." To regulate, direct, and manage black people, the estate owner situated himself to be viewed ("for miles around") in the center; and this authoritative location enabled the planter to observe ("his entire estate") a 360-degree vista of his power. Centralizing both to be seen and to see was critical for maintaining the controlling gaze.

Similarly, the spacial arrangements of particularly designated black workers' (especially women's) cabins reveal more of the signification, symbolic nature, and apparatus of privilege in the master-slave dynamic. Chattel women assigned to work in their shacks adjacent to the Big House experienced a unique rank, site, and function. Ex-slave Lucy reports that this specific type of shack "was whitewashed; it was closer to the [Big] house, you see, so the white folks could get to them easy if they wanted them; and they had to have it that way to keep from spoiling the looks of the big house." Within the overall scheme of spacial orchestration, some nigger shacks played intimate roles in proximity to the Big House, providing quick access for white desires, and an intentional harmony for aesthetic consistency.[49]

Control and repetitive rituals indicated the further implementation of slavemasters' creation and re-creation abilities. Repeated daily and weekend activities, scripted by white Christians with multiple advantages, established frameworks to transform the old free African self of being Yoruba, Hausa, Ibo, etc., into a new enslaved African American in the New World. Regularized restrictions accented both the apparent all-powerful reality of whites and the predictable movement of blacks.

William Wells Brown, in his autobiography written on free soil, renders the following true tale of his former slave life:

> My master owned about forty slaves, twenty-five of whom were field hands . . . who were summoned to their unrequited toil every morning at four o'clock, by the ringing of a bell, hung on a post near the house of the overseer. They were allowed half an hour to eat their breakfast, and get to the field. At half past four, a horn was blown by the overseer, which was the signal to commence work.

Ex-chattel Mrs. Wright, when interviewed for her slavery recollection, recalled rising with her fellow slaves at 3 A.M., feeding stock, bypassing their own breakfast, and then proceeding directly to the fields to labor. Other accounts note the use of various alarm clocks: ram horns (by the overseer), bugles (by the master's son), and conch shells (by the master).

The completion of field work did not signal the end of the day's work. Tom Hawkins testified: "Dey come in 'bout dark. Atter supper, de mens made up shoes, horse collars, and anything else lak dat what was needed; de 'omans spun thread and wove cloth." Finally, for their weekday obligation, African Americans had to undergo a bed check. Emmaline Heard tells of a bell ringing at midnight to signal the ceasing of spinning and lights out. Others remembered the overseer checking each individual cabin, and some former slaves spoke about a roll call system of control.[50]

The weekend rituals further intensified the redundancy of control by limiting blacks' times and choices. Saturday was a workday, though on certain plantations slaves could have the evening time for leisure such as dancing. But after dinner, most washed, ironed, cleaned up their shacks, and prepared tools and other equipment for the coming week. Rachel Adams attested to nothing but work for enslaved blacks throughout the year: "Dey hardly knowed what Sunday was. Dey didn't have but one day in de Christmas, and de only diff'unce dey seed dat day was dat dey give 'em some biscuits on Christmas day. New Year's Day was railsplittin' Day."[51]

An anonymous slave summed up the insightful theological awareness of chattel who connected slavemaster Christianity to a seemingly religious regularity: "Mistress was a mighty church member . . . had one of these cockle shells just like a snail shell that she blowed for the hands to come to dinner."[52] Slave owner Christians segmented African Americans' time and space.

Repetitive rituals regularized and routinized slave life—their bodies, thinking, expectations, and time. Regularity, in former slave accounts, suggested predictability and thus subservience to someone else's parameters of time and scheduling. Likewise, predictability meant programming the African American community to react and think in expected manners. A routinized way of life, like that of a mule with blinders that plows up the dirt in preparation for planting, indicated a visceral existence full of constant blind recapitulations. A routine, force of habit existence, slave stories suggested, was to inaugurate the day in response to the sound of those who had enslaved black people. It was not to respond to the natural sounds of birds, trees, and the winds around you, but, rather, to react to the artificial constraints imposed to privilege others who acted in the capacity of earthly lords. Moreover, as lords in their own "kingdom" space, plantation owners deployed sound to organize the movements of slave communities with military precision.

Fundamentally, control attempted to trivialize the slaves' own spiritual, intellectual, and physical capabilities by violently (that is, non-voluntarily) framing the waking hours of chattel from sunup to sundown within the agenda of the master and mistress. Repetitive rituals acted like a form of theater in which the rehearsal of repetition engendered a skewed way of thinking about life, knowing about life, and visioning life's possibilities. Enslaved African Americans, therefore, were entangled in a plot penned by others; and their casting in contingent roles sought to dull completely their sensibilities and faith in the sacred power dwelling in themselves.

RECLASSIFICATION

Coupled with control and discipline, the third process in remaking the enslaved African American in the context of a Protestant culture of racial difference and American beliefs in superior-inferior social hierarchy entailed reclassifying slave identity. Recategorizing yielded a forced abdication of black self-identity and a violent attack on the Africans' self-definition. Fundamentally, to remake blackness called forth an essential question: What was the meaning of being black or black being in the Christian "New World"? Reclassification resulted from persuading public opinion, rearranging the black body, and labeling the slaves' names.

Newspapers served as essential tools in reclassifying chattel identity in the public's eye, providing distinct images for the public of the value and meaning of black slaves. Owners posted slave notice ads such as this 1837 announcement in the *Mobile Register and Journal* of Mobile, Alabama:

> SLAVE NOTICE
> FORTY DOLLARS REWARD
> Ran away from the subscriber about seven weeks since, a Negro girl named Fanny. The said girl is about thirty-five years of age and about five feet, six inches in height, is rather black, grey headed, has an uncommon large mouth, and takes long strides in walking. She is probably lurking somewhere about in the city. All persons are forbidden harboring or employing her. The above reward will be paid for the apprehension and delivery to me, at 58 St. Francis Street.
>
> M. Hovendon.[53]

Such ads appeared as regularly as similar notifications for the sale and purchase of livestock or farm equipment. But even more, slave notices transformed African American humanity from fellow human beings of the larger community into some mixed phenomenon between an animal and an inanimate object. The public read the predicament of this fugitive slave as a text inscribing an infantile adult, biological descriptors, and specific motor inclinations, instead of the sanctity of the human person being defended for fleeing incarceration. The oxymoron of an infantile adult, after repeated public advertisements, eventually made rational sense to the white reader enjoying the pleasurable act of experiencing black people's reclassified identity. The "said girl" is both child and adult. The age of thirty-five and the height measurement five feet, six inches underscored that these were not characteristically traits of adulthood, but the markings of a child. The designation of the fugitive as a child obliterates in the white reader's mind the age-height details. For the reader-voyeur, primary attention goes to the centrality of the "girl" label; all else remains supporting and corroborating evidence.

The physical description of "an uncommon large mouth" and the ambiguous notation of "takes long strides" both trivialize the identity of this woman and universalize the danger for all black female slaves. Fanny's unique identity, in this portrayal, is lost because the defining substance of her humanity is replaced by subhuman markings. Furthermore for the white public, any "Negro girl" (that is, any black female adult with a large mouth and long stride) could possibly suffice according to how the slaveholding community interpreted the text of this advertisement. Thus blacks became objects viewed for their lip size and nuance of their walks.

In addition, the newspaper medium fostered the continued criminalization of enslaved African Americans within American culture; that is how the dominating culture in the United States absorbed a criminal depiction of blacks into the reflexive instincts of this culture's racially privileged worldview. The slave notice depicts a dangerous creature "lurking," as if the Negro girl-adult were a werewolf biding its time to pounce murderously upon the white community at an unexpected moment. The "lurking" picture aided the tightening of the white community's collective muscle tension whenever a black appeared on the scene unsupervised, unattended, or unexplained by a white person. (The identity of an African American was not a free-standing, independent possibility due to its derivative reality and contingent relation to a white.)

As criminal, now sanctified by the authoritative position of the newspaper, the Negro girl-adult becomes an outlaw not only for the owner, from whom she has escaped, but also for all of society. The ad closes off her legal connection to other humans with the threat of criminal prosecution; all are forbidden to harbor or employ her. A material incentive in the form of monetary reward, however, persuades the public to abide by this interpretation of Fanny as a criminal non-person.

Similar advertisements appeared for free blacks captured, the sale of slaves, their hire or renting, and the public declaration of taxes on chattel. A Mr. Levi Stanly suffered the loss of freedom when a sheriff jailed him because Stanly claimed to be free. The related newspaper notice (titled "Slave Claiming To Be Free") states that Stanly "professes to be a free man. His owner is requested to come forward." Between the idea that Stanly thinks he is free and the sheriff assuming he has an owner lies the subtext and projected sign of silence that typifies the crafting of black identify as questionable, suspect, and guilty until proven otherwise by a white person.[54]

Similarly, Christian principles of love, reconciliation, and freedom were suspended when it applied to notifying the white public regarding the sale, hire, and documentation of taxes on black people. *The Times* of Charleston, South Carolina (April 3, 1810) published an ad for the sale of two "wenches" along with a "saddle horse." Ads were placed not only for private sale but also for auction sale. Apparently by law, owners of human chattel were required to publicly announce taxes paid on all their possessions. The existence of blacks in these documented lists denoted the complete transformation of reclassified slaves into private property, capital, commodities, and investment.[55]

Reclassifying the identity of the enslaved body often attempted to force African American chattels' self-perception from focus on a free ability to a wounded physical humanity. Torture of the black body could result from the master reading into and interpreting the eye or the tongue of a servant as representing independence of vision or speech. In this instance, the violent reaction against such "insubordination" resulted in rewriting the contours of black people's physical being with whatever weapon the plantation owner found at hand. Here the master's intolerance for any look (that is, vision) or word (language) of insubordination on the part of the chattel translated into understanding the body of the servant as a site for violent pain as punishment for independent thinking and empowering talk.[56]

Two additional accounts of former slave interviews affirmed this focus on recategorizing the corporeal dimension of black reality. In each of these cases, the slave mistress was attracted to the art of disfiguring a female servant's hair. One unnamed former slave rehearsed memories of the mistress redefining hair: "Mistress uster ask me what that was I had on my head and I would tell her, 'hair,' and she said, 'No that ain't hair, that's wool.'" The body has to be reclassified out of the human sphere into the plant and animal domain to both provide new images in the slave's mind and to elevate the truth of real hair possessed by the mistress. If both mistress and servant were equal in biological traits (that is, if they both naturally had real hair), perhaps they should be equal likewise in social standings. Similarly, Mrs. Dora Wilkins recalled the visceral reaction to the times the mistress allowed her (the mistress's) daughter to shear Mrs. Wilkins' African American hair and force her to wear a red bandanna handkerchief. This ritual shaving perhaps implied the daughter's perception of black hair as that of a personal pet or doll baby toy. But the violent imposition of the handkerchief also intimated that the reorganization of the slave woman's head from full hair to handkerchief covering meant the truth of black female existence was one of serving. Female chattel often covered their heads in deference and in the capacity of catering to their owners.[57]

Perhaps the most radical alteration of identity was the renaming process conducted by the master. The power to name denoted direct power in racial social relations, particularly bringing to the surface the contradiction between, on the one hand, private property exercising the right to identify him- or herself and, on the other, the owner's sacred claim to lordship over all of his enslaved creation. One ex-slave, in his autobiographical statement, surmised the following signification in the naming act:

> There were two reasons given by the slave holders why they did not allow a slave to use his own name, but rather that of the master. The first was that, if he ran away, he would not be so easily detected by using his own name as by that of his master. The second was that to allow him to use his own name would be sharing an honor which was due only to his master, and that would be too much for a negro, said they, who was nothing more than a servant. So it was held as a crime for a slave to be caught using his own name, a crime which would for a slave to be severe punishment.[58]

Abdication of naming surrendered one of the natural and sacred rites of passage that parents shared with their offspring and that adults also engaged in when, for instance, they underwent a major conversion experience. It was the name, therefore, that linked forever the slaves' social location and ownership reference point, especially when plantation masters had their initials branded onto the black chattel's body. Escape from the restrictions of the bondage system would prove futile as long as the white owner's identity covered the reality of the black person. Furthermore, on a spiritual level, the owner denied the slave this naming right because the black would be too puffed up with pride and self-importance, harboring sentiments of a mutually shared honor with the master. In a word, closely linked to self-naming and identity was self-claiming and equality. The bond servant system had to discipline the black body, control the slave's life, and reclassify labels, of which the naming ritual remained paramount.[59]

This was true because the invention of the African American as a premier foundation of a democratic society meant that, for the theological and religious predisposition of Christian owners, blacks were property. The Rev. Green recalls how his former mistress, who was a white liberal follower of Jesus Christ and rather easy on her chattel, acted in concert with conservative owners when the bottom line question concerned curtailing black independence and ensuring continual Euro-American wealth. "[M]y mistress was not so hard on her slaves. She was a Christian woman. As I think back now I wonder why she didn't free us, but I guess she thought, like all the rest, that slaves were just so much property."[60]

The above larger conversations regarding the reconstruction of the African American as object by way of (a) a black labor complex for white profit and (b) a network of discipline, control, and reclassification served to embody the totality of a hegemonic organism termed "from sunup to sundown," in the context of Protestantism and American culture. The final and most concentrated Christian constituent of the world the slaveholders made materialized in the multidimensional architecture of slavery churches for blacks.

Architecture of Slavery Churches

White Christians with power and privilege in Protestantism and American culture established an elaborate architecture of slavery churches to remake the black self into a new entity—a slave commodity. Upon a theological apparatus and a religious mechanism (thus a multidimensional architecture), Christian whites ensured a complex institution of slavery churches to maintain white Protestant potency and cultural hegemony.

Slavery churches were those religious gatherings brought about by white Christians taking the initiative to force feed enslaved blacks a gospel message harmful to African Americans' full humanity. These religious formations had a specific *purpose*, identifiable *type*, and cohesive *content*.

However, there were two exceptions in which religion was not used as a tool of domination. First, there were rare individual exceptions within the Christian community who refused to be both Christian and slaveholder. And, secondly, not all Christian slaveholders used the strategy of subverting black humanity by introducing the way of Jesus Christ. Pennington's autobiographical narrative underscores the intransigent practice of his slave owners regarding Christian pedagogy for slaves: "Neither my master or any other master, within my acquaintance, made any provisions for the religious instruction of his slaves." Concurring with Pennington's experience, another former slave emphatically stated, "If a nigger got religion [plantation owners] said you was crazy."[61] Clearly, the tool of Jesus Christ was not used for the domination and exploitation of black property on every plantation.

PURPOSE

Still overwhelmingly, Jesus Christ and the attendant faith mythologies of Christianity were employed to construct slavery churches. In this building process, slavery churches served various purposes.

First, white Christians initiated confessional gatherings in an attempt to *socialize* the entire black race into an abject, groveling state of absolute *obedience*. Put differently, the ultimate goal of churches provided for African Americans was not to teach the individuals faith in Jesus Christ, but to mold slaves into believing in and acting as if the white race were God on earth. This was the foundational purpose for the Protestant masters' introduction of the alien religion of Christianity to an oppressed ebony people whose own indigenous faith background emerged out of West African religions. Rarely, if ever, did masters, mistresses, plantation owners, and other individual white Christians preach to the chattel a gospel of liberation to overthrow wicked, earthly principalities and powers in the form of either individual or systemic manifestations. Sometimes an owner might go as far as to theorize about a black person being free and express this *privately* to the enslaved. Yet a private individual opinion about theory coupled with continued oppression in fact can often be as frustrating for the oppressed as a consistent opinion for and practice of oppression.

Perhaps the equivocation and double standards of the liberal white Christian offered the most difficult and perplexing obstacle in black-white relations. Former chattel Mrs. Browne substantiates this fact regarding a white mistress named Miss Betsy:

> Miss Betsy, though a warm-hearted woman, was a violent advocate of slavery. I have since been puzzled how to reconcile this with her otherwise Christian character; and, though she professed to love me dearly, and had bestowed so much attention upon the cultivation of my mind, and expressed it as her opinion that I was too pretty and white to be a slave, yet if any one had spoken of giving me freedom, she would have condemned it as domestic heresy.[62]

Here one encounters the best of the liberal Protestant mainstream during slavery: a tradition that educated its slaves, openly confessed love for blacks, expressed words in support of African American freedom, and maintained a rational, non-emotional, pacific character. If in practice the issue of allowing blacks to think and act independently and to make decisions without the mistress or master present arose, however, then Miss Betsy immediately reverted to a violent schizophrenic posture equating the possible non-contingent status of blacks as a heresy, that is, an affront to Jesus Christ.

More specifically, the first purpose of slavery churches (that is, socialization for absolute obedience) included the fracturing of black spirituality, willpower, and imagination in order to (a) ensure profitable labor commodities and (b) condition blacks to fear whites simply because they were white.

If chattel swallowed the theology of the slavery churches, then the house, field, and other types of African American plantation workers would automatically act as complacent and complying labor units. From the 1620 Pilgrims' Protestant compact with God to subdue the verdant landscape of the New World to the American cultural contract enshrined in the 1787 Constitutional Convention to sanctify American citizenship only for white men with property, an unbroken thread in the spirituality of vision and the materiality of practice of slavery had been the deployment of labor for the accumulation of wealth in North America.

The conditioning of blacks to fear whites simply because they were white was, as discussed earlier, partially achieved by disciplining the black body through violence, maiming, and torture. In addition to this brutal method, the socialization for obedience in the slavery churches spawned new (nonphysically damaging) dimensions of cultivating the fear of white people. For instance, laws aimed pointedly at regulating the courage-fear factor in black religious existence were passed.

> If any slave or free person of color shall preach to, exhort, or harangue any slave or slaves, or free person of color, unless in the presence of five respectable slave-holders, any such slave or free person of color so offending, shall, on conviction before any justice of the peace, receive, by order of said justice of the peace, thirty-nine lashes for the first offence, and fifty lashes for every offence thereafter; and any [white] person may arrest any such slave or free person of color, and take him before a justice of the peace for trial.[63]

Christian statutory intimidation conditioned the African American faith community to hesitate and reflect on the implications of not trembling at the seemingly omnipotent plantation owners. Thus instilling in slaves a fear of what it meant to be white comprised an important dimension of socialization for obedience, the first purpose of plantation churches for blacks.

Second, the slavery churches maintained the purpose of *institutionalizing* an oppressive theological *language* among the black population. In particular, masters dreaded the possibility of African Americans worshiping Jesus Christ on their own and became extremely anxious about the nature of faith discourse professed from the unchaperoned mouths of black chattel. One master, after learning that two of his female workers had sneaked over to another plantation for prayer meetings, "came there and whipped 'em and made 'em go home." Continuing her reflections, ex-slave Sara Byrd inferred, "I reckin he thought us wuz praying ter git free." Apparently, deep within the theological or logical consciousness of plantation owners, they realized the subversive language of body and spiritual liberation embedded in the Christian gospel. Such a metaphorical message, harboring multidimensional possibilities different from what the owner desired, had to be aborted and replaced by an institutionalized language about God that further fostered the oppression of ebony servants. In a word, the master had to control what religious language came out of the mouth of the slave.

Third, slavery churches offered plantation masters the opportunity to *display their personal blacks* like prize horses to the public. Those with wealth (here black private property signified accumulation of wealth investment and returns) bragged about their own importance and rich standing by offering African American servants for the visual consumption of other white voyeurs. After training in slavery churches, private property went on exhibition as evidence underscoring the achievement of Protestant theological instruction, American cultural acclimation, and the triumph of the Judeo-Christian civilization. "They took us to the camp meetings," articulated one former slave, "the white folks had the meetings; they would carry you there to show you to their friends. 'I'll show you my niggers,' they would say to each other, and they would come 'round and look at each other's niggers."[64] The Christian church, the site where the believer worshiped in an encounter with the liberating spirit of Jesus Christ, was transformed into a faith text inscribed by one group of Protestant plantation owners so that their colleagues could gaze at black flesh conditioned by a slavery church.

Fourth, the final purpose of slavery faith institutions encompassed the *replacement of the intermediary being of Jesus Christ* with white authority functioning as the only door to God. Specifically, when a believer or a new convert sought the new way to God, she or he would desire fellowship with God by offering to enter the community of faith—the household of Jesus Christ. According to traditional Protestant doctrine and practice, the primary go-between facilitating union of the supplicant and God was the "Son of God." No one came to the "Father" except through the "Son." But when such ecclesial affirmations were applied to black chattel, the rules of faith were altered. "When a slave wanted to 'jine the church,'" in the memory of Shade Richard, "the preacher asked his master if he was a 'good nigger', if the master 'spoke up for you', you were 'taken in,' but if he didn't you weren't."[65] The word of the master on earth replaced the authority of the Master in heaven. Slavery churches imbued black servants with the notion that their old divinity, before their Christian conversion, had been replaced by a new, more powerful one: the plantation owner with his God complex.

TYPE

Masters constructed various types of institutional arrangements to facilitate the purposes of slavery churches. White Christians propagandized their religion in diverse segregated worship conditions. David Gullins recollects: "Going back to the church services, we slaves attended the white folks churches. There were galleries built for the slaves in some of the churches, in others, there was space reserved in the back of the church for the colored worshippers." When a pastor and the plantation owners who paid him commissioned the design and erection of a religious edifice, part of the original blueprint for fellowship and worship entailed specifications for separate racial accommodations: either up near the ceiling or barricaded in by a partition in the back. Certain landscapes of worship comprised parallel seating arrangements: "us niggers sat on one side and de white folks sat on the other." Whether blacks were "up near heaven," roped in in the rear, or seated side by side across the aisle from whites, the white Methodist, Baptist, Presbyterian, and Episcopal churches labeled these designated places the "Negro pew."[66]

This theological notion of a segregated pattern within one house of worship upheld racial separation consistently. Where there were baptismal pools inside the church, the going under and coming up ritual (imitating the dying and rising of Christ) likewise was segregated. Furthermore, despite the fact that enslaved blacks could join the church and put their meager money in the collection baskets, the democratic right to participate in the franchise and the leadership of the faith community was quarantined and reserved for white male members only. The history of one white slavery church records: "The office of the pastor, elders and deacons are recognized and it is agreed that they shall be elected by the vote of the congregation.

That each white male of the age of twenty-one, who contributes twenty-five cents to the support of the congregation, shall be entitled to vote."[67]

Just as the founding document of government and civic society (the United States Constitution) enshrined a negative affirmative action for white males with wealth, so too did the foundations of disparate Protestant churches in America.

With its leadership offices and baptismal rites separated by Christian white supremacy, this first type of segregated churches existed where slave and master belonged to the same church and attended the same ecclesial gathering, though spacially divided. Other types of slavery churches were segregated too, but with a slight difference. Some Christian gatherings of slave owners and their families and supporters refused to allow any dark people across the threshold of the church. Only on special occasions, as Queen Elizabeth Bunts recalls, were the blacks "allowed to stand outside" the window and listen to the playing and singing of music for the glory of God. Moreover, Robert Henry's owners did not desire the white Christianity and God to be anywhere near that of his servants; consequently there were two churches on the plantation, "one fer de white folks and one fer de niggers."[68]

In addition to these three types of slavery churches (segregated inside one building, positioned outside the window of churches for white Christians, and strictly distanced by skin color in two separate religious edifices), other types included white preachers propagandizing an all-slave pew, black preachers delivering sermons under the watchful eye of a white male authority figure, and the more tender method of individual mistresses giving Christian instructions to an intimate group of slave children.[69]

Slavery churches for black private property hinged on segregation of the races as a cardinal principle of the plantation owners' Christianity and their paid clergy's theology. Apartheid, the separation of the races, signified how whites joined spacial distance of pigmentation to salvation by color. They perpetually positioned their lighter selves closer to the pulpit, the preacher, and the cross as if to trust metaphorically that whiteness of skin plus closeness to the Bible would yield admission into heaven. Relatedly this racial apartness intimated the slavemasters' need to separate the clean—the plantation owners and all who supported their kingdoms—from the unclean, the tattered and tired chattel. The slavemasters' theology appeared to harbor the assumption that since God created humanity dissimilar and unequal, therefore, the house in which the divinity was worshiped necessitated a demarcated order of difference.

Furthermore, the separation found in the various types of slavery churches suggested a definite appreciation of Christ ("who do they say that I am?") as one who was not only for an apartheid Christianity, but also for a superiority-inferiority, hierarchical institutionalization of faith. This brought to the surface the question of identity. Put differently, the self-naming dynamic of a white Protestant church deployed the marker of difference from a(n) (inferior) black church. The former's identity relied and thrived on the existence of ebony chattel. Instead of embracing self-definition from Jesus Christ, the plantation owners' faith gatherings gained their defining moment from containing and putting boundaries around black private property.

A final characteristic of various slavery church types included the introduction of violence in Protestant houses of worship whenever blacks participated in these religious meetings. After offering a sober observation and assessment of the nature of Christian gatherings provided by the master for the slave, former chattel Alec Bostwich concluded—"All de time dat overseer wuz right dar wid his gun."[70] This type of slavery church, in the Protestant remaking of African Americans, comprised not only place segregation and oppositional self-delineation, but also violence in salvation.[71]

CONTENT

Slavery churches in Protestantism and American culture fabricated the new phenomenon of an enslaved African American with a two pronged attack in content: catechisms and sermons.

Though it is not necessarily the exact text that every white denominational group propagated in the slavery churches, the biblical themes manifest in this standardized Episcopal catechism—a collection of religious lessons, educational guides, and spiritual formations—typifies the Jesus Christ message amenable to the masters' Christianity.[72]

In the characteristic query-response mode, the initial interrogation demanded of the slave is this:

Q. Who was the first negro?
A. Cain.
Q. How did he become so?
A. The Lord set a black mark upon him.

> Q. Did the Southern slave come from him?
> A. Yes.

Note the linguistic level and distinct derivation of divine sanctioned color hierarchy. "Black" is a metaphor for everything evil related to people of darker hue; "black" was made to symbolize the demonic dimensions prevalent in American culture and theology. Originating from God, the color black, then, was inscribed on the physical bodies of dark-skinned people as a natural, biological, and genetic inevitability. Given their color, African American genealogy linked them directly to Cain.

Resuming the catechism:

> Q. When Abraham took his 318 slaves, and pursued the kings, why did they not run away, as slaves do now?
> A. Either because Abraham had his hounds along, or because God had taught them better.

In this instance, substantiation and justification for white superiority and black inferiority hauled the Old Testament patriarch into the field of play. Not only did the righteous Abraham possess human private property and Yahweh bless him with over three hundred personal chattel, but Abraham kept law and order by employing hound dogs. The word "hounds" was a signifier (an expression) for that which was signified (the content) and every black servant understood the code (rules for unlocking a sign-signifier-signified dynamic) that enabled an interpretation of universal meaning and truth within the ethos of the colonial and antebellum United States. Each enslaved African American acknowledged "hounds" in any narrative as a sober warning for the potential of bitten black flesh. In a word, Yahweh, Abraham, and the Bible mandated plantation owners to embrace the possibility of violence to perpetuate the race relations status quo.

> Q. Have the negroes been held as slaves in all ages of the world?
> A. Yes.

Now, in this part of the catechism, one discovers that enslaved blacks linked back to Cain through Abraham were Negroes and Negro chattel existed throughout the geography, history, and eons of the world.

> Q. Did Christ and his apostles approve of Roman slavery?
> A. Yes.
> Q. How do you know?
> A. They didn't say any thing against it.

Christ, in ruling class theology, condoned chattel race relations due to Christ's silence; thus the New Testament corroborated the Old.

> Q. Was Paul a good man?
> A. Yes, he was a holy saint.
> Q. What did he do?
> A. He sent back a run-away slave.

Likewise Paul, the authority figure subject only to Jesus' command in the New Testament, sanctified slavery.

The final question posed to the enslaved African American was:

> Q. What does U.S.A. stand for?

The slave ends the catechism with the correct Protestant response:

> A. United Slave-holding America.

Therefore, the fact that those of European descent had decisive dominion and definite determination over Africa's progeny was a pre-ordained reality institutionalized in the true nomenclature and character of the republic.

But it is in a related catechism that one encounters the essential profit motive intent and incentive in God's granting permanent decision-making power to masters.

> Q. Did Adam and Eve have to work?
> A. Yes, they were to keep the garden.
> Q. Was it hard to keep that garden?
> A. No, it was very easy.
> Q. What makes the crops so hard to grow now?
> A. Sin makes it.
> Q. What makes you lazy?
> A. My own wicked heart.
> Q. How do you know your heart is wicked?
> A. I feel it every day.
> Q. What teaches you so many wicked things?
> A. The Devil.[73]

Learned by heart, this catechism syncretized God, the Devil, and human labor; specifically, the immediate, long-term, divine, and ultimate purpose of black humanity (that is, its theological anthropology) was to work for the masters' wealth. The question was one of definition. Christian masters refused to abdicate to the servants the right to determine how African Americans felt and imagined their own relation to a higher divinity. The masters assumed that their authority to make up theology in a peculiar fashion and a singular method came only from God.

Sermons, the final aspect of the content in slavery churches, pursued a parallel purpose to catechisms. Published specifically to aid white clergy in their edification of the Negro servant, a standard Protestant sermon professed:

> If, therefore, we would have our souls saved by Christ; if we would escape hell and obtain heaven, we must set about doing what he requires of us, that is, to serve God. . . . Almighty God hath been pleased to make you slaves here, and to give you nothing but labor and poverty in this world, which you are obliged to submit to, as it is his will that it should be so. . . . Your bodies, you know are not your own: they are at the disposal of those you belong to; but your precious souls are still your own.[74]

This telling excerpt operates on several theological and doctrinal levels. It links christology and salvation ("saved by Christ"), thus fixating the slaves' faith posture on essential matters of life and death. Eschatology or the advent of God's kingdom on earth (heaven) would result from correct Christian witness ("doing what he requires of us"), the latter interpreted as self-sacrifice for the plantation owners' benefit. God's providence ("Almighty God hath been pleased to make you slaves") smiled upon the face and condition of the black worker. The doctrine of the two worlds required a dichotomized surrender of the African American's split self: the body belonged to the earthly white human master and the soul belonged to the white heavenly Master.

In another section of this sermon, the preacher argued: "All things whatsoever ye would that men should do unto you, do ye even so unto them." This was interpreted as meaning that the African American chattel, if they were masters, would require the same religious obligations and theological injunctions of their white slaves. The logic of this conclusion presupposed an antagonistic either-or philosophy and christology: Christ wanted either whites to win at the expense of blacks, or blacks to win at the expense of whites. The primal fear of the masters obscured and skewed alternative truth meanings in the golden rule. The plantation owners' racial lens of white-skinned privilege failed to interpret and understand Jesus' golden rule in a third way—justice for the colors of all God's creation; all could be equal and free.

The sermon and the catechism in slavery churches facilitated the thwarting of God's word in the Bible and, therefore, made God into a liar. They served to magnify the power of evil and leverage the presence of the demonic in Scripture and theological doctrine with exclusive benefit for the owners. The departure point arose from the concern to keep the plantation masters under divine authority and enslaved blacks under demonic subordination. Whites prayed that the uncritical repetition of catechisms and the redundant hearing of sermons would effect certain results on the African Americans: dull their intuitive senses about right and wrong; position self-doubt deep within their minds' corridors; and seduce their spiritual yearnings for full humanity, so much that the employment of physical violence would be unnecessary.

Perhaps the collective theological intention to manipulate personal property for religious gain was symbolized in this historian's account:

> In some of the older slave States, as Virginia, and South Carolina, churches, in their corporate character, hold slaves, who are generally hired out for the support of the minister. The following is taken from the Charleston Courier, of February 12th, 1835. "Field Negroes by Thomas Gadsen. On Tuesday, the 17 Instant, will be sold, at the north of the Exchange, at ten o'clock, a prime gang of ten Negroes, accustomed to the culture of cotton and provision, belonging to the Independent Church, in Christ's Church Parish."[75]

Not only did individual plantation owners seek the theological justification from the ministers of God's word. The minister and the corporate church entity delved and traded in human flesh, too.

Conclusion

We have engaged the multileveled religious undoing of the Africans (and their offspring) who were brought to the so-called New World in 1619. The unraveling process took place largely in the unholy time, space, and place designated as sunup to sundown, when black labor instruments toiled from "can't see to can't see." In this matrix of Protestant belief-practice and American cultural milieu, plantation owners attempted to create a new reality unheard of or seen before in the history of humankind, that is, the phenomenon called the African American. Whites acted like God and invented a new racial religious identity—the black American. The foundation for perpetual racial interaction occurred in the groundbreaking intervals of the colonial and antebellum periods. Religion played an essential part in this pervasive process, for the 1620 Pilgrims (as well as the Anglicans of 1607 Jamestown, Virginia) perceived themselves on a divine mission to proclaim the Christian European way of thinking, believing, feeling, and acting unto the far corners of the earth. Consequently, questions of faith stances and practical mandates flowed through their theological prism into the overall culture.

Systemically and institutionally, European and European American founding Protestants created the African Americans into a civilized, human, slave population by manufacturing (a) a black labor complex for white profit, (b) a network of discipline, control, and reclassification, and (c) a multidimensional architecture of slavery churches for African Americans.[76]

The masters initiated these three broad areas, which we might call "technologies of re-created power," and based them on the Holy Bible, divine implantation, natural ordination, Constitutional legality, aesthetic sensibility, genetic information, investment returns, Christian duties, violent dismembering, interpretive privileges, and rational argumentation. Moreover, technologies of re-creation power maintained the hierarchical status quo, grounded on racial monopolization of wealth, truth, and meaning, by deploying scenarios shot through with strict racial identities, concentration of wealth, microsubstructures of domination, metaphorical and symbolic language, and signs coded in texts.

In the reality termed "from sunup to sundown," the pleasure to create ebony chattel into objects of plantation owners' knowledge formations resided in white hands. This was one impulse in Protestantism and American culture. At cross-purposes to such an attempted objectification, a competing trajectory within religious communities and the national will seized the initiative "sundown to sunup."

In this latter trajectory, was it possible for an oppressed religious people to lie dormant under such a barrage of assaults on their human person? Was it possible for the enslaved blacks to abdicate their African heritage completely and deny their own capability of forging a novel syncretistic theological worldview? Answers, pointers, and indications may be found in the religious reality and cultural cosmos black workers (with the presence of the holy) made for themselves and the plantation owners. Black folk's struggle for liberation and the practice of freedom verify the ever present room for maneuvering, resistance, and self-creation even within the strictest abuse of power.

NOTES

1. The catechism is found in Quarles, *The Negro in the Making of America,* 71; and the ex-slave quote is from The John B. Cade Library Archives, Southern University (Baton Rouge, La.), no page number. Hereinafter, these archives will be cited as "Cade Library Archives."

2. Hodges, ed., *Black Itinerants of the Gospel,* 89.

3. For an examination of and an engagement with the creation of whiteness in the "New World," see, Toni Morrison, *Playing in the Dark: Whiteness and the Literary Imagination* (Cambridge, Mass.: Harvard University Press, 1992); Ruth Frankenbery, *White Women, Race Matters: The Social Construction of Whiteness* (Minneapolis: University of Minnesota Press, 1993); Dana D. Nelson, *The Word in Black and White: Reading "Race" in American Literature 1638–1867* (New York: Oxford University Press, 1993); Theodore W. Allen, *The Invention of the White Race,* vol. 1, *Racial Oppression and Social Control* (New York: Verso Press, 1994) and vol. 2, *Class Struggle and Social Control: A Pattern Established* (New York: Verso Press, 1995); David R. Reedier, *Towards the Abolition of Whiteness: Essays on Race, Politics, and Working Class History* (New York: Verso Press, 1994); Kenyan Malice, *The Meaning of Race: Race, History and Culture in Western Society* (Washington Square, N.Y.: New York University Press, 1996); Steven Gregory and Roger Sinjuku, eds., *Race* (New Brunswick, N.J.: Rutgers University Press, 1994); David Theo Goldberg, *Racist Culture: Philosophy and the Politics of Meaning* (Cambridge, Mass.: Blackwell, 1993); Charles W. Mills, *The Racial Contract* (Ithaca, N.Y.: Cornell University Press, 1997); Joseph Barndt, *Dismantling Racism: The Continuing Challenge to White America* (Minneapolis: Fortress, 1991); Matthew Frye Jacobson, *Whiteness of a Different Color: European Immigrants and the Alchemy of Race* (Cambridge, Mass.: Harvard University Press, 1998); and Lee D. Baker, *From Savage to Negro: Anthropology and the Construction of Race, 1896–1954* (Berkeley: University of California Press, 1998).

4. See Noel Ignatiev, *How the Irish Became White* (New York: Routledge, 1995).

5. *Unwritten History of Slavery,* 110.

6. Isaac Johnson, a former slave, in Cornel Reinhart, ed., *Slavery Days in Old Kentucky by Isaac Johnson, a Former Slave* (1901; reprint, Canton, N.Y.: Friends of the Owen D. Young Library and the St. Lawrence County Historical Association, 1994), 25–26.

7. "Zion Church and Frierson Settlement in Maury County, Tenn.," pp. 12–13; found at the UNC Southern Historical Society.

8. Cade Library Archives, no page. In the same archives (with no page), former slave Dora Wilkers states: "The slave did all the work on the farm, in the kitchen, in the big house, in the weaving room, and everything else to be done." And again in the same collection (with no page number), ex-chattel Jash True claims: "We had to work hard like dogs, our master did not care

for us." Clearly, if there was one category of being alive which all blacks shared in the eyes of whites, it was the classification of labor. The totality of slave existence was dominated by a primary obligation to work for the benefit of Euro-Americans.

9. David Walker, *David Walker's Appeal to the Coloured Citizens of the World, but in Particular and Very Expressly, to Those of the United States of America,* ed. Charles M. Wiltse (1829; reprint, New York: Hill and Wang, 1965), 16.

10. Found in the slavery box, Louisiana State University Archives, Hill Memorial Library.

11. The Cornelia reference comes from *Unwritten History of Slavery,* 144.

Other parts of the fence opener quote relate the following: The white master "would get up early in the morning and get on his horse. A man had to be in front of him to let the fence down and put it up again, or to open the gate and close it when he had to go through. He just tended to the horse and followed him around all day." In this instance, blacks are lower than livestock. The particular horse, chosen by the master that day, enjoyed the privilege of having a black serve it (tend to the horse and follow it around all day). As a labor commodity, therefore, the slave, here, saves the owner not only time (by enabling him not to descend and ascend his horse for gate opening) but money. He is capital that maintains the master's capital (that is, the horse). (See *Unwritten History of Slavery*, 24)

The Julia statement comes from George P. Rawick, ed., *The American Slave: A Composite Autobiography*, Georgia, supplemental series 1, vol. 3, pt. 1 (Westport, Conn.: Greenwood Publishers, 1972, 1977, 1979), 320. Here the worth, value, and identity of a female slave is determined by how she sustains the durability and cleanliness of a white Christian woman's cloth. *The American Slave* comprises forty-one volumes of interviews of ex-slaves. From now on, it will be referenced by title, name of the state, series, volume, and part.

12. See Quarles, *The Negro in the Making of America,* 39.

13. Northup's comment is found in Solomon Northup, *Twelve Years a Slave* (1854; reprint, New York: Dover Publications, 1970), 225; Davis' remembrances are taken from the Cade Library Archives. William Grimes likewise comments on Negro drivers in his "Life of William Grimes, the Runaway Slave" in *Five Black Lives,* 67.

14. References are from the following sources: Bell McMillan, Cade Library Archives, no page number; Ned Lacy, Cade Library Archives, no page number; the peafowl feather waver, *Unwritten History of Slavery,* 25. From *The American Slave*: Addie Vinson, Georgia, vol. 13, pt. 4, 101; Susan Castle, Georgia, v. 12, pt. 1, 181; and Tom Hawkins, Georgia, vol. 12, pt. 2, 128.

15. Both Callie Hopkins's and Mary Calhoun's testimonies come from Cade Library Archives, no page numbers. Mrs. Claibourn's interview is found in *The American Slave,* Georgia, vol. 12, pt. 1, 187–88.

16. See *Unwritten History of Slavery*, 29–30.

17. See Frederick Douglass, *Life and Times of Frederick Douglass* (rev. ed., 1892; reprint, New York: Crowell-Collier Publishing Company, 1962), 59; and for the "slept under the stairway" reference, see *Unwritten History of Slavery*, 111–12.

18. Austin Steward, *Twenty-Two Years a Slave and Forty Years a Freeman, Embracing a Correspondence of Several Years While President of Wilberforce Colony, London, Canada West*, 2d ed. (Rochester, 1859), 31–32.

19. Lula Washington was interviewed in *The American Slave*, Georgia, vol. 13, pt. 4, 135; and the unattributed quote is from *Unwritten History of Slavery*, 148.

Other references to the house laborers' better treatment and self-perception of superiority can be found in: *The American Slave*, Georgia, vol. 13, pt. 4, 196 ("On the plantation of Mr. House the house slaves thought themselves better than the field slaves because of the fact that they received better treatment"); and Georgia, vol. 13, pt. 3, 67 ("De house servants hold that dey is uh step better den de field niggers").

20. Henry Bibb, *Narrative of the Life and Adventures of Henry Bibb*, 136.

21. See *Unwritten History of Slavery*, 2. Ex-slave Jennie Burns was the daughter of the white master on her plantation. In her case, she did not have to endure the brutal hardships of other slaves. She nursed children and performed whatever her father-master required her to do. Still her basic life purpose was labor. See Cade Library Archives, no page.

In her autobiography, Harriet A. Jacobs testified: "The secrets of slavery are concealed like those of the Inquisition. My master was, to my knowledge, the father of eleven slaves." See her *Incidents in the Life of a Slave Girl Written by Herself* (1861; reprint, Cambridge, Mass.: Harvard University Press, 1987), 35.

22. *The American Slave*, Georgia, vol. 13, pt. 4, 133.

23. See *Unwritten History of Slavery*, 1, no name. Ward's reflections are found in *The American Slave*, Georgia, vol. 13, pt. 4, 133. Harriet Jacobs stated bluntly: "Women are considered no value, unless they continually increase their owner's stock. They are put on par with animals" (*Incidents in the Life of a Slave Girl*, 49).

24. In Octavia V. Rogers Albert, ed., *The House of Bondage or Charlotte Brooks and Other Slaves* (1890; reprint, New York: Oxford University Press, 1988), 107.

25. See examples in Cade Library Archives; unfortunately these archival materials lack pagination. On the instances of the broom, glass of water, and lamp, see *Unwritten History of Slavery*, 89.

26. See *Unwritten History of Slavery*, 99.

27. See Jacobs, *Incidents in the Life of a Slave Girl*, 38. Other references to black children under slavery can be found in the "Preliminary

Report: Touching the Condition and Management of Emancipated Refugees;
Made to the Secretary of War, by the American Freedman's Inquiry Commission June 30, 1863," 69, in the Slavery Section, National Archives, Washington, D.C., file 3280, 1863, microfilm roll 199; *Unwritten History of Slavery,* 29–30, 56, 100, 108; and Cade Library Archives, no page number; and in "Extracts from Debates on the Adoption of the Federal Constitution, Relating to Slavery," of the American Freedmen's Inquiry Commission, 1863–64, microfilm roll 200, no page number, at the Library of Congress, Washington, D.C.

28. Refer to Katz, ed. *Five Slave Narratives,* 32. Other references to aged blacks can be found in Still, *The Underground Railroad,* 429; Albert, ed., *House of Bondage,* 15; Jacobs, *Incidents in the Life of a Slave Girl,* 16; and *Life and Times of Frederick Douglass,* 99.

29. Both texts mentioned come from the Cade Library Archives; not paginated. Other issues of separation are found in this same Archives of interviews pertaining to Florida, the Mississippi Valley, Alabama, Texas, and Louisiana. Also review Nichols, *Many Thousand Gone,* 20; Jacobs, *Incidents in the Life of a Slave Girl,* 38; *Life and Times of Frederick Douglass,* 28; and *Unwritten History of Slavery,* 19, 59, and 86.

The "humane and Christian" note is from Craft, *Running a Thousand Miles for Freedom,* 9.

30. Descriptions and interpretations of the poor religious treatment of dead slaves are found in *Unwritten History of Slavery,* 54 and 151.

31. The effectiveness of recreating African Americans into labor suppliers of white people's profit is revealed in the fact that in "the quarter of a century preceding the Civil War, the cotton fields of the South were producing three-fourths of the world's supply." See Quarles, *The Negro in the Making of America,* 63.

32. Creel, *A Peculiar People,* 79. References to South Carolina and New Jersey are found on pages 79–80 of Creel.

33. The eight-year-old's account is from *National Anti-Slavery Standard,* October 22, 1840, 78 (Widener Library, Harvard). And the "gashes . . . skin" text comes from an interview with ex-slave Mrs. Florence Bailey in Cade Library Archives, no page number.

34. The cat torture mechanism is found in *The Liberty Almanac,* no. two, 1845 (Syracuse, N.Y., Tucker & Kinney, Publishers). Text of Thomas Jefferson's nephews can be read in *The American Anti-Slavery Almanac for 1840,* vol. 1, no. 5. Both documents are found in Cornell University Slavery Collection.

35. See Peter Still and Vina Still, *The Kidnapped and the Ransomed: The Narrative of Peter and Vina Still After Forty Years of Slavery* (1856; reprint, Philadelphia: The Jewish Publication Society of America, 1970), 195; introduction by Maxwell Whitman. For the "stock" reference, review former slave Robert Smalls' testimony in "Extracts from Debates on the Adoption of the Federal Constitution, Relating to Slavery" of the American Freedmen's Com-

mission, 1863–64, microfilm roll 200, no page number, at the Library of Congress. Regarding Old Mack Williams, refer to interview of ex-slave William Ward in *The American Slave,* Georgia, vol. 13, pt. 4, p. 133. The barrel citation comes from the same volume and part, 297.

Other references to the variations of the "runaway's irons" or "chokers" can be investigated in "The Emancipated Slave Face to Face with His Old Master: Valley of the Lower Mississippi: Supplemental Report (B); American Freedmen's Inquiry Commission by James McKaye," 27, found at the National Archives, Washington, D.C., file 3280, 1863, microfilm roll 199.

36. This excerpt from *Slave Life in Georgia; A Narrative of the Life, Sufferings, and Escape of John Brown, a Fugitive Slave, Now in England* (London, April 1865) edited by L. A. Chamerovzow, Secretary of the British and Foreign Anti-Slavery Society, London, is found in *The Anti-Slavery Advocate,* 257, at the Boston Public Library.

37. Brown in Katz, ed., *Five Slave Narratives.* Reference to the holed paddle is found in an interview with former chattel Joe Johnson, in the Cade Library Archives, no page number; to the ox-whip in an interview with former slave Sam Gray in the Cade Library Archives, no page number; and to the bullwhip in *Unwritten History of Slavery,* 134.

As the Civil War unfolded, many observers in the South wrote letters to the federal government on the conditions of enslaved blacks. Regarding the types of whips used, one author wrote: "There was the whip of knotted hempen-cords; the whip with the twisted lash of dried bulls hide; the coach-trace whip and the paddle." Flat handsaws were also employed as whips. See page 18 of "The Emancipated Slave Face to Face with His Old Master: Valley of the Lower Mississippi: Supplemental Report (B); American Freedmen's Inquiry Commission by James McKaye," found in the Washington, D.C. National Archives, file 3289, 1863, microfilm roll 199.

38. Regarding the stocks, see interview with Roy Refield in *The American Slave,* Georgia, vol. 13, pt. 4, 304. And references to the buck are found in *The Anti-Slavery Advocate,* London, November 1853, 109, Boston Public Library; and in *Unwritten History of Slavery,* 132. The log is described in an interview with ex-slave Bill Collins, the Cade Library Archives, no page number; the stake in a Cade Library Archives interview with ex-slave Jennie Burns, no page number; and the tree in *Unwritten History of Slavery,* 49.

39. See Jefferson Henry's opinion in *The American Slave,* Georgia, vol. 12, pt. 2, 185; William McWhorter in vol. 13, pt. 3, 96; Easter Brown in vol. 12, pt. 1, 137; and the unnamed slave in *Unwritten History of Slavery,* 111.

40. *Life and Times of Frederick Douglass,* 51. The reference to slaves fearing masters can be found in an interviewer's account of Nath Perkins found in Cade Library Archives, no page number; see *Unwritten History of Slavery,* 63, regarding punishment for reading; review *The American Slave,* Georgia, vol. 13, pt. 4, 180, George Womble's interview on beating for fun.

41. See page 83, no name, microfilm roll 201. "Letters Received by the Office of Adjutant General (Main Series)," National Archives, file 3280, 1863.

Reference to Mrs. Flint can be found in Jacobs, *Incidents in the Life of a Slave Girl*, 12. In another case, a white deacon "in good and regular standing" in the same church with his slave, would regularly whip his female property "nearly to death." See Gilbert Osofsky, ed., *Puttin' On Ole Massa: The Slave Narratives of Henry Bibb, William Wells Brown, and Solomon Northup*; reprint San Francisco: Harper and Row, 1969), 191.

42. See Harriet Jacobs's account in her autobiography, *Incidents in the Life of a Slave Girl*, 70.

43. *Life and Times of Frederick Douglass*, 55–56.

44. See Milton Hammond in *The American Slave*, Georgia, vol. 12, pt. 2, 94. For another reference to weekly allowance, see Heard Griffin, Georgia, vol. 12, pt. 2, 75; Lewis Favor, Georgia, vol. 12, pt. 1, 319; James Bolton, Georgia, vol. 12, , pt. 1, 93; and James L. Smith, *Five Black Lives*, 152. The "bread and water" reference comes from Eli Coleman, Texas, Cade Library Archives, no page number; the "sour milk" comment from Mrs. Sutton, *Unwritten History of Slavery*, 13, Tenn.; the "buttermilk and corn bread" statement from *Unwritten History of Slavery*, 29–30; and the "pick up crumbs" testimony from Lue Boman, Cade Library Archives, no page number.

Hundreds of testimonies about food control abound. Further samples can be found in the following: interviews with Jennie Hagens, Florence Bailey (a house slave), Martha Jackson, Rufus Houston, Ned Lacy, and John W. White, all found in Cade Library Archives, no page numbers; Pennington in Katz, ed., *Five Slave Narratives*, 65; *Unwritten History of Slavery*, 4–5, 105, 130, 140; and Rachel Adams, *The American Slave*, Georgia, vol. 12, pt. 1, 3.

Exceptions were granted on some plantations: blacks might be allowed to plant a little garden or fish and hunt, whenever these activities did not disrupt the whites' assignments and obligations.

45. For reference to the "trough" and "feet," see Milton Hammond, *The American Slave*, Georgia, vol. 12, pt. 2, 93; and for the "bowl" and "dip in it," see Annie L. Burton's "Memories of Childhood's Slavery Days," in *Six Women's Slave Narratives*, The Schomburg Library of Nineteenth-Century Black Women Writers (reprint, New York: Oxford University Press, 1988), 4–5. Other statements on children eating out of troughs can be found in interviews of Saul Williams and Amelia Daniels, Cade Library Archives, no page numbers; and Willis Cofer, *The Slave in America*, Georgia, vol. 12, pt. 2, 203. For detailed descriptions of children's diets see: interviews with Ben Wooley and Ben Simpson in the Cade Library Archives, no page numbers; Rachel Adams, *The Slave in America*, Georgia, vol.12, pt. 1, 93; and *Unwritten History of Slavery*, 55.

46. "Supply allowance of clothing" reference is from *Life and Times of Frederick Douglass*, 55–56; "coat" descriptions are from James L. Smith, *Five Black Lives*, 151, and *Unwritten History of Slavery*, 130; "sack shirt" statement is found in *Unwritten History of Slavery*, 24; and "no underwear" remarks are from *Unwritten History of Slavery*, 3 and 109. See Emma Hur-

ley in *The American Slave,* Georgia, vol. 12, pt. 2, 275 regarding "no shoes"; other no "shoe" references can be found in the interviews of Florence Bailey in Cade Library Archives, no page numbers; and Callie Elder in *The American Slave,* Georgia, vol. 12, pt. 1, 309.

For investigations and interpretations of meaning concerning the forced rationing of clothes for slaves, see: Willis Cofer, *The American Slave,* Georgia, vol. 12, pt. 2, 203; John Bates, Bell McMillan, Lue Boman, and Eli Coleman, Cade Library Archives, no page numbers; *The Kidnapped and the Ransomed,* 141; Jefferson F. Henry, *The American Slave,* Georgia, vol. 12, pt. 2, 184; *Unwritten History of Slavery,* 150; and Moses Grandy in Katz, ed., *Five Slave Narratives,* 6.

47. For citations pertaining to slave houses, see interviews of: Joe Johnson, John Bates, Charlie Bassett, and Mary Johnson in Cade Library Archives, no page numbers; Willis Cofer, *The American Slave,* Georgia, vol. 12, pt. 2, 203; Benny Dillard, Georgia, vol. 12, pt. 1, 289; Leah Garrett, Georgia, vol. 12, pt. 2, 15; Lewis Favor, Georgia, vol. 12, pt. 1, 322; Minne Davis, Georgia, vol. 12, pt. 1, 254; an unnamed former slave, Georgia, vol. 13, pt. 4, 363; Robert Shepherd, Georgia, vol. 13, pt. 3, 251; in *Unwritten History of Slavery,* an unnamed ex-slave, 94, Mr. Huddleston, 14, and Mrs. Sutton, 14; and the autobiographies of James L. Smith, *Five Black Lives,* 151; Moses Grandy, in Katz, ed., *Five Slave Narratives,* 18; and Daisy Anderson, *From Slavery to Affluence, Memoirs of Robert Anderson, Ex-Slave* (1927; reprint, Steamboat Springs, Colo.: Steamboat Springs Pilot, 1986), 3.

48. Rev. Green, in Clifton H. Johnson, ed., *God Struck Me Dead: Religious Conversion Experiences and Autobiographies of Ex-slaves* (1945; reprint, Philadelphia: Pilgrim Press, 1969), 87.

49. Review the interview of Rhodus Walton, *The American Slave,* Georgia, vol. 13, pt. 4, 123, for the elements pertaining to seeing, being seen, and at the center; and Lucy, *Unwritten History of Slavery,* 5 for the issues of proximity, mobility, and aesthetics.

50. William Wells Brown's remarks are found in Osofsky, ed., *Puttin' On Ole Massa,* 180 and Mrs. Wright's in *The American Slave,* Georgia, vol. 13, pt. 4, 195. The types of "alarm clocks" are noted in the interviews of Cicely Cawthon, Georgia, supplemental series 1, vol. 3, pt. 1, 183; Julia Cole, Georgia, vol. 12, pt. 1, 233; Charlie King, Georgia, vol. 13, pt. 3, 17; and Rev. W. B. Allen, Georgia, supplemental series 1, vol. 3, pt. 1, 6. See Georgia, vol. 12, pt. 2, 149 for Emma Heard's comments. And Charley Basset (Cade Library Archives, no page numbers) and Callie Elder (Georgia, vol. 12, pt. 1, 309) deal with "roll call" and "overseer night checks", respectively.

51. See Rachel Adams's interview, *The American Slave,* Georgia, vol. 12, pt. 1, 6. Other "weekend" comments found in Minnie Davis words, Georgia, vol. 12, pt. 1, 259, and Carrie Hudson's statements, Georgia, vol. 12, pt. 2, 215.

Other references to weekday rituals can be noted in the following interviews: Amanda Jackson, Georgia, vol. 12, pt. 2, 289; Easter Huff, Georgia, vol. 12, pt. 2, 248; and the unnamed ex-slave, *Unwritten History of Slavery*, 109.

52. See *Unwritten History of Slavery*, 148.

53. See the *Mobile Register and Journal* of Mobile, Alabama, August 13, 1837; Library of Congress, Manuscript Division, Slave Narrative Project, Box A891.

54. See "June 12, 1830, Mobile Alabama," Library of Congress, Manuscript Division, Slave Narrative Project, Box A891.

55. For a sampling of newspaper advertisements, see: "For sale, a Bargain, Two fishing Negroes," *The Times* (Charleston, S.C.), April 6, 1810, p. 1; "Negroes for Sale, For Cash, Produce, or Credit," *The Times*, April 3, 1810, p. 1,; "For Private Sale, A Few Prime Africans," *The Times*, April 3, 1810, p. 1; notice of auction sale, *The Times*, April 3, 1810, p. 1. (These issues of *The Times* can be found at the College of Charleston, Special Collections, Charleston, S.C.) "Mobile Slave Notice of 1828," *Mobile Commercial Register*, Mobile, Ala., June 4, 1837, Library of Congress, Manuscript Division, Slave Narrative Project, Box A 891; "Wanted on hire," *The Times*, April 3, 1810, p. 1; notice of city taxes, *The Times*, April 5, 1810, p. 2; and "State and County Taxes for 1848," Louisiana State University Archives, Hill Memorial Library, Slavery Box.

56. See James W. C. Pennington's autobiography in Katz, ed., *Five Slave Narratives*, 9.

57. These two accounts can be found in *Unwritten History of Slavery*, 37, and Dora Wilkins's interview, Cade Library Archives, no page numbers.

58. "My Life in the South," found in Katz, ed., *Five Slave Narratives*, 14. Other documentation of the reclassification by way of naming can be found in the following ex-slave interviews: William Ward, *The American Slave*, Georgia, vol. 13, pt. 4, 130; George Caulton, Georgia, supplemental series 1, vol. 3, pt. 1, 171; unnamed interviewees, 20, 93, 150, and Mrs. Chapman, 33, all in *Unwritten History of Slavery*; and Mary Davis and J. Johnson, both in Cade Library Archives, no page numbers. Also review "Life of William Grimes the Runaway Slave, Brought Down to the Present Time" (original, 1855) in *Five Black Lives*, 70.

59. White Christians and the privileged who supported an American culture of difference employed a division of labor or apparatus of power mechanisms in order to discipline, control, and classify black chattel.

Poor whites were willing tools in this technology of reformulating the truth and meaning of who and what was an African American in the New World. Poor whites served as: *patrollers*—those white males who, by legal obligation, worked night shifts to catch any unauthorized black moving about; *overseers*—employed white men who used violence and its threat to keep the field hands productive; *nigger hunters* with *nigger dogs*—those white men whose profession was to be authorities on the ways of unruly blacks, particularly runaways; and *hired whippers*—whites contracted by some masters or mistresses to perform the cutting of black skin.

Middle- and upper middle-class whites had their roles, too: as *speculators*—speculating on the market that bought and sold Africans and African Americans; *slave traders*—usually those men who forced slaves on foot from one state to another; *negro pen* and *auction block* owners—the owners of the holding cells for blacks prior to sale or relocation, and the owners of the stands upon which stood the slave property being tendered for sale.

On the patrollers, see: "Report of the Captain of the Guard, City Hall New Orleans Jan. 13 to 14, 1818" and the "Jan. 14 to 15" records in the Louisiana State University Archives, Hill Memorial Library, Slavery Box; the interviews of ex-slaves—Callie Elder, *The American Slave*, Georgia, vol. 12, pt. 1, 311, Mr. Huddleston, *Unwritten History of Slavery*, 14, John Bates, Cade Library Archives, no page numbers; and Ruby Lorraine Radford, Georgia, vol. 13, pt. 4, 321; and the autobiographies of Northup, *Twelve Years a Slave*, 237, and Stephen Jordon in Albert, ed., *House of Bondage*, 106.

On the overseers, see: interviews of Emman Malone, Cade Library Archives, no page numbers; unnamed interviewee, *Unwritten History of Slavery*, 153; Alex Bostwick, Georgia, vol. 12, pt. 1, 108; and Northup, *Twelve Years a Slave*, 165; William W. Brown in Katz, ed., *Five Slave Narratives*, 21, and *Five Black Lives*, 75.

On nigger hunters and their dogs, see: "New York Misc. Papers, 1762–1831," especially the June 10, 1806 letter of Richard Bogardus of Boston writing to Abraham Huffman of New York, found in the UNC's Southern Historical Collection; "Christian Politicians" magazine, recorded in the *May Anti-Slavery Pamphlets 40,* p. 18, which describes a white Baptist clergyman who was a nigger hunter with nigger dogs, and the newspaper ad of another nigger hunter on page 19 of the same *Pamphlets 40,* found in Cornell University's Slavery Collection; the interviews of Rev. W. B. Allen, Georgia, supplemental series 1, vol. 3, pt. 1, 3–4; James Bolton, Georgia, supplemental series 1, vol. 3, pt. 1, 7; an unnamed person, *Unwritten History of Slavery*, 130; and the unnamed interviewee, Cade Library Archives, no page number; and the autobiographical account of Uncle John in Albert, ed., *House of Bondage*, 77–78.

On hired whippers, see: Katz, ed., *Five Slave Narratives*, 39.

Regarding speculators and slave traders, refer to: Julia Brown, Georgia, vol. 12, pt. 1, 143; Moses Grandy in Katz, ed., *Five Slave Narratives*, 33; Rev. Allen, Georgia, supplemental series 1, vol. 3, pt. 1, 5; Bibb, *Narrative of the Life and Adventures of Henry Bibb*, 102; unnamed sources, *Unwritten History of Slavery*, 1, 20, 29–30, 129; and Henry Houston and Harve Quanles, both found at the Cade Library Archives, no page numbers.

For notations of the negro pen and auction block review: *National Anti-Slavery Standard*, June 3, 1841, p. 206, found in Widener Library, Harvard; "From Johnson's Lake Shore Home Magazine, Vol. No. 1, Jan., 1896. Romances and Realities of the Underground Rail Road," p. 22, found in *The Underground Railroad in Washington, DC*, in Box 70, Collection 116 of the Siebert Papers; Lewis Favors, Georgia, vol. 12, pt. 1, 323–24; William W.

Brown, in Katz, ed., *Five Slave Narratives*, 83–84; *Unwritten History of Slavery*, 13, 17, 99, and 133; and Reinhart, ed., *Slavery Days in Old Kentucky by Isaac Johnson*, 9–11.

60. Johnson, ed., *God Struck Me Dead*, 71.

61. Pennington, in Katz, ed., *Five Slave Narratives*, 66; on the second reference, see *Unwritten History of Slavery*, 150. Other instances of whites failing to introduce Christianity to their property can be found in: Easter Brown's interview, *The American Slave,* Georgia, vol. 12, pt. 1, 138; and *Unwritten History of Slavery*, 2 and 86.

62. Martha Griffith Browne, *Autobiography of a Female Slave* (New York: Negro Universities Press, 1969, originally published in 1857 by J. S. Redfield), 12.

63. Eric Foner, ed., *Nat Turner* (Englewood Cliffs, N.J.: Prentice Hall, 1971), 118.

64. *Unwritten History of Slavery*, 57. Sara Byrd's reflections are found in *The American Slave,* Georgia, vol. 12, pt. 1, 170–71.

65. *The American Slave,* Georgia, vol. 13, pt. 3, 203.
Also note similar accounts in: "Slavery and the Slaveholder's Religion: As Opposed to Christianity," (p. 35) by Samuel Brooke. This tract was published by the author in Cincinnati, 1846; found in *May-Anti Slavery Pamphlets 40*, Cornell University Slavery Collection; the diary of Harriet Eaton, vol. 1, March 12, 1854, deposited in the UNC Southern Historical Collection; and in the interviewer's account of how Elmina Henry joined a church: "She just gave the Boss man her hand and the white lady (his wife) said 'Yes we will receive Elmina into the church. She is so obedient to her master and mistress'"; found in the Cade Library Archives, no page number.

66. See Birney, *The American Churches*, 6–7 for further clarification of the Negro pew; and Marshall Butler's interview regarding parallel worship experiences. David Gullins' remarks are found in *The American Slave,* Georgia, vol. 12, pt. 2, 85.

67. See "Zion Church and Frierson Settlement in Maury County, Tenn.," UNC Southern Historical Collection. This archival material continues: "the colored people were not neglected, and also that the privilege of contributing to the salary of their old and beloved pastor should be enjoyed by each member"; see pp. 14–16. Thus the blacks had taxation without representation.
Also, the remarks on segregated baptism can be found in the remembrances of Martha Colquitt, *The American Slave,* Georgia, vol. 12, pt. 1, 246.

68. See Robert Henry, *The American Slave,* Georgia, vol. 12, pt. 2, 197, and Queen Elizabeth Bunts, Georgia, supplemental series 1, vol. 3, pt. 1, 122.

69. See the diary entries of Rev. Francis Hanson, a white cleric paid by the slave owner to preach and baptize the latter's servants. One of the entries reads: "On Sunday, August 19th, I preached in the morning in St. Andrew's

to the white congregation. In the afternoon I preached to the servants in the Church" in "From the Diary of Rev. Francis Hanson," found in the UNC Southern Historical Collection.

Other references to a white preacher rendering homilies to a black pew: "Diary of Harriet Eaton, vol. 1, March 12, 1854," also found in the UNC Southern Historical Collection; "Journal of Mary Susan Ker," found in the Louisiana State University Archives, Hill Memorial Library; Martha Everette, *The American Slave,* Georgia, supplemental series 1, vol. 3, pt. 1, 238; Addie Vinson, Georgia, vol. 13, pt. 4, 106; Alice Hutcheson, Georgia, vol.12, pt. 2, 286; Berry Clay, Georgia, vol. 12, pt. 1, 190–91; Hannah Austin, Georgia, vol. 12, pt. 1, 20; Celestia Avery, Georgia, vol. 12, pt. 1, 25; *Unwritten History of Slavery,* 20, 23, 24, 45, 53, 64, and 135; and in the Cade Library Archives, see interview of Florence Bailey, no page numbers.

References to an African American preacher with a white authority figure present can be found in: interviews of Annie Price, Georgia, vol. 13, pt. 3, 181; Susan McIntosh, Georgia, vol. 13, pt. 3, 83; Leah Garrett, Georgia, vol. 12, pt. 2, 16; Lewis Favors, Georgia, vol. 12, pt. 1, 323; and see *Unwritten History of Slavery,* 46, 60, and 73.

Notations on mistresses teaching slaves can be reviewed in the diary of Rev. Francis Hanson, especially the Sept. 20, 1858 entry in "From the Diary of Rev. Francis Hanson," found in the UNC Southern Historical Collection; and in the interviews of Cicely Cawthon, *The American Slave,* Georgia, supplemental series 1, vol. 3, pt. 1, 182; and Wheeler Gresham, Georgia, vol. 12, pt. 2, 69.

A host of ex-slaves offer their interpretational experiences with slavery churches in William C. Emerson, M.D., *Stories and Spirituals of the Negro Slave* (Boston: Gorham Press, 1930), 18, 20, 23, 30, 35, 42, and 78.

70. Found in *The American Slave,* Georgia, vol. 12, pt. 1, 109.

71. Two recognitions would be helpful in closing out the "type" subsection. First, not all owners provided a "type," that is, neither formal nor informal religious instruction/worship was present in all situations of master-slave interactions. (For references, see Pennington's autobiographical account in Katz, ed., *Five Slave Narratives,* 66; and *Unwritten History of Slavery,* 2, 86, and 150.)

Second, there existed, in addition to types of slavery churches, independent African American denominational institutions. See, for example, James Melvin Washington, *Frustrated Fellowship: the Black Baptist Quest for Social Power* (Macon, Ga.: Mercer University Press, 1986).

72. Taken from *The Liberty Almanac for 1848,* no page number, found in the Slavery Collection at Cornell University, Ithaca, New York. For additional such injunctions, see *The Anti-Slavery Advocate,* London, July 1854, p. 176, found in the Boston Public Library; Quarles, *The Negro in the Making of America,* 71; the Rev. J. R. Balme, *American States, Churches, and Slavery* (1862; reprint, New York: Negro Universities Press, 1969), 38; and Jacobs, *Incidents in the Life of a Slave Girl,* 7–8.

73 See p. 176 of *The Anti-Slavery Advocate,* London, July 1854, found in the Boston Public Library.

74 See "'Slavery and the Slaveholder's Religion; As Opposed to Christianity' by Samuel Brooke. Published by the Author, Cincinnati, 1846"; found in the *May Anti-Slavery Pamphlets 40,* 29–33, Cornell University Slavery Collection.

For other samplings of slavery church sermons, review the interviews of Benjamin Johnson, *The American Slave,* Georgia, vol. 12, pt. 2, 325; Tom Hawkins, Georgia, vol. 12, pt. 2, 131; George Lewis, Georgia, vol. 13, pt. 3, 49; Martha Johnson and Charley Bassett, both in the Cade Library Archives, no page numbers; the unnamed source in *Unwritten History of Slavery,* 154; examine the Northup autobiography, *Twelve Years a Slave,* 128; and also note the October 1852 edition of *The Anti-Slavery Advocate*, p. 2, published by the Anglo-American Anti-Slavery Association of London, found at the Boston Public Library.

75. Birney, *The American Churches,* 7.

76. For excellent manifestations of the mindset of the plantation owners in welding these three dynamics together, review "Extracts for a Christian Slaveholder's Diary. Sabbath, May 21, 18—", in *The American Anti-Slavery Almanac for 1836,* vol. 1, no. 1, p. 38, deposited at Cornell University's Slavery Collection; and p. 134 of *The Anti-Slavery Advocate*, February 1854, published in London, found in the Boston Public Library.

CHAPTER 3

From Sundown to Sunup: The African American Co-Constitutes the Black Self

I is waitin' now for judgement day and the time when I won't have to work no more. They tells me there is black angels with black wings and I is prayin' I will be one of them black angels.

Mamie White, ex-slave

The folks would sing and pray and testify and clap their hands, just as if God was right there in the midst of them. He wasn't way off in the sky. He was a-seeing everybody and a-listening to every word and a-promising to let His love come down. . . . Yes sir, there was no pretending in those prayer meetings. There was a living faith in a just God Who would one day answer the cries of His poor black children and deliver them from their enemies. But the slaves never said a word to their white folk about this kind of faith.

Simon Brown, ex-slave

There [in West African religions] we have a description of a vigorous religion, whose followers blend it with all their activities. What matters is the intention by which nothing is profane. It is only the practitioners of a feeble religion who categorize their service as variously religious or profane. God cannot have intended that one who cultivates the land should cease to be holy during his work, or that one who works on the water should have to wait for the propitious hour for liturgical celebrations in a church, etc. Each person should ensure by his intention that everything, even his walking and breathing, should become religious activities putting him in constant contact with God. [1]

PROTESTANTISM AND American culture were saturated with technologies of re-creation power—a black labor complex for white profit and pleasure, a network of discipline, control and re-categorization, and an architecture of slavery churches. This was the sunup to sundown period invented by the slave master. In contrast to this faith perspective and way of life, enslaved Africans and African Americans maintained a determined desire to reconstitute and re-create their own new reality through methods of the black self (that is, to know oneself and to take care of oneself) inspired by a sense of the transcendent. By what religious means, theological myths, and regularized rituals could and would African American chattel redraw the boundaries between externally imposed definitions and internally initiated lifestyles grounded in fundamental faith claims? How could the African American subject arise by transgressing established systemic parameters of white Christians? What alternative could be presented to oppose the sunup to sundown time?

In an attempt to clarify this battle of beliefs and meanings of existence in the New World, black people added their own interpretation, understanding, and truth to Protestantism and American culture. It is this attempt, sometimes actual and other times figurative, that defined sundown to sunup, a dimension often hidden from the plantation owners, though it might be displayed before their unseeing eyes.

In the sundown to sunup time, we find enslaved Africans and African Americans re-creating themselves with divine purpose. They accomplished this divine-human constitution of the black self by using methods of the self. They made do with what they had at hand. Specifically, in this chapter, methods of the self include: *Seizing Sacred Domains,* the *Divine Right to Resist,* and *Constructing a Syncretized Religion.* Restated, the methods of the self are the means for the re-creation of the African American self from the old self of sunup to sundown to the new liberated self—one that practices freedom with divine purpose, during the sundown to sunup period.

To carry out this re-creation process, they had to lay a firm foundation that acted as the substructure upon which they could then imagine, build, and refine methods of the self—seizing sacred domains, the divine right to resist, and constructing a syncretized religion. This foundation or substructure was made up of their common-sense folk wisdom, a reinterpretation of the Christianity presented to them by the slave masters, and aspects of African religions. Regardless of what methods of the self were used (in addition to the three methods in this chapter, chapters four through six draw on other methods), the foundation on which they built the re-creation process with God was the blending of wisdom, Christianity, and Africa. These three ingredients, once welded together, acted as the substructure for every proactive struggle undertaken by black folk in America since their forced and violent arrival in 1619. On the basis of this foundation, African Americans were able to forge various forms of methods of the self. Thus, before a full investigation of the methods, we must examine this substructure.

In other places, I have elaborated on commonsense folk wisdom and how black people reinterpreted Christianity[2] (two of the ingredients in the substructure that then allowed black folk to carry out their method of self re-creation with divine intent). Therefore here we look only at the third ingredient: indigenous West African faith experiences brought across the Atlantic. To grasp and engage the African religious aspects embedded in black religious reality, one has to understand the worldview, theological sensibilities, and religious importance of indigenous religions of Africa, especially as reflective of the West Coast from which the majority of the Africans departed.

West African Religions: A Background

Enslaved Africans were not tabula rasa, empty heads without a tradition of religious practices and conceptual faith systems. And even as the African American phenomenon was eventually and partially created by the introduction of Christianity to black chattel, retentions of West African religions persisted. Africans and African Americans brought their own commitments to previous concepts and visceral lifestyles, a comprehensive spirituality, into the rituals and regularities of slavery churches. Slaves and masters could hear, repeat, and swear to the same biblical text, catechism, or sermon but think, feel, and interpret differently.

Thus the Christian mythos influenced the pre-existing African faith sensibilities. Likewise, in a dynamic process, African precepts renegotiated the substantive terms of Christian plumb lines. Consequently, the voluntary acceptance of what the slavemaster thought was his Christianity by his human property occurred both because a fundamental structure in West African religions was somewhat compatible to a (reinterpreted) slave Christianity and because the malleability of African American chattels' creativity wove together select portions of mainstream biblical teachings with remnants of the West African religious worldview.

Though they spoke an arguably pidgin white English or a new (black) English, enslaved Africans and African Americans were intelligent and pious human beings despite the oppressive theology standardized by slavemaster Christians. Consequently, in addition to a reconfigured Christianity (and occasional life and death belief mandates derived from commonsense folk wisdom), West African religions persistently pervaded the black faith spectrum, whether as the comprehensive manifestations of the first-generation enslaved Africans or as the fragmented remnants resulting from the new creation called African Americans.

Like Christianity, religions of the west coast of Africa held in highest esteem God the Supreme Being, comprised of absolute creating powers, unique in that nothing existed prior to this all powerful Spirit. For in West African indigenous faith "God, or the Supreme Being, is outside the pantheon of gods. He is the eternal Creator of all the other gods, and of men and the universe. This makes Him absolutely unique, and He is differentiated from the other gods in having a special name. This name is always in the singular."[3]

Captured and enslaved Africans, as they arrived on the shores of the thirteen British colonies and the United States of North America, did not know Jesus Christ, hence were not Christians; still they worshiped one God with similar attributes. For them there was only one ultimate divinity. This One was known by various local names but consistently embodied the same essential characteristics—creator, power, justice, beneficence, omniscience, and eternity. The Supreme Being constituted the beginning and the ending of all time, space, breathing, and non-breathing. God held power over life, death, rewards, and punishments. God was the final authority.[4]

Likewise, the theological and philosophical understandings of intermediary divinities were not foreign to the heart and thinking of the new African arrivals. Where Jesus Christ and the Holy Spirit served as intermediaries for and practical workers of the divine Christian godhead (of the Father, Son, and Holy Ghost in traditional patriarchal language), an indigenous West African worldview deployed a pantheon of belief comprised of the ancestors and lesser divinities. The ancestors were venerated (not worshiped) because they were the living who had traveled or passed over into the realm of closer proximity to the divine dwelling. Thus they could be called on to mediate between the living on earth and God, interpret the divine signs and happenings on earth, and offer both protection and success for surviving family members. Power of the ancestors derived not from their being gods, but from their spacial relation to God.

Intermediary divinities came after the ancestors in the traditional pantheon of faith. Like all of creation, divinities were limited creatures due to their derivative status from the Supreme Being.

These lesser deities received their power from God and functioned in more focused charges assigned to them by God. They could be either good or evil, female or male, and dwell in bodies of water, hills, trees, certain animals, and rocks. They were spirits inhabiting other creatures. Put differently, the Supreme Being controlled nature through servants.[5]

Those living on earth (and then the unborn) completed the faith and ritual aspects of West African religions, an extended family proceeding from the reality of the Supreme Being and returning through those who had not physically appeared on earth (that is, the unborn).[6] Such a broad kinship network necessitated certain codes of conduct, order, and expectations. In Christian terminology, the practitioners of indigenous religions possessed and performed a theological anthropology and an ethical way of life.

Perhaps the most encompassing testament to the divine purpose for humanity and the moral compunctions in traditional African religions could be summed up as balance and interrelatedness between Creator and creation and within creation. In the words of one African scholar: "By African Traditional Religion, we mean the wholeness of African life: the African perception of self vis-à-vis environment, attitude towards life, values and self-awareness. The concept takes into consideration variations within the African continent and the dynamism which is present in African culture."[7]

Matters of faith or belief dramatized a way of life whose purpose entailed maintaining right relationship with fellow human beings and the environment, both physical and spiritual. Consequently, a complete harmony intertwining the spiritual world, society, nature, and humanity was the radical (in the sense of root) pursuit. Understandably, such a journey consumed all of life; indeed, to the Akan (roughly occupying present-day Ghana), life was religion breaking down borders between "sacred" and "secular" or "holy" and "profane." One Ghanaian religious scholar asserted: "It may be said, without fear of exaggeration, that life in the Akan world is religion and religion is life, and to understand the Akan, a thorough knowledge of his [or her] religion is imperative."[8]

To be human was to be ethically communal in outlook and life. For instance, a paramount case would involve the sin of one community member and its dire effects on the sinner's neighbors. Signifying the communal ethic and its socioeconomic consequences, the Yoruba of Nigeria, who practiced indigenous religions, upheld an apt proverb:

> If a member of one's household
> Is eating poisonous insects
> And we fail to warn him (to desist)
> The after-effect of his action
> Would rob neighbors of sleep.[9]

The moral maintenance of balance in a religious system encompassed by and circumscribing all of life left no room for belief in individualism because such a sinful act, a break in harmonized relations, fractured the cardinal belief that no person existed on her or his own. To be human was not to be individualistic, a casting into a non-human and non-being state. The dynamic of individual rights and familial-neighbor obligations weighed more toward the latter. The positive state of individuality, in contrast to the negative stance of individualism, surfaced out of a sea of prior commitments to communal survival and overall freedom. In the words of one African proverb: "Life is when you are together, alone you are an animal."[10]

Communality and obligation manifested strongly in indigenous religious practices and understandings of the family—from the future presence of the unborn to the ancestors who lived in another kind of existence but were still all around their survivors. The existence of the ancestors constituted one of the most important features of indigenous religions. "In fact, after God, who is the Final Authority in all matters, the One who is pre-eminent in all things, the ancestors come next in importance."[11] Thus the elders, those who had journeyed into the spirit realm and those close to that sacred threshold, held traditions of the people and lived in closer proximity to the Supreme Being. Veneration of ancestors offered identity to the group through disclosure of traditions and opportunities of receiving goodness and blessings from God.

Naming rituals and the power to name likewise underlined the vital interplay between the individual's connection to community and the communal obligation to the person. To name indicated cultural identity and definition within the sacredness of the group.

> There are many naming customs all over Africa. . . . There is a naming ceremony, attended by members of the family, relatives, neighbors and friends. The name is considered in African societies to be very much part of the personality of the person. Therefore it is taken seriously, and chosen with care and consideration.[12]

Meanings of the person's personality, abilities, and prospects—all of which influenced social relations—comprised the name. Consequently the religious ritual of naming drew family and neighbors (who functioned as the extended family) together to ensure the collective wisdom about and discernment of God's desire for the name of the unborn who was now born. Moreover, to have power over the name granted authority over the individual and determined how that person would grow to her or his full humanity: a humanity either anathema to the well-being of others or one harmonized with the overall will. The need for family connection, as a religious duty and life-giving force, therefore, permeated all occasions in group living.

In summation, faith in God, interrelatedness, communality, and balance suggested an epistemology of the self (that is, awareness of one's consciousness) anchored in awareness of others' existence and needs (of ethical obligations). To know oneself was to know the other and share in her or his spiritual and material necessities of life. Only in relationship did one become conscious that one was a human being with privileges and responsibilities to God, the self, the family, the community, and creation.[13] In a word, aspects of African indigenous religions acted as a key ingredient for the creation of and co-constitution of the black self in the United States. Black folk in America did not begin in slavery; they began in West Africa.

With a firm foundation made up of West African religions, their commonsense folk wisdom, and a reinterpretation of the slave masters' Christianity, enslaved black folk could then imagine, build, and refine methods of self care upon these three ingredients. The end result of this process of the method of the self offered a new space and a novel lens in Protestantism and American culture, in the colonial and the United States periods.

New structural signs/codes, multilayered metaphors/symbols, macro and micro apparati of power appropriated for constitution of the self as subject, and racial and cultural identity strategies emerged from the enslaved black religious experiences. African American chattel, therefore, had to map and remap the space, place, time, and pleasure given by the plantation owners, as well as negotiate a vantage point for the present and the future out of the elements of a disrupted past.

This rearrangement of faith, time, space, place, wealth, language, and identity also redefined what it meant to be and who constituted Protestantism and American culture. Following 250 years of slave religious experiences and an irrevocable African American voice (directly and indirectly)[14] within the larger national way of life and personality, no longer could one describe Protestantism and American culture exclusively as the "white" mainstream and black religious belief and everyday sacred practices as non-mainstream.

First, there existed no singular unilateral Protestantism in North America. In fact, Protestantism was a rainbow and quilt of diverse revelations in particularities. (This does not deny the fact that numerous white church leaders, religious scholars, and lay people in Euro-American churches wrote religious history with this silent presupposition of one—white—theological tradition. Similarly, by unconscious reflex, most white Christians and scholars immediately meant white people when referring to Protestantism and American culture.)

And second, Protestantism and American culture acquired their definitions and identities by their opposition to black religious faith claims and African American humanity. In other words, Protestantism and American culture would not have been what they were if the experiment in the importation of Africans and the creation of African Americans in the New World had not been successful. Consequently within the formation and ongoing re-creation of white American Protestantism and culture, one discovers an African American presence lodged at the center of its configuration; just as black religion and culture are partially constituted by white American presence, represented in the phrase "African [and] American."

During sundown to sunup, enslaved Africans and African Americans, wrapped in the arms of the sacred, re-created themselves by seizing initiative in the crevices and pauses left vacant by the plantation system. If sunup to sundown (time claimed by the slave system) marked the multiplicity of assaults to turn black workers from their divine created origin and intent (being created freely and created to be free), then from sundown to sunup (time claimed by the enslaved) indicated the black chattels' turn from the evil creation of the master to the original divine origin and intent. Accordingly, as mentioned earlier, enslaved blacks drew on various strands from West African religious remnants, common folk everyday wisdom, and a reinterpreted Christianity to co-constitute the black self with God.

Based on these three ingredients acting as foundation or substructure to black folk's existence, African American workers did not allow for a separation between sacred and secular. Understandably so, such a move would displace God's sovereignty from all of creation. Since the High God molded time, space, place, breath, the living, and the dead, then no second could be considered absent from the divine time and space. Indeed, the holy presence pervaded even intervals of laughter and fun. From the Old and New testament witnesses, Yahweh and Jesus brought sacred community to all aspects of living, loving, laughing, dancing, and dying.

Likewise, indigenous West African religious memories, in particular, imbued the enslaved blacks with sensibilities honoring all of creation and space as holy. The ongoing influx of fresh arrivals from Africa to North America reinforced indigenous African religions and philosophical outlook (claims of ultimate truth, knowledge, and meaning) from 1619 to 1807. The year 1807 marked the de jure cessation of the international slave trade. But traditional ways of life and thought from the African west coast continued to replenish the body of knowledge of slaves in North America because, as we documented in chapter two, the de facto international slave trade ended only with the 1865 conclusion of the North American Civil War.

Building on top of the foundation made up of ingredients from African indigenous religions, common sense folk wisdom, and a reinterpretation of the Christianity forced upon them by their slave masters, the constitution of the African American self as creatures of God involved knowing about oneself and taking care of oneself. To know oneself as both an object of and co-laborer with divine initiative emboldened one to act in a self-initiating manner. Because one's ultimate authority was greater than the plantation hegemony, black chattel could seize space and time of self-assertion in some of the most least expected instances. To know oneself as belonging to the divine, in a word, empowered one to claim opportunities for life. Consequently, to take care of oneself, in the establishment of the black self as conscious agents of God, was a religious act.

Restated, God created African Americans as members of the holy community. And divine grace made them free to pursue their holistic liberation—both incremental and complete, both spiritual and material—signifying theological acts of free self-care wherever black folks found themselves. To know oneself and to take care of oneself was to release the enthusiasm in determining how one wanted to be in the world along with a God who liberates one from an old self and frees one to a new self.

To know about oneself and take care of oneself manifested as three overarching religious methods of the self co-constitution with God: specifically, a *Divine Right to Resist, Creating a Syncretized Religion,* and *Seizing Sacred Domains.* Self co-constitution with God was a religious cultural act—a total way of life saturated with a quest for ultimate meaning. Self co-constitution with God was an epistemology of faith and a practical nurturing of an emancipatory way of being in the world on a daily basis.

Seizing Sacred Domains

Before exploring the divine right to resist and creating a syncretized religion below, we examine the seizing of sacred domains as the first broad method of the self and a religious cultural act of ebony chattel. For Africans and African Americans, at least three crucial issues constituted the sacred domains—the theology of pleasure, sacred word power, and resource redistribution.

A THEOLOGY OF PLEASURE

As part of their theological strategy of re-imaging and living as free creations of the divine in a comprehensive holy environment, enslaved Africans and African Americans stole and claimed the sacred domain of pleasure, either as fun times or during corn-shucking episodes or other labors initially organized by the plantation master. Even in pleasure, black workers knew who they were and how to nourish themselves.

Numerous slave accounts attest to the religious feel of and almost ultimate desire for fun times. Black chattel seemed to experience near ecstatic behavior, to be transported to another reality. Indeed, the pleasures and amusements of fun times literally hoisted African Americans up into a novel spiritual current and sped them far away from the life-denying and time-controlling power of the plantation system and sensibilities. In enjoyment, blacks liberated themselves by merely having fun in a situation that allowed relatively few openings for free breathing by slaves, an entanglement of oppressive social relations and symbols where to be black was to have derivative status from whites. The simple control of fun times in the theology of pleasure (that is, an area under sacred domain) marked one form of rebellion and re-creation of the African American self.

Former chattel Florence Bailey recounted the act of reclaiming ultimate space of seized pleasure and the faith of protection in the supernatural presence in an overturned pot: "Sometime a group of slaves would leave the house and go on the branches to talk and have pleasure among themselves and when they got ready for such meetings they would turn a pot down to keep the sound from going in the direction of their master's house."[15] The phrase "among themselves" is key in this representation of black fun. To be with their own oppressed kind where they could talk, walk, and have pleasure signified the risk of their surreptitious gathering suffering from discovery and punishment. Yet talking among themselves brought them power to be themselves alone in the midst of God's created nature—"on the branches." They could only talk when they were isolated in the space of nature's surroundings because talking implied thinking freely with liberal interchanges without hierarchical designations, interruptions, or coded body languages. They could now walk freely without contrived body postures of bowed head, bent shoulders, and scratching where there was no itch—all representing the intense muscle tension and doubletalk inevitable when conversing with agents of the plantation system and its negative spirituality.

The inability to talk and walk in the space and time from sunup to sundown meant that blacks were not humans but mere respondents to the master's whims and purposes. The forced stammering or absolute loss of tongue made enslaved African Americans non-persons. The silenced tongue (that is, the passive reactor) on the non-person (that is, the subservient slave) negated freedom of enjoyment (that is, a vivacious spirituality).

But talking and walking in nature without the permission of the plantation authorities granted a true freedom and place for pleasure in the midst of their faith in a protective power greater than themselves. In this time and space, one sees and hears illegally created new creatures communing in holy greenery ("on the branches") and speaking in a liberated tongue unknown to the masters. Here groups of outlaw blacks became new persons of pleasure with a life and death belief in the potent protection of a drum-like pot which embraced and sheltered their spirit-filled sound from the clutches of the master's control and direction. The drum-pot of pleasure times enhanced their faith by containing their playful sounds within sacred nature space. The drum-pot kept evil at bay and provided a respite for renewed spirits of survival.

In fact, these fun times in the theology of pleasure imaged a religious revival working up Christians to peak places of near total tiredness. Former slave Dora Roberts contends:

> De colored folks had dey fun as well as dey trials and tribulations, 'cause dat Sat'day night dance at de plantation wuz jist de finest thing we wanted in dem days. All de slabes fum de udder plantation dey cum ta our barn an' jine in an' if dey had a gal on dis plantation dey lob, den dat wuz de time dey would court. Dey would swing to de band dat made de music. My brother wuz de captain ob de quill band an' dey sure could make you shout an' dance til you wuz nigh 'bout exhausted.[16]

Like their bodily motions swept away by the sacred spirits in their more explicit illegal religious woods gatherings (called the Invisible Institution), this quill band induced spiritual slaying of black dancers and realized similar effects. Trials and tribulations were forgotten, and, consequently, black chattel finally had an opening to escape from pain and sorrow. People whooped and hollered with contorted torsos flailing in the rhythms of freedom, possessions of another world where shouting and dancing transformed into ecstatic behavior ("nigh 'bout exhausted"). Black workers from surrounding plantations arrived to be made new under the leadership of the quill band captain and to begin or deepen further the potential new romance life with lovers.

Theirs was an urge for an ultimate time of pleasure (a superlative time signified by the "finest thing we wanted in dem days") where uncontrollable music induced a collective spirituality of liberated bodily nimbleness. It was a proactive realization of desiring to sing, to shout, to dance, and to be exhausted together. Caught up in the collective spirit of a time and geography uncontrolled and undefined by the earthly master, enslaved African Americans sustained themselves (therefore participating in self-creation) through positive communal interaction without the sinister and shrewd eye of plantation prohibitions. They recreated self-identity and self-space through the larger power of the communal gathering, which was greater than the individual; a collective power built up individuals and gave them courage and strength.

In the words of former chattel Mrs. Sutton who captured the holy presence in the midst of fun times: "I danced all night long. . . . You'd hear the darkies, 'Promenade on,' and that was the time to promenade all over the place. Of course, I know what I felt and see, too. It appeared as a voice from heaven."[17]

In addition to fun times, the theology of pleasure included the disputed dynamic of corn-shucking. The ritual of corn-shucking, from the masters' perspective, served the macropolitical economy of the southern agrarian way of life. Ostensibly the labor of corn-shucking mapped out a work zone defined by the hegemony of plantation owners, but the powerful quantitative presence of enslaved African Americans transformed qualitatively the spiritual authority reigning over the corn-shucking ritual. "Sometimes four or five hunners" [hundreds of] slaves assembled, commented former slave James Bolton. During this work time–fun time (a brilliant maneuver and magnificent metamorphosis from subservient labor into panoramic pleasure), the collective slave self renamed the sweat of their vivified energy as a new identity—poor blacks participating in the act of communal pleasure. The corn, the sounds, the earth, and the pace became controlled (at least, until the end of the day) by the initiative of ebony chattel. Resuming, Bolton triumphantly exclaimed: "Some years we 'ud go to ten or twelve corn-shuckin's in one year!"[18]

The corn-shucking ritual occurred during harvest season. Slave gangs from surrounding plantations would sing as they approached the particular plantation where a huge mountain of raw corn ears waited to be stripped of their outer skins. Upon arrival, two teams of workers were chosen, with either one or two "generals." After the designated signal, each general urged on his team, all hoping to be the first to finish shucking their section of the mountain of raw corn. The generals led their teams in song, laughter, and joking. After the pile had been sheared of the outer skins, all the slaves shared in a banquet. Then the master was hoisted up into the air and he and the mistress were made fun of by the black folk. Under the cover of frivolity, enslaved African Americans could say what they wanted about the master. Next came dancing and more singing. Finally, the various slave gangs returned to the roads as they sang their ways back home.

Rachel Adams, a former slave, maintained fond memories of corn-shucking: "'Bout de most fun slaves had was at dem cornshuckin's. De general would git high on top of de corn pile and whoop and holler down leadin' dat cornshuckin' song 'till all de corn was done shucked. Den come de big eats, de likker, and de dancin'."[19]

Theologically, corn-shucking was the superlative pleasurable encounter ("de most fun") with a life counter to the strictures and language of the normative slavery system. "In corn shucking time," stated one ex-slave, "no padderrollers would ever bother you."[20] Even the patrollers or padderrollers (whose legal role in the slavery system was to seek out, detain, and in certain instances, terrorize blacks lacking permission to move around) were put at abeyance. Shucking became a spiritual event in which enslaved blacks created a communal space subverting the master's usual role as spectator before a faceless, groveling black mass of silent flesh. In fact, the spiritual determination and ingenuity of these African Americans' booming voices transformed themselves as the spectacle and centered the desires of the oppressed at the top of the master-slave configuration. Chattel chipped away at the all-powerful gaze of the plantation owner. What the master hoped would be a spectacle of buffoons and a theater of fools was seized by African Americans and re-imaged into a novel world of self-knowledge and self-care. For a moment, they remade themselves out of an accumulated willpower that became greater than any one person.[21]

They talked back to the master in their joking and "roasting" of him, his mistress, and their way of life. They claimed the master's space in front of the master's face. They usurped the power of decision making by choosing teammates in the corn-shucking contest. They regulated the time needed to finish the shucking in order to take time to enjoy one another. They experienced a rare event: the power to eat from a massive menu, the right to choose which foods to eat, and the pleasure of having a feast cooked by someone else. ("Dere wuz barbecue and chickens, jus' a plenty . . . , and corn bread . . . , light bread . . . , and lots of 'tato pies and all sorts of good things."[22]) They employed a rhythmic call and response way of being in the world when they sang throughout the ritual act. In a sense, the highly charged and seemingly ecstatic singing and dancing were ways of giving thanks to life and invoking a new tempo, opportunity, and presence among them. Movement and sound became acts of freedom.

SACRED WORD POWER

The theology of pleasure, with its fun times and corn-shucking antics, was accompanied by instances of sacred word power—especially incarnated in the written word, prayer, spirituals, and naming.

Enslaved African Americans seized the written word as sacred word power in order to gain literacy for reading and interpreting the Bible. Though legally restricted from learning how to read, black chattel subverted this mechanism of power (that is, the holy scriptures employed as a false instrument anchoring oppressive sermons, catechism, and ethics of the master and his paid clergy) by reappropriating and claiming the biblical word from their vantage as those at the bottom of the plantation political economy. By seizing a power withheld from them, African American workers could deploy the Bible as a technique of constituting the black person's self-initiating being. Surreptitiously reading the biblical story enabled them to know the world for themselves, to be made whole by expressing their intellect, and to master a sacred text.

To maintain their divine power over black slaves, masters issued one of their strongest bans against learning to read, particularly the Bible. When asked what would have happened if she had learned to read, former slave Ferebe Rogers replied: "I'd had my right arm cut off at de elbow if I'd a-done dat. If dey foun' a nigger what could read and write, dey'd cut yo' arm off at de elbo, or sometimes at de shoulder." Such mutilation of the black body resulted from the master's perceiving reading as contrary to the absolute mandates of God. Ex-slave Henry Nix had an uncle whose master removed a forefinger because the slave uncle had stolen a book. The theological rationale of this brutalized "sign for the rest" of the black servants was that, in the master's language, "Niggers wuz made by de good Lawd to work" and not to read and write.[23]

However, for the enslaved, reading the Bible was a miraculous resurrection of the black intellect from the hell of whiteness and ignorance. In fact, in his autobiography, runaway freedman Henry Bibb termed the constrictions of slavery as the "grave yard of the mind."[24] The seizure of the sacred text, then, symbolized a journey from imprisonment to a new religious being, one liberated, at least on the cognitive level, in a new space claimed within the physical bonds of captivity.

Similarly, Frederick Douglass agreed that the God in the Bible was an enabler in the constitution of the new black person. Douglass received this novel revelation about the transformative power of the written text partly from overhearing his master's prohibitions against teaching enslaved blacks how to read. His slavemaster stated the following about denying Douglass instruction in reading: "'If he learns to read the Bible,'" exclaimed Douglass's master, "'it will forever unfit him to be a slave. He should know nothing but the will of his master, and learn to obey.'" For Douglass, hearing this statement was like a bolt of lightning from heaven, converting his old confused self into a resolute self bent on emancipation. In his awestruck words, Douglass testified: "This was a new and special revelation, dispelling a painful mystery against which my youthful understanding had struggled, and struggled in vain, to wit, the white man's power to perpetuate the enslavement of the black man. . . . And from that moment I understood the direct pathway from slavery to freedom."[25]

The sacredness of reading removed Douglass forever from the potency of the master's domain and propelled Douglass in a free space both in terms of his sense of his own identity and self-knowledge, and literally by providing that decisive push to run away to the north. Biblical knowledge through reading made him unfit to remain a slave. The enslaved re-created self and context—facilitated by a vivified holy text—by perceiving the master's language games and power dynamics and then by transforming them for liberation of the victim.[26] With his knowledge of the language, Douglass took care of himself on the road to freedom.

The potency of the praying word, like that of the written word, enabled black chattel to be transported and to relocate themselves into novel horizons beyond the demonic clutches of those who would snuff them out. In a not so uncommon scene, a group of black workers had assembled illegally in a slave shack to worship to their own souls' satisfaction and enjoy some real preaching conducted by one of their own. But the religious exhorters "made more noise than we were aware of" thus attracting the violent arrival of nearby white night patrollers. Armed to the teeth, the captain of the patrol entered, whereupon the assembled fell to the ground "and prayed that God might deliver us." Indeed the seemingly miraculous occurred. The captain's "knees began to tremble, for it was too hot, so he turned and went out." For the ex-slave who remembered this story, the divine presence had intervened in response to the victim's prayer. The former chattel concluded the following: "As God had delivered us in such a powerful manner, we took courage and held our meeting until day-break."[27] Prayer could shake the foundations (e.g., exemplified by the knee trembling of the captain) and bring heat upon those anointed to sustain and nurture evil systemic restrictions around the utterers of words to the sacred realm.

Consistently, ex-chattel recounted stories of heartfelt prayers receiving responses. The praying word reached God's ear and moved the divinity who was power. Prayers, therefore, were not in vain. On the contrary, they yielded positive and effective results by humbling perpetrators of violence against those without wealth or political connections. Similarly, prayers reconfigured symbolic and metaphorical signs of potency offering a language of reversal from the victims' vantage. Prayer, moreover, relativized hierarchical social relations and emboldened slaves born with the wrong color identity. Prayer aided the structurally marginalized to endure, and to triumph in the end. The power of prayer was the certitude of faith.[28]

The singing word (particularly the spirituals, the unique religious songs originating in the African American enslaved community) offered a spontaneity in creation leading toward black psychological wholeness, part of the dynamic to take care of oneself. A former chattel recalled how his master ordered him to receive one hundred lashes. At the "praise meeting dat night dey [the other slaves] sing about it."[29] The communal absorbing of the hundred-lash pain of the individual, though not necessarily lessening the mortal lacerations, allowed the individual a psychological reintegration derived from participation in community. Invention of a group song provided a way to nurture, heal, and create the self in a communal procedure.

Similarly, in the surreptitious gatherings of enslaved African American worship, black chattel proclaimed their faith, predicament, and future hope through song. For instance, a representative song in such a secret gathering included holy lyrics displaying the power to know oneself and to acknowledge to whom one belonged.

> See these poor souls from Africa
> Transported to America;
> We are stolen, and sold to Georgia,
> Come sound the jubilee!
> See wives and husbands sold apart,
> Their children's screams will break my heart;
> There's a better day a coming,
> Will you go along with me?
> There's a better day a coming,
> Go sound the jubilee!
> O, gracious Lord! when shall it be,
> That we poor souls shall all be free;
> Lord, break them slavery powers—
> Will you go along with me?
> Lord Break them slavery powers,
> Go sound the jubilee!
> Dear Lord, dear Lord, when slavery'll cease,
> Then we poor souls will have our peace;—
> There's a better day a coming,
> Will you go along with me?
> There's a better day a coming,
> Go sound the jubilee![30]

The first stanza of this song recalled history, tradition, and origin. The second stanza comprised future hope underscored by the enslaved's self-initiative, thus acting as historical agents. The third verse presented a plaintive and joyful cry unto the Lord—expressing both a query to and a faith in the divine ability to render freedom. The final stanza equated the cessation of slavery with peace and the sounding of Jubilee.

The sacred power of the singing word, in the final analysis, reflected not simply the solo effort of the ebony enslaved. Indeed, the divine gift of potent song (in the words of one ex-chattel: all a black person "gotta do is open his mouth and a song jes nachally drops out."[31]) emanated from loftier heights of a sacred horizon. In the retrospective of former slave Rev. Reed: "Some of them old slaves composed the songs we sing now. God revealed it to them."[32] Thus the revelation of divine lyrics and holy rhythm implanted in the aesthetic harmonizing of beautiful dark tongues signified the co-laboring exertion of God and humanity in the reconfiguration of the black self. African American servants knew about themselves and how to take care of themselves.[33]

The potency of the naming word exemplified similar attributes and theological import as did reading, praying, and singing words. Moreover, given the religious consequences of naming rituals in certain indigenous West African worldviews and practical witness, to give an enslaved African or African American a name denoted or implied ultimate significance in one's self-identity, communal relations, and being in the world. As one Ghanaian theologian referenced traditional ways of life: The Akan of Ghana link divine naming to God's "love of justice and fairness." Quoting Akan sacred folk wisdom, he resumed: "Since God does not like wickedness, He gave every creature a name."[34] Indeed black chattel (at least in the South Carolina and Florida regions, and probably in other areas) were aware of the West African practice of endowing names with the presence of the holy.[35]

Consequently, one fought to maintain one's accepted family name, not one's given slave name. Harry Robinson, after sale to the Harper plantation, rebelled by holding on to his family's last name. "My father was named Robinson, so I kept his name after I got free."[36] The master's name equalled slavery; a family name equalled freedom. Slaves went to the extreme of lying to their masters about their true feeling regarding their names. Toward the white supremacy of the plantation structure, they presented the descriptions prescribed by the slavery system while "among themselves they use[d] their [own] titles."[37]

RESOURCE REDISTRIBUTION

The daily struggle for the co-constitution of the self (sacred and human) persisted on several levels. Reallocating wealth was one example of the sacred domain of resource distribution. Enslaved African Americans related to wealth and materiality within the presence, power, and purview of the holy. Black chattel, in the face of the earthly lordship of the racialized plantation system, not only survived but, in some cases, became entrepreneurs. At first glance, such a survival undertaking producing and deploying limited wealth resources suggested a further accommodation to slavery strictures. Yet on closer examination, blacks engaged in business power plays were attempting to be in the world by pressing and pressuring the barricades around and against black life. Not only were the manipulation and seizure of resources ways of simply forcing against imposed obstacles and legal restraints, they actually fostered a certain freedom within but also beyond chattel confines. The times and places when some black folk could nurture and negotiate power over limited wealth resources positioned them in the force field and sacred space of an authority unbounded by, thus higher and more potent than, the master's slavery.

For instance, in some plantation areas, black bondspeople received a liberal master's permission or secretly acquired the wealth to sell food and goods to whites and blacks. Former bondwoman Cornelia confirmed such an occurrence:

> My father had a garden of his own around his little cabin, and he also had some chickens. . . . The floor of our cabin was covered with planks. Pa had raised up two planks, and dug a hole. This was our storehouse. . . . Sunday, Master Jennings would let Pa take the wagon to carry watermelons, cider and ginger cookies to Spring Hill, where the Baptist church was located. The Jennings were Baptists. The white folks would buy from him as well as the free Negroes of Trenton, Tennessee. Sometimes these free Negroes would steal to our cabin at a specified time to buy a chicken or barbecue dinner. . . . Pa was allowed to keep the money he made at Spring Hill, and of course Master Jennings didn't know about the little restaurant we had in our cabin.[38]

From one angle, this is merely a narrative of a black person imitating a white, or perhaps only seeking income for the sake of money. But more than that, an enslaved person organizing, planning, managing money, marketing, distributing, taking risks, accounting, and counting was a leader whose allegiance and authority derived from borders beyond the chattel system. Seemingly unfolding within slavery but actually flooding the porous nature of the plantation hierarchy, the accumulated rituals of African Americans configuring limited capital income bred self-confidence, leadership skills, and visions of possibilities stretching across the parameters of the visible. From actual ability and practical performance arose a spirituality not derivative of the master. Caught up in that spirit, some slaves could perceive potent potentialities in other arenas.[39]

A theology of resource redistribution entailed not only a reallocation of wealth but also a redefinition of landscaping, particularly pertaining to land ownership, the building of slave quarters, and pathway construction. Former slave Bayley Wyat argued persuasively and theologically about the sacred and ancestral right of black people to reap the rewards of the materiality and spirituality poured into the earth by unpaid black hands for decades.

> Freedman Bayley Wyat of Yorktown, Virginia, in a speech given in 1865, was most explicit about his people's claims: "We has a right to the land where we are located. For why? I tell you. Our wives, our children, our husbands, has been sold over and over again to purchase the lands we now locates upon; that the reason we have a divine right to the land. . . . And den didn't we clear the land, and raise de crops ob corn, ob cotton, ob tobacco, ob rice, ob sugar, ob everything?"[40]

God gave the land to all, signifying holy communal ownership of the land of life; hence ownership of the land is a divine right. And the accumulated memories of bodies, pain, and pleasure invested by ancestral spirits ensured an eventual return of ownership to those who had labored. Moreover, the past of the dead blanketed the present and compelled the living to claim their right to the black soil. A God-given, natural land title evolved out of the location of extended family spirituality, thus decentering hegemonic plantation spirituality. Land contestation was, among other things, contestation on the spiritual realm.

For instance, one black woman willed her land to her offspring and swore she would come back to haunt them if they lost that sacred possession.[41] Part of co-constituting the self enveloped in sacred intent was not only recapturing the holiness of one's name or spirit; it denoted, furthermore, a concrete piece of the earth, a sign of wealth to be possessed and passed down generation to generation. To be fully human, then, enslaved African Americans perceived freedom as foolish unless they owned the actual land in the United States. Otherwise, the long term implication meant that they and their offspring would forever dwell in a warped configured space of dispossession. A method of the self (to know and take care of oneself) meant forever keeping one's eye on God's gift of the earth to those who worked it.

African Americans redefined landscaping also by taking creative initiative in the practice of an architecture of resistance; taking the building designs and housing constructions of the masters and restructuring them for black purposes toward a full humanity. Though these acts of rebellious redefinition of aesthetics and beauty did not necessarily lead to an overthrow of the macropower of white supremacy on the political economic level, they were signs of a certain guerrilla warfare in the realm of microtechnologies—maneuvering within the allowed and seized crevices of the macrotechnology of the slave system.[42]

Plantation owners preferred geometric order in the geography and layout of the plantation blueprint—preferably with the Big House sitting on a hill and slave shacks in the same construction and in strict lines at some distance from the master's main dwelling. In rebellion, the forty-one black workers who labored on a slave plantation in Mt. Vernon, for instance, "located their cabins randomly among the trees and at the edge of the cleared fields." And an observer of a rice plantation in Georgia noted that when given the opportunity to build their own abodes, the enslaved "wanted their cabins in some secluded place, down in the hollow, or amid the trees." Similarly on J. J. Smith's cotton plantation in Beaufort, South Carolina, black folk's cabins "were set at odd, irregular angles to one another.[43] Though shacks, these black homes and their placement were an affront to the plantation hierarchy and racial order in the social and economic world the slave owners made (that is, from sunup to sundown). The secluded designs imaged a cry for control over some safe space to be oneself away from the master's gaze and geography.

Such a general landscape suggested that African Americans also possessed a different worldview not beholden to white people's imposed viewpoints. Architecture, as a contested front of struggle for a full spiritual and material humanity, signified buildings of spontaneity (rather than of stultifying classification), dwelling with the divine in the woods (rather than under the eyes of slave owners), and breathing creativity in their homes (rather than the suffocating regularity and prohibitions in the Big House and the slave owner's fields).

Some of the Africans and African Americans sought a conscious reconnection to their cultural identity. While inhabiting slavery time, their architectural inclinations took them back to an African past time. One former chattel recalled the following: "Ole man Okra he say he wahn a place lak he hab in Africa so he buil im a hut. I membuh it well. It wuz bout twelve by foeteen feet an it hab dut flo an he buil duh side lak basket weave wid clay plastuh on it. It hab a flat roof wut he make frum bush an palmettuh an it hab one doe an no winduhs."[44] The pleasure derived from seizing a memory of past home life transported and performed in the present challenged the power of naming one's identity in a foreign land. This re-imaged hut from the African continent no doubt stood as a cultural reminder not only about where one came from but to whom one belonged. Clearly, such an offense to white definitions of black living indicated that some blacks knew themselves as living under an authority not sanctioned by their earthly masters.

African Americans' construction of paths for walking marks the final symbolic redefinition of landscaping as a vital indicator of the moment to reconstitute the black self. And like the entire creative dynamic of African Americans seeking full humanity on all levels, these paths served a multileveled practicality known only to the black hearts that had been initiated into the domain of sundown to sunup. In particular, paths and trails into the countryside of Virginia revealed the way to surreptitious multipurpose meetings—sometimes defined by explicit religious worship, other times by fiddling and dancing, and, more than likely, other times by illegal gathering for slave resistance—creative meetings for the Spirit to empower and black folk to enjoy. Paths across the fields to slave quarters indicated the movement to a slave shack or hut that was a clandestine storehouse of reappropriated food. Another set of paths through the woods enabled those brave enough to test the vigilance of the white patrollers to attempt a risky rendezvous with neighboring plantations. In a word, a parallel and clandestine territorial system emerged in the midst of slavery's evil.[45]

A Divine Right to Resist

A divine right to resist, along with the method of co-creating the black self by seizing sacred domains, also fueled black folk's struggle to reconstitute and regenerate their own new reality. To claim control over and freedom for the black body (either individual or collective) was to assert that one's humanity reflected sacred creation—an attempt to position an ebony body for self-determination of space (that is, a political dimension) and for self-identity (that is, a cultural dimension). Both revolutionary aspects in the context of the slavery system removed one literally from the domain of the evil ones and their structures to sacred ground—a place where one sought a new life, "born again" in the hoped-for reality of new macro (political economic), micro (the everyday ordinary), linguistic, and cultural identity dimensions of what it meant to be a child of God struggling for a full humanity. The moment of exercising the divine right to resist, therefore, comprised a theological dynamic.

Individual rebellions manifested in suicides, an affront to dominating Christian theology but congruent with certain West African notions of returning home or to an originating space. For example, numerous Africans committed suicide on the Middle Passage by jumping off slave ships bound for the New World. Similarly, upon arrival, certain Ibos brought to the North American mid-Atlantic shores turned around and walked back into the water headed for Ibo land.[46] With the acts and scenes of suicide, enslaved blacks either drew on streamlets of African cosmology (consciously or unconsciously) or (and perhaps both-and) rebelled to flee the domain of evil—a theatrical performance asserting one's humanity.

An antislavery pamphlet of the 1840s documented various suicide attempts on the part of incarcerated blacks. In Baltimore, one woman leaped out of a window and headed for the nearest body of water to drown herself. In Richmond, a male "negro," with hands tied, bolted for water and drowned himself. Pursued by dogs in New Orleans, a black man climbed a tree and hanged himself, using cords which he had prepared in advance of this ritual of self-delivery from evil. After being lacerated by the pounding of his master's boots, another black man killed himself in a nearby pond, "having tied a stone to his own neck."[47] Other enslaved blacks slit their own throats rather than be returned to the land of Satan.[48] Suicide suggested an ultimate determination to remove an unpaid labor commodity from the slavery system and, consequently, was a blow against macropolitical economy.

Running away to the north provided another avenue for the collective and individual right to resist. In this process, African Americans employed a coded language of freedom, marking preparation for their departing illegally from a plantation. Sarah Bradford, the biographer of Harriet Tubman, surmised the following from Tubman's testimonies: "Slaves must not be seen talking together, and so it came about that their communication was often made by singing, and the words of their familiar hymns, telling of the heavenly journey, and the land of Canaan, while they did not attract the attention of the masters, conveyed to their brethren and sisters in bondage something more than met the ear." In fact, Tubman sang these words to her fellow slaves as she prepared to run away from Delaware slavery to freedom up north:

> When dat ar ole chariot comes
> I'm gwine to lebe you
> I'm boun' for de promised land
> Firen's, I'm gwine to lebe you.

I'll meet you in de mornin'
When you reach de promised land
On de oder side of Jordan
For I'm boun' for de promised land.[49]

The use of liberation language indicated that the coast was finally clear for one more soul's journey to freedom. And it was a joyful song symbolic of praising the power of God's grace over oppression. Moreover, it covered as deception for any potential white listeners by employing a multivalent and melodious sign of song.

A jubilant portrayal of slaves' preparation for the final removal into black folk's own liberated space, time, and pleasure, Frederick Douglass' eyewitness account of runaway slaves' setting out for free soil displayed the markings of a religious revival. "We were at times," he wrote, "remarkably buoyant, singing hymns, and making joyous exclamation, almost as triumphant in their one as if we had reached a land of freedom and safety." The songs they sang denoted duplicitous theological, spiritual, and earthly meanings. Of the songs, he wrote: "On the lips of some it meant the expectation of a speedy summons to a world of spirits, but on the lips of our company it simply meant a speedy pilgrimage to a free state, and deliverance from all the evils and dangers of slavery."[50] Wherever the New Jerusalem beckoned, black bodies ran away to a northern horizon (horizontally) or upward to spiritual freedom (vertically) as a religious conversion from the old self of slavery to a new self of God; that is, they ran away from the demonic domain of evil.

Maroons, communities of runaways, indicated the concentrated collective will and rebellious daring of enslaved blacks. In some states as early as the 1650s, organized separate new communities of runaways survived either in or on the borders of areas that later became-Virginia, North and South Carolina, Louisiana, Georgia, Florida, Mississippi, Alabama, and Oklahoma. For their cultural, political, and economic sustenance, they apparently drew on both African indigenous worldviews and a reinterpreted Christianity. In the colony of Virginia, at least thirty years after the first group of Africans were brought as slaves to Jamestown, some Africans had fled white control and established their own maroon societies in the outlying areas, in swamps, woods, forests, and hills. There were reports of fugitive Africans trying "'to form small armed groups in various sections of the colony and to harass neighboring plantations, at the same time creating bases to which others might flee.'"[51]

These Africans had not been broken by colonial European or Euro-American philosophies and divested of their indigenous West African religious sensibilities and beliefs. They harbored conscious memories of what it meant to be a human being created by the Supreme Being, to remain in proximity to the presence and protection of the ancestors. Their faiths and cosmologies had not been totally shattered or damaged by the warped Christian catechism and preaching from hired plantation preachers. Indeed, they represented first generation and "Saltbacks" (that is, freshly imported) Africans with the spiritual markings, "theological" intuitions, and religious rituals of their old country. For them, there existed no separation of sacred and secular; everything, including walking, breathing, laboring, and lovemaking, was deemed a religious activity putting the person in constant contact with God.[52] Religion appeared in the practice of their political economy, linguistics, culture, and microdimensions of being in the world. They took care of themselves as Africans— quite aware of the knowledge of who they were as stolen strangers in a foreign land.

In addition to the West African religious substratum constituting many of these villages, a Christian thread wove itself into other outlying communities. For instance, a group of Louisiana runaways built a maroon society in the alligator swamps. Pursued by hired professional slave catchers, the black clan successfully braved the jaws of alligators while crossing the water. But when the slave catchers' blood hounds jumped into the bayou, the alligators ate six of them. Asked later why the alligators ate the dogs but did not touch the runaways, one former slave offered two answers depicting his polyvalent black linguistic expertise (and perhaps a duplicitous ethic of employing cryptic confusion and speaking deceptive humor to his white master): "'dun' no Massa, some ob 'em said dey tought it was God, but for my part I tink de alligators love dog's flesh better'n personal flesh.'"[53]

Grounded in both West African religions and their version of Christianity, maroon settlements were virtually self-sufficient spiritual New Jerusalems or refashioned Ibo lands. "Citizens" of this new earthly Common Wealth raided nearby plantations for food and livestock; often using the reconnaissance skills of enslaved blacks on those plantations. Many built military forts and conducted periodic armed sorties in guerrilla war fashion. With communities sometimes reaching several thousand in number and sustaining themselves for decades, maroon dwellers often provoked terror in slaveholding areas, causing politicians to debate their existence and pass laws calling for the termination of their open military rebellions and the extermination of participants.

Indeed, the Virginia colony passed such a law in 1672. One slave-holder (in 1787) in Purrysburgh, South Carolina, complained to the governor and the legislator that unless violent measures were taken to kill these runaways "the matter may become of too serious a nature, as hereafter to give ourselves farther trouble about the matter more than quietly submit our Families to be sacrificed by them & probably by our own indoor Domestics."[54] Throughout the south, the federal administration dispatched troops in attempts to exterminate the maroons; often armed slaveholders sought to take matters into their own hands.

Maroon societies, in some cases, signified what the new North America could become, a paradigmatic setting of cultural and racial cooperation of resistance to injustice and the creation of peace with justice. For example, one report noted:

> In the summer of 1841 serious difficulty arose in what is now Okla-homa and was then known as Indian Territory. A contemporary source declared that "some 600 negroes" formerly from Florida, as well as additional runaways from among the slaves of Choctaws, Cherokees and white planters, uniting "with a few Indians, and perhaps a few white men" had associated themselves together.[55]

Undergirded by African indigenous and reformulated Christian spiri-tualities, Africans and African Americans fought for their heaven on earth to signal the dawning of a new day. Maroon societies offered havens for other runaways, harassed plantation owners and politi-cians (including the federal government), exemplified intransigent rebellion and straightforward insubordination, supplied ready leader-ship, and struck a direct blow to the labor commodities that built North America. But it was a spirituality of constituting the black self and of showcasing what North America could potentially be that brought horror to the owners of wealth and the originators of a lan-guage that classified freedom as racially circumscribed in white Christian skins.

However, opposition and rebellion, another aspect of the divine right to resist, did not occur only on the maroon outskirts of God-fearing white Christian communities. Instead, the spirituality of naming and claiming oneself through rebellion took place on planta-tions themselves. On January 19, 1811, in a region near Louisiana and Mississippi, a letter was sent to the commanding officer at Fort Adams reporting "intelligence of an insurrection of the slaves."[56]

The *Missouri Democrat* newspaper linked black religion and African American plantation rebellions directly when it stated:

> For the past month the journals from different Southern States have been filled with numberless alarms respecting contemplated risings of the negro population. In Tennessee, in Missouri, in Virginia, and in Alabama, so imminent has been deemed the danger, that the most severe measures have been adopted to prevent their congregating or visiting after night, to suppress their customary attendance at neighborhood preachings, and to keep a vigilant watch upon all their movements, by an efficient patrolling system.[57]

Others fused the religious occasions of funerals to organize armed insurrection. "According to their custom they went in the night, and taking a monstrous big coffin, would bury it in the woods." Such coffins, of course, were full of guns and ammunition, and, at some appointed date, would be resurrected to "live" again.[58]

A final representative sampling of black people's efforts to achieve full humanity beyond the confines of the evils of slavery are the explicit West African–Christian armed rebellion scenarios of Gabriel Prosser, Denmark Vesey, and the Baptist clergyman, Rev. Nat Turner. Through a syncretistic religious ethos combining African conjuring and biblical apocalypse, these signifiers of claiming and constituting the black self established a novel linguistic faith and political witness through an attempt at creative metaphorical religion steeped in an anticipated appropriation of the slavemasters' wealth on earth.

For Gabriel Prosser, the apocalyptic day of judgment and the establishment of God's new sacred earth derived from his interpretation of the Bible; he saw it from the perspective of one enchained in body but not entrapped by a restricted intellect and deformed faith. Prosser, overwhelmed by the spiritual imperatives in the book of Judges, established a network of one thousand slaves to deal the final rebellious death blow to the kingdom of Satan (that is, the slaveholding system) in August 1800 in Henrico County, Virginia. Samson of the Hebrew Scripture imaged the true picture of God's ordained servant.

Like his hero, Samson, Prosser wore his hair long and believed firmly that God had set him aside since childhood to liberate his fellow slaves. He proselytized his followers with messages paralleling the condition of blacks under slavery with appropriate stories in the Bible, underscoring "the necessity of rising up against the Philistines—the slaveholders." The final and ultimate goal entailed erecting "a new black kingdom in Virginia with himself as ruler." Though his Christian strategy and radical religion failed, "according to the official report, about one thousand actually met at the rendezvous outside of the city." Prosser latter confessed that he had assembled roughly ten thousand men primed to wreak havoc on the white supremacist structures of chattel control. Gabriel's biblical hermeneutic expanded beyond the narrow confines of one state. In fact, the governor "of Mississippi said that as many as fifty thousand slaves were in complicity with Gabriel."[59]

Twenty-two years later in Charleston, South Carolina, Denmark Vesey resurrected the spirit of Prosser, imbuing it with a syncretized African and Christian religious worldview revised with a Pan-African expectation. (Vesey hoped for reinforcements from Haiti and Africa.) Gullah Jack, Vesey's lieutenant and a conjurer, came directly from Africa, as did several of the other conspirators. All of the leadership were leaders in the Charleston African Church, hence the coexistence of two complementary religious belief systems—Christianity and African indigenous faith. Indeed the idea for the insurrection commenced with the founding of the African Church. And Vesey's interpretive skills were grounded on a reading of the Hebrew Scripture's exodus theme, Luke 11:23 ("Whoever is not with me is against me"), Josh. 6:21 ("Then they devoted to destruction by the edge of the sword all in the city"), and Zech. 14:1-3 ("See, a day is coming for the Lord").

The African- and Christian-inspired insurrection, while unsuccessful, included nine thousand rebels. Vesey employed an almost catechismic interrogation method during his recruitment of fellow black Christians. For instance, questioning a potential conspirator, Vesey engaged in the following antiphonal rational argument: "Did he Bacchus [the potential recruit] sleep on as soft a bed as his master—No—who made his master—God—Who made you—God—And then ar'nt you as good as your master if God made him and you, ar'nt you as free, yes. Then why don't you join and fight your master."[60]

Testifying after the abortive rebellion, one black witness exposed Gullah Jack as an African conjurer with supernatural powers: "all those belonging to the [Christian] African Church are involved in the insurrection, from the country to the town—that there is a little man amongst them [Jack] who can't be shot, killed or caught. [And there existed] a Gullah Society [a society of Angolans] going on which met once a month."[61] Sixty years prior to the start of the Civil War, with the continued illegal importation of blacks from Africa, West African religions permeated various parts of the black belt south and gravitated naturally to a liberation theology's metaphorical and literal embracing of the Bible.

Finally, the Baptist Rev. Nat Turner exhibited the most graphic traits of the mystic, prophet, and possessed leader. Handling new religious language steeped in symbolic and metaphorical discourse tinted with encoded significance only Rev. Turner could decipher, he eventually confessed the following when captured and put on trial: "I reflected much on this passage ['Seek ye the kingdom of Heaven and all things shall be added unto you."]. . . . As I was praying one day at my plough, the Spirit spoke to me. . . . [It was the same] Spirit that spoke to the prophets in former days." After two years of contemplation and prayer, he concluded that he "was ordained for some great purpose in the hands of the almighty." Turner brought together a radical biblical understanding from the perspective of the bottom of society, the third person of the Trinity, and prolonged and profound prayer with an acceptance of a vocation directly ordained by the Christian God. Because Christ had laid down the heavy burden of a yoke, Turner believed that "I should take it on and fight against the Serpent."[62]

Individual and group actions exemplified the divine right to resist. Along with seizing sacred domains and the divine right to resist—both employed in the dynamic of co-creating the black self in concert with the sacred presence—the third manifestation of methods of the black self was creating a syncretized religion in the Invisible Institution.

Creating a Syncretized Religion

"Stealin' the meetin'," what enslaved religious blacks called the secret (reinterpreted) Christian gatherings—commonly termed the Invisible Institution—were the institutional location out of which the future black theology of liberation emerged. Such surreptitious congregations often reached huge numbers.[63] The intricate dynamic of "stealin' the meetin'"—its types, content, and forms—located the syncretistic or hybrid reality of African American religious experience.[64] In the Invisible Institution, a novel substance was molded from remnants of African indigenous religion, everyday common folk wisdom, and a reinterpreted Christianity. Only in secret communion with God could black folk both speak freely about the God that had liberated the Hebrew people and act out the self that they created away from the presence of white power.

TYPES

Enslaved religious blacks configured several types of the Invisible Institution in the hope that God would make a way out of no way. One such type was the secret society. After the Civil War, one freedman, a Robert Smalls, responded with a common doubletalk and apparent contradiction (contradictory to the Christian slavemaster's logic) to the query: "Were there any societies among the colored people for discussing the questions of freedom?" Smalls replied: "I do not think there are any secret societies except the Church societies and they do not introduce that subject there. They pray constantly for the 'day of their deliverance.'"[65] The mindset and philosophical inclinations of the oppressed Christian were diametrically opposed to those of the oppressor.

Smalls probably saw no contradiction in his response. The white interrogator left the question open by not specifying any particular societies. Thus Smalls could answer that there were no general societies that spoke of freedom. However, there was a particular secret society—the black church—that prayed for the deliverance of the African American. Had the white questioner asked about specific societies, then Smalls could not have answered as he did. But the master of both an unfettered thought pattern and a creative linguistic acrobatics, Smalls could truthfully say that there were no general societies discussing freedom, but a secret religious one that prayed to God for deliverance. Moreover, in his own nuanced theological thesaurus of liberation, there existed a definite distinction between "freedom" and "deliverance"; thus, again, for him, he provided no contradiction. Enslaved African Americans were masters of their own discourse.

African Americans knew that their God would not forsake them, so they sought all means and types of prayer opportunities. They actually believed a prayer was answered once it was lifted up to divine heavens. Sometimes they prayed in the fields ("We often waited until the overseer got behind a hill, and then we would lay down our hoe and call on God to free us"). When black chattel became too loud in their singing at night in slave shacks, plantation owner Dr. Little, gave stricter orders for quiet. Consequently, in the report of ex-slave Mary Ferguson, "us tuck to slippin' off to a big gully in de pastur to sing and pray whar de white fokes couldn' hear us." Field praying was a sacred occasion positioning hearts in tune. While beseeching God's grace and glory at the top of their lungs, enslaved black voices were protected by the powerful silencer of the iron kettle. "Meetings back there meant more than they do now. Then everybody's heart was in tune, and when they called on God they made heaven ring. . . . They would steal off to the fields and in the thickets and there, with heads together around a kettle to deaden the sound, they called on God out of heavy hearts."[66]

Another type of stealin' the meetin' or the Invisible Institution was prayer in the woods. At an appointed hour, African Americans sneaked off in the blackness of night to the woods. Some simply had "a good time talking about their mistress and master"; others assembled around a big fire on the edge of the woods "whar deir racket wouldn't 'sturb de white folks"; while others knelt and prayed with faces turned toward the ground to deaden the sound of their supplication and heartfelt longings for themselves and future generations: "I know that day we'll be free and if we die before that time our children will live to see it."[67]

Illegal house prayer and worship embodied an additional expression of the African American attempt to recreate the self hidden from the white plantation owner's purview. Key to this dimension of self-constitution under divine presence was the overturned pot. At times the pot was positioned in the middle of the house to catch the sound before it travelled out to the master or overseer. An unnamed ex-chattel recalled: "I've known them to have to turn down a pot to keep the sound in. . . . I've never known them to get caught while the pot was turned down at my home." In one instance, the pot was stationed outside the door as if it were a supernatural sentinel, one who had supernatural powers to silence the ecstatic expressions of the black worshippers and to warn the gathered of an approaching enemy. Mrs. Sutton, a former slave, recounted: "They would get a big ole wash kettle and put it right outside the door, and turn it bottom upwards to get the sound, then they would go in the house and sing and pray, and the kettle would catch the sound. I s'pose they would kinda have it propped up so the sound would get under it."[68]

Not all types of the Invisible Institution manifested in group activity; some African Americans desired solitude as they placed heavy burdens before God or offered up thanksgivings of joy. Elija Davidson bore such an onerous weight that all he could do was bow before God. "My work was so hard that I would go out in the barn and fall on my knees and pray to my God to set me free." For him, the strength to carry on for another day resulted from a personal God ("my God") who offered hope for an ultimate day of deliverance. Similarly, Charlotte Brooks, in her autobiography, opted for clandestine individual prayer as she called on the name and power of God: "O, my blessed Lord, be pleased to hear my cry; set me free, O my Lord."[69]

Perhaps the most elaborate constructions of secret sacred places in which to develop their own Christian sensibilities and, thereby, recreate themselves away from the demonic Christianity of plantation ethos were the bush arbor gatherings. Bush arbors epitomized black hands and hearts creating space for the poor to encounter the holy in permanent structures of worship. Bush arbors, therefore, symbolized permanent seizure of space, invested with elaborate preparations and thought. The architectural sacredness of the building complemented the holiness of the geographical location of the gathering. Pierce Cody, ex-slave, offered the details upon which the following bush arbor picture was created:

> As a beginning, several trees were felled, and the brush and forked branches separated. Four heavy branches with forks formed the framework. Straight poles were lain across these to form a crude imitation of beams and the other framework of a building. The top sides were formed of brush which was thickly placed so that it formed a solid wall. A hole left in one side formed a doorway from which paths extended in all directions. Seats made from slabs obtained at local sawmills completed the furnishings.[70]

It is in the collective preparation to worship God that the poor not only fashion their secret and novel approach to the divinity, but also resist and reinvent themselves over against oppressive strictures. Bush arbors were hidden holy conversations out of the slavemasters' earshot, allowing a domain of real preaching and testifying to unfold. While theologizing in liberation tongues, African Americans also formed a communal self unlike that ordained by their forced chattel existence. To boldly position a permanent "church" dwelling in the midst of slavery country, to organize the details of work to construct the edifice, and to take slabs from local sawmills without detection took the ability of a people hemmed in to accept the empowering motivation of worship as grace. It appears as grace in the woods for free worship and as grace engendering the constitution of new black selves: fearless, bold, and risk taking.

CONTENT

Creating a syncretized religion—a Christian black faith of liberation—meant definite content and explicit substantive claims on the part of enslaved African Americans. First this new Christianity of spiritual and material freedom called forth a politics that seized space and place for those without wealth resources. Politics, here, suggests the right of the poor to call on God to work with them in implementing the right of self-determination. The power of this space-place dynamic would make a way—a new location and a novel horizon where black workers could openly worship their freedom God and be their freely created new selves.

Bill Collins reminisced about this political right of self-determination when he recalled: "On Sunday we would go to the barn and pray to God to fix some way for us to be freed from our mean masters."[71] One could not be a new creation or embrace a God of power unless there were acts of deliverance. In fact the co-constitution of the self through politics can be seen in how their faith in God enables the blacks to physically move to a new and safe place-space (for example, the barn) in expectation, through prayer, that their God would then facilitate their ultimate deliverance from the realm of structural slavery.

The political content of black syncretized religion was never one of selfish faith claims, individualistic witness, and provincial expectation. The movement out of the chains of "Egypt" and the realization of self-determination brought a universal note, if not for those gathered in prayer, at least for their offspring and ultimately for all humankind. Alice Sewell remembered the arduous physical journey of moving from plantation pathos to penultimate free space and the hope that black freedom places engendered for free spaces for the unborn and a more healthy social relation for people of all races. "We prayed for dis day of freedom. We come from four and five miles to pray together to God dat if we don't live to see it, to please let our chillen live to see a better day and be free, so dat dey can give honest and fair service to de Lord and all mankind everywhere."[72]

The content of black Christian syncretized religion included a cultural strand also. In this instance, culture signifies the ability of poor black people to realize the right of self-identity. Who has the right to name a person? Who has a right to contradict and subvert a person's belief that God grants one the right to identify oneself as part of the self-constitution process? Apparently, from his early years, former slave William Wells Brown grasped the identity and self-creation interplay around naming when he wrote: "And I received several very severe whippings for telling people that my name was William, after orders were given to change it. Though young, I was old enough to place a high appreciation upon my name. . . . So I was not only hunting for my liberty, but also hunting for a name."[73] Taking not only the political right of self-determination of space and place but also the cultural right of calling himself whatever he freely wished to be called empowered Brown to undergo repeated whippings for refusing to yield either of these two rights.

Furthermore, the right of self-identity, in this instance, entailed a struggle over naming as a word accepted by the oppressed individual in radical distinction to an imposed word identified by oppressors. The word "William," accepted by Brown and denied by supporters of the plantation system, was part of a struggle over language power and metaphorical imagination. By holding on to his accepted name, Brown fought for all the polyvalent meanings such a title imaged—a language of free self-creation, a word of self-initiative.

Moreover the content of the hybrid Invisible Institution religion includes the risk for its followers of theological marginalization; that is, they assume the potential danger of following a faith argument of "thus saith the Lord" against wicked spiritual and material powers. The danger of these theological claims being tainted as marginalized, according to dominating theological norms, is in reality the good news of apocalyptic deliverance and eschatological hope for dispossessed communities. Former chattel Peter suggests how what is marginal Christian belief to the mainstream public definers of theology is actually the Christian gospel of hope for the oppressed and subversive discourse within the mainstream of marginalized believers. His summaries of enslaved black preachers' sermons from the hidden margins of plantation life indicate such a critiquing and prophetic content for black theology of liberation.

> The preachers were inspired by this bright hope of freedom, and as it grew nearer its imagined fulfillment they preached it to their people with thrilling eloquence. "'Taint no dream, nor no joke," cried one of these; "de time's a'most yer. Der won't be no mo' whippin', no mo' oversee's, no mo' patrollers, no mo' huntin' wid dogs; everybody's a gwine to be free, and de white mass'r's a gwine to pay 'em for der work. O, my brudders! de bressed time's a knockin' at de door! in dis yer world, bof white and black, is gwine to live togedder in peace."[74]

A true word preached from the margins transforms into the immediacy of a critical theological discourse proclaiming freedom and peace for all humanity "in dis yer world."

FORMS OF WORSHIP

Part of thinking about God differently, the construction of black theology, and recreating oneself in sacred space, the co-constitution of the black self, involved establishing novel forms of worship as celebration with God and resisting evil's presence. In the autobiographical reminiscences of slave secret meetings, Isaac Williams commented: "There would seldom be silence in our meetings, waiting for each other to speak, as I am told there is often in a white man's prayer meeting. We were always ready, that is the religious ones, to testify, and felt much better for doing so."[75]

Jubilant continuous testimony delineates one form of black religious ingenuity. For blacks, silent moments in the presence of divine power and grace were supplanted by a total yielding of the self to spiritual possession. To keep silent (that is, to keep one's thoughts and joy to oneself) before God reflected a form of individualism in radical contrast to rejoicing in communal activity. Though each individual African American had to "come through religion" and be converted to the divinity by her- or himself, such an individual conversion embraced a communal context of an extended family of believers as well as an obligation to report back to the public all sacred experiences. In other words, in the Invisible Institution, the secret, sacred gathering of black folk, marked the time for poor people to assert themselves in one voice openly and aggressively, the time to tell God all about their lives.

Jubilant continuous testimony was accompanied by the form of embodied ecstatic singing particular to black worshippers. Once free, James L. Smith penned the following testimony in his autobiography:

> The way in which we worshipped is almost indescribable. The singing was accompanied by a certain ecstasy of motion, clapping of hands, tossing of heads, which would continue without cessation about half an hour; one would lead off in a kind of recitative style, others joining in the chorus. The old house partook of the ecstasy; it rang with their jubilant shouts, and shook in all its joints.[76]

In this novel form of communing with God, singing comes from the body; in fact the body sings praises to the divinity by the empowering presence of the Holy Spirit. Embodied ecstatic singing is a theological expression because the sacred immanence moves the poor community to an otherworldly realm, to a horizon of a new self whose new constitution begins in a spiritual plane, and then relocates this transcendent event in this world by re-impacting the physical bodily presence.

Singing is an extended family chorus, in which one bonds with the neighbor through words of songs. Former slave, Alice Sewell, remembers, "when we all sung we would march around and shake each other's hands." Indeed, another ex-chattel indicated that this ritual of communal family feeling of comradery was encoded in song; one verse stated—"Our little meetin's about to break, chillen, and we must part. We got to part in body, but hope not in mind. . . . We walk about and shake hands, fare ye well my sisters, I am going home."[77]

Thus walking, physical movement, united with the singing and buoyed the gathered throng. The more they walked in the secret worship, the more they sang, the more they united as an extended family of sisters and brothers in the presence of the holy. The increased bonding of the horizontal plane of human interaction coupled with the thickness of the spiritual embrace from the vertical plane emboldened poor folk and prepared them to enter the realm of evil plantation owners with a renewed sense of faith and a newly constituted self blessed by the divinity. As bodies separated after secret meetings, the remembrance of the song served as spiritual glue to recall all who had gathered clandestinely.

The connection between the religious forms of the ring shout dance (of enslaved African Americans in secret worship) and the memory of the drum (of their West African ancestors) displayed the vital sacred relation between black theology and the indigenous religions of West African communal practices. The ring shout-drum memory, an additional form of syncretized religion, underscores the claim that enslaved blacks knew who they were as African people. Such knowledge, derived from an African indigenous lineage, appeared consciously for those blacks closer to their West African heritage and unconsciously in the layered fiber of the newly created black religion in North America.

The drum had become the object of virulent and rabid attacks from European colonizers in West Africa. In the analysis of one West African scholar: "In the beginning of the colonial period, both administrators and missionaries waged a merciless war against the drum for various reasons. . . . Christian missionaries found in the drum an excuse to wage a war against African traditional possession cults. They took away and destroyed thousands of drums."[78] White Christians feared the drum because, for them, it acted as an instrument in the political resistance against the military attacks of Christian colonialists and was associated with the presence of divine powers. In fact, whites were correct in their assessments. Another West African interpreter concurs in this appraisal when he writes: "drumming accompanied most, if not all, religious occasions in traditional society." Religion and the drum are wedded together in West African indigenous religions because the High God saw fit to prioritize it in creation. One Akan saying claims:

> God in creating the world
> Has suffered to create.
> What did he create?
> He created the Drum.
> Divine Drum,
> Wherever you are
> In nature,
> We call upon you,
> Come.[79]

As God's creation, the drum is part of God, belongs to the sacred realm, engenders human-divine relationship and re-creative powers. The drum hinges the constitution of the self with the holy. For the Akan of West Africa, the drum summons the divinity and the ancestors to the worship event of the devotees, conveys the message of God to those gathered, and sends divine spirits and ancestors back to their place of dwelling.

Along with the drum, religious practices in Congo-Angola, Dahomey, Nigeria, the Gold Coast, Sierra Leone, and Togo, (areas of origin for blacks in North America) involved movement in a ring in religious rituals venerating ancestors. Specifically the Ibos, Yorubas, Ibibios, and Efiks of southern Nigeria engaged in a slow, counterclockwise motion embodying a "wave-like ripple which runs down the muscles of the back and along the arms to the fingertips. Every part of the body dances, not only the limbs."[80]

Once Africans crossed the Atlantic and were denied by law the usage of the drum and, therefore, were forced to worship God secretly, they incorporated the memory of the drum sound and function in their newly crafted ring dance. They performed the memory of the drum into a ring shout. One contemporary observed the following:

> The good-natured ingenuity of the Negroes in circumventing plantation rules speaks well for their ready wit, and it always rouses my admiration to see the way in which the McIntosh County "shouters" tap their heels on the resonant board floor to imitate the beat of the drum their forebears were not allowed to have. Those who hear the records of the musical chants which accompany the ring-shout . . . cannot believe that a drum is not used, though how the effect is

achieved with the heels alone—when they barely leave the floor—remains a puzzle.[81]

The ring shout showed the theatrical alteration of poor Christians' state of consciousness and the syncretistic form of Invisible Institution religion, a religion possessed by the Christian Holy Spirit's power of changing the old self into a new self. It contained partial remnants of West African indigenous spirituality grafted into a reinterpreted Christianity to produce black theology.[82] This novel New World syncretism showed forth in the possessed sound and motion of drumlike feet circling while worshipers shouted divine praises in a frenzy.

We return to the turned-over pot as a final form created by enslaved African Americans in the secret worship of God. Here too, one could argue for a syncretistic synthesis between West African indigenous faith practices and a reconfigured Christian belief system. Based on extensive field work among African communities, Surinam in particular, anthropologists Melville and Frances Herskovits link ecstatic dancing to the theological dimension of drums. They claim, first of all, that Africans perceived dancing as a sacred way of life. Next they observe the body positions of worshipers relative to the holy drums. Lastly, they conclude that dancing around the drum signified an affirmation of God dwelling in these divine instruments. The religious dancers "face the drums and dance toward them, in recognition of the voice of the god within the instruments."[83]

There are similar associations between African American Christian worshipers and the sacredness of the overturned pot, which may be a remnant of the West African sacred drum. For example, an unnamed former slave recalled: "Time has been that [slavemasters] wouldn't let them have a meeting, but God Almighty let them have it, for they would take an old kettle and turn it up before the door with the mouth of it facing the folks, and that would hold the voices inside."[84] Here this interviewee associates in linguistic thought forms God's permission with an overturned kettle. Though slavemasters denied Christian worship, this former slave believed that God held all might over all creation including the earthly masters on the plantation. And in the thought process and sentence construction of this former chattel's talking, God of all might enabled poor blacks to have safe time and ample space in which to forge their own theology by means of (in the interviewee's word "for") an old kettle which held the power to protect the voices of those secretly praising God.

In another former slave's thought association, we find epistemological clarity as God's gift of grace. "In some places that they have prayer meetings they would turn pots down in the middle of the floor to keep the white folks from hearing them sing and pray and testify, you know. Well, I don't know where they learned to do that. I kinda think the Lord put them things in their minds to do for themselves, just like he helps us Christians in other ways."[85] The knowledge to take care of themselves, in a situation in which yearning for faith practices are effected in spite of lethal threats from earthly slavemasters, derived from the pedagogical gift of God. Divine kindness (that is, grace) instructs oppressed African American Christians to craft an ingenuity to subvert evildoers who would prevent the spiritual self-care required in situations of subordination.

In this sense, the pot or kettle becomes holy knowledge, the power for blacks to make a way out of no way. It therefore facilitates not only their taking care of themselves but also enables temporal and spacial conditions for African Americans to co-constitute their theological worldview in addition to forging a new humanity amidst deleterious circumstances. Put differently, this former slave's rhetoric (akin to persuasive discourse) juxtaposes evil's denial of worship, God's allowing a way for the oppressed, and the kettle's making real a divine knowledge. At the same time, the ex-chattel's logic (akin to rational argument) links the mouth of the kettle to God's power somehow. Pedagogy, rhetoric, and logic are embodied in the kettle's expediting the remaking of both a subversive Christian faith claim and a reconstituted slave status for self-initiative.

More pointedly, Patsy Hyde remembers slavery days in which the overturned pot indeed revealed directly the presence and power of God to those surreptitiously gathered in faith. "De slaves would tek dere old iron cookin' pots en turn dem upside down on de groun' neah dere cabins ter keep dere white folk fum hearin' w'at dey wuz sain'. Dey claimed dat hit showed dat Gawd wuz wid dem."[86] The phrase "Gawd wuz wid dem" echoes the Christian notion of Emmanuel, an honorific title for Jesus the Christ, denoting "God is with us." In their mindset, blacks were certain in their claim that divinity resided in their midst; this holy nearness of God's appearance was more powerful and more protective than any force on earth. And an old iron cooking pot had something to do with this sheltering, liberating power.

Conclusion

Part 1 of *Down, Up, and Over: Slave Religion and Black Theology* has laid the contextual backdrop for the development of doctrinal statements on God, Jesus, and human purpose in a constructive black theology, which Part 2 takes up.

In Chapter 1, we saw how Protestantism and American culture began with two arrivals—that of the hopeful Pilgrim in the Christian voluntary journey to Massachusetts aboard the Mayflower in 1620 and the involuntary advent of dread experienced by twenty West African practitioners of indigenous religion who were dragged to Jamestown, Virginia, in 1619 on a Dutch man-of-war. Both signify symbolically and substantively a duplicitous dimension of Protestantism and American culture.

The Pilgrims fled the Old World for freedom of religion and a new life. Ever since then, mainstream theology and ways of life in North America would incarnate a push toward equality and a God of democracy and a pull to racial hierarchy and demonic oppressions. It was as if a set of twins, born from the same parents, had undergone a genetic moral defect, making one take the high ethical ground accepting all people based on the content of an individual's character and the other instinctively seek the lowest, inhuman path in social relations.

To the first twenty Africans, religion had been a way of life linked to their high God, ancestors, spirits, and the unborn—a faith and practice marking balance, individual-communal ethics, partiality to the least in the community, openness to the stranger, justice for the forlorn, and so on. To be wrenched violently out of context by Christian whites posed a fundamental dilemma for black people. What could they expect from their new captors and the latter's strange religion? How would they sustain themselves in this new land and what faith resources could they draw on to forge both a new theology and new selves?

In Chapter 2, we examined what Africans received of their expectations. Protestantism and American culture, with occasional exceptions, institutionalized a political economy that made Africans and African Americans commodities for white pleasure and profit. Culturally, a way of life and systemic social patterns that privileged white skin over black in the national identity were set in motion. Linguistically, metaphors, symbols, syntax, and rhetoric emerged that encoded and reinforced black-white asymmetries. On a micro level, issues of time, space, ritualization, bodies, geography, architecture, surveillance, laughter, and others further made problematic what it meant to be black in North America. This was one layer in Protestantism and American culture.

In this chapter, we have touched on how Africans and African Americans sustained themselves and what faith resources they drew upon. They laid the basis for a second layer within Protestantism and American culture. In a sense they had to knock down, break up, and jump over the structures, forces of habit, worldview, and theological constructs revealed by mainstream Protestantism and American culture. They sought to accomplish this constructive theological effort through methods of black self-knowledge and self-care—seizing sacred domains, actualizing the divine right to resist, and institutionalizing a syncretized religion.

Throughout this chapter, the investigation has offered evidence that from sundown to sunup, enslaved black folk believed that God gave the earth's resources to all (political economy), created an identity of universal human beauty (culture), acted as a word of liberation for the oppressed (language), and operated on multiple levels of everyday human interaction (microrealities). Essentially, Africans and African Americans sowed the seeds for a systematic black theology by synthesizing a reinterpreted Christianity, everyday commonsense wisdom, and remnants from West African indigenous religions.

Throughout Part 1, the argument has embellished the basic thesis that, within Protestantism and American culture and toward the invention of a novel faith practice of freedom, African Americans have constructed a black theology of liberation with universal implications and co-constituted themselves with God's grace of freedom. Part 2 systematizes the thesis in the liberation doctrines of God, Jesus, and human purpose. A spiritual and material full humanity requires a statement of constructive theology. Black theology calls on the black church to struggle for liberation and to practice freedom granted by the Spirit of liberation.

NOTES

1. Quotes one through three are found in the following sources, respectively: William C. Emerson, M.D., *Stories and Spirituals of the Negro Slave* (Boston: The Gorham Press, 1930), 78; William J. Faulkner, *The Days When the Animals Talked*, 54; and Jacob K. Olupona, ed., *African Traditional Religions in Contemporary Society* (New York: Paragon House, 1991), 127.

2. For more on this synthesis, see my *Introducing Black Theology of Liberation* (Maryknoll, N.Y.: Orbis, 1999), ch. 1, and my *Shoes That Fit Our Feet: Sources for a Constructive Black Theology* (Maryknoll, N.Y.: Orbis, 1993), ch. 1. Other texts relevant to African retentions in black culture that

also have an impact on religion (given the fact that religion is part of black culture) are: Peter J. Paris, *The Spirituality of African Peoples: The Search for a Common Moral Discourse* (Minneapolis: Fortress, 1995); Joseph E. Holloway, ed., *Africanisms in American Culture* (Bloomington and Indianapolis: Indiana University Press, 1990); J. L. Dillard, *Black English: Its History and Usage in the United States* (New York: Random House, 1972); Geneva Smitherman, *Talkin and Testifyin: The Language of Black America* (Detroit: Wayne State University Press, 1977); Winifred Kellersberger Vass, *The Bantu Speaking Heritage of the United States* (Los Angeles: Center for Afro-American Studies, University of California at Los Angeles, 1979); Eileen Southern, *The Music of Black Americans: A History* (New York: Norton, 1983); William D. Piersen, *Black Legacy: America's Hidden Heritage* (Amherst: University of Massachusetts Press, 1993); Roger D. Abrahams, ed., *Afro-American Folktales: Stories from Black Traditions in the New World* (New York: Pantheon, 1985); Mel Watkins, *On the Real Side: Laughing, Lying, and Signifying—The Underground Tradition of African-American Humor that Transformed American Culture, from Slavery to Richard Pryor* (New York: Simon and Schuster, 1994); and Mechal Sobel, *Trabelin' On: The Slave Journey to an Afro-Baptist Faith* (Westport, Conn.: Greenwood, 1979).

3. Kofi Asare Opoku, *West African Traditional Religion* (Accra, Ghana: FEP International Private Limited, 1978), 5.

4. Opoku, *West African Traditional Religion*, 9–10.

5. See Opoku, *West African Traditional Religion*, 54 and John S. Mbiti, *Introduction to African Religion*, 2d ed. (Portsmouth, N.H.: Heinemann, 1991), 41.

6. John S. Mbiti, *African Religions and Philosophy* (New York: Anchor Books, 1970), 136–37.

7. See J. N. K. Mugambi and Laurenti Magesa, eds., *Jesus in African Christianity* (Nairobi, Kenya: Initiatives Ltd., 1989), 2.; and Opoku, *West African Traditional Religion*, 13.

8. Kofia Asare Opoku, "Aspects of Akan Worship," in C. Eric Lincoln, ed., *The Black Experience in Religion* (Garden City, N.Y.: Anchor Books, 1974), 286; Opoku, *West African Traditional Religion*, 1, 13; Mbiti, *Introduction to African Religion*, 29; and Pobee, 44.

9. See Olupona, ed., p. 102.

10. Opoku, *West African Traditional Religion*, 91–92.

11. Opoku, *West African Traditional Religion*, 36.

12. Mbiti, *Introduction to African Religion*, 92–91.

13. Other texts on African religion are: Laurenti Magesa, *African Religion: The Moral Traditions of Abundant Life* (Maryknoll, N.Y.: Orbis, 1997); and Thomas D. Blakely, Walter E. A. van Beek, and Dennis L. Thomson, eds., *Religion in Africa: Experience and Expression* (Portsmouth, N.H.: Heinemann, 1994).

14. In addition to the near genocide of American Indians, the European and Euro-American initiated slave trade fashioned the wealth, politics, language, culture, and racial face of the founding of the United States. This negative imprint of the black figure on the U.S. nation was accompanied by African Americans' resistance and public protest, along with the abolitionist organizing of some whites. Moreover, the U.S. Constitution is based on slavery (e.g., the infamous "three-fifths" clause). And throughout slavery, white politicians, clergymen, and plantation owners spoke, wrote, and preached about "the Negro problem."

15. The words of Florence Bailey as told to a narrator can be found at the Cade Library Archives, no page numbers. Other references to the overturned pot can be found in *Unwritten History of Slavery*, 150, and in the interview with Martha Johnson in the Cade Library Archives, no page number.

16. Dora Roberts, *The American Slave*, Georgia, vol. 13, pt. 3, 206.

17. Mrs. Sutton, *Unwritten History of Slavery*, 15. Other references to dances can be found on pp. 4 and 150 of the same book; and separate interviews with Jake Roberts, Saul Williams, Tom Holl, Lee Bridget, and Dora Wilkins at the Cade Library Archives, no page numbers.

Similar fun times occurred at quilting parties (see *Unwritten History of Slavery*, 9, no name of interviewee given) and at Christmas (refer to the separate interviews of Harve Quanles and John W. White in the Cade Library Archives, n.p.)

18. James Bolton, *The American Slave*, Georgia, vol. 12, pt. 1, 99–100.

19. Rachel Adams, *The American Slave*, Georgia, vol. 12, pt. 1, 7. For other references to corn-shucking, see unnamed, *Unwritten History of Slavery*, 46, 34–35; Jasper Battle, Georgia, vol. 12, pt. 1, 71.

For a thorough description of the entire corn-shucking ritual, see Roger D. Abrahams, *Singing the Master: The Emergence of African American Culture in the Plantation South* (New York: Pantheon Books, 1992).

20. Unnamed interviewee, *Unwritten History of Slavery*, 50.

21. Regarding the issue of status elevation and reversal, see Victor W. Turner, *The Ritual Process* (London: Routledge and Kegan Paul, 1969), 172.

22. Willis Cofer, *The American Slave*, Georgia, vol. 12, pt. 1, 209.

23. The Ferebe Rogers reference comes from *The American Slave*, Georgia, vol. 13, pt. 3, 215; and that of Henry Nix from p. 144.

Other accounts of slaves struggling to read can be found in "The Emancipated Slave Face to Face with His Old Master: Valley of the Lower Mississippi: Supplemental Report (B); American Freedmen's Commission by James McKaye," National Archives, Washington, D.C., file 3280, 1863, microfilm roll 199, pp. 12–13; Tom Hawkins, *The American Slave*, Georgia, vol. 12, pt. 2, 130–31; Emma Hurley, Georgia, vol. 12, pt. 2, 274; Alice Green, Georgia, vol. 2, pt. 2, 42; *Narrative of the Life and Adventures of Henry Bibb*, 31–32; and unnamed, *Unwritten History of Slavery*, 148.

24. *Narrative of the Life and Adventures of Henry Bibb*, xi.

25. *Life and Times of Frederick Douglass*, 79–80.

26. See the following references for further insight on reading, the Bible, and self-constitution: "The Emancipated Slave Face to Face with His Old Master: Valley of the Lower Mississippi: Supplemental Report (B), American Freedmen's Inquiry commission by James McKaye," National Archives, Washington, D.C., file 3280, 1863, microfilm roll 199, pp. 12–13; Tom Hawkins, *The American Slave*, Georgia, vol. 12, pt. 2, 130–31; Henry Nix, Georgia, vol. 13, pt. 3, 144; Ferebe Rogers, Georgia, vol. 13, pt. 3, 215; Emma Hurley, Georgia, vol. 12, pt. 2, 274; Alice Green, Georgia, vol. 12, pt. 2, 42; *Narrative of the Life and Adventures of Henry Bibb*, xi and 31–32; Stephen Jordon in Albert, ed., *House of Bondage*, 11; *Unwritten History of Slavery*, no name, 148; William McWhorter, Georgia, vol. 13, pt. 3, 97; Hodges, ed., *Black Itinerants of the Gospel*, 113; Craft, *Running a Thousand Miles for Freedom*, 98; Rev. Reed, *Unwritten History of Slavery*, 20; Rachel Adams, Georgia, vol. 12, pt. 1, 5; Dosia Harris, Georgia, vol. 12, pt. 2, 109; and Thomas H. Jones, *The Experience of Thomas H. Jones, Who Was a Slave for Forty-Three Years* (Boston: Bazin & Chandler, 1862), 20–21.

27. *Five Black Lives*, 167.

28. See other instances of the power of prayer: Johnson, *Slavery Days in Old Kentucky*, 39; Celestia Avery, *The American Slave*, Georgia, vol. 12, pt. 1, 24; and "Extracts from Debates on the Adoption of the Federal Constitution, Relating to Slavery," American Freedmen's Inquiry Commission, 1863–64, National Archives, Washington, D.C., microfilm roll no. 200, no page number.

29. Nichols, *Many Thousand Gone*, 102.

30. Quoted in William Wells Brown, in Osofsky, ed., *Puttin' On Ole Massa*, 197.

31. Stated by Callie Chatman, *The American Slave*, Georgia, supplemental series 1, vol. 3, pt. 1, 195.

32. Rev. Reed, *Unwritten History of Slavery*, 20–21.

33. For commentary on spirituals and examples of this song genre, see: the quotation of Frederick Douglass (p. 14) in Nichols, *Many Thousand Gone*, 98–99; the quotation of Harriet Jacob (pp. 108–9) found in *Many Thousand Gone*; Mary Glady, *The American Slave*, Georgia, vol. 12, pt. 1, 25; Katz, ed., *Five Slave Narratives*, 67; Anderson, *From Slavery to Affluence*, 4–25; "Charles Howard Family Domestic History," 173–74, found at the UNC Southern Historical Collection; and Sterling Stuckey, *Slave Culture: Nationalist Theory and the Foundations of Black America* (New York: Oxford University Press, 1987), 62.

34. Kofi Asare Opoku quoted in "Aspects of Akan Worship," in Lincoln, ed., *The Black Experience in Religion*, 299.

35. See Robert L. Hall, "African Religious Retentions in Florida," in *Africanisms in American Culture*, ed. Joseph E. Holloway (Bloomington: Indiana University Press, 1990), 101; and Creel, *A Peculiar People*.

36. *Unwritten History of Slavery*, 122.

37. See the responses of former chattel Robert Smalls in "Extracts from Debates on the Adoption of Freedmen's Inquiry Commission, 1863–64," National Archives, Washington, D.C., microfilm roll 200, no page number. Other relevant references to the naming ritual are discovered in: testimony of Mrs. Holmes, *Unwritten History of Slavery*, 90; and William Wells Brown in Osofsky, ed., *Puttin' On Ole Massa*, 217.

38. Ms. Cornelia, *Unwritten History of Slavery*, 144.

39. Other references to my interpretation of the theology of resource allocation can be found in: Henry Barnes' testimony in *The American Slave,* Alabama, supplement series one, vol. 1, 40; and Mr. Huddleston, *Unwritten History of Slavery*, 15.

40. See John Michael Vlach, *Back of the Big House: The Architecture of Plantation Slavery* (Chapel Hill: University of North Carolina, 1993), ix.

41. See Will Coleman, "'Coming Through 'Ligion': Metaphor in Non-Christian and Christian Experiences with the Spirit(s) in African American Slave Narratives," in *Cut Loose Your Stammering Tongue: Black Theology in the Slave Narratives,* ed. Dwight N. Hopkins and George Cummings (Maryknoll, N.Y.: Orbis Books, 1991).

42. Regarding architecture and space as contested categories, see Michael Parker Pearson and Colin Richards, eds., *Architecture and Order: Approaches to Social Space* (New York: Routledge, 1994), and Sophie Watson and Katherine Gibson, eds. *Postmodern Cities and Spaces* (Cambridge, Mass.: Blackwell, 1995).

43. See Vlach, *Back of the Big House*, 14.

44. Former slave Ben Sullivan in Georgia's Writers' Project, *Drums and Shadows* (Athens: University of Georgia, 1940), 179.

45. Vlach, *Back of the Big House*, 13.

46. The idea of returning to home was popularized in the mytho-documentary film *Daughters of the Dust,* directed by Julie Dash.

47. All accounts are taken from *May Anti-Slavery Pamphlets 40* found in the Cornell University Slavery Collection.

48. See the *National Anti-Slavery Standard*, December 10, 1840, 106, found in the Widener Library, Harvard; and the narrator's account of formerly enslaved Jennie Kendricks, *The American Slave,* Georgia, vol. 13, pt. 3, 5.

49. See Sarah Bradford, *Harriet Tubman: The Moses of Her People* (Secaucus, N.J.: The Citadel Press), 27–37.

50. *Life and Times of Frederick Douglass*, 159–60. In Box 69, Collection 116 of the Siebert Papers (no page given), a December 6, 1892 letter mailed to Siebert from an unknown correspondent from Sardinia, Ohio, renders this memory: One slavemaster arrived in Ohio pursuing his runaways and described one—"One of them was a young mulatto, with sense enough for a Congressman and religion enough for a whole Church." Many runaways were intellectually brilliant and religiously faithful.

51. Quoted in Harding, *There Is a River*, 30.

52. Vincent Mulago's "Traditional African Religion and Christianity," in *African Traditional Religions in Contemporary Society,* ed. Jacob K. Olupona (New York: Paragon House, 1991), 127.

53. "The Emancipated Slave Face to Face with His Old Master: Valley of the Lower Mississippi: Supplemental Report (B); American Freedman's Inquiry Commission by James McKaye," National Archives, Washington, D.C., file 3280, 1863, microfilm roll 199, pp. 23–26.

54. Herbert Aptheker, *To Be Free: Studies in American Negro History* (New York: International Publishers, 1948), 13.

55. Aptheker, *To Be Free,* 26. For fuller accounts of maroon societies, see Aptheker, *To Be Free,* 11–30; Nichols, *Many Thousand Gone,* 93; Katz, ed., *Five Slave Narratives,* 62–63; and in the Cornell University Slavery Collection, *The American Anti-Slavery Almanac* for 1839, vol. 1, no. 4, 42–43.

56. This letter signed by a David Holmes is found in the Louisiana State University Archives, Hill Memorial Library.

57. Boston Public Library, Rare Books section, *The Anti-Slavery Advocate,* February 1847, 14–15.

58. Boston Public Library, *The Anti-Slavery Advocate,* London, July 1861, 443. Also see the Louisiana State University Archives, Hill Memorial Library, specifically the April 25, 1811 account found in the William C. C. Claiborne document regarding the governor's act repaying white slave owners for blacks executed or killed in the latter's rebellion, as well as compensation for houses burned down. Found in the same archives is the New Orleans. November 18th, 1804 letter from Louisiana Governor William C. C. Claiborne to a Col. Butler describing black folk's preparation for armed rebellion in Point Coupee (no page numbers).

59. Gayraud S. Wilmore, *Black Religion and Black Radicalism* (Maryknoll, N.Y.: Orbis Books, 1986), 54–55.

60. Quoted in Sterling Stuckey, *Slave Culture,* 45. Also see the Louisiana State University Archives, Hill Memorial Library, Ferguson (Samuel Wragg) Papers, Folder 3, no. 1416, p. 6, and the elaborate account given in Wilmore, *Black Religion and Black Radicalism.*

61. Stuckey, *Slave Culture,* 50.

62. Foner, ed., *Nat Turner,* 43. Also review *Five Black Lives* for a former slave's interpretation of the effects of Turner's Christian insurrection.

63. One former slave remembered: "Notwithstanding our difficulties, we used to steal away to some of the quarters to have meetings." On one occasion, "where we assembled about fifty or seventy of us in number," found in *Five Black Lives,* 165. And the phrase "stealin' the meetin'" comes from John Cade, "Out of the Mouths of Ex-Slaves," *Journal of Negro History,* 20 (1935), 330.

The final section of this chapter explains the syncretized African and Christian witness of an oppressed people of faith in the secret recesses of the plantation routine and ritual. However, one should note that African Americans spiritually fought within and disrupted the established typologies of slavery churches elaborated in Chapter 2. In the presence of white preachers and segregated white supremacist Christians, blacks would often disturb the normal liturgical flow of worship. In a word, despite slavery churches, some blacks fought for space within these demonic spaces because, once filled with the Holy Spirit, they became liberated enough and bold enough to invade white spaces (by coming down to the white segregated section of churches) while shouting for joy. They broke spacial, architectural, legal, sacred, and noise prescriptions of plantation Christianity. For stories substantiating this claim, see Martha Colquitt, *The American Slave,* Georgia, vol. 13, pt. 1, 247; the diary of Harriet Eaton, vol. 1, March 12, 1854, found in the UNC Southern Historical Society; and the December 20, 1846 letter from Jarsh Scuddeo to his brother, found in the Louisiana State University Archives, Hill Memorial Library.

64. For a reference on the battle over the term syncretism, see *Syncretism/Anti-Syncretism: The Politics of Religious Synthesis,* eds. Charles Stewart and Rosalind Shaw (New York: Routledge, 1994).

65. "Extracts from Debates on the Adoption of the Federal Constitution, Relating to Slavery." American Freedmen's Inquiry Commission, 1863–64, National Archives, Washington, D.C., microfilm roll no. 200, no page number.

66. Quotes in this section on the praying in the field type can be found in *The American Slave,* Georgia, vol. 12, pt. 1, 174 and 328; and in Johnson, ed., *God Struck Me Dead,* 76, no name.

67. See Cade Library Archives, no name, no page, Texas; Georgia Johnson, *The American Slave,* Georgia, vol. 12, pt. 2, 333; and Mr. Womble, Georgia, vol. 13, pt. 4, 192.

68. See *Unwrittten History of Slavery,* no name, 23; and Mrs. Sutton, *Unwritten History of Slavery,* 15.

69. Brooks in Albert, ed., *House of Bondage,* 55; and Davidson, Cade Library Archives, no page.

70. *The American Slave,* Georgia, vol. 12, pt. 1, 197–98; also see Amanda Jackson, Georgia, vol. 12, pt. 2, 292; Della Briscoe, Georgia, vol. 12, pt. 1, 127; and Charlie Bassett, Cade Library Archives, no page.

71. Bill Collins, Cade Library Archives, no page.

72. Alice Sewell in Norman R. Yetman, ed., *Life Under the "Peculiar Institution": Selections from the Slave Narrative Collection* (New York: Holt, Rinehart and Winston Inc., 1970), 263.

73. Williams Wells Brown in Osofsky, ed., *Puttin' On Ole Massa,* 217. Similarly, the interviewer of ex-slave Samuel Simeon Andrews relates this account of Mr. Andrews and his siblings gaining their freedom: "they all dropped the name of their master, Lane, and took the name of their grandfather, Andrews"; found in *The American Slave,* Florida, vol. 17, 17.

74. Peter Still and Vina Still, *The Kidnapped and the Ransomed,* 160.

75. Isaac Williams, *Sunshine and Shadow of Slave Life. Reminiscences as Told by Isaac D. Williams* (East Saginaw, Mich.: Evening News Printing and Binding Company, 1885), 67.

76. James L. Smith, *Autobiography of James L. Smith*, (Norwich, Conn.: Press of the Bulletin Company, 1881), 27.

77. The song comes from Albert, ed., *House of Bondage*, 12; and Alice Sewell's remarks are taken from Yetman, ed., *Life Under the "Peculiar Institution*," 263.

Mary Gladdy of Georgia recalled a song sung in their secret worship meetings which indicated the ongoing process of creating each member into a new brother-sister collective self geared toward liberation. She explained how the following song was performed right before dawn after an all-night session of relating religious experiences through story, song, prayer, and shouting. Their essential desire was freedom, recounts Mrs. Gladdy. She states, moreover, that participants were touched by the Spirit just before dawn, would then sing the following song for twenty minutes or so, and shake hands as they departed into the greyness of the morning hours.

> Jest befo' day, I fees 'im. Jest befo' day, I feels 'im.
> My sister [or my brother], I feels 'im. My sister, I feels 'im.
> All night long I've been feelin' 'im.
> Jest befo' day I feels 'im. Jest befo' day I feels 'im.
> The sperit, I feels 'im. The sperit, I feels 'im!

(narrator's report on Mary Gladdy, in *The American Slave,* Georgia, supplemental series 1, vol. 3, pt. 1, 258–59).

78. Olupona, ed., *African Traditional Religions in Contemporary Society,* 81.

79. Olupona, ed., *African Traditional Religions in Contemporary Society,* 84–85; see John Pobee for quote on the drum accompanying religious occasions, *Toward an African Theology,* 66.

80. Stuckey, *Slave Culture,* 11 and 19–20.

81. Lydia Parrish, *Slave Songs of the Georgia Sea Islands* (Athens: University of Georgia Press, 1992), 16.

82. See Creel, *A Peculiar People,* 298–99. Historian Creel, in her study of descendants of slaves off the coast of North Carolina on the Gullah Islands, claims: "The background of the Gullah ring shout, a manifestation of possession trance, was West African in origin and in important characteristics of the initiation process," 299.

83. Quoted in Stuckey, *Slave Culture,* 20.

84. *Unwritten History of Slavery*, 19–20, no name.

85. *Unwritten History of Slavery*, 10, no name.

86. Patsy Hyde in *The American Slave,* Tennessee, vol. 16, 34. Other testimonies regarding the overturned pot are found throughout ex-slaves' testimonies from the different states, evincing a phenomenon that crossed regional and state boundaries. See John Hunter, Arkansas, vol. 9, 364; Johnson, ed., *God Struck Me Dead*, no name, 69; Saul Williams, Cade Library Archives, no page; and Sister Kelly, *Unwritten History of Slavery,* 82.

PART 2

Constructive Black Theology:
The Spirit of Liberation

IN THE CONTEXT of slave religion, Protestantism and American culture, how does one construct a black theology of liberation and, in a related manner, co-constitute the self with God? In Part 1, we engaged Protestantism and American culture and the co-constitution of the theological self as backdrop—an indication of novel ways in which oppressed religious communities seize and syncretize that which is given by oppressor groups with creative resources indigenous to the oppressed community.

In Part 2, we develop a constructive black theology of liberation. Our basic claim is that, based on the Bible and the faith experiences of enslaved black folk, a constructive black theology today understands, feels, and lives out the Spirit who manifests total liberation in macro-, micro-, linguistic, and racial-cultural identity realities in the dynamic of co-constitution of the self for a full spiritual and material humanity (goal or telos). Chapter 4 argues that God is the Spirit of total liberation for us (theology); Chapter 5 that Jesus is the fulfillment of God's promise to be the Spirit of total liberation with us (Christology); and Chapter 6 that human purpose is God's Spirit of total liberation in us (theological anthropology).

In the final analysis, a constructive black theology of liberation accompanies the co-constitution of a new self and a new Common Wealth, on earth as it is in heaven.

CHAPTER 4
God—The Spirit of Total Liberation for Us

And Mary said,
"My soul magnifies the Lord,
And my spirit rejoices in God my Savior,
For he has looked with favor on
*   the lowliness of his servant.*
Surely, from now on all generations will call me blessed;
For the Mighty One has done great things for me,
And holy is his name.
His mercy is for those who fear him
*   from generation to generation.*
He has shown strength with his arm;
He has scattered the proud in the thoughts of their hearts.
He has brought down the powerful from their thrones,
And lifted up the lowly;
He has filled the hungry with good things,
And sent the rich away empty."

Luke 1:46-53

SINCE THE TWO foundational arrivals of 1619 and 1620—markers of Protestantism and American culture—and contextualized by the sunup to sundown period of the slavemasters' religious strictures, enslaved African Americans used the space and time from sundown to sunup to co-constitute themselves with divine intent into their own racial religious formation. They hoped for and pursued a liberated humanity. They forged themselves as a new African American people of faith embodied in an everyday practical knowledge anchored in their existential encounter with the Spirit of freedom and in their own hermeneutical reading of the biblical text. In a word, the liberating Spirit met them and worked with them both in material experience and in textual deciphering. Yet this dynamic formation was not only a practical reconfiguration at the level of religious experience. It was also the crafting and deployment of faith—a quasi-theology from the oppressed African American perspective.

From this religious occurrence and emerging, fragmented faith statements, we can be informed in the construction of a black theology of liberation. Specifically we can learn from enslaved African American racial religious formation and biblical insights to seek the development of doctrinal statements on God, Jesus, and human purpose. Therefore, we can claim that a black theology today perceives the Spirit of total liberation who manifests in macro, micro, linguistic, and racial cultural identity dimensions (those disciplines of creativity or methods of the self that bring knowledge of the self and are the sites for taking care of the self in the practice of freedom) as part of self co-constitution for a full spiritual and material humanity. God, in constructive black theology, is the Spirit of total liberation for us. Jesus is the fulfillment of the Spirit of total liberation revealed to be with us. And human purpose is the Spirit of total liberation in us. The struggle for liberation and the practice of freedom unfold in the incarnation of these three theological doctrines.

In this chapter, we discover that God is for us through divine acts, being, and knowledge. And these forms of God's presence are given to the least in society and to the brokenhearted through various divine attributes.

The Acts of God—Ethics—What Does God Do?

The primal hope act of God is the exodus story. It signifies the paradigmatic expression of covenantal partnership of co-constitution of the oppressed self into a new liberated self. Divine intent works with marginalized humanity through liberation to exit out of physical restraints of Egyptian bondage (or wherever it exists today) and into material free space undergirded by a spiritual belief in the power of Yahweh and the human community. The Spirit of total liberation or holistic freedom of Yahweh is never in itself, but is always an empowering "ruach" (breath) for poor humanity. The finger of God is for us; and the divine Spirit breathes on us for us.

To encounter the identity of God's liberating Spirit—the divine face of freedom—we look for what God is doing in the ongoing process of embedded transcendent ethics of holistic spiritual and material humanity. Divine ethics (the doing of God) do not escape us in an ephemeral invisibility or in a distant space acting on us absent from us. The work of God is actively present for us in the attempts of the poor to construct themselves anew. God for us is always socially located with the poor communities on this earth. To believe otherwise is to deny and fracture the original covenant of the Spirit's presence for broken humanity. God does wherever and whenever marginalized humanity cries out in the pain and pleasure of forging a new self. Divine activity is revealed in the voice of the marginalized fighting to make a way out of no way. There is the action of Yahweh.

The acts and ethics of God are also in direct response to the monopolizers of power in society who project their fears upon the Other (for black theology, the Other is the African American oppressed community in solidarity with other groups who struggle). Somewhat similar to the Israelites of old, black people today embody the otherness assigned them by a skewed system of social relations, skewed not in their favor. For instance, the new king who came to power in Egypt stated: "'Look, the Israelite people are more numerous and more powerful than we. Come, let us deal shrewdly with them, or they will increase and, in the event of war, join our enemies and fight against us and escape from the land.' Therefore they set taskmasters over them to oppress them with forced labor" (Exod. 1:9-11). In today's society, the perception of the black race remains a negative indicator of evil and untrustworthiness. It serves, for those with resources to propagate such a vision, as a thesaurus for criminality, slovenliness, sexuality, entertainment, and non-intellectual labor. The social location of racial formation is either outstanding or standing out. The black self is perceived to excel beyond the norm (therefore an outstanding exception) or is expected to fail (hence standing out as a palpable disaster that, in commonsense understanding, is the African American norm); the black self is perceived to be either an unbelievable herculean success or a predicted collapse beneath the pressures of life. Race matters still in Protestantism and American culture as demonic presence (with accompanying synonyms) and as truncated two options of standing out or out standing.

The projected threat of a community defined by color pigmentation then operates at multiple levels. The monopolizers of power in society define a mission to "oppress them with forced labor" (as the Egyptian king would have it). The oppression of African Americans (particularly the poor) is spiritual and material. The latter oppression is to extract profit, either by a disproportionate presence in the ranks of the unemployed or by a general asymmetrical income and wealth scale detrimental to African American workers. On the spiritual plane, the attempt is to crush the memory, vision, and desire of African Americans to struggle for liberation and to practice freedom. Consequently, the monopolizers of power seek to anesthetize marginalized African American people, who then would have a blurred perception of who has the power to create a threat with them as the Other. And oppressive power holders attempt to implement a systematic locking out of the majority of black humanity from the earth's resources created by God. In contrast and in response, God works with the oppressed black community to co-constitute a new liberated, spiritual and material humanity. God is the Spirit of freedom for us—for those who suffer anti-black racism and other forms of oppression.

The fundamental act of God (that is, the doing and ethics of the divinity of liberation for us) is earthly emancipation for those in bondage, both spiritual and material, and this act operates in a co-constitutive fashion. The poor and brokenhearted are co-agents with divine intent to fashion a new emancipated human self. In a word, God works with us through the act of freedom as we constitute ourselves from oppression to a full reality of the highest potential of a liberated humanity. God liberates us totally and holistically. The basis of the new self is found in the ethics of divine freeing on earth. As one former slave asserted in faith: "Indeed I, with others, was often told by the minister how good God was in bringing us over to this country from dark and benighted Africa, and permitting us to listen to the sound of the gospel. To me, God also granted temporal freedom, which man without God's consent, had stolen away."[1] Though sacred power pervades the spiritual dimension, the giving of full humanity—the Spirit of liberation for us—is all the time manifest in the temporal realm as well. For the earth's dispossessed, "the sound of the gospel" is temporal freedom. We cannot encounter the language of the gospel, the work of Yahweh, without it being embedded or embodied in the tangible. The temporality of freedom might manifest in miniature acts of God or in obvious major divides in the fracturing of restraints which enchain oppressed humanity. Regardless, God's ethics and doing come to us or are granted to us as a sign of divine grace: the gift of the Spirit of total liberation is the manifest presence of a holy, omnipotent God whose constancy of being for us is eternal and whose glory appears in mercy, whose patience in working with and for us (despite our frail limitations) reflects the fullness of divine wisdom. The power of God to work on behalf of the oppressed never ceases.

God offers a liberating presence. We are not alone, for the covenantal engagement between Yahweh and the oppressed (both on the spiritual and material plane) arises out of the haunting testimony of the enslaved African American poor and the cries of the biblical witness. In the exodus drama, Yahweh proclaims to those in bondage: "'I have observed the misery of my people who are in Egypt; I have heard their cry on account of their taskmasters. Indeed, I know their sufferings, and I have come down to deliver them from the Egyptians, and to bring them up out of that land to a good and broad land" (Exod. 3:7-8). The power of God to work for the oppressed is eternal. In the divine time of patience and knowing all about the plight of the poor, Yahweh's demonstrative glory comes as the harnessing of divine might for the "little ones" of this earth. For the marginalized believer, God's acts are real.

In this believing of those without access to resources to live their full humanity, we discover a faith to act on the covenantal promise of Yahweh. The doctrine of God is liberation for those who believe and act on this faith: faith in liberation from personal and collective demons and for the practice of freedom in a new God-centered self and life. Having departed from slavery, Etna Elizabeth Dauphus confessed the following to an interviewer: "In setting forth her reasons for escaping she asserted that she was tired of slavery and an unbeliever in the doctrine that God made colored people simply to be slaves for white people; besides, she had a strong desire to 'see her friends in Canada.'"[2] Etna Dauphus exemplifies the co-constitution of the self, the divine and human agreement of transformation from the old to the new humanity. God provides the faith in liberation (as the divine intent for us) which frees the sufferer to act (in response to and in accord with that which is offered by Yahweh) on the word or doctrine of the freedom Spirit.

The divine gift of God, therefore, is both the active presence of the Spirit for us (that is, Yahweh acts on the hearing of the cries of the oppressed) and the granting of free agency as liberating common sense to the oppressed. The doing of the Spirit for us is the might of God made manifest and the gift to us is to act freely with divine purpose. As one fugitive ex-slave penned in her autobiography: "In no situation, with no flowery disguises, can the revolting institution [of bondage] be made consistent with the free-agency of [humanity] which we all believe to be the Divine gift."[3] The intertwining of divine act, human faith, divine gift, and human agency is the empowering covenant for a God-human co-constitution of oppressed humanity.

Moreover, often Yahweh's act of liberation deploys others on behalf of the oppressed. Though the marginalized of society, fundamentally, work in response to and in concurrence of God's doing, the divine grace of acting for and with the oppressed manifests in signs not necessarily from the marginalized community. Indeed, there are times when the poor have to be shrewd enough to perceive divine doing in the camps of the non-oppressed. Divine ethics of liberation can be, at times, clouded by the agency chosen by God to implement divine intent.

For instance, former chattel Rev. W. B. Allen relates how he, during slavery, refused to pray for the southern whites who wanted slaves to beseech God for Confederate victory. In contrast, Rev. Allen continued to pray for the victory of the northern forces, not out of any love for the Yankees, but because God's plan demanded the enslaved African American to achieve emancipation. Therefore, in response to divine initiative, black folk had to pray for the fulfillment of God's liberation ethics. Rev. Allen commented in reference to his white plantation owners: "I then told them that God was using the Yankees to scourge the slave-holders just as He had, centuries before, used heathens and outcasts to chastise His chosen people—the Children of Israel."[4]

In order to work with God, the oppressed must be open to and astute in reading the signs of the times that indicate God's doing. Consequently the marginalized have a vocational necessity to respond to and co-labor with God, even when the Spirit of liberation for us appears in non-oppressed sectors of society. In other words, the constitution of the self (through a covenant between God and poor people) requires the majority of society, those at the bottom of society, to employ a hermeneutics using a liberative lens. Otherwise the gift of the Spirit of liberation can be obscured by ruling sectors of any community claiming that they are acting for the least of the community. An interpretive liberative lens perceives the divinity of freedom employing whomever to aid the victims in the latter's movement for emancipation, even if the poor share no affection for the emancipation tools used by Yahweh.

Rev. Allen, displaying a radical interpretation from the perspective of the poor, stated: "Of course, I didn't have any love for any Yankees." It is in the dynamic of our act of prayer for emancipation responding to God's act of manipulating forces on the poor's behalf that we must carry out a consistent interpretive worldview in the reading of the signs of the times.

The Being of God—Ontology—Who Is God?

The Spirit of total liberation for us is expressed not only in God's acts but also in the being of God; God is an emancipating being for the oppressed of the earth and frees humanity spiritually and materially in an ongoing manner. This suggests the total and holistic being of the divinity as a constant dynamic, a process without beginning and without end. When Yahweh responded to the cries of the oppressed Israelites, Yahweh announced the ontology of God in the following proclamation: "God said to Moses, 'I AM WHO I AM.' He said further, 'Thus you shall say to the Israelites, "I AM has sent me to you." ' . . . This is my name forever, and this my title for all generations'" (Exod. 3:14, 15). The I AM God is a verb, to be, one of the simplest yet most complex and versatile action verbs in human languages. Thus the I AM God is both present, in the sense that the divinity exists here and now, and future present, in the sense that the sacred one will always be I AM WHO I AM. Yahweh not only acts on behalf of and in conjunction with the oppressed and poor, but, moreover, God is a God whose being is I WILL BE WHO I WILL BE. I AM and I WILL BE signify a oneness and eternity in the Spirit of liberation for us. God is for us and God will always be for us. For instance, while running away from slavery, Henry Bibb contemplated boarding a steamboat to a free state and immediately beseeched the being of God to embolden him in his emancipation journey from chattel states to northern territory. "Before I took passage, I kneeled down before the Great I Am, and prayed for his aid and protection, which He bountifully bestowed even beyond my expectation; for I felt myself to be unworthy. I then stept boldly on the deck."[5] I AM is the Spirit of unceasing aiding, protecting and rendering boldness. For the oppressed, in this moment, I AM becomes a comforting and defiant mood that transforms the human frail temperament of passivity and fear into one of empowered feelings for freedom. In the fearless disposition (that is, where the Spirit situates the liberating attributes of the I AM) of the human person, one discovers a profound transference of I WILL BE WHO I WILL BE. God shares with and gives us a part of God's being of holistic freedom—what former slave Henry Bibb termed a bountiful bestowing beyond the human expectation. Precisely in the holy transfer point of divine being into the human being is where one confronts the co-constitution of the marginalized from the poor, obsequious, insecure self into a comforted and dauntless new humanity.

The comforting of the Great I AM, moreover, comes to the being of the poor not in a general character but in a familiar way which allows the liberating Spirit to more easily deposit its aiding, protecting, and bold self into the weak and brokenhearted. Ex-chattel Kate Drumgoold offered a graphic portrayal of the familiar personality adopted by I AM. "So God has been a father and a loving mother and all else to me, and sometimes there has been enough of trials in this life to make me almost forget that I had this strong arm to save me from these trials and temptations; but when I fly to him I find all and in all in Him."[6] I AM assumes both parental genders, is both mother and father, so that the fear of the weak and marginalized will open itself more quickly to familiar personalities and allow the entrance of divine liberating comfort. Therefore the divine being is not a patriarchal reality with the attendant trappings of subordination of women. On the contrary, to fully be the Spirit of liberation for us, the very nature of God's being, the sacred ontology and who God is, is gender equality with full powers of emancipating comforting shared between mother and father, woman and man.

Any being masquerading as God but suffering from a designation as only male (without the equal sharing of spiritual and material power and a simultaneous naming as female) is a demonic personality whose intent, consciously or unconsciously, is not to bring freeing comfort to the oppressed. Instead such a demonic being can only construct an oppressive hierarchical configuration among the earth's marginalized voices. The very name of the Spirit of liberation for us is gender inclusive and free of gender asymmetry. Therefore the transference of emancipatory comfort shared in the human spirit of fear and hesitation must image the mother-father ontology of the God I WILL BE WHO I WILL BE. The Great I AM's being is gender inclusive and holistic, not privileging either gender, while ensuring the full liberation of all regardless of gender or skin color.

In other words, if the I AM brought comfort to the poor and wounded only in a male personality, then the familiarity of the female (in the above quote, the female and male personalities assumed the well known mother and father roles) would cease being part of I AM's ontology. God would be male only, thus denying the complementary and complex process of comfort yielded in a holistic parental expression. Just as children "fly to" their parents for aid, protection, and bold empowerment of themselves, so too do the oppressed interact with God's maternal and paternal being, the eternal dynamic of total liberation for us.

I AM not only encompasses mother and father. Ex-slave Kate Drumgoold's testimony asserts the all-inclusive nature of the liberating spirit: that God is "all else" connotes a sovereign being extending beyond any parameters, parental or otherwise. At another section of her slave narrative she also connects the co-constitution of the self and divine being with sovereignty imagery when she writes: "Lord, lead me on day by day. . . , and is not God the One that I should serve? And I love to serve Him and honor Him, for He is my all in all."[7]

Here an ex-slave's verbal witness implies the classic designation of God's sovereignty as Lord—the intimation that God rules the entire globe as God's kingdom. Though couched in a monarchical connotation of lordship sovereignty, the actual substance of God's rule ("all in all" suggests a sacred rule of the entire earth) surpasses such an exploitative medieval terminology. The real content of the Great I AM's lordship sovereign rule, in contrast, enables the human person's self-transformation and, therefore, bursts asunder the common linguistic understanding of an ancient monarchical dominion. In fact, the divine being as sovereign facilitates the weak and downtrodden to gain the glorious victory when they meet the reality of empowering sovereignty with trust. Again, the co-constitution of the self in full victory becomes operative in God's ontological reality when human initiative (that is, trust) meets and thereby co-labors with I WILL BE WHO I WILL BE's offering of a newly defined jurisdiction (that is, "the God of all this broad earth"). The reconfiguration of kingdom-sovereignty language associated with the divine being met by human trust engenders a triumphant fulfillment for the weak who remain faithful.

Like Kate Drumgoold, David Walker, a free black living in the northern section of the United States during the slavery period, links the sovereign rule of God with a reinterpreted ontological substance defining sovereignty as God being for the oppressed. "God rules in the armies of heaven and among the inhabitants of the earth, having his ears continually open to the cries, tears and groans of his oppressed people and being a just and holy Being will at one day appear fully in behalf of the oppressed, and arrest the progress of the avaricious oppressors."[8]

In addition, God is a just and holy being whose justice is the partiality to the groans of those who are heavy laden with unjust oppression. The justice of I AM becomes known or appears only in relation to the lack of justice expressed in the cries of the downtrodden and brokenhearted. Therefore in order for the divine being of liberation justice to become operative, the suffering cries of the marginalized must go up to God. The being of God is never in and of itself, but is always in a co-creative posture with those who are locked out of a society.

Closely related to justice is the holy dimension in the ontology of divine freedom. Holiness is sacred glory—a manifestation of the brilliant power and presence of liberation offered by the divine to the poor in cooperation with their cries of pain and resistance. Like justice, holiness or glory shines forth like the sun; it brings new life to those in need, but can burn the oppressive demonic and systemic configurations strangling those without resources, keeping them from realizing their full humanity. The holy glory of the being I AM operates in a dual fashion. The isness of God appears as justice for the weak, but destroys and "arrests the progress of the avaricious oppressors."

Knowledge of God—Epistemology—How Does God Reveal?

Our knowledge of God, the Spirit of total liberation for us, flows from the divine revelation which accompanies the acts and being of the divine freedom in cooperation with the efforts of self-affirmation by the oppressed. In a word, God not only acts on behalf of and with society's marginalized and presents a sacred being to be with those with suppressed voices, the Spirit of total liberation is also for the poor in an epistemology of liberation.

In the beginning as witnessed in the narrative of Genesis, God created all the resources of the earth: heavens, water, animals, birds, plants, light, the entire universe, and women and men. The creation of all that is visible testifies to the macrorevelation of the Spirit of liberation for us. For us, God gave the breath of life into the larger biological and material systems on earth. Originally, all of humankind had access to the created, visible resources; the totality of creation, therefore, locates on a grand scale our knowledge of God's reality and intent of equal sharing of the earth's rich resources for all humankind. The poor only have to observe the manifestation of nature to remember the divine revealed purpose that all that exists belongs to all of God's humanity. Whatever access to any part of creation is blocked by other human beings who may have committed the sin of monopolization of any aspect of creation should remind the poor that their journey toward full spiritual and material humanity necessitates a struggle to regain equal ownership and distribution of God's gift to all, daily displayed in the creation before us and for us.

Escaped slave James Curry shared his story of bondage in an antislavery meeting, his beliefs and biblical interpretation corroborating this knowledge of God found in the liberation creation account.

> When my master's family were all gone away on the Sabbath, I used to go into the house and get down the great Bible, and lie down in the piazza, and read, taking care, however, to put it back before they returned. There I learned that it was contrary to the revealed will of God, that one man should hold another as a slave. I had always heard

it talked among the slaves, that we ought not to be held as slaves; that our forefathers and mothers were stolen from Africa, where they were free men and free women. But in the Bible I learned that "God hath made of one blood all nations of men to dwell on all the face of the earth."[9]

Divine revelation (that is, the Spirit of total liberation for us displayed epistemologically) becomes evident when the slave's biblical inter-pretation suggests Yahweh's creation comprising two parts. One man-ifestation allows us to know God's emancipatory nature through the definitive creative act in equality among all nations and human beings. For the oppressed, the Bible verifies the original intent of equality among and non-privileging of skin colors. Despite the evil of racial discrimination brought about by the acts of white skin privi-leges, the poor know of divine purpose for the ultimate sharing of power in social relations—symbolized by the "one blood" shared by all people, regardless of color.

The second dimension of creation of the Spirit for us is God's allocation of the created earth for all humanity in the realm of geog-raphy and movement on a grand scale. The actual lands of the earth reveal knowledge about divine intent being the dispersal of all peo-ples freely throughout the globe. No one should suffer impediments in their movements, nor should anyone endure forced removal from a corner of God's earth. The stealing of others from one section of the earth and the monopolization of land and resources by a small elite contradict Yahweh's revelation. To know God, therefore, we can look to the visible testimony of the expansive globe—"to dwell on all the face of the earth." The epistemology of God embodying the liberating Spirit for us is also a macro-ecology marked by spacial and mobility arrangements.

Not only do we know God through major issues of power, wealth, and macroresources, God also reveals the divine liberating spirit for us in smaller, more focused social relations. This is not to say that the macro-issue of political economy, the structural relationships that command the exigencies of political economy, does not pertain to narrower, less global concerns. On the contrary, even on a micro level, we find God's self-epiphany given to us as an offer for the poor and all who side with them to co-constitute the self with sacred intent and to achieve a full spiritual and material humanity. In this regard, micro-epistemological unveilings manifest, among other things, as God inspired cartography and love between individuals.

The Song of Songs exhibits love as an everyday, microsocial relationship. A sacred bond of spiritual and sexual relationship between a man and woman embodies the possibility of full humanity defined by holy love. Part of the Spirit for us, therefore, is the recognition of the need for men and women to be free to love each other equally on diverse levels; and this is authenticated by the biblical witness. Though this book of Hebrew Scripture has often been interpreted by Jews as an analogy for Yahweh's relation to a chosen people and by Christians as Christ's connection with the church, nevertheless, both interpretations concur that a sacred intimacy of being loved and giving love in freedom applies. For my purposes, the text also reveals knowledge of God's emancipatory love between men and women.

> [Man]
> How graceful are your feet in sandals,
> O queenly maiden!
> Your rounded thighs are like jewels,
> the work of a master hand.
> Your navel is a rounded bowl
> that never lacks mixed wine.
> Your belly is a heap of wheat,
> encircled with lilies.
> Your two breasts are like two fawns. . . .
> O loved one, delectable maiden!
> You are stately as a palm tree,
> and your breasts are like its clusters.
> I say I will climb the palm tree
> and lay hold of its branches.
> Oh, may your breasts be like clusters of the vine. . . .
>   (7:1-3, 6b-8a)
>
> [Woman]
> I am my beloved's,
> and his desire is for me.
> Come, my beloved,
> let us go forth into the fields,
> and lodge in the villages;
> let us go out early to the vineyards,
> and see whether the vines have budded. . . .
> There I will give you my love.
>   7:10-12

Part of being fully free and present with one's lover in a divinely sanctioned intent, thus locating a site of knowledge about God, is appreciating the natural beauty of the other. An epistemology of sacred freedom is an aesthetics of natural attraction on a micro level. It is, moreover, an embracing of the physical body of one's lover in harmony with metaphors from nature, thereby underscoring a truly liberated intimate human union as a congruent nondominating connection to the naturally created order. The trembling and eagerness for love and the giving of love also mark an awareness of sacred presence in the midst of a monogamous consummation. The giving of the self in a free equality of sharing, sanctioned in holy intimate love, testifies to one form of self-constitution of the self that displays to the self, the other, the community, and nature, the reality of how God reveals God's purpose of liberation.

After love between individuals, the second microrelation, cartography (that is, mapping as an additional revelation of God for us on a micro level) is expressed in an ex-slave spiritual. The partial lyrics speak to calling on the appearance and knowledge of divine presence to be a pilot in a barren space: hence the cartography and mapping dimension of sacred reality. The slave song testifies to the oppressed person's comprehension when the holy appears as pilot: "Guide me, O thou great Jehovah, Pilgrim through this barren land." Here, through song, oppressed humanity calls out from a restricted and deleterious space for aid from God. To know God, then, is commensurate with how the marginalized understand the sacred-human connection and constitution not only in macropictures inclusive of political economic resource configurations, but also in space (barrenness), geography (land), and cartography (holy mapping).

In addition to micro- and macroconfigurations, racial cultural identity serves as a third site for divine knowledge of God for the oppressed. The identity of the marginalized African American race and culture within an unequal society does not materialize at the expense of other races and cultures. Precisely because of the enforced de-centering of oppressed African American race and culture from stated and unstated normative claims in the United States, God reveals God's self to affirm that which evil systems and persons suppress. Another ex-chattel attests to this epistemology of aesthetics and way of life (that is, race and culture) in the following: "The Lord, in His love for us and to us as a race, has ever found favor in His sight, for when we were in the land of bondage He heard the prayers of the faithful ones, and came to deliver them out of the Land of Egypt. For God loves those that are oppressed, and will save them when they cry unto him, and when they put their trust in Him."[10] Knowledge of sacred love for the oppressed race displays itself in the divine favor for the racial dimension of the oppressed; in a word, God embodies holy self within the color of the downtrodden. On this racial cultural identity level, among others, Yahweh is for the liberation of the black race as the divine-human dynamic (of the faithful crying out and trusting and the divinity hearing and delivering) unfolds.

Similarly, former slaves' biblical interpretation depicts knowledge of who God is for oppressed humanity today.

> He says that Ethiopia shall yet stretch forth her hand and all nations shall bow unto her. I long to see the day that the Ethiopians shall all bow unto God as the One that we should all bow unto, for it is to Him that we all owe our homage and to be very grateful to Him for our deliverance as a race. If we should fail to give him the honor due there would a curse come to us as a race, for we remember those of olden times were of the same descent of our people, and some of those that God honored most were of the Ethiopians, such as the Unica and Philop, and even Moses, the law-giver, was of the same seed.[11]

God expresses what God's actions and being are in the racial heritage of the biblical witness and its genealogy down to present African American people. The Ethiopia paradigm locating divine intent, consequently, speaks to the awareness of God in black races and culture and to the need for all who would support marginalized black humanity to acknowledge divine intent (that is, for "all nations [to] bow unto her"). Ethiopia, in the biblical story, embodies polyvalent purposes. On the one hand, it accents a special place for poor African Americans by affirming ("God honored most") their confidence in their black phenotypical selves and ebony way of being in the world. Ethiopia underscores acceptance of racial cultural identity. At the same time, and not in contradiction, God presents comprehension of the sacred self to all who would engage and embrace Ethiopia for their own relation to God. Ethiopia underscores a universal epistemology for all by all accepting African American racial cultural identity.

Knowledge of God comes through language, a final exemplar of sacred epistemological encounters. Language, especially proclamation of what God has done for the unlettered and the outcast, acts as a powerful medium for God's making God's self known. Usually it is in the attempt of the oppressed to claim her or his voice in a context of demonically stifling circumstances that one discovers God's ordaining significance for the poor to speak with liberating power. One African American woman during slavery instructs our contemporary juxtaposition of talking and sacredness:

I also held meetings in Virginia. The people there would not believe that a coloured woman could preach. And moreover, as she had no learning, they strove to imprison me because I spoke against slavery: and being brought up, they asked by what authority I spake? and if I had been ordained? I answered, not by the commission of men's hands: if the Lord had ordained me, I needed nothing better.[12]

Preaching, in this instance the prime example of language, comes from the commissioning of Yahweh's ordination of a poor black, unlettered woman who suffered both from the white Christian community and from backward theological perspectives in her own oppressed community. Moreover, the potency of the poor accepting divine holiness in language can even cause oppressors to be fearful and, consequently, threaten imprisonment of the oppressed voice asserting its God-given right to utter a word about the goodness of God. The fear of losing racial, gender, and formal educational privileges brings to the surface the demon within the victimizing group and forces the restriction of authority in sacred language matters to a human hierarchy, with the bottom rung occupied by black women.

In this regard, by supporting the restructuring of hierarchy into equality by lifting up the bottom rung, recognition of black women's preaching or saying a sacred word aids the knowledge of God by perceiving divine revelation in the African American poor woman's voice. Furthermore, as another black female former slave indicates, the language reality of God's knowledge offered to the least in society, accompanies a divine-human co-constitution dynamic: "Chile, God's a talkin' man an' you gotta talk back to him."[13]

The Attributes of God

The characteristics of God's actions, being, and knowledge given as grace to and for the co-constitution of the poor (in particular the African American oppressed) through macro, micro, racial cultural identities, and linguistic formations express themselves in disparate attributes. Put differently, divine attributes work within the oppressed community to offer hope in and continued struggle for the Spirit of total liberation or holistic freedom for the full spiritual and material humanity of the marginalized.

GLORY AND UNITY

The glory of God is God's unity. It shines forth in signs of liberation like the brilliance of the sun's rays bringing nurturing life to struggling and growing plants freeing themselves from the encasement of too restricting seed shells. The evidence of divine holistic freedom for the poor, therefore, pours out as a radiant light signifying God's acts, being, and knowledge presented from Yahweh to the marginalized of society. The God of liberation is one in a brilliantly manifested sacred unity with women and men and in a singular divine intent to co-labor with the dispossessed in their journey to full humanity. In a word, divine glory and unity offer a light of hope in the realization of freedom for those brokenhearted confined by various levels of oppression.

For instance, the commentary of a former slave about the cessation of the Civil War and the legal termination of slavery testifies to the nexus between God brilliantly supplying emancipatory signs and the obligation of the exploited to decipher and embrace what divinity provides for the oppressed. "God gave us war signs which spoke of the dissolution of the Union." For the underside of history, momentous earthly events regarding freedom indicate confirmation of biblical injunctions in which Yahweh shows forth the unity of the holy will. Continuing his commentary, the former slave asserted: "when the proclamation of freedom was proclaimed; it sent a thrill of joy through every avenue of my soul. I exclaimed, 'Glory to God, peace on earth, and good will to men,' for the year of jubilee has come!"[14]

The oppressed perceive sacred glory because of their ability to decode so-called secular signs by deploying the rules of faith granted to those who hold on to the brilliant hope indicators evident in both the biblical story and in the poor's commonsense folk wisdom experience. And though the process of deciphering such freeing signs offers a transitory uncertainty about the exact contours of the new that is breaking in like sun rays at dawn, God's glory of eventual liberation is one certainty. Sacred glory, therefore, signifies the appointed time for the letting go of God's people in bondage, thus predicting the ultimate new humanity of the poor to come (and thereby all peoples) and reenacting a primal sign of the Exodus story in which Yahweh calls forth to Pharaoh to "let my people go."

Furthermore, when God's glory shines forth for the poor, its dazzling light covers all of humanity, because in the liberation of the majority of the earth's people, the minority who monopolize multi-level resources (that is, macro, micro, linguistic, and racial cultural identity) attain an equal status with the rest of empowered humankind. The removal of the majority as the basis for the rule of the minority enables the minority to change its status within a new democratized relation of equality and freedom for all. That is why a sign of emancipation for the marginalized renders "peace on earth, and good will to" all women and men. In the particularity of the marginalized community, one encounters the universal implications of holistic emancipation.

Moreover the liberative light of the divinity shining glory on the marginalized community is the condition of possibility for the now freed poor to offer praises of glory back to God ("I exclaimed, 'Glory to God'"). The sacred act of glory coexists with the victim's praising glory in a co-constituting dynamic of transforming and creating a new humanity of liberation.[15]

God's glory is divine unity; the one definite and unified intentional brilliance of the holy is the freeing of those who believe, cry out, and struggle for full humanity. When sacred grace shines upon those in captivity, it is accompanied by the execution and reaffirmation of the liberating divinity. Yahweh freed the oppressed and bound Hebrews and made a covenant to forever liberate them as long as they felt obligated to recognize the oneness of a God of liberation. "You are my witnesses, says the LORD, and my servant whom I have chosen, so that you may know and believe me and understand that I am [God]. Before me no god was formed, nor shall there be any after me. I am the LORD, and besides me there is no savior" (Isa. 43:10-11).

Arguing against a multiplicity of white supremacy gods during the slavery period, an African American abolitionist penned these similar remarks: "God made [humanity] to serve Him alone, and that [humanity] should have no other Lord or Lords but Himself—that God Almighty is the sole proprietor or master of the whole human family. . . . God is a God of justice."[16] The unity in the lordship of God is not a blind unity of a peasant to a feudal lord, but one conditioned and defined by justice and liberation. Lordship, in this liberative instance, connotes and denotes the enhancement of full spiritual and material freedom of oppressed people, particularly those suffering from racial discrimination.

In the poor African American woman, however, the fullness of the oneness of the divinity of freedom becomes even more apparent because here one encounters God's multidimensional liberating acts. Old Elizabeth, remembering her trials and labors as chattel property of white plantation owners, recalled the advice given to her. "At parting my mother told me that I had 'nobody in the wide world to look to but God.' . . . [The overseer] tied me with a rope, and gave me some stripes of which I carried the marks for weeks. After this time, finding as my mother said, I had none in the world to talk to but God."[17] Black women endure a tripartite pain—the exploitation of labor, the discrimination of race, and the oppression of male supremacy. Hence, in the tradition of female generations passing on commonsense theological wisdom to succeeding generations, God's brilliance of freedom is one for all three dimensions of poor and working-class African American women.

In sum, God is one in sacred acts, being, and knowledge, united in the purpose of liberation. God is one in the divinity's uniting with the poor for the total emancipation of the victims. And God is one in that all other gods seeking allegiance elsewhere are false. The radiant signs of the sacred are one in freedom.

RIGHTEOUSNESS AND OMNIPRESENCE

God's righteousness is always present, whether the poor and the rich are clear in its recognition or confused in its interpretation. The righteousness of God is justice for the downtrodden and brokenhearted. In his epistle to his former master, escaped slave Henry Bibb proclaimed the following in faith:

> I mean that you shall know that there is a just God in heaven, who cannot harmonize human slavery with the Christian religion: I mean that you shall know that there is a law which is more binding upon the consciences of slaves than that of Congress, or any other human enactment—and I mean that you shall know that all of your slaves have escaped to Canada, where they are just as free as yourself, and that we have not forgotten the cruel treatment which we received at your hands while in a state of slavery.[18]

The law of divine justice surpasses the contrived human impediments and exploitative stumbling blocks manufactured by even the highest arbitrators on earth. Sacred justice, at least in the mind of the poor, dwells deep within the psychological and moral recesses of the least in society. God's righteousness, therefore, protects the downtrodden, saves them from evil entrapments, and gives them victory in the end ("In you, O LORD, I seek refuge; do not let me ever be put to shame; in your righteousness deliver me" Ps. 31:1). Because God is (in the present tense) justice for those in need of salvation right now, they know and believe that God's grace of protection surrounds them in the midst of daily and long-term battles. Victory is certain because God defeats the enemies of the least in society. The biblical witness provides the historical certainty of the current efficacy of divine victory by way of justice: the saving of the poor from personal and systemic evil, in the past and now and for always.

Even within excruciating circumstances, one in which ordinarily death appears imminent, God rearranges the situation if the oppressed are involved in order to provide a safe haven for the abused. For instance, runaway slave Old Joe escaped to the woods to keep from receiving a whipping from his master.

> You ought to hear him tell about the rattlesnakes that used to keep him company in the woods. He said the snakes got so used to him that they stayed under his moss bed at night. Sometimes he could hear them turning over under him. The snakes would go off in the day and come back at night. He could kill them if he wanted to, but he was glad to have them for company. You see, my child, God will take care of his people.[19]

No space or place evades the all pervading presence of God's justice. God even makes it right for the fugitive in the midst of nature's deadly creatures. Because it is unfair for the natural creatures of death to harm the fugitive, God tames the seemingly harmful things or situations and turns their relationship into one of friendship, comforter, and fellow traveler. Whether in the heavens, among humans, or deep within the recesses of nature, God is there in old and new times. "And I heard a loud voice from the throne saying, 'See, the home of God is among mortals. He will dwell with them as their God; they will be his peoples, and God . . . will be with them; [God] will wipe every tear from their eyes. Death will be no more'" (Rev. 21:3).

The nature of this heavenly voice speaking out in full and perpetual presence is a heartwarming and encouraging voice of liberation. The beauty of God's justice voice accompanying the downtrodden is that God's righteousness does not depend on our strength. Quite the contrary, our weakness is God's present strength. Even in times when the realization of righteousness on earth stares us in the face and is within our grasp, we often stumble. Because the full victory of material and spiritual freedom requires a co-constitution of both human effort and divine effort, we cannot make it alone. That is where God enters to carry us through. The presence of the divine vision toward liberation breathes an invigorating energy for us to press on toward the mark. In the memory of one runaway slave:

> I sat down by the road-side and wept, prayed, and wished myself back where I first started. I thought it was all over with me forever. . . . I thought one [*sic*] while I would turn back . . . and give myself up to be

captured; then I thought that would not do; a voice spoke to me, 'not to make a fool of myself, you have to go far from home . . . , keep on towards freedom, and if you are taken let it be heading towards freedom.' then I took fresh courage and pressed my way onward towards the north with anxious heart.[20]

God manifests total presence with a perspective of liberation especially in our hour of doubt.

It is the very nature of God to give a liberating perspective because God acts as judge high above the minutiae of everyday human pain. Such a height gives a panoramic view of all creation. God watches from above in order to best perceive where to realize justice among humankind. For example, Robert Carr ran away from Maryland and remarked that his former master could not escape from a right relation with God. The master's "religious pretensions might pass among slaveholders, but that it would do him no good when meeting the Judge above."[21] Because the divinity is above suggests a permanence which permeates all time.

Indeed, because righteousness guides God, God can bring about right relationship at any time, whether past, present, or future. God's presence for society's abused means the divine can reach back into time (which then becomes God's present time), intervene in the contemporary time (which is the present time experienced by humanity), and stretch forth the long hand of justice into the future (which is to bring the ultimate taste of right relations back into human present time).

Former slave Samuel Northup, in particular, confirms this permanent time presence on the divine scale. Northup witnessed the brutal beating of a female slave and thought the following about justice and time for his cruel master: "Thou devil, sooner or later, somewhere in the course of eternal justice, thou shalt answer for this sin!"[22] Though God sits high, the divinity looks low and involves God's self in the arbitration of right and wrong on earth. And this arbitration occurs in eternity as eternal justice. It is present for all time for the doers of evil and the victims of unjust social relations.

The unjust relations caused by those with oppressive power (on the racial, class, gender, or sexual orientation levels) will suffer the decision of God's ever present righteousness. Injustice is evil and a curse on the created order. The created ecology was originally intended for peace and equal sharing of all of God's resources without a hierarchy of exploitation where, by virtue of skin color, gender designation, or wealth ownership, some parts of humanity attain the height of advantage over other parts. Only God sits high and looks low. And even the divine sitting above is because the ethics, being, and knowledge of God are all liberation for the poor and abused of society.

Therefore when there exists a disruption in justice relations among people, it is an affront to God's nature of justice, a curse affecting both the least in society and a challenge against God. Such a curse compels God to act and to be in the presence of the voiceless. Evil social relations suffer consequences of retribution—the realignment of unjust human connections. Ex-slave Lucy Delaney from St. Louis, Missouri, knew this fact when she cried out: "Slavery! Cursed slavery! What crimes has it invoked! And, oh! What retribution has a righteous God visited upon these traders in human flesh!"[23]

The presence of righteousness, however, does not align itself with any sector of society because of any power or privilege that particular sector has. Even in the case of the poor, abused, and locked out, God grants the presence of righteousness because God does not endorse evil. Present righteousness goes to the poor because poverty contradicts God's ethics, being, and revealed knowledge of divine intent. Rev. G. W. Offley, born a slave in Maryland, substantiated this claim when he wrote: "Our family theology teaches that God is no respecter of persons, but gave his son to die for all, bond or free, black or white, rich or poor. If we keep his commandments, we will be happy after death."[24] Moreover, this is additional good news for the poor. Why? Because righteousness in our time is blind, all are equal before the divine bar of justice of God. The poor and marginalized should see themselves and act out in the now as free persons. The divine judgment bar employs a norm of freedom.

Divine justice, furthermore, requires us in the present moment to fulfill the mandates of struggling for liberation and practicing freedom. In this instance, this means an ethics of justice. The biblical witness calls us to this challenge and way of life: "Learn to do good; seek justice, rescue the oppressed, defend the orphan, plead for the widow" (Isa. 1:17).

CONSTANCY AND ETERNITY

Closely related to divine righteousness and omnipresence is God's constancy and eternal nature. The constant fact of God as the Spirit of liberation for us endures throughout eternity. This does not change, and it will be real even if all else perishes. The biblical witness attests to the following: "The Spirit is the guarantee that we shall receive what God has promised his people, and this assures us that God will give complete freedom to those who are his" (Eph. 1:14). God the Spirit for us insures consistently the practice of freedom for the poor in their struggle for liberation. And this freedom is complete; a multilevel, polyvalent freedom on various levels—the macropolitical economic, the micro everyday, the linguistic, and the racial cultural identity. Therefore the actual ongoing process of liberation from evil targets a multiplex reality of race, class, gender, and sexual orientation discriminations.

God works with us within the complex snares of life from which we attempt to seek liberation. At the same time, the divinity offers the gift to assume a proactive posture and actually live our lives as if we are free; to live with God's gift is to practice freedom. God gives complete, not partial, freedom to the oppressed and brokenhearted. What we can rely on is this constant fact of God being God in a complete and holistic revelation of grace forever. Again, it is the assurance that makes all this possible, this divine-human co-laboring that renders a new life for the faithful who struggle and practice that which is offered to oppressed humanity.

And if God is constant in the divine promises, then we too must act in faith and witness in a constant fashion. One ex-slave speaks to the necessity to answer one's calling to follow this way: "Our family theology . . . teaches that if God calls and sanctifies a person to do some great work, that person is immortal until his work is done; that God is able and will protect him from all danger or accident in life if he is faithful to his calling or charge committed by the Lord."[25] Constancy does not abandon those human beings who work with the divine plan and respond in faith. Constancy does away with all fears because it signifies God's sanctification in the calling to work with the Spirit of liberation for us. Moreover, this sanctification or being made holy protects the person and makes her or him immortal to the evils that will attempt to thwart one's commissioning or anointing. Immortality in the work of the Spirit of liberation for us means that we are committed by and accompanied by God's constant gift of complete freedom until our work is finished.

And the constancy of this assurance comforts the weak because this complete freedom lasts forever. "Long ago you laid the foundation of the earth, and the heavens are the work of your hands. They will perish, but you endure; they will all wear out like a garment . . . and they pass away" (Ps. 102:25-27). God who is the Spirit of liberation for us reveals to us a guarantee and a promise that serve as cornerstones to the foundation of our faith that forever and ever the constant gift of complete freedom will reign. Total liberation is always, with no beginning, middle, or end.

OMNIPOTENT AND MERCIFUL

God is the only being who is both all powerful and merciful. "Our God is merciful and tender. God will cause the bright dawn of salvation to rise on us" (Luke 1:78). The mercy of God reveals in God's power to help the captives go free, to save them from their enemies, to enable them to serve God's intent without fear, and to lead them into a peace of freedom. God has the power to "cause the bright dawn of salvation to rise on us" for us. As one ex-slave records:

> When the time had arrived for us to start, we blew out the lights. Knelt down, and prayed to our Heavenly Father mercifully to assist us, as he did his people of old, to escape from cruel bondage; and we shall ever feel that God heard and answered our prayer. Had we not been sustained by a kind, and I sometimes think, special providence, we could never have overcome the mountainous difficulties which I am now about to describe.[26]

Linked to the working and poor people's faith in the historical record of what God has done, mercy is the divinity assisting the downtrodden to flee from persecution or unjust situations. Mercy hears and answers and offers a special kind hand to sustain the marginalized on their journey into freedom space and time. Therefore, all these parts of mercy enable the voiceless to get over a mountain of tribulations. Again, the emancipation process combines a co-constitution dynamic in which divinity and humanity labor together for full spiritual and material freedom. In other words, the mercy of an all powerful God does not exist all by itself. The poor must maintain faith in the heat of the struggle to simply live daily and to gear up for the long-term journey. Many times, given the sinister nature of race, class, gender, and sexual orientation stumbling blocks, the least in society will endure trials and tribulation as a test of their faith in the Spirit of total liberation for us. The co-constitution of the new liberated humanity derives from God's mercy and the poor's faith in action (1 Peter 1:3-7).

In God's mercy there is power, moreover, because the very name of God is El Shaddai, meaning "I am God almighty" (Gen. 17:1). And this God does whatever the divinity pleases (Ps. 115:3); God is a mighty powerful Spirit of liberation for us. David Walker confirms God who does whatever is needed for the bottom of society. "There is a God the Maker and preserver of all things, who rewards in this and in the world to come,—we may fool or deceive, and keep each other in the most profound ignorance, beat, murder and keep each other out of what is our lawful rights, or the rights of man, yet it is impossible for us to deceive or escape the Lord Almighty."[27]

Walker's testimony verifies God as the all powerful one who makes, preserves, rewards now and later, and knows all things. Divine power even employs nature to realize God's potent commitment to just relations. An unnamed former slave remembers one of the cruelest white masters in the entire chattel institution. "Bob Lampkin was the meanest slave owner I ever knowed." This master would beat his slaves and any other black chattel he saw. The ex-slave resumes the story: "He was so mean 'til God let him freeze to death. He come to town and got drunk and when he was going back home in his buggy, he froze stiff going up Race Creek Hill."[28] Divine power calls into service the natural elements to remove the oppression of the wicked from the innocent.

Often, the wicked hide beneath the cloak of established religion, especially the mantle of Christianity. Somehow, evil deploys the name of an accepted religion as a more effective mechanism to attempt the subversion of God's power and mercy. Oppressors, by going to church on Sundays, partaking of the Holy Communion, calling themselves Christians, and owning a Bible seem to think that one's self-designation as Christian can block or hide one's practice of domination over individuals or groups. The power of God breaks through correct rhetoric to discern incorrect practice. In particular, religious clergy who oppress or misuse the poor participate in a grave affront against God's calling to them to preach good news to the captives, let the downtrodden go free, and to facilitate their ownership of the earth's resources. Former chattel Leah Garrett recalls:

> In dem days, preachers wuz just as bad and mean as anybody else. Dere wuz a man who folks called a good preacher but he wuz one of the meanest mens I ever seed. When I wuz in slavery under him he done so many bad things 'til God soon kilt him. . . . [The slavemaster put one of his slave women] up in what us called de swing, and beat her 'til she couldn't holler. De poe thing already had heart trouble; dat's why he put her in de kitchen, but he left her swingin' dar and went to church, preached, and called hisself servin' God. When he got back home she wuz dead.[29]

When it comes to the well-being of the poor, no one is exempt if they trespass against the helpless. Even Christians and pastors cannot use their religion or their "backwards collars" to evade the potency of divine justice. Even the power of the institutionalized religion of Christianity cannot protect the guilty from the Spirit's power of liberation.

Finally, because God's quest with the poor to constitute a full spiritual and material humanity on many planes touches both the victim and the victimizers, God works not only on the oppressed but also on the oppressor. Divine mercy and omnipotence know no boundaries and exclude no one. The grace of merciful omnipotence extends out to the perpetrators of institutional and individual exploitation. An ex-bondperson writes: "When I considered him accusing me of stealing, when I was so innocent, and had endeavored to make him satisfied by every means in my power, that I was so, but he still persisted in disbelieving me. . . . I forgave my master in my own heart for all this, and prayed to God to forgive him and turn his heart."[30]

God has power over all of creation and over one's spiritual and material life and death, whether one is poor or rich. The power of the merciful God is a divine mercy which realizes potency in forgiveness and pity. Similarly, it is an omnipotent God of mercy who grants the power of the poor in history. For it is impossible for the One to forsake the little ones; this is contrary to God's being, acts, and revelation. To be the only force who is all power is an awesome beingness. Yet it is omnipotence tempered by compassionate mercy. Whoever engages in the immediate and long-term effort to be with and at the service of the least in society will enjoy the gift of this all powerful mercy and this merciful power. "For mortals it is impossible, but not for God; for God all things are possible" (Mark 10:27). Deliverance through salvation from oppression is the compassionate revelation of divine potency.

GRACE AND HOLINESS

Grace is an undeserved gift coming from the holy. The spirit for us grants us the gift of liberation. Paul states: "Now to one who works, wages are not reckoned as a gift but as something due. But to one who without works trusts [God] who justifies the ungodly, such faith is reckoned as righteousness" (Rom. 4:4-5). Faith and belief in a God of liberation is the co-constituting precondition for God's grace of salvation and liberation. Co-constitution of the free self derives from the oppressed person's belief, on the one hand, and, on the other, the actual event of the divine working with the oppressed to realize salvation and liberation. Grace, therefore, exhibits a divine gift in spite of frail efforts, whether progressive or reactionary, on the part of the poor; for the emancipation of the latter never materializes on its own. Only through belief and faith in the Spirit for us (that is, that which is in us but greater than us) will total liberation eventuate. It is in this sense that grace is not contingent on human efforts.

However, once grace pervades the human person of faith, her or his actions for freedom fall within the sphere of and are anointed by the effects of divine grace. The efforts of the poor at constituting the new self of freedom become purposeful when they base their struggle on the faith in the Spirit of freedom for us. The divine and human constitution of the liberated new humanity and full humanity occurs with the presence of grace, faith, holy action, and human action guided by holy purpose.

In this way, grace is a gift of freedom of God's spirit of liberation for us. It freely comes to those at the bottom of society and to those experiencing pain. The very nature of God is I AM for the weak. The very ethics of God is God's actions for the downtrodden. The very knowledge of God is divine revelation with the little ones in society suffering alone and with oppressed communities.

One former slave verifies the attribute of divine grace in the following story:

> My master and Burrow [a white man who did whippings of blacks] went forward, and I followed behind. I looked up to heaven and prayed fervently to God to hear my prayer, and grant me relief in this hour of adversity; expecting every moment to be whipped until I could not stand; and blessed be God that he turned their hearts before they arrived at the place of destination: for, on arriving there, I was acquitted. God delivered me from the power of the adversary. Blessed be his name, he heard my prayer in the hour of adversity, and delivered me from the enemy. . . . [I] put my trust, and offered my prayers to my heavenly Father, who heard and answered them.[31]

Here we find an African American worker boxed in by an earthly master and an agent hired to inflict pain on a black body. Perhaps the latter was "guilty" of impudence, thinking differently from his master, or even running away. At the lowest point, just on the threshold of punishment, this victim has no other human option of resistance. Consequently, he surrenders to prayer and hopes for a miracle of deliverance through grace. Thus there is nothing that the poor can do on their own to bring about their own release from pain. To create the new liberated humanity, they must turn to faith in a God who grants freedom freely. This free gift of grace means that the poor and the brokenhearted do not have to do anything as solitary victims of spiritual and earthly forces in the guise of wicked people who attempt to usurp God's authority, attempt to turn them away from God, and whip them into submission. If the oppressed struggle to reconstitute themselves only on their own efforts, this would mean a contradiction of sacred power. In reality (in the reality of divine time offered for us), God is, acts, and knows us freely.

The lesson from Ephesians, furthermore, underscores divine grace: "For is it God's grace that you have been saved through faith. It is not the result of your own efforts, but God's gift, so that no one can boast about it" (Eph. 2:8-9). There is a mutual interplay between the oppressed's faith in the grace of liberation and the freedom of God's gift of liberation. Put differently, no human actions alone yield the freedom of the new human being (that is, one who struggles for liberation and practices freedom). However, because the captive turns to God (the Spirit for us whose action, being, and knowledge is liberation) with faith, God chooses freely to set the captive free. It is a co-constituting process with divine grace vivifying our embracing of faith and amplifying our efforts to be full spiritual and material human beings. If the poor and the oppressed misinterpret the grace dimensions of the God-human co-constitution, then the victims of society stumble into hubris.

Though the freedom of the oppressed and the forlorn comes about through human effort, it is, nevertheless, the accent on divine grace that humbles the victims in their struggle for personal and social transformation. Otherwise the poor are subject to inflated arrogance and a disproportionate sense of exaggerated self-awareness, thereby splintering the dynamic interpenetrating process of the Spirit of liberation for us who empowers our faith and our acts.

Moreover, grace is a complete gift. God's grace speaks to us in a language that the poor can understand and this divine word has always been offered freely. The gospel according to John testifies to divine voice being ever present: "In the beginning was the Word, and the Word was with God, and the Word was God" (John 1:1). God's grace affirms our created self as good (Gen. 1:31); that is to say, our racial cultural identity as created by divine breath or spirit for us is valued in God's sight just as we are without trying to change our physical, cultural, or racial selves into something else. God's grace gives us stewardship and protection over all the wealth, income, and power in society. It is a collective gift for all, especially granting dominion to the majority of the world, the poor and working people.

Dominion means collective ownership of all wealth and resources whereby no one person or small group has a monopoly on God's gift of creation (Gen. 1:27-30).

Furthermore, God's grace means that God promises never to leave the mistreated ones alone during any moment of the day, because God knows the very hairs on our head. Grace is an everyday micro-event. This is what the Negro spiritual means when it states that the divinity constantly watches over us—"My eye is on the sparrow because I know God watches over me."

Therefore, grace is complete on many levels. Ex-chattel William McWhorter elaborates this point when he confesses: "Folks ought to git ready for a better world dan dis to live in when dey is finished on dis earth, and I'se sho glad our Good Lord saw fit to set us free from sin and slavery. If he hadn't done it, I sho would have been dead long ago."[32] Grace brings a total life away from death. It frees both on the level of individual sin and on the societal or systematic level.

For a black theology of liberation, regardless of one's station in life, God freely liberates us and is for us in a total manner. Nothing escapes divine presence. More specifically, divine freedom is holiness. Holiness covers a totality of situations, oppressed conditions, and individual pain—women and men, black and white, diverse sexual orientations, and the well-being of nature and all creation. And through the poor of all colors without wealth, it opens up the possibility that all classes will become one as collective stewards of wealth. Holiness is the grace of God's freedom that sets the whole creation free. "The holy God of Israel sets us free—God's name is the Lord Almighty" (Isa. 47:4).

Not only does holiness encompass a diversity of situations and peoples, it is, furthermore, the holiness of God that acts for us in the secular and sacred realms of the everyday. Indeed, there is no separation of the sacred from the secular. If there were, God's grace of freedom and liberation would become fractured, partial, and provincial. On the contrary, the sacred appears, manifests, embodies all of creation, and dwells especially in each vicissitude of the poor, the lonely, and the weak. The opportunity that God grants for us to be free persons spiritually and materially has no boundaries, because God will leave no space, place, time, or event unchallenged or undisputed in the divine work to make each individual and each oppressed community whole.

The grace of holiness to the oppressed and the poor, though freely given, demands, in addition, that the victims of society also have faith in and live by the grace of freedom and liberation. Holiness makes a normative claim for a belief in and a witness for liberation. Holiness, in this sense, is not a cheap grace. To be in the sphere of God's holiness (that is, as God encompasses a diversity of situations and peoples, and as God's presence permeates the secular and sacred) denotes a covenantal response on the part of the oppressed and the weak.

In order for "kings" to release the "deeply despised" and the "servant of rulers" and in order for the marginalized to receive the honor and respect of earthly powers and principalities (Isa. 49:7), those at the bottom of society must fulfill their obligation to the grace of holiness. They must move out on rock-like faith in the God of salvation. As Hannah proclaims in 1 Samuel: "There is no Holy One like the Lord, no one besides you; there is no Rock like our God" (1 Sam. 2:2).

WISDOM AND PATIENCE

God's wisdom includes knowledge of all things, but particularly about those enchained to forces of spiritual and material harm. God's wisdom knows all things about the conditions, feelings, and thoughts of the abused. And God's wisdom knows how to deliver and save them from these harmful situations. We can draw theological lessons from former slave William Summerson when he proclaims the following: "While I was in the Court-House, and the traders were examining me, I lifted my heart to the Almighty, and besought him to make a way for me to escape. After I left the Court-House, I went back to the store, and that night, the last that was left me, as I prayed and groaned before the Almighty, He put a plan into my head which carried me safely to freedom."[33] A divine plan flows from the all-knowing God always willing to extend sacred wisdom into the depths of the very mind of the individual victim caught and held for unjust punishment. In contrast to the rulers and abusers of power, God does not keep understanding and knowledge from the little ones of society. God democratizes the flow of information so that no one has advantage or privilege over another. In fact, the spread of this information is not a neutral act in and of itself. More concretely, this plan presents a path of escape to a safe haven away from any type of oppression (that is, people and situations that cause danger).

Not only is wisdom intertwined with the safety of the individual, it also covers an entire class of exploited people. "Great is our Lord, and abundant in power," writes the Psalmist. "His understanding is beyond measure. The Lord lifts up the downtrodden; he casts the wicked to the ground" (Ps. 147:5-6). This understanding cannot be measured because that would put boundaries around and control the divine way of being and acting for the downtrodden. Thus God's wisdom is boundless for oppressed sectors of society and realizes a power that, on the one hand, overflows in the direction of the victims, and, on the other, flows over the wicked, throwing them down from their own human created arrogance and evil. The wisdom of God is the Spirit of liberation for us.

In addition, Proverbs sums up the diverse dimensions of divine wisdom:

> For the Lord gives wisdom; from his mouth come knowledge and understanding; he stores up sound wisdom for the upright; he is a shield to those who walk blamelessly, guarding the paths of justice and preserving the way of his faithful ones. Then you will understand righteousness and justice and equity, every good path; for wisdom will come into your heart, and knowledge will be pleasant to your soul; prudence will watch over you; and understanding will guard you. It will save you from the way of evil.
>
> Prov. 2:6-12

God offers freely: knowledge that is sound and not weak or off-the-cuff; understanding that makes righteousness, justice, and equality real in communities broken by incorrect and oppressive relations between and among people; a guard that will preserve and watch over the correct path to maintain justice; and ultimately salvation, which is the sacred acting with the victims in the process of being delivered from evil.

Furthermore, divine wisdom acts like a strong and guiding hand. Though this takes place on a daily and minute basis, often it becomes more apparent in major social conflicts between evil (for example, the systemic privileges and oppression caused by race, class, gender, or sexual orientation) and good (the individual and groups struggling to realize the full humanity of all). The Civil War provided such a macrotheater of decisive conflict for former slave James L. Smith:

> When President Lincoln called for men to defend the country, the call was for white men. Our martyred President, proud in the strength of his high position said, "the Union must be saved with slavery, if it can, without it, if it must." Did he forget that at the great wheel of state there was a guiding hand, stronger and mightier, and more just than his. Truly, "God moves in a mysterious way, His wonders to perform.[34]

In this instance, an official of privilege, Lincoln, "proud in the strength of his high position" gives himself to pride in self-knowledge coupled with an assumption that he is the ultimate arbiter over the affairs of a nation. Yet the difference between divine wisdom and its relation to the victims, on the one hand, and the self-centered wisdom of society's ruling representatives, on the other, is precisely the fact that the latter rely on the wicked things of this world (self-importance and privileged dominance over others). In distinction, the God-poor wisdom encounter gains a life activated by God's infusing of a knowledge perspective yielding holy victory.[35] Restated, the wisdom of God for us is like a guiding hand.

Sacred wisdom will most definitely bring about salvation and freedom for the sufferers in this world even though divine patience is often confusing to the oppressed. The wisdom of God can require a profound appreciation of the patience of God during the process of deliverance. Rephrasing one Negro spiritual, we can discern the interrelationship between patience and time: "God may not come when you call God, but God is always right on time."

God's patience takes on diverse forms from the human perspective, at once slow and at other times much faster. However, from the divine perspective and action, patience and time surpass human contemplation. Regardless, patience provides salvation and deliverance from evil on earth. For God, divine patience overrules the human understanding of time. "But do not ignore this one fact, beloved, that with the Lord one day is like a thousand years, and a thousand years are like one day" (2 Pet. 3:8-9). For some of the poor, afflicted by pain resulting from unjust social systems, God's patience manifests in an instance. Former chattel Orleans Finger experienced instantaneous results from God's patience revealed on time:

> I'm puny and no 'count. Ain't able to do much. But I was crippled. I had a hurting in my leg, and I couldn't walk without a stick. Finally, one day I went to go out and pick some turnips. . . . My leg hurt so bad that I talked to the Lord about it. And it seemed to me, He said, 'Put down your stick.' I put it down, and I ain't used it since. I put it down right there, and I ain't used it since. God is a momentary God.[36]

For Mr. Finger, perhaps God the momentary divinity did not act with an extended patience because of immediate relief given for the hurt in his leg. But for God, this moment could have been like a thousand years. The conclusion of divine patience was concrete results, in this scenario, for individual relief.

In other situations, it might appear that God's patience takes on the characteristics of years for those burdened with societal oppression and spiritual dis-ease. Clayborn Gantling, an ex-slave, remembers the patience of God displayed in a longer time interval. "I tell you chile, it was pitiful, but God did not let it last always. I have heard slaves morning and night pray for deliverance. Some of 'em would stand up in de fields or bend over cotton and corn and pray out loud for God to help 'em and in time you see, He did."[37] In time, God's patient time, help arrives and deliverance is realized.

Ultimately, divine patience is the Spirit for us to be fully human, spiritually and materially, and to enable those ensnared within the oppressive clutches of death and social disease to struggle for liberation and to practice freedom. Maria Stewart, in her on autobiographical spiritual narrative confirmed the following:

> Certainly, God has not deprived [enslaved blacks and northern African Americans] of the divine influence of his Holy Spirit, which is the greatest of all blessings, if they ask him. Then why should man any longer deprive his fellow-man of equal rights and privileges? . . . I am firmly persuaded, that he will not suffer you [white slavemasters] to quell the proud, fearless and undaunted spirits of the Africans forever; for in his own time, he is able to plead our cause against you. . . . We will tell you that our souls are fired with the same love of liberty and independence with which your souls are fired.[38]

The Holy Spirit is the greatest of all blessings for oppressed black folk, whether free or unfree, north or south. And this spirit for us denotes specifically patience (in God's own time and not forever) described as equal rights, privileges, liberty, and independence. In a word, divine patience helps the victims to become full liberated and independent human beings over against certain races and groups who monopolize privileges given by God equally to all. God created all as one body embodying the same internal Spirit. But the souls of the oppressor activate this Spirit of "liberty and independence" at the expense and on the backs of the same impulse found in the "undaunted spirits of the Africans." Yet God's patience is on time to spark this Spirit implanted deep within oppressed black folk.

The militant black northern abolitionist David Walker summarizes the broader framework of divine patience experienced in the advent of victory for the bottom of society. "God will not suffer us, always to be oppressed. Our sufferings will come to an end, in spite of all the [white] Americans this side of eternity. Then we will want all the learning and talents among ourselves, and perhaps more, to govern ourselves.—'Every dog must have its day,' the American's is coming to an end."[39] The patience of God will not stand idly by and allow the oppressed to be the oppressed "always." This fact provides a certainty in divine patience because it yields results of salvation and deliverance from all forms of spiritual and material evil. Relieved of the weight of painful burden, in the patience of God's own time, the now emancipated victims can truly become who they were created to be by acquiring learning and talents (that is, the right of self-identity) and by taking charge of the necessary resources to govern the wealth around them (the right of self-determination). Every dog must have its day culminates out of divine patience on the side of the poor and the brokenhearted.

God, through the Spirit for us, elects the poor not to sacralize poverty, but because poverty is demonic. In fact, sometimes the poor oppose the will of God for liberation, the normative yardstick for all humanity. God chooses the poor: because the ethics, ontology, and epistemology of God is total liberation by which human beings can reach their highest divine creativity; because the majority of black folk in the United States do not own the wealth, lack affirmation of their racial cultural identity, are controlled on a daily basis by demands outside of themselves, and suffer abuse for using their own language; and because of the universal implications of freeing the poor for all humanity.

Once the poor work with God to remove obstacles to that goal of co-constituting themselves with divine purpose, then the small group in America that monopolizes power, privilege, right of self-identity and the right of self-determination will no longer have anyone to oppress. Thus they too will be liberated from their intricate web of causing lethal harm and will be able to achieve their fullness simply as additional members of the human race. Remove the object of oppression and exploitation, and oppression and exploitation cease. This is the ultimate goal of the Spirit of total liberation for us.

In summation, the Spirit of liberation for us works with oppressed black folk and other peoples underneath the heel of victimization through the interplay of God's glory and unity, righteousness and omnipresence, constancy and eternity, omnipotence and mercy, grace and holiness, and wisdom and patience. Through these divine attributes, we encounter the revelation of God's acts, being, and knowledge. To further the role of this Spirit as a vivifying agent in the co-constitution of a full material and spiritual humanity in the new Common Wealth requires further inquiry in to the Spirit of liberation with us: that is to say, the reality of Jesus with us today.

NOTES

1. "Narrative of Lunsford Lane" in Katz, ed., *Five Slave Narratives*, 20.
2. Still, *Underground Railroad*, 458.
3. Martha Griffith Browne, *Autobiography of a Female Slave*, 242.
4. In *The American Slave*, Georgia, vol. 12. pt. 1. 13. For the connection of God's act of using the Yankees in the Civil War to other divine acts, see Bradford, *Harriet Tubman*, 106.
5. Bibb, *Narrative of the Life and Adventures of Henry Bibb*, 48.
6. Kate Drumgoold, "A Slave Girl's Story: Being an Autobiography of Kate Drumgoold" in *Six Women's Slave Narratives*, 30. Kate Drumgoold was born a slave in Virginia.
7. *Six Women's Slave Narratives*, 16.
8. Walker, *David Walker's Appeal*, 3.
9. Blassingame, ed., *Slave Testimony*, 131.
10. Kate Drumgoold in *Six Women's Slave Narratives*, 3.
11. Kate Drumgoold in *Six Women's Slave Narratives*, 23–24.
12. Old Elizabeth, "Memoir of Old Elizabeth, A Coloured Woman," in *Six Women's Slave Narratives*, 17.
13. Nancy Williams, in *Weevils in the Wheat: Interviews with Virginia Ex-Slaves*, ed. Charles L. Perdue, Jr. (Bloomington: Indiana University Press, 1980), 319–20.
14. Autobiography of James L. Smith in *Five Black Lives*, 195 and 198.
15. Other former slaves speak about the signs of God's glory. See William Adams from Texas who relates: "The old folks in them days knows more about the signs that the Lord uses to reveal His laws than the folks of today. It am also true of the colored folks in Africa, they native land. . . . It am knowing how the Lord reveals his laws" (Botkin, ed., *Lay My Burden Down*, 37.
And Mrs. Virginia Hayes Shepherd concurs: "The Negroes said God had sent a sigh to white folks worning them not to be cruel to the Negroes," in Perdue, ed., *Weevils in the Wheat*, 258.
16. Walker, *David Walker's Appeal*, 4 and 5.
17. Old Elizabeth, in Maryland, 1766, was sent away from her slave mother to another plantation; from *Six Women's Slave Narratives*, 4.
18. Blassingame, ed., *Slave Testimony*, 52.
19. In Albert, ed., *House of Bondage*, 46–47. Similarly, female slave Hattie commented on how she survived in the woods after running away: "'All I can tell, God took care of me in these woods'" p. 71 of the same book.
20. *Five Black Lives*, 173.
21. Still, ed., *Underground Railroad*, 463.
22. Northup, *Twelve Years a Slave*, 258.
23. Lucy Delaney, "From the Darkness Cometh the Light or Struggles for Freedom," in *Six Women's Slave Narratives*, 14; see a similar notion of curse, omnipresence, and righteousness in the statement of ex-slave L. M. Mills in Blassingame, ed., *Slave Testimony*, 504.
24. *Five Black Lives*, 134–35.

25. Rev. G. W. Offley in *Five Black Lives*, 134–35.

26. Craft, *Running A Thousand Miles for Freedom,* 40.

27. Walker, *David Walker's Appeal,* 36.

28. Unnamed ex-slave in *The American Slave,* Georgia, vol. 13, pt. 4, 291–92). Also, former chattel Julia Brown states: "There was a white man, Mister Jim, that wuz very mean to the slaves. . . . Mister Jim wuz jest a mean man, and when he died we all said God got tired of Mr. Jim being so mean and kilt him" (Georgia, vol. 12, pt. 1, 144–45).

29. Leah Garrett, in *The American Slave,* Georgia, vol. 12. pt. 2, 12.

30. *Five Black Lives,* 99.

31. *Five Black Lives,* 73–74.

32. In *The American Slave,* Georgia, vol.13, pt. 3, 103.

33. Blassingame, ed., *Slave Testimony,* 700.

34. *Five Black Lives,* 196.

35. In Prov. 3:7 we find: "Do not be wise in your own eyes; fear the Lord, and turn away from evil." Similarly in 1 Cor. 1:20b-21, we read: "Has not God made foolish the wisdom of the world? For since, in the wisdom of God, the world did not know God through wisdom, God decided, through the foolishness of our proclamation, to save those who believe."

36. Botkin, ed., *Lay My Burden Down,* 34.

37. In *The American Slave,* Florida, vol. 17, 142.

38. Maria W. Stewart's "Productions of Mrs. Maria W. Stewart, Presented to the First African Baptist Church & Society of the City of Boston," in *Spiritual Narratives*, ed. Schomburg Library of Nineteenth-Century Black Women Writers (1835; reprint, New York: Oxford University Press, 1988), 18 and 19.

39. *David Walker's Appeal,* 15.

CHAPTER 5

Jesus—The Spirit
of Total Liberation with Us

The Spirit of the Lord is upon me,
Because he has anointed me
To bring good news to the poor.
God has sent me to proclaim release to the captives
And recovery of sight to the blind,
To let the oppressed go free,
To proclaim the year of the Lord's favor.
   Luke 4:18-19

The Spirit of the Lord God is upon me,
Because the Lord has anointed me;
God has sent me to bring good news to the oppressed,
To bind up the brokenhearted,
To proclaim liberty to the captives,
And release to the prisoners;
To proclaim the year of the Lord's favor,
And the day of vengeance of our God;
To comfort all who mourn;
To provide for all who mourn in Zion.
   Isa. 61:1-3

Mistress's religion did not make her happy like my religion did. I
was a poor slave, and everybody knowed I had religion, for it was
Jesus with me every-where I went.
   Charlotte Brooks, ex-slave[1]

IF GOD IS THE Spirit of liberation *for* us, then Jesus, in black theology, is the fulfillment of the Spirit of total liberation *with* us. Jesus is the Emmanuel—the decisive revelation of God with us. This revelation of the sacred with us occurs not in abstract, ethereal spirituality. In fact, Jesus' spirit appears with us in macro, micro, linguistic, and racial cultural identity formations among the black poor and working people, and, through them, the global poor. Moreover, this freeing spiritual presence works with us in the co-constitution of the new African American self: that is to say, in the ongoing creation narrative of divine-poor co-laboring for a new Common Wealth on earth. In a word, the Spirit labors with us in the vocation to struggle for liberation and to practice freedom so each person achieves full spiritual and material humanity.

In the present chapter, we examine the theological implications of Jesus by exploring the goal of liberation with us, the road to that goal, the fruits of the journey, and the co-constitution of the new self and new Common Wealth. In this part of constructing a black theology from slave religious experiences and biblical stories, we continue to attend to the various excluded and locked out voices in society. In addition, we engage the different levels of their exclusion and the diverse ways they pursue the theological development of resistance and creation.

The Goal of Liberation with Us

THE PURPOSE OF JESUS

The public inaugural sermon preached by Jesus in Luke 4:18-19 as a continuation of Isa. 61:1-3 contextualizes the entire purpose of Jesus' advent, birth, life, death, resurrection, and second advent. No understanding of Jesus (the anointed liberation Spirit with us) can appear with clarity without this foundational word of God. Combining Luke 4:18-19 and Isa. 61:1-3 with the social location and enduring faith of those at the bottom of society, former slave J. W. C. Pennington summarizes concisely the divine intent for oppressed humanity:

> that blessed Saviour, who came to preach good tidings unto the meek, to bind up the broken hearted, to proclaim liberty to the captives, and the opening of the prison to them that are bound. To proclaim the acceptable year of the Lord and the day of vengeance of our God; to comfort all that mourn. To appoint unto them that mourn in Zion, to give unto them beauty for ashes, the oil of joy for mourning, the garment of praise for the spirit of heaviness, that they might be called trees of righteousness, the planting of the Lord that he might be glorified.[2]

Preached by Jesus, this call sermon and inaugural proclamation live, first of all, among the earth's meek; Jesus anchors his intent to be "with us" within a definitive social location. Because the lowly need to hear good news, Jesus preaches good tidings to them. They require, moreover, a spirit with them that can repair their broken hearts, fractured by wicked spiritual and physical powers on earth. The intent to proclaim liberty to the captives denotes a holistic salvation and liberation encompassing the entire dimensions of the poor (macro, micro, linguistic, racial cultural identity, material, spiritual, private, and public). The bursting asunder of prison doors suggests both metaphorically and literally how Jesus acts today to remove the poor from all manner of prisons and from any obstacles preventing them from struggling for liberation and practicing freedom.

Jesus comes to announce, in addition, a freedom calendar, where now is the day and year acceptable to God. Consequently, the poor need to act in response to this divine gift of Jubilee by conducting themselves already as if the new Common Wealth has arrived. However, this is not a cheap grace; it is not an easy gift. All must go before the bar of judgment day, the day of vengeance. At that historical juncture, rich and poor, black and white, and peoples of all colors and all stations of life have to submit their lives to an accounting. Did they or did they not strive to co-constitute the new self with Jesus—the Spirit of total liberation with us now?

Yet, even in the midst of the "day of vengeance of our God," Jesus provides comfort for those who mourn as a result of unjust injury, and nurture for those suffering from the scars of exploitation. The divine spirit of liberation with us is mother and father who elevates and clothes the downcast spirits with "a garment of praise." And moreover, Jesus affirms their natural beauty in place of the negativity cast upon their created racial identity. Joy with the poor in their mournful state comes from Jesus.

Furthermore, Jesus' purpose encompasses a paradigm of servanthood for the outcast, a model that all humanity is to emulate. Ex-slave William Adams offers this profound theological insight:

> Bout special persons being chosen for to show the power, read your Bible. It says in the book of Mark, third chapter, "And He ordained twelve, that they should be with Him, that He might send them forth to preach and to have the power to heal the sick and to cast out devils." If it wasn't no evil in people, why does the Lord say, "Cast out such"? And in the fifth chapter of James, it further say, "If any am sick, let him call the elders. Let them pray over him. The prayers of faith shall save him." There 'tis again. Faith, that am what counts.[3]

The intent of Jesus ordains us to be with him; Jesus does not simply come into this world for us, but calls us out to work with the

Spirit of liberation, that we "should be with Him." Fundamentally, this being with entails the giving of power from Jesus to those who accept the call and the power to servanthood for the least in society. Yes, Jesus manifests power, but, at the same time, this Spirit of liberation with us chooses to share this power with those accepting the mandate to serve others—"being chosen for to show the power."

How does Jesus work with humanity who accepts the purpose of servanthood? First, pursuing servanthood with Jesus means embracing divine power and preaching the good news of this power of liberation with us. Power and preaching, transformation and proclamation collaborate in the process of forging the new human being. This movement from the old self as oppressed black working people (and the universal poor) to the new practice of freedom without hierarchy of wealth ownership (but with all things owned in common as in Acts 2:44-45) embodies transformation on the levels of the spiritual (that is, the psychological, the soul, and the determination to reach the new Common Wealth) and the material (the concrete communal ownership of all of the Spirit's creation and the tangible respect between people without automatic white skin privileges).

It means, moreover, focusing on the bruised and least in society. The latter are sick because of systemic restrictions preventing free and adequate health care and because of financial and cultural pressures forced upon working class and poor individuals and families. And their bodies and minds are racked internally by psychological demons created by larger macrostructures circumscribing attempts to live a daily micro-existence of full spiritual and material humanity. Closely related to healing and casting out psychological pain, prayer over the sick (that is, those ill from physical, spiritual, and social maladies), relates to, again, the least in society suffering from various forms of oppression and exploitation that engender socially induced sicknesses. For instance, to be working class or poor and to be black implies the experience of attacks on one's ability to control one's own humanity—that is, to lack control of wealth and God's resources for a full humanity as well as to lack the outlets for expression of one's beautiful cultural identity. The stifling of the right of self-determination and the right of self-identity causes illnesses on psychological, physical, and social levels.

Jesus is with the oppressed, gives power for the poor to use power to fight evil, and offers faith for salvation, in a word, full deliverance. By working with Jesus—the Spirit of liberation with us—the victims of society pursue the role of servanthood for salvation; they administer power to the powerless, proclaim a freedom word, heal the sick, cast out demons, and pray over the ill ones. "The prayers of faith shall save him."

JESUS AT THE BAR

We understand further the goal of Jesus by working back from the last day when all of humanity will be judged by one clear norm and level yardstick, what was done to assist in realizing the full spiritual and material humanity of the poor on earth. That final day will expose the entire living human race (those alive on earth and the live spirits of dead ancestors) at the bar of adjudication presided over by the Spirit of liberation with us.

At the end of time, when Jesus the Spirit of liberation with us comes to co-constitute the new spiritual and material humanity for the new Common Wealth on earth, the sole criterion will be justice for the poor and weak in society. Matt. 25:31-46 sets the divine foundational questions to be asked at the bar of Jesus' judgment. Paraphrasing this biblical passage, Henry Bibb describes how Christ will demand of those with privileges whether or not they based their entire daily life on bringing concrete liberation for the least of these. When "the judgment of the great day" comes, Christ "shall say to the slaveholding professors of religion, 'Inasmuch as ye did it unto one of the least of these little ones, my brethren, ye did it unto me.'"[4]

Out of the sixty-six books of the Bible, Matthew 25 is the only citation where we discover Jesus' goal at the end time, at the judgment bar. Nowhere else are the step by step criteria elaborated for entering into heaven, the new Common Wealth. Sitting on "the throne of his glory" at the bar, Jesus will ask all individuals—the living, the ancestors, and the unborn—whether they facilitated the establishment of social and spiritual structures to give food to the hungry (that is, to reallocate priorities, wealth, and technology to abolish hunger), to give water to the thirsty (since the primary use of earth's waters is for the masses of the globe and not the pleasure of the wealthy), to welcome the stranger (for example, to accept all undocumented workers), to clothe the naked (to provide free clothing first to those at the bottom of society before the wealthy can receive them), to care for the sick (that is, to provide free health care and the best medical professionals to work first on the poor), and to visit the prisoners (that is, to bring all of society's resources to bear on rehabilitating the prisoners who are overwhelmingly poor, working class, black, and people of color).

Therefore, whoever helps the poor (whom Jesus calls the least in society and members of God's family) in the struggle for liberation and the practice for freedom will be with Jesus. Whoever works with the Spirit of liberation to alter oppressive macro, micro, linguistic, and racial cultural identity formations will receive salvation from Jesus at the bar. This is the presence of the Spirit and humanity working to co-constitute the old self into a new spiritual and material humanity.

Thus the goal of Jesus is to be with us—to bring all humanity to the bar and to get all humanity successfully through the tests of liberation for the poor. For instance, in critiquing his slavemaster and, by implication, those individuals today who have parallel wealth, education, class, and white skin privileges, and other asymmetrical negative affirmative actions, James Pennington gives the following admonition:

> [Those who are the victims] will all meet you at the bar. . . . What excuse could you offer at the bar of God, favoured as you have been with the benefits of a refined education, and through a long life with the gospel of love, should you, when arraigned there, find that you have, all your life long, laboured under a great mistake in regard to slavery. . . . I can only say then, dear sir, farewell, till I meet you at the bar of God, where Jesus, who died for us, will judge between us.[5]

Again, Pennington reinforces the notion that what we do on earth to the marginalized of society will be questioned at the bar by Jesus. Things of this world (such as the monopolization of wealth, the best educational credentials, long membership in a church, etc.) will not suffice for membership in the new society organized on liberation principles. At the bar, it will be too late to change one's historical record; evidence cannot be falsified.

Furthermore, the past atonement of Jesus, the anointed spirit of liberation, embodied in Jesus' victory over the death of poverty and pain on the cross through his definitive resurrection of victory links directly to the final time at the bar of Jesus' judgment session. In this sense, the goal of Jesus intertwines atonement and the eschaton. For instance, another former female slave raises a rhetorical question about whether or not black Americans are "excluded from the grace of that atonement." Because the powerful and the wealthy attempt to keep black folk outside of Jesus' gift of liberation grace, these same privileged sectors of society will undergo strict interrogation at the bar and "will stand with a fearful accountability before the Supreme Judge."[6] Here too, we find a clear broadening of atonement from simply an individual confession of personal sins to include atonement as reconciliation or radical transformation of wicked systems like slavery. Whoever fosters the atonement benefits ushered in by the resurrection will benefit at the bar at the end time.

Finally, Jackson Whitney (a slave who ran away and wrote a letter back to his former master) teaches us that the goal of Jesus with us encompassed in "at the bar" stands at the core of our entire understanding of Jesus the Spirit of total liberation with us. Indeed, without this central piece, there would be no use for Jesus with us or God for us. Jackson writes: "But if you want to go to the next world and meet a God . . . who says "Inasmuch as you did it to the least of them my little one, you did it unto me" . . . [you] had better repair the breaches you have made among us in this world [through concrete justice actions]. . . . If God don't punish you for inflicting such distress on the poorest of His poor, then there is no use of having any God, or talking about one."[7]

This christological statement (the understanding of Jesus' identity and mission with us) by Whitney regarding the nature of one's faith and practice with Jesus resonates with the biblical narrative enunciated by Jesus. "So when you are offering your gift at the altar, if you remember that your brother or sister has something against you, leave your gift there before the altar and go; first be reconciled to your brother or sister" (Matt. 5:23-24). One cannot be liberated and free from internal demons of oppression and seek such a full humanity if that person (or stratum of the rich and powerful) creates oppressive structure harmful to others. Likewise, one cannot attain one's fully created potential if one has done harm against someone on the everyday level of existence, such as those who are objects of white supremacy. The hope and pursuit of salvation and liberation become empty rhetoric when divorced from concrete restitution and tangible amends given and made to the oppressed community or injured party. Hence, to be with Jesus now and forever, to become a new full self co-constituted with the Spirit of liberation, requires standing at the bar without the destructive baggage of any manifest wrongdoing.

Former chattel Mrs. Lizy McCoy sang an old slave song of common folk wisdom: "God don't love ugly, Don't care nothing beauty, All he want is your soul."[8] God don't like ugly, otherwise God would not be God all the time. And one example of that saying reveals in the goal of "at the bar."

JESUS' GOSPEL

Ultimately, the goal of Jesus is to provide the Spirit of liberation with us in the good news gospel. Such a clarion call of visionary hope and comforting nurture covers all aspects of the lives of the oppressed. It does not neglect the microsins of individual transgressions. Nor does it avoid the wickedness of macrosystems. With the Spirit of liberation, it combats the spirit of injustice that pervades the entire land. Whether that injustice is the form of slavery prior to the Civil War or the slavery connected with monopoly capitalism's payment of unfair wage and benefit packages to working people, "the holy will [does not] sanctify it."

In a word, "the gospel rightly understood, taught, received, felt, and practiced, is anti-slavery as it is anti-sin. Just so far and so fast as the true Spirit of the gospel obtains in the land, and especially in the lives of the oppressed, will the spirit of slavery sicken and become powerless."[9] The good news gospel, as a goal of Jesus with us, has meaning when the true Spirit of liberation with us becomes the norm and "obtains in the land." Just as fast and as far as we work with Jesus among the poor (the criterion for a new humanity), the new humanity will come into being. Faithful witness unfolds in the co-constitution of the free self. At the same time, the Spirit reveals its fullness through the oppressed and, from there, to the rest of humanity. The Spirit is partial to the poor because Jesus is with those enchained by poverty. Poverty and domination are contrary to the good news. By breaking demonic forces of monopolized power, asymmetrical privilege, and harmful internal spirits, the oppressed free themselves from the restraints of the oppressor. When the oppressor has no one to oppress, then the oppressor ceases to cause discrimination and has the opportunity to be equal to the formerly oppressed who are now free. The Good News works in time and space, levels hierarchy, and realizes equality for all people. "Especially in the lives of the oppressed" brings universal salvation and justice, a struggle for liberation and the practice of freedom. The gospel goal of liberation is with all humanity.

The Road to the Goal

JESUS' GIFTS

The goal of Jesus—that is, the fulfillment of God's promise of the Spirit of total liberation not only to be for us, but also to be with us every day—is attained along a road filled with gifts which Jesus provides so that the poor might pursue the way to the goal. Restated, the goal is for the Spirit of liberation to be with us, and, while we pursue this ultimate quest, Jesus remains with us in the struggle for liberation and the practice of freedom.

The first important gift given by Jesus to suffering and brokenhearted people is faith and courage. Without these, no one would have the strength to sustain oneself against wicked spiritual and material attacks, let alone marshal enough energy to pursue the practice of freedom proactively. As an instruction of belief to his disciples, Jesus stated: "Because of your little faith. For truly I tell you, if you have faith the size of a mustard seed, you will say to this mountain, 'Move from here to there,' and it will move; and nothing will be impossible for you" (Matt. 17:20).

Faith lets the poor know that trouble does not last always. And despite all appearances of persistent excruciating pain internally and formidable oppressive systems externally, the least in society know how Jesus is with them through the resurrection's victory over the death of poverty and pain. Because the ultimate power of poverty's death and sin's grip has been defeated through victory, then the black poor and other working people can believe that a difference has been made not only in the cosmic realm, but also in their daily lives. With this belief and knowledge they can have courage to pursue a vision in which their lives and their children's lives will be free to attain their full potential as human beings.

Rev. Squires Jackson, once freed from the status of an oppressed black worker under slavery, responded to the question of how "he got over": "He says that the treatment during the time of slavery was very tough at times, but gathering himself up he said, 'no storm lasts forever and I had the faith and courage of Jesus to carry me on,' continuing, 'even the best masters in slavery couldn't be as good as the worst person in freedom, oh, God, it is good to be free, and I am thankful.'"[10]

Jesus gives the poor the gift of faith and courage and, with these, the poor are able to see what faith has provided for them (that is, the fact that the ultimate victory is certain) and what courage brings to their personal predicament (the ability to pursue the culminating victory of faith).

Jesus also offers the gift of his sacrificial blood of love, and the response on the part of the least in society is to track these blood guideposts of love. Each love drop indicates a way along the road toward the goal of full humanity. Each blood remnant empowers our memory that Jesus gave the poor and marginalized the victory in the triumph of the resurrection over the death on the cross. Because blood was shed and victory gained, the ultimate systems of domination and dehumanization (such as racial oppression, class exploitation, gender discrimination, and heterosexism) have no authority and no lasting power. Final authority exists in the Spirit of liberation with us; consequently, the authority of this "with us" supercedes any earthly human being regardless of color or privilege. Yahweh of the Hebrew Scriptures and Jesus of the Christian witness are one in the denial of worship of any other gods or spirits before the one God. Similarly, unjust systems and psychospiritual demons have no lasting grip on the existence of the victims and lonely ones of this earth. Blood drippings of love remind and comfort the weak to not surrender themselves to the fear of evil's presence, because "joy will come in the morning."

An unnamed ex-slave corroborates this claim in his recollection of Negro spirituals created by the collective black voice during the slavery system:

> They'd sing:
> "Jesus have gone to Galilee.
> And how do you know that Jesus is gone?
> I tracked him by his drops of blood,
> And every drop he dropped in love."[11]

The offering of sacrificial blood drops of love become real when they are tracked by those who have faith and courage to risk the struggle for liberation and the practice of freedom. Otherwise, these signs of blood love cannot be perceived without a response of risk. This gift from the Spirit of liberation with us challenges the poor to act in a different way, against the exploitative norm and for one's own freedom. It means pursuing the signs, indicators, and manifestations along the path to the goal of full spiritual and material humanity. Jesus offers the gift; the poor must work with these gifts in order to co-constitute the new self. The writer of Hebrews confirms the need for faith, courage, and blood. "Therefore, my friends, since we have confidence to enter the sanctuary by the blood of Jesus, . . . let us approach with a true heart in full assurance of faith. . . . Let us hold fast to the confession of our hope without wavering, for he who has promised is faithful" (10:19-23).

Along the path to the goal of a new Common Wealth where the poor, the majority of the world, attain full spiritual and material humanity, Jesus furnishes us with the gift of prayer in addition to blood love. Prayer emboldens the oppressed especially in situations in which the only thing they can do is claim their spirit as a gift of God. In those extreme situations, prayer assumes for the individual a deep dimension of liberation from any type of external or internal wickedness. The gift of prayer fosters a faith in the Spirit of liberation with us, even at the expense of surrendering the body. The spirit of defiance and obedience to Jesus with us (that is, obedience to the struggle for liberation and the practice of freedom) surpasses any constraints experienced on earth.

In his testimony, for example, praying Jacob prayed three times a day regardless of his work assignment or the hour of day. His slavemaster once pointed a gun at Jacob and threatened to blow out his brains if he did not cease praying. The narrator of this story resumed: "Jacob would finish his prayer and then tell his master to shoot in welcome—your loss will be my gain—I have two masters one on earth and one in heaven—master Jesus in heaven, and master Saunders on earth. I have a soul and a body; the body belongs to you, master Saunders, and the soul to master Jesus. Jesus says men ought always to pray, but you will not pray, neither do you want to have me pray."[12] The ritual of prayer, in response to this gift of Jesus, foreshadows partially the co-constitution of the new self, even while in chains. Prayer subordinates the earthly oppressor's control over the victim to a higher realm. Prayer enables the victim to determine his or her own hours of the day, in opposition to the assigned periods to perform labor, and thus presents an affront to the macropolitical economy of exploitation. At this juncture, a microdaily act of spiritual resistance impacted the macrosystem of material profit. Though the victim may tell an earthly oppressor that the victim's body belongs to this wicked one with earthly privileges, in fact, by justifying the rebellious actions of prayer as necessary for the soul, the victim also removes the body from the commands of the oppressor. By pursuing prayer and surrendering the body to death at the hands of the oppressor, the victim likewise removes the body from the context of the oppressor. With the event of death, the body returns to the earth and is literally freed from the oppressor's ownership. The prayer dictates of the Spirit with us reconfigures the social relations between the oppressor and the oppressed. In a word, the freedom of the soul through Jesus is a liberation which no person can undo or circumvent. Therefore soul freedom can put the poor beyond the clutches of the oppressors. Prayer, in other words, is the medium of deliverance for those who suffer: "Is anyone among you suffering? He [or she] should keep on praying about it" (Jas. 4:13).

Finally, Jesus (the anointed Spirit of liberation with us) gives the oppressed, especially the African American oppressed folk, racial equality. To be with Jesus and not to depart from him obligates all to affirm the beauty and racial equality for oppressed blackness in the United States. The dominant norm in North America, to the contrary, is white skin privileges—a contradiction opposed to Jesus that will block the achievement of full humanity along the path toward the goal of liberation and the practice of freedom. To continually assert in practice, if not in word, that white Christians should lord their phenotype over black folk is to usurp the power of Jesus and to leave him by himself on the way toward the final goal. This would constitute an act of sin against the co-constitution of a liberated self. Thus the strong and persistent affirmation of the racial cultural identity of black folk is a definite marker of the presence of Jesus with us in the struggle for liberation. Denial and silence on this question will leave Christians in America without Jesus. David Walker grasped this point in his agitation against slavery:

> Can the [white] American preachers appeal unto God, the Maker and Searcher of hearts, and tell him, with Bible in their hands, that they make no distinction on account of men's colour? Can they say, O God! thou knowest all things—thou knowest that we make no distinction between thy creatures, to whom we have to preach thy Word? Let them answer the Lord; and if they cannot do it in the affirmative, have they not departed from the Lord Jesus Christ, their master?[13]

White churches, religious institutions, and the broader society make racial classifications that discriminate against the biological make-up and physical characteristics of black folk. Yet Jesus condemns color supremacy because the forced normativity of whiteness creates a false idol as the center of all humanity. In this schema, all other colors must bow down to, worship, and revolve around the automatic and often unstated value of whiteness. In North American society, race still matters, due to the wicked spirit of white supremacy: that is, the default position of whiteness, and daily (but often unmentioned) application of accustomed advancement and assumed affirmative action if one is white, especially if one is white and has power. Therefore, an affirmation of the divine nature of blackness in instances of white superiority serves to promote racial equality for all. The Spirit of liberation with us does not discriminate based on color. In fact, in order to underscore the equality of all, the Spirit frees blackness from the superior and demonic values of whiteness. Against the demon of whiteness, the Spirit affirms that black is beautiful because, like all others, black is created by God. Therefore, to stand in solidarity with Jesus' presence with the black oppressed is to stand with Jesus.

Black folk who are free with Jesus know that the liberating Spirit co-labors with African American working people to the very end. Former slave Rev. Hale confirms this reality: "Now what do Solomon say about wisdom? 'The beginning of wisdom is to fear God and keep His commandments.' What nationality was Solomon? He was a black man. 'Forsake me not because I am black!' Who was it that bore the cross when Christ was wagging the cross up Calvary Hill? He was a black man, Simon of Cyrean."[14] On the path to short-term death and long-term resurrection life of the new humanity, Christ co-labored up the arduous and bloody trail of Calvary Hill accompanied by a black man. It is, likewise, the black person (female and male) who chooses to be with Christ (the anointed Spirit) in the oppressed and exploited conditions facing the least in society who will reap the victory of the co-constituted full material and spiritual humanity once the goal is attained. Salvation and liberation have a special place for black working people and poor people.

In the particular asymmetrical racial situation in North America, Jesus is with the black poor by accenting and affirming that part of their full humanity that declares black is beautiful. Furthermore, Jesus (the Spirit of total liberation with us) is with the black people who are free to accept their own natural hair texture, nose, eyes, and body parts. The achievement of full humanity means not destroying one's hair, eyes, nose, and other body parts in order to look like white people. To be with Jesus is to love the beauty of black folk just as they are. To do that, one has to start with loving oneself and accepting this gift of beauty that Jesus offers with his presence on the path to the final goal.

POWER OF JESUS' NAMES

In addition to gifts, the power of Jesus' names facilitates the journey of the poor on the path to the ultimate goal—the fulfillment of God's promise of the Spirit of total liberation with us in freedom every day. Indeed the very name of Jesus causes the poor to survive, re-energize, and pursue a new humanity with their own voice. Former chattel Charlotte Brooks recalled: "Aunt Jane used to sing 'Jesus! The name that charms our fears.' That hymn just suited my case. Sometimes I feel like preaching myself."[15] The very name of Jesus (which is the liberating Spirit with us) embraces a powerful energy enhancing the will, the determination, and focus of poor folk to struggle for a new humanity now. The name itself calms the fears of oppressed and marginalized folk who today are enslaved by all types of harmful conditions external to their being and negative feelings inside of their soul. Jesus' name is not simply innocuous, nor a casual title; it has the potency to defeat pain, thus acting as a balm. It defeats a weak will, therefore building courage. It defeats any warring internal conflict of the poor, therefore yielding peace and balance in the soul in order to keep struggling for justice.

The title "doctor" like the name "Jesus" also strengthens the least in society in the journey toward full spiritual and material humanity. Kate Drumgoold, a poor black ex-slave, affirms the omnipotence and salvific nature of this title: "I had many a hard spell of sickness . . . and the doctors said that I could not live beyond a certain time, but every time they said so Doctor Jesus said she shall live, for because I live she shall live also; and He came to me and laid His strong arm around me and raised me up by the power of His might."[16]

Doctor Jesus baffles the knowledge base and technological progress of those who would relinquish all hope of recovery for the poor who are sick. The Spirit of liberation with us envelops the sick in the strong arm of liberation and frees them from the grip of illnesses. Thus the lame and the downtrodden are raised up from their prone and subservient positions. Ex-slave Charlotte gave a similar response when asked about her survival ability. "'Why, I can't see what kept you alive, Aunt Charlotte, till now!' 'The dear Lord and Saviour kept me alive.'"[17] Life does not depend on the elite rulers and the recognized leadership on earth. Quite the contrary, Jesus determines who lives and who dies. And because Jesus has opted to be with the poor (in general) and the black poor (in particular), ultimate accountability lies with his prescription: pursuing relentlessly the path toward holistic liberation and the realization of freedom. Doctor Jesus, for the poor and the least in society who endure pain, keeps them from death because the "medicine" provided is not of this earth. The liberating Spirit with the poor is transcendent in the sense that it is not confined to or bound by the visible world. Though the medicine materializes in the tangible, the will, determination, discipline, hope, and focus to continue toward the goal come from faith in Jesus' prior record of doctoring successfully and, consequently, hope in the future certainty that he will again prevail. In a response to how she bore all of the spiritual and material oppression of slavery, an old black Granny stated: Jesus "held me up. I'd'er died long ago widout him."[18]

Jesus likewise has invigorating and guiding power in the name "pilot." The poor lack the ability to perceive all the snares and dangers that confront them. In these instances, they cannot co-constitute the new human being without a leader to navigate the rough terrain of life defined by multilevel oppression and many a tormenting trial. With exploitation manifesting in the political economy of unfair practices against black working people; with attacks on the worth of the color of blackness; with a dismissal of black English and the profound cultural world to which it opens up; and with the daily assaults against microrealities of black life (whether in the form of derisive laughter, psychological pressures on the black family, or destruction of the black body), the masses of folk require more than their own antennae to decode and detect destructive disasters on the way to freedom. For one ex-slave, like so many of the black poor throughout history and today, the name of Jesus "has led me through paths seen and unseen and has been my pilot, for we have been called to pass through many a dark trial."[19] Pilot Jesus directs the feet of the poor on the path to the final goal of full humanity. He holds the compass and the map and becomes the primal cartographer; he discerns the seen and obvious, and the unseen and hidden.

However, a pilot does not only detect what acts against the poor of society, she or he, in the case of Jesus, creates new pathways and provides new proactive opportunities for the weak. David Walker put forth such a description to oppressed black workers under slavery: "Never make an attempt to gain our freedom or natural right, from under our cruel oppressors and murderers, until you see your way clear—when that hour arrives and you move, be not afraid or dismayed; for be you assured that Jesus Christ the King of heaven and of earth who is the God of justice and of armies, will surely go before you."[20] While Jesus pilots the way of black working people enchained by material and spiritual constraints, he takes on "those enemies who have for hundreds of years stolen [their] rights," in Walker's words. Yet at the same time, Jesus the pilot goes before and with the poor to empower them with a time and space to move which is not defined by the oppressor. Here the victim co-labors with Jesus to become a self-determining and self-identifying subject negotiating her or his own routes in life, in spite of the malicious mapping on the part of the wealthy and privileged. The pilot chooses the appointed hour most favorable for those disadvantaged due to multi-layered oppressions,

ines the natural environment most conducive to travel.
rable and conducive time and space along the way to the
s called "kairos." Jesus is a kairotic pilot.

ial name of Jesus that brings joy to black working people
and u.. universal poor is "soul sweetener." Oppressed people who
maintain faith in the Spirit of total liberation with them have no
other allegiance competing for this final goal. Once they attain this
loving level, their souls are at rest. A restful soul denotes a sweet
status where the victim's spirit is no longer troubled and determined
by outside oppression, but defined now by a pleasurable posture of a
proactive, self-determining, self-identifying, and self-affirming agency. Often, this pleasing position arrives with us when we discover
ourselves in the most physically binding restraints. Charlotte Brooks
narrates the candied nature of Jesus: "I'd be in prison on Sunday. I'd
sit all day singing and praying. I tell you, Jesus did come and bless me
in there. I was sorry for marster. I wanted to tell him sometimes
about how sweet Jesus was to my soul; but he did not care for nothing
in this world but getting rich."[21]

In radical contrast, if the wealthy (of class privilege), men (of male
gender privilege), whites (of racial privilege), and heterosexuals (of
sexual privilege) choose to subordinate their lives to addictions to
these varied privileges, they cannot enjoy the pleasure of a sweet
soul. Desiring the option to be over against another echoes the stance
assumed by the victimizer in the above story: "he did not care for
nothing in this world but getting rich."

We discover a desire of allegiance to anything but Jesus the soul
sweetener in Jesus' encounter with a certain rich man. To embrace
the vocation of following the path and reaching the goal of full material and spiritual humanity, to struggle for liberation and to practice
freedom, Jesus tells this rich man to sell all that he owns, distribute
the money to the poor, and follow the path of the Spirit of total liberation with us. The rich man's soulful disposition turns sour and his
spiritual composition becomes sad, "for he was rich." In response,
Jesus retorts with a forceful and definitive exclamation: "How hard it
is for those who have wealth to enter the kingdom of God!" While for
those poor who have surrendered all to the allegiance to Jesus, they
receive sweet souls and, furthermore, will acquire great abundance
"in this age, and in the age to come," on earth as it is in heaven. But
"it is easier," Jesus continues, "for a camel to go through the eye of a
needle than for someone who is rich to enter the kingdom of God"
(Luke 18:18-25).

LANGUAGE

Pursuing the path toward the immediate and final goal of the Spirit of liberation with us entails more than Jesus offering empowering gifts and providing motivational names. It signifies a liberating language from the liberating spirit with us. At times this emancipating language assumes the form of words of inspiration that urge and enable the victim to flee from all kinds of oppression to her or his own free space and leisure time. Inspiring words can be with the oppressed and work with them to reconfigure their inner and outer selves, whether this be an actual transformation of an external architecture of systemic oppression or an alteration of a stultifying internal edifice of psychological enslavement. Jesus' inspirational words engender the imagination to envision a different life from the constraints surrounding poor and working people. This captivating language, in addition, acts as a catalyst for social transformation and cognitive independence. In a word, the Spirit's inspiration language is a kind word of freedom for the oppressed.

Writing back to his former master after escaping to Canada, Jackson Whitney reveals the motivational thrust that resulted eventually in his having time, place, and space of his own. "But I rejoice to say that an unseen, kind spirit appeared for the oppressed, and bade me take up my bed and walk—the result of which is that I am victorious and you are defeated."[22] For Whitney, the kind spirit is the Spirit of liberation with him, which is Jesus. The words of inspiration cited as enlivening him to get on the path to freedom match the narrative in the book of Matthew where Jesus heals a lame person. For Whitney, his suffering under slavery as an exploited worker parallels the physical condition of the paralyzed man in Matthew. For the latter, Jesus offers simple words: "Stand up, take your bed and go to your home" (Matt. 9:8). Freed from the restrictions causing a painful contorted body, one can then walk and go home. For Whitney, home became freedom, a location to move freely about on one's own accord. Similarly, for the former paralytic, home became a new location where he could now walk about unrestricted by the disfigurement of his body. Therefore, Jesus says words of encouragement that enable those in pain to walk the road to the final goal of victory.

The essential characteristics of words of inspiration derive their power from two basic claims of Jesus. First, the Spirit of liberation with us means being in the world for the least in society, for the poor, and for those who have less privileges than we have. No matter what one's station is in life, until the new Common Wealth arrives on earth,

profit driven and scapegoat designed economic and cultural sys-
ns in the United States engender social stratification. Hence to be
ith the Spirit is to dwell in a constant phase of helping those who
cannot fully help themselves as a result of macrosystems operating
against the poor.

Second, the co-laboring dynamic of Jesus Emmanuel with
oppressed humanity entails defining our humanity based on the full
attainment of others' humanity. We should do unto others what we
desire to have done to ourselves by others. In other words, to achieve
our individual humanity in community (that is, to have others in the
Common Wealth provide conditions for our own human potentiality),
we have to exemplify a positive posture toward others' human potential. One person cannot be fully human, spiritually and materially,
until all others achieve their full humanity. The wealthy cannot be
fully human unless they share in common the wealth with all the
poor, thereby making all equal in relation to God's created resources
on earth. The white cannot be fully human unless the black (and the
red, brown, and yellow) is also verified as normative in all of society.
All levels of society will mirror the racial make-up of the society without granting privileged positions based on white skin privileges. The
man suffers from a loss of humanity until the male gender is redefined as being fully a man only when women reach their full potential. And heterosexuals can only enjoy their full identity when they
affirm homosexual sexual orientations. However, the norm, key, and
consistent principle is how all sectors of society stand with the poor
in diverse communities. Here we discover the touchstone for all manifestations of full humanity.

Escaped slave Henry Bibb's letter of admonishment to his former
master encapsulates these two claims of Jesus: "Listen to the language of inspiration: 'Feed the hungry, and clothe the naked: Break
every yoke and let the oppressed go free.' 'All things, whatsoever ye
would that men should do unto you, do ye even so unto them, for this
is the law and the prophets.'"[23] Bibb, for his flight on the path toward
freedom, draws on Jesus' words in Luke 4:18-19 and those in Matt.
7:12. Using his own commonsense wisdom mixed with biblical
instructions, Bibb teaches us that the sound, substance, and significance of inspiring words is our humanity for the marginalized.

The liberating language of Jesus with us on the way to the new
human being enables the victim to assume her or his voice. The poor
can never achieve the goal of freedom without recognizing the need
for their own voice, finding that voice, and asserting it with all their

might. One of the profound tragedies and sinister schemes of the oppressor is to convince the oppressed that the voice (or interest) of the oppressor is the same as for the oppressed. Hence to think like, interpret like, and talk like those who control oppressive systems is one of the surest ways for the poor to participate in their own exploitation and discrimination. Echoing the voice of the oppressor acts so powerfully that the victims identify with the oppressor in the act of oppression; all the while the victim thinks she or he lives in freedom and not in the shadow of a deadly system, both spiritually and materially, personally and systemically. Voice, like culture, embodies a complete way of life; it opens up the entire daily existence and thought patterns of an individual and a group. Speaking embraces, reflects, and creates reality—either an authentic or counterfeit life.

In the following theological hymn from blacks during slavery time, the importance of Jesus the Spirit with us enhancing the victim's voice is illustrated.

> Shout brother He never said a mumbling word,
> They took my blessed Jesus and taken him to the woods
> And they made him hew out his own dear cross and he wagged up
>   Calvary.
> Shout brother He never said a mumbling word.
> They taken my blessed Jesus and whipped him up the hill
> With a knotty whip and a raggedy thorn and He never said a mum-
>   bling word.
> Shout brother He never said a mumbling word.
> Two angels come from heaven and brought that mighty loud
> As the heaven door partd, the Israelites squalled and
> The watchmen all fell dead, and the watchmen all fell dead.
> Shout brother He never said a mumbling word.
> Go tell Mary and Martha the Savior has risen
> Has risen from the dead and will live forever more
> And won't have to die no more and won't have to die no more.
> Shout brother, etc.[24]

The line "Shout brother He never said a mumbling word" indicates that the connection between Jesus not saying a mumbling word and the voice of the oppressed victim speaking (in this case a black person under slavery claiming his or her voice) go together. In a word, Jesus is with the victim. Moreover, because this refrain occurs over and over again, with Jesus' silent voice and the victim's booming voice juxtaposed in the same line, thus in the same breath of the singer, we know that Jesus is with the marginalized of society forever.

This permanence, both in the tight relationship between Jesus and the oppressed and in the unending repetition of the song, underscores that the Spirit of liberation with us facilitates and brings power to the oppressed to claim their voice.

In particular in the first stanza, throughout the process of crucifixion (the evil done against the liberating spirit), Jesus does not speak. However, divine silence does not mean silence for poor folk. Quite the contrary, the silence of Jesus, at least the momentary silence on the cross, calls forth loud yelling on the part of the victim. In fact, because both "silence" and "shout" are held together so tightly, the Spirit of liberation instructs the poor to do just the opposite of not saying a mumbling word. It tells the poor that silence is not the way ("Shout brother"); Jesus' lack of a mumbling word is and will be only with the oppressed as long as the victim claims her or his own voice.

Initially, here in the first stanza, it may appear that the Spirit of liberation capitulates to the defilement of the efforts to pursue the goal of liberation, because of "never said a mumbling word." But even in the seeming despair and silence of this Spirit with us, Jesus commands the victim to shout out for himself. Restated, never should the poor, under any circumstances, allow the forces of evil to dominate their material and spiritual well-being. Jesus, by contrasting silence, commands those at the bottom of society to speak out and talk back in whatever forms are appropriate for the circumstances.

Voice plays such a decisive role (whether in opposition to racial attacks, abuse of women, harassment of gay people, or the arrogant exploitation of workers) because the liberating Spirit cannot manifest in complete silence. Again, a surface contradiction seems to appear if Jesus never says a mumbling word in this black spiritual. However, a closer look reveals a partnership between Jesus' apparent lack of sounds and the slave victim's outcry. In a word, the Spirit of liberation with us can only reveal itself through the victim's voice; the Spirit does not speak by itself. It chooses to work with (in the sense of Emmanuel or God with us) and through the materiality of the poor's existence. Jesus makes a conscious decision, even in silence, to locate the divine voice in the oppressive context and neighborhood of the oppressed. Therefore, to hear the voice of Jesus calling on the path toward the goal of practicing freedom, we must go to where poor and working people live.

Yet, though with us, Jesus does not deny the intensity of certain periods of discrimination and violence against the little ones of this world. The second verse denotes how even the Spirit of liberation seems, at times, on the defensive under the excruciating pain caused by the powerful ("whipped him"). The grip of evil, whether systemic or individual, external or spiritual, personal or public, can give the impression of absolute hegemony. Nonetheless, throughout it all, Jesus' silence beckons the victim to claim her or his voice in a big way. Furthermore, in consonance with this divine beckoning to speak, heaven's door unlocks and angels come forth toward the least in society to bring good news that the stammering tongues of the oppressed are unleashed. Those men of the oppressive systems and situations fall dead, either literally or figuratively and, thereby, are removed as obstacles to the nonstammering tongue of the broken-hearted and exploited.

Similarly, in the fourth verse, it is the steadfast faith of the women, Martha and Mary, to whom the Spirit with us comes commanding them to pursue a public witness as disciples (Matt. 28:1-15). The commissioning of the women suggests a direct laying on of hands by God's representatives (that is, either the angels or the Spirit). With this authority, the poor can look toward the leadership of women because they have received direct direction from and careful connection to heaven's intermediaries. Thus the good news of the women sent as missionaries to the world assists the poor in both shouting out against layers of oppression and shouting for their right to be full human beings liberated from internal spiritual demons and harmful external social structures.

The victim's voice, the embodiment of language, must have a proper location in the very being of the oppressed, in radical contrast to the oppressor. Because language does not merely reflect passively one's circumstance in life but, in fact, engenders right relation with the Spirit with us in the co-constitution of the new liberated self, the location from which one speaks one's voice about the divine word bears grave implications on the everyday level. The rhetoric of voicing has its own logic and logical location. A break at any level of this spoken and situated logic can bring havoc on the poor or an opening to follow the Spirit's way. Former slave Nancy Williams accents the necessity of correct positioning and origination of voice. "Dat ole white preachin' wasn't nothin'. When de services was near over, ole waitman would come back to de plantation an' tell all de slaves to come on to church. All had to go too, 'ceptin' de cook. Ole white preachers used to talk wid dey tongues widdout sayin' nothin' but Jesus told us slaves to talk wid our hearts."[25] Jesus, the Spirit with us, instructs and commands the least in society how to preach or speak the divine word; and the poor embody this very knowledge in themselves, despite the oppressive catechism and homilies of the oppressor. The perpetrators of a harmful white theology and Christian religion talk "widdout sayin' nothin'" because they simply engage in a wagging of tongues and spew forth empty discourse. The commandments of Jesus, however, emerge from the depths of warm spirit-filled hearts of the slaves of society. A deceitful tongue reflects the deceit inside the preacher or talker. But "to talk wid our hearts" signifies that speech in line with the Spirit with us originates from a heart overflowing with the presence of the Spirit. What comes out of the mouth reflects the truth of the heart. Thus words, as acts of creation, manifest in the co-constitution of the self and symbolize the fruit of the pureness of the heart acting as the seed of divine presence with the oppressed. The origin and articulation of a liberating discourse follow a consistent logic. Echoing the testimony of former slave Nancy Williams, the psalmist wrote: "With my whole heart I seek you; do not let me stray from your commandments. I treasure your word in my heart, so that I may not sin against you. Blessed are you, O LORD; teach me your statutes" (Ps. 119:10-12).

Finally, to claim one's voice from the heart filled with the Spirit with us brings on the oppressor's wrath and potential literal or metaphorical death for all the victims at the bottom of society. Though momentary trials and tribulations can and, in certain cases, will result in harm and death, the ultimate result of speaking one's voice of the true liberated self realizes the ultimate deliverance into final freedom—that is to say, the voiced word surpasses anything that evil can bring down on the oppressed. Ex-slave Jimmy yielded to a martyrdom that displayed a doublelayered instance of a theatrical performance of the Spirit with us. As he toiled in the field, Uncle Jimmy was set on fire and burned to death because he refused to stop singing his voice of praise and freedom in Jesus-with-us. "De overseer come on back down in de fiel an' took Uncle Jimmy cross de fiel ov' de fense. Made de po' man dig a hole in de groun wid his nacked han's. Den dey put straw in de bottom of de hole an' po'd on de tar. Den he chained po' Uncle Jimmy an' th'owed him in de hole an' lit a match to him. Lawd! Lawd! But dis ain' stop him. Uncle Jimmy say, 'Ise fixin' to die to live agin' in Christ.'"[26]

On the one hand, Uncle Jimmy's musical voice amidst a fiery inferno of a black bodied, charred lynching serves as a theater of pleasure for white folk's voyeuristic gaze. On the other hand, his final song of praise serves as his own theatrical goodbye; an affront to the slavemaster and an affirmation that "the world didn't make him and the world can't take him away" (paraphrasing black folk religion) from the Spirit of liberation with him. Once those enchained by internal spiritual demons or external systematic structures take the risk against the forces of death, the fullness of one's spiritual and material humanity becomes apparent when one, through faith in Jesus' pledge to proclaim freedom for the oppressed, sings one's voice into liberation and emancipation. The more the victims claim their voices, the more steadfast their preparation to become freely human. The paradox of faith in, witness for, and pursuit of the Spirit of liberation with us is a momentary death but an ultimate and inevitable victory for the majority of the world (for the poor, working people, and the brokenhearted). To the very end of every life-threatening challenge, the voice of the least in society cries out: "'Ise fixin' to die to live agin' in Christ."

Fruit of the Journey

Jesus, the Spirit of total liberation with us, not only offers various dimensions of the goal (of liberation and the practice of freedom) and the road to that goal. Jesus continues to be with the least in society and the brokenhearted by granting them fruit on their journey's path to co-constitute with God's spirit the new self of liberation and freedom. And this fruit of the self consists of new methods of the self, expressions of the full spiritual and material humanity in larger social structures, local ordinary daily life, language articulations, and positive racial cultural affirmations.

ONGOING REVELATION WITH THE POOR

A primary fruit gained by the poor on their journey of freedom is the event of the Spirit of liberation speaking to them. It is an event that reveals itself as a form of communication understood by and needing the interpretation of the least in society. Experiencing this language, a divine gift of communicative action, the poor realize and feel the ever present reality of the Spirit. Jesus, as this spirit, is the divine reality with the bottom sectors of society. That is why Jesus is Emmanuel—the Spirit with us.

Yet demonic spirits of the oppressor and evil will deny continually that the poor are visited by Jesus and, therefore, the poor, from the demons' perspective, do not have the capability of being the receptors and interpreters of the language act of the Spirit's revelation. In radical contrast, white supremacist Christians, male chauvinists, heterosexists, and those with class privileges all claim that God has revealed God's spirit of liberation with us only to each of their own particular privileged groups. They seek to monopolize the revelatory language as an exclusive event of the Spirit being only with them. In effect, once they create or interpret a theological and religious canon in their favor, oppressors and those with privilege close off further revelation in an attempt to deny the inevitable communication from and to the Spirit. But this ongoing ritual of revelation is at the heart of the poor's faith that they will always and continually hear a direct word of liberation from the Spirit in their journey along the way to a new humanity.

Old Elizabeth presents this profound point as she travels along the road to proclaim the good news of liberation for the downtrodden and oppressed during the slavery era. Born in 1776 in Maryland, freed at age thirty and called to preach to the enslaved and free blacks, Old Elizabeth felt ordained by the Spirit with her to remain in her own slave territory to be a witness for the journey. She faced not only the physical possibility of a return to the institution of slavery. But also, she faced "the slings and arrows" on the spiritual and language levels of her everyday existence. For instance, white supremacist clergymen routinely questioned her authority to preach. In her response, she claimed the reward of proclaiming the gospel as a result of direct communication through revelation.

> As I traveled along through the land, I was led at different times to converse with white men who were by profession ministers of the gospel. Many of them, up and down, confessed they did not believe in revelation, which gave me to see that men were sent forth as minister without Christ's authority. In a conversation with one of these, he said, "You think you have these things by revelation, but there has been no such thing as revelation since Christ's ascension." I asked him where the apostle John got his revelation while he was in the Isle of Patmos. With this, he rose up and left me, and I said in my spirit, get thee behind me Satan.[27]

Christian ministers who support a status quo of oppression cannot open themselves up or receive the ongoing manifestation of Jesus' persisting gift of liberation for those least in society. Even more, they cannot imagine or envision the possibility that a former enslaved black female worker could have anything to say about the good news of freedom. Such male proclaimers of a Christianity of oppression continue to be blind to revelation today. They fail to connect the appearance of the Spirit of liberation in the Bible (bringing about the full humanity of the outcasts in the biblical narrative) with the continual issuance of this same Spirit from the mouths of the least in today's society. In a word, the Spirit of liberation with the oppressed in the Hebrew and Christian Scriptures is the same Spirit laboring with the downtrodden and broken hearted in the contemporary context.

We discover divine revelation wherever Jesus struggles with the marginalized as they move to co-constitute themselves into a new liberated full humanity. Christian ministers with a truncated faith and stifling theology embody a legion of spirits from Satan because they limit revelation to Jesus' ascension. Oppressors do not have the power to contain the omnipresence of the Spirit of liberation. They cannot close the canon on where Christ chooses to be. From biblical witness and the oppressed's own location, Jesus' resurrection from the dead signifies the ongoing hope of Jesus' presence with them.

TO LIVE WITH JESUS

Rev. W. B. Allen, ex-slave, testifies to an additional fruit along the journey to full humanity. The poor and forsaken gain the inevitable hope of living with Jesus. Rev. Allen shares this song he remembered his mother singing while a chattel.

> Our troubles will soon be over,
> I'm going to live with Jesus—after
>   while;
> Praying time will soon be over,
> I'm going home to live with Jesus
>   after while.
> All I want is Jesus; you may
> have all the world.
> Just give me Jesus.[28]

To live with Jesus is a subversive hope with an initial paradox. At first glance, this song from the mouths of the oppressed appears to indicate a pliant surrender to all of earth's resources and, thereby, a cowardly surrender of the fight on earth to the oppressor. However, the radical reversal in this black theology demands further investigation. The oppressed do shun "the world" because this world in which they live today, with unequal social relations, is not the way the world will ultimately look. In this sense, they abdicate all allegiance to the current world of oppression. Yet, the hope lies in a world reconfig-ured radically by the home that is Jesus; that is to say, a world where the full spiritual and material humanity of the poor becomes evident. Hope in this new home on earth and in heaven with Jesus brings a condemnation of today's world of discrimination.

At the same time, the poor have hope in inevitable salvation and liberation into a new humanity co-constituted with the Spirit with us (that is, Jesus) because the Spirit calls for no other gods before it. Abundance for the poor, found in the existence of Jesus' presence with them, can only become a realized hope of truth and actualized meaning of faith when nothing in this world is put before Jesus. Again, another paradox appears. By surrendering all of this old world, the poor receive all of a new world. By placing other demons and gods before Jesus, oppressed humanity would lose all human hope in homeness and abundance with Jesus, who is the time and location of liberation and freedom. Only by letting go and letting the Spirit guide their faith can the oppressed of any society receive the fruit granted in a realized hope. To paraphrase slave religious folk wisdom, grounded in the vivid context of excruciating pain and a warped social relations stacked against them, "this world ain't my home." This common sense wisdom is, thus, a rigorous "no" to oppression and an invigorating "yes" to a new self in Jesus.

Harriet Gresham, ex-slave from Florida, recalled a similar song from the slavery period; similar in the sense of theological truth and meaning.

> T'ank ye Marster Jesus, t'ank ye,
> T'ank ye Marster Jesus, t'ank ye,
> T'ank ye Marster Jesus, t'ank ye,
> Da Heben gwinter be my home.
> No slav'ry chains to tie me down,
> And no mo' driver's ho'n to blow fer me
> No mo' stocks to fasten me down
> Jesus break slav'ry chain, Lord
> Break slav'ry chain Lord,
> Break slav'ry chain Lord,
> Da Heben gwinter be my home.[29]

This black theology rendered in music instructs us about the impor-tance of context as one angle to discern the liberation impulse in the hope of living with Jesus. Under the slavery system with white supremacists bringing death to hopes for a novel time and place for an independent black self, this song would assume an otherworldly text for those listening but not initiated into the polyvalent and multilayered black English of the least in society. When oppressed people are hemmed in, they often voice a hope in being at home with Jesus in a far off heaven, someday and somewhere. The discourse of homeness with Jesus entails a truth and falsehood. Poor folk and oppressed folk often employ double language as a strategy to disguise their hope for immediate transformation of their (or at least their children's generation's) circumstances. Double meaning language becomes a space and experience seized by the marginalized where they can assert their true voice and assert their true self in spiritual and physical safety. So "Da Heben gwinter be my home" can be offered to the nearby oppressor as a harmless balm of "darkies" musing philosophically about the afterlife, without an apparent impinging on the macropolitical economy of slavery or capitalism.

Yet the yearning for immediate earthly freedom (as well as heavenly emancipation), as another interpretive discourse for hope to live with Jesus, lingers not too far beneath the surface of each word in this Negro spiritual. In fact, when emancipation came, the formerly enslaved African Americans sang into freedom their hope in an already realized homeness with Jesus symbolized by the abolition of slavery. In fact, this song was actually sung right when freedom was declared. Thus the context of post-slavery time enunciates more stridently the pre-slavery sub-text of a hope in Jesus' gift of homeness (that is, full spiritual and material humanity) on earth.

Moreover, the hope in the nearness of living with Jesus at home is revealed in the description of what "Da Heben gwinter be my home" looks like. This sustaining hope in the home of Jesus is very concrete; it is the elimination of all forms of oppression, discrimination, and exploitation. It is being with Jesus where no forms of chains can bind the downtrodden, where no one or no situation can tie down the movement or the tongue of the least in society. A formerly oppressed person can go where he or she pleases without the fear of hate crimes of racism, domestic violence, rape, or antigay attacks. It offers a place and time where the muted tongue of the formerly enchained person can speak whenever and wherever she or he desires. At the same time, "no mo' driver's ho'n to blow fer me" symbolizes the ending of people with power and privilege lording their oppressive behaviors over those lower on the totem pole of capitalist civilization. One in the home of Jesus no longer suffers from any threatening summons or backbreaking instructions. And "no mo' stocks to fasten me down" means the cessation of imprisonment for those who go against institutions and instances of sin; whether on the level of insults of micro everyday living or the constraints of macro structural evil. To live with Jesus, therefore, is to have hope in the fruits of the journey toward the goal of liberation and freedom imagined and institutionalized when "Jesus break slav'ry chain."

The doublenatured discourse of this song occurs not only in the pre-slavery period. In the post-slavery era, the oppressed folk's song (in their faith and hope in living with Jesus) also assumes double meaning. True, the context of post-slavery emancipation allows the oppressed to conjure up more forthrightly the pre-slavery content of earthly homeness of living with Jesus. Hoping to live with Jesus, here, denotes actual and material transformation of this earthly world. Yet, the second dimension of this hope, even in the context of emancipation, consists of a faithful hope that there will be a better life with Jesus (and one's family) in heaven after death. Consequently there is no contradiction between the now and the not yet. Indeed, the struggle to bring life to the living with Jesus now on earth ("Jesus break slav'ry chain") is a foretaste of the heavenly expectation of the ultimate fruit of eternal life. That is why the oppressed can struggle in hope for the "already" possibilities of earthly freedom and the "not yet" of full realized liberated and freed humanity living with Jesus in heaven. "T'ank ye Marster Jesus, t'ank ye, Da Heben gwinter be my home" occurs in the temporal present and in the far off time. The Spirit of liberation with us is the hope to live with Jesus now and in the future.

SAVIOR AND LIBERATOR

As the poor travel the journey toward the goal of liberation, in addition to receiving the ongoing revelation of the Spirit with them and the grace of Jesus living with them, they also experience the fruit of Jesus as savior and liberator. Even when the marginalized of society articulate through song words similar to what oppressors might offer in their Christian praise, the excruciating and painful context of oppression impacts greatly the meaning and truth of the salvific and deliverance words of those treated as objects by the social elites. To those pressed against the wall by overarching structures of exploitation, hemmed in by duplicitous rules stacked against them, and racked with the demons internal to their own spiritual, psychological, and emotional well-being, Jesus presents balanced energizing gifts.

More specifically, these salvific and liberative moments and blessed dynamics of the Spirit with them appear in at least two forms—an evangelical and a political co-constitution of the new self. On the one hand, the brokenhearted undergo a profound metanoia (or change) on the inside. They are filled with and consumed by the Spirit warring against internal demons and fighting their previously hopeless battles against anger, self-doubt, insecurities, loss of voice, self-effacement, and capitulation to the painful and lonely rule of evil. Jesus fills their soul with the Spirit's potency; and the objects of society no longer have to rely only on themselves and be without the presence of Jesus. This marks the salvation dimension brought on by the fruit of evangelical power along the journey. It is what black folk spiritual wisdom characterizes as: "I looked at my hands and they felt new. I looked at my feet and they did too." Newness of a constituted self with the Spirit begins on the inside of the soul: the soul surrenders to Jesus' presence and victory over internal demons of self-defeat in the old self, and now experiences a new realm of joy, peace and serenity. Joy on the inside proves sufficient to appreciate the new self and to bear the attacks from external afflictions. Peace offers a balanced sense of calm interior space that enables the poor to get off the spiritual, psychological, and emotional roller coaster run by the ever present legions of the demonic, to know their true identity and to attain their own voice. Serenity rewards them with the assurance that they no longer will pursue the same old journey while expecting different results. The presence of the evangelical Spirit yields a novel feeling that in fact for the oppressed appears to produce a new body.

For instance, the biblical witness narrates the story of a certain man (a non-specific marker symbolizing all who suffer) possessed by demonic spirits, a man who dwelled in the graveyard. Being possessed, he had great strength, for not even handcuffs and shackles could subdue him. But in fact, the legion of internal demons presented a false and harmful power that caused this suffering man to inflict brutal pain upon himself. His false sense of power and control brought destruction to his body. Thus instead of becoming a new self with new hands and new feet, he continually reduced, through self-inflicted injury caused by the internal demonic, his body to morbidity and a slow death. No other human was strong enough to subdue this man and heal him of his false and dangerous sense of power and control. The more he attempted to heal himself, the more he found the internal wicked, possessed state too formidable an opponent. The more others tried to control him and change his wretched state of pain and poverty, the more he reared up in stark opposition. Only when Jesus came to be with him and called on the presence of the Spirit of liberation with him (that is, Jesus as that spirit) did this oppressed man reap the fruit of joy, peace and serenity on the inside. Jesus spoke to the demons within, and through this speaking of the Spirit, the demon identified itself: "My name is Legion; for we are many." And with that encounter, Legion departed the soul and body of the man who, now recovered, went forth to enjoy the fruits of his journey (Mark 5:1-20).

Simultaneously, as the Spirit with us conjures up a consuming evangelical presence within the soul of the demonically possessed, the Spirit bears fruit on the political front of oppression—that is, the external dimensions of painful systems. Conversion and sanctification imply a forthright engagement with multileveled systems of demonic power outside of oneself in the larger political, social, and civic realms. Without the participation of the Spirit with the little ones of society in their victimization by and struggles against the macrostructures of racial discrimination, sexual oppression, homophobic bias, and class exploitation, then the old self of demon possession would prove victorious. Restated, the Spirit is with us in changing us from the old state of subservience and self-injury while, at the same time, it pursues the journey with us in a constant enlivening. The move toward the life of the new self entails a continual reaffirmation of that self along life's way. And this conversion and sanctification movement (with the Spirit) emboldens the poor to struggle against and claim their victory over external systemic evil and harmful social asymmetry. The certainty of evangelical change and sustenance fuels the tenacity of the efforts against larger oppressive systems. Likewise, engagement of political structures fosters radical transformation of space and time that activate and animate the oppressed to further realize the new self.

The dramatic portrayal of the realized gift of the Spirit's salvation and liberation (that is, soul-filled evangelical joy and structural political victory on the journey to a full humanity) becomes quite evident in major social realignments of harmful arrangement and constricting instances where the least in society adorn their new selves with the grammar and habits of soothing songs and pleasurable practices. Slave religious experiences verify this claim. The daughter of former chattel, Sara Crocker, remembered the jubilant equation of salvation and liberation when enslaved African Americans finally won their freedom in 1865 after the Civil War. The newly liberated ebony selves chanted and danced for joy while offering songs of praise: "I am glad salvation is free for us all,/ I am glad salvation is free."[30] These words were sung and danced upon hearing of slavery's death.

When the oppressed achieve a measure of freedom found in the newly co-constituted self accompanied by the Spirit with us, they enunciate very clearly, through resilient rituals, the dynamic interplay between the fruit of salvation and liberation. Jesus brings salvation along with earthly freedom. An evangelical spirit-filled soul parallels and dovetails with a spirit-induced social transformation. The fuller salvation and liberation manifest together, the fuller the presence of Jesus with us. Salvation (evangelical witness) and liberation (political witness) are both exemplars of the Spirit of total liberation revealed to be with us as fruits on the journey to a total spiritual and material humanity. Evangelical salvation alone yields the negative fruit of narcissistic inwardness. Political liberation alone yields a fruitless celebration of perpetual rebellion.

ONE MASTER

Moreover, Jesus, the Spirit of liberation with us, offers one of the most freeing fruits of all: an emancipated status in this world where no other person, place, thing, or situation has absolute supremacy over those suffering. This beneficial effect liberates the hearts and spirits of those who are the least and at the bottom of society to seek allegiance, not to earthly principalities and powers, but to one with them along their journey to full humanity. At first, the acceptance of the Spirit with us as one master might connote a slavish transference of one obligation of servility to another. However, one master (that is, Jesus) walks with the oppressed to co-constitute themselves anew in the image of and in accordance with the will of the one master. Acceptance of this positive outcome becomes an affront against earthly systems that carve out harmful parameters limiting the full potential of the voiceless.

In fact, the actual surrender to the one master obligates the poor to be themselves in spite of the nagging aches in their soul and the arrogance of ruling elites and privileged people who lord a demonic master relationship over them. One cannot serve both the master that is the hegemony and influence of evil and the realm and righteousness of the master offering freedom to be free. Because the one master's (that is, Jesus') will emboldens the oppressed to seek their own pathway toward liberation and the practice of freedom, service to Jesus the one master with them implies the subservience of the poor to their own goal of total liberation. In this sense, the more the brokenhearted and voiceless adhere to the one master, the more they are actually undertaking a journey toward that which is in their own best interests (their own freedom). To transfer accountability to Jesus brings a more resolute way toward attaining voice and place on earth.

David Walker, free black and abolitionist against all earthly proclaimers of evil masterhood, refuted the white supremacists of slavery during his day. For Walker, both the oppressed and the oppressor must surrender obedience to one master who is the bearer of good news for the forlorn and the enchained. "Have we any other Master but Jesus Christ alone? Is he not their Master as well as ours?—What right then, have we to obey and call any other Master, but Himself?"[31] The revolutionary implications of one overarching lord and master subverts the hierarchy of demonic structures and levels the social relations between the haves and the have-nots. Because we all owe obligations to the Spirit with us, even the oppressors are called to recognize the lordship of the one master with us all. Therefore, to undertake the process of the co-constitution of the new self with the Spirit with us gives the oppressed a feeling that they can walk this land freely because there is one who is greater than themselves. At the same time, this one reigns greater than and above even the rich and the powerful. Master Jesus removes the internal chains of self-doubt, chaos, lack of focus from the spirits of the oppressed and enables them to wake up each morning "with their minds stayed on Jesus," to paraphrase a Negro spiritual.

Furthermore, learning from the example of Walker, freedom to be oneself aligned with one master alters one's perception of possibilities. If the Spirit of God's freedom with us has created all, then all on earth belong to Jesus and not to the narrow claims of any one class, race, gender, or sexual orientation. The creation through and possession of all resources by Jesus bring equality in social, political, and cultural relations among humankind. No one can take that which has been brought about by Jesus. Hence the voiceless and least among us have the same rights to equality of daily life, affirmation of a particular identity, articulation of unique languages, and ownership of capital—that is, to all the methods of the self-actualization of full humanity—as do the most powerful and rich among us. The powerful are humans and subject to Master Jesus' purpose of total liberation with us, just as are the weak. The poor and those at the bottom of society alter their worldview from one in which they cringe in subservience before a skewed notion of authority and a deleterious hierarchy of credibility. Now, with Jesus the Master, the poor perceive the powerful as vulnerable, finite, and regular human beings.

The one master gives the ultimate gift of freedom; Jesus sets the downtrodden free. Those converted to the path of a newness of life do not gloss over or water down the radical reality of the Spirit bringing the gift of freedom. Former slave Green Willbanks articulates the normative nature of the fruits of the Spirit of liberation with us being to set free.

"I think Abraham Lincoln was a all right man; God so intended that we should be sot free [set free]. Jeff Davis [president of the Confederate States of America] was all right in his way, but I can't say much for him. Yes mam, I'd rather be free. Sho! Give me freedom all the time. Jesus said: 'If my Son sets you free, you shall be free indeed.'"[32] Mr. Willbanks, in his unique discourse, expresses faith in and the rewards of one master by a language of leveling. He first acknowledges the humanity of Lincoln by claiming this president was an "all right man." Yet the true master with the power to determine the will and way of Lincoln was Jesus, the one who sets free. While rendering recognition of Lincoln, Mr. Willbanks indicates that the final arbiter of justice is Jesus because he fixed the intention and put the deliverance will into Lincoln's ambition and inclination. Lincoln becomes subservient to Jesus. Likewise, Mr. Willbanks offers an affirmation of the humanity of Jeff Davis (the head of the southern white supremacist states). Though he cannot say much for Davis, still the latter "was all right in his way." Here too, Mr. Willbanks relegates Davis beneath the decisive bestowal of freedom—the Spirit of total liberation with us. The oppressed, in this situation, give no divine authority to earthly elites, whether of the northern liberal racist or southern white supremacist ilk. Jesus offers the Spirit of liberation with us in a supreme lordship.

In this manner, the poor, who open themselves to receive the fruit of one master on the journey to freedom, will indeed receive one who sets free. The reception of the gift, which calls on the least in society to claim their own new self on life's way, will in turn bring about a continual emancipation to a full self. Willingness to receive the Spirit with us on the way will yield the fruit of removing allegiance from the oppressors, asserting the mere humanness of the oppressors, and articulating the true self's need to be truly liberated. The one master presents the potential gift of freedom for those who would alter allegiances from either a selfish focus on the self or a demonic hegemony. Simultaneously, the one master as lord solidifies the poor's and brokenhearted's certainty, determination, and joy of being liberated and practicing freedom, "all the time." The blessing of one master accompanies the blessing of ongoing freedom.

A NEW SELF

Jesus, the Spirit of total liberation with us, is an event of life and death movement from an old self of stultifying sin and servile submissiveness to the I AM WHO I AM nature of God (the Spirit of liberation for us) which grows within the poor communities and humbled sectors of society. This divine nature or image of God (or imago dei) has been dormant or subject to attacks on all sides, both internal and external, spiritual and material. Jesus comes as a process of action and dynamism and literally re-turns the poor to the path of their full potential. Conversion, that re-turning, defines the most decisive work of the Spirit with us. Only through the re-turning of conversion can the oppressed have the courage, vision, energy, and, above all, faith to pursue the newness of their own individual lives as well as the new social configuration that the Spirit works with them to co-constitute, that is, the new humanity in the new Common Wealth.

The message of the Gospel proclaims freedom for the captives, liberation for those blind, emancipation for the brokenhearted, and the accepted "year of the Lord's favor" (Luke 4:19), which is an ultimate jubilee celebration. Yet sin of the old self, personal and structural, prevents the marginalized of society from seizing the goal, pursuing the road, and enjoying the fruits of their journey to the good news. They cannot live into the healing and revolutionary grace offered by the Spirit for them and the Spirit with them. On one level, they suffer at the apparent power and mystifying might of the controlling sectors and rulers of society. Economically poor and working people do not have the abundant material wealth and social networking connections to experience the bounty of the earth created for all of humanity. Women, on their own, lack sufficient resources to overcome a male-centered culture and nation geared to maintaining the majority of positions of decision making for one gender only. Black folk still endure a legacy in which the heartbeat of slavery echoes throughout every level of what it means to be an American; the norm remains white. And lesbians and gays risk death merely because of public displays of human affection.

On another level, the pangs and pains of sin within the victims' own souls prevent them from moving toward the goal of their full humanity. Fear, self-doubt, anger, resentment, jealousy, depression, compulsive behavior, hedonism, and an assortment of addictions and abuses verify that no part of the human community has a monopoly on truth and liberation. The legion of demons within the self affects adversely and tears down definitively not only the self, but the family, the community, and even the church, including the African American church. Without a healing turn away from such harmful entrapments, the poor and the oppressed cannot seize the time of jubilee. In other words, the new humanity and the new Common Wealth require a process away from self-focused deleterious practices and a journey away from those manifold expressions of structural confinement.

At this juncture, the paramount position of "being with" defines the core of Jesus. Jesus works with those forced to be obedient objects for others and frees them from the passive posture of reacting to people, places, things, and systems. Conversion sums up this creative and freeing process. The Spirit of liberation with us anchors such an ongoing dynamic of becoming new "born again" human beings constructing innovative systemic social relations. Conversion empowers and, therefore, enables the weak to move about this world as if this world belonged to them. They organize themselves to reflect the image of God within them and the Spirit with them, even risk rearranging the political economy to embody the feel and structures of a the new Common Wealth. In that way, the weak become strong.

Strength, however, dwells not in a fortified sense and exclusive practice of being over against the other. This would reflect a mere inversion of the oppression perpetrated by the oppressor. Conversion is not an instantaneous coup with those outside the castle walls simply replacing the current occupants of a skewed structure. On the contrary, the sacred event of conversion is toward the democratization and equalization of all resources, languages, racial cultural formations, and classes of people. The democratic ownership and equalized decision making and positive self-affirmation signify the in-breaking of the new journey of the Spirit with us. With the oppressed, Jesus labors in this struggle to change from the death of the old to the life of the new self, individually and collectively.

In fact, the dying and rising with Jesus begins on the inside of the oppressed and causes a major initial disruption, symbolizing Jesus' struggle to defeat the internal demons preventing the poor from changing their external circumstances. Sister Kelly's three-week conversion process signals the picturesque ebb and flow of "coming through religion."[33]

> Well, I walked along . . . and 'pear like to me something said, "You never shall die a sinner." Well, I jest trembled and shook like a leaf. . . . Well, I heard that voice three times, and every time it said, "You never shall die a sinner." It seem like it was inside of me. . . . And seem like a clear loud voice said, "You is jest in God's hands, and you must praise and bless God all the time." . . . I knowed no more about it than this here rock, but I sho felt something and I heard something too.

After many days of wrestling with the presence of Jesus with her, Sister Kelly encountered a deepening of her conversion experience.

> I tell you the gospel's truth, I kin go and put my hand on the spot right now, where I jest fell; face foremost—something just struck me. . . . I fell to crying, jest like I was crazy; I felt right crazy, too, praise God, but I wasn't; it was just the grace of God I had done been looking for, lo them many weeks. . . . I tell you it's a wonderful feeling when you feel the spirit of the Lord God Almighty in the tips of your fingers, and the bottom of yo' heart . . . I knows now when I feel that spirit arising in my body, yessire. . . . When I got up from prayer, I felt like I was brand new—I had done been washed in Jesus' blood . . . 'cause I sho' been through a great fight with the devil. . . . That morning, seem like Jesus said to me, "My little one, what makes you so hard to believe, when you know I am the one and only God?" . . . I heard him all on the inside.

Ultimately in the conversion dynamic, Jesus, the Spirit of liberation with us, frees her from fear of any person, situation, or thing. "Well, the last time the Lord spoke to me, he said, 'My little one, I have carried you out of this world, and you is no more of this world, but of another world, the holy world, and they will hate you for my sake.' That's the truth, ain't it. I don't fear no man but Jesus. He is my God, do you hear me?"[34]

Conversion originates with the least in society undergoing a terrifying encounter with fear. Fear stands at the root of the oppressed person's entrapment to macropolitical structures of discrimination and microspiritual demons of self-imposed restraints. Working people fear the implications of struggling to claim the resources and wealth that God has given all humanity. Women face the physical strength of men; blacks (and other people of color) confront an entire edifice of white supremacy; and lesbians and gays experience the fickle and volatile whims of the entire heterosexual population. At the same time, the least in society experience a silent killer; the profound self-imposed fear acting as glue for self-doubt, low self-esteem, harmful anger, resentment, and lack of enough self-love.

However, the Spirit of liberation with us goes to work on the inside to render a sense of a full self and full voice to the downtrodden. This is what Sister Kelly meant when she said the voice of Jesus "seem like it was inside of me." Transformation begins within and racks the entire body as well as activates all of the corporal senses. Primarily the event of the Spirit with us entails a procession of bodily sensations. Initially one does not become aware intellectually. Knowledge which one does acknowledge is an epistemology and a pedagogy of the body. It is a feeling and a hearing way of understanding and interpreting meaning and truth. The feeling becomes a location of fierce contestation between who will possess and rule the physical nature of the oppressed. Will it be "the devil" or Jesus the Spirit with us? In fact, the manifest victory of the Spirit over the legion of demons becomes a stark reality when the oppressed undergoes "the struck dead" phase of conversion. Now, through this death, the least in society can rise with the Spirit. In a parallel manner, Paul narrates a similar motion of down and up, dying and rising with Christ in the baptismal ritual for the oppressed and in the crucifixion-resurrection ritual with Jesus.

> But if we have died with Christ, we believe that we will also live with him. We know that Christ, being raised from the dead, will never die again; death no longer has dominion over him. The death he died, he died to sin, once for all; but the life he lives, he lives to God. So you also must consider yourselves dead to sin and alive to God in Christ Jesus. Therefore, do not let sin exercise dominion in your mortal bodies, to make you obey their passions. No longer present your members to sin as instruments of wickedness, but present yourselves to God as those who have been brought from death to life, and present your members to God as instruments of righteousness.
>
> Rom. 6:8-13

Fundamentally, the journey of conversion with Jesus involves a returning to the will of God, the goal of comprehensive and holistic freedom. To get there, one has to be struck dead to sin and made alive to Jesus.[35] It brings on "a great fight with the devil" (as Sister Kelly says) in the body. And coming through this faithful religious experience includes the final marker of blood. In a word, with the defeat of "the devil" and its legion of psychological, emotional, and visceral demons, Jesus offers the washing of the oppressed soul with Jesus' own blood as a balm to heal the internal racking of the body brought on by the birth of the new self (with Jesus) out of the death of the old self (with "the devil"). In that sense, the poor can say, "I had done been washed in Jesus' blood."

Cleansed in this final indicator of victory, the poor can claim a fear of "no man but Jesus." "No man" means that no human person or system on earth has authority over the least in society or the ability to make them bow down to oppressive powers. On the contrary, the oppressed are now in fear of Jesus. But Jesus is not a tyrannical lord. Rather, he is the Spirit of total spiritual and material liberation with the poor, the marginalized, the exploited, the brokenhearted, and the least in society. Thus to fear Jesus is to fear not working with Jesus to realize the final goal of liberation and the practice of freedom; that is, the co-constitution of the full self. Sister Kelly remembers: "I tell you, honey, you got to be touched from the inside, and be struck by his hand like I was 'fore you feel that holy uplifting spirit."[36]

The uplifting holy spirit yields a giddy sense of newness in one's soul and body. Sister Kelly shouted "I felt like I was brand new" after her conversion experience. Moreover, being with the Spirit in soulful transformation accompanies the re-turn toward God in social transformation. Sojourner Truth's testimony enlightens us on this point. The following excerpt comes from her narrative as told to an editor:

> She desired to talk to God, but her vileness utterly forbade it, and she was not able to prefer a petition. . . . At length a friend appeared to stand between herself and an insulted Deity; and she felt as sensibly refreshed when, on a hot day, an umbrella had been interposed between her scorching head and a burning sun. But who was this friend? became the next inquiry. . . . An answer came to her, saying distinctly, "It is Jesus." "Yes," she responded, "it is Jesus."[37]

The power of conversion enabled Sojourner Truth to become one of America's leading antislavery advocates and ardent supporters of women's rights. Consequently, she defied the life-threatening crowds of white supremacists and male chauvinists because Jesus worked with her, through conversion, as she became a radical witness for the fundamental overhaul of American society. Here, the internal spiritual allegiance to a new self with Jesus translates into a new self in motion to rearrange social relations in the public sphere for a new Common Wealth: the democratization and equalization of God's resources for all humanity. The Spirit of liberation with us, Jesus, heralds the dawning of intense and persistent efforts towards social transformation. Conversion confronts configurations of slavery (that is, white oppression and class exploitation) and women's subordination while claiming victory over the the death of demons inside of the oppressed. The spiritual is political and the political is spiritual.

Similarly in his autobiography, a former slave offered a direct correlation between the spiritual death and life resurrection dimension of conversion with Jesus to the material liberation from earthly structures of dehumanization. In his words: "He who has passed from spiritual death to life, and received the witness within his soul that his sins are forgiven, may possibly form some distant idea" of what freedom means.[38] In other words, in his attempts to depict what his newfound freedom felt like (now that he had departed from the slavery system), the only parallel of any significance and substance was the conversion experience of Jesus; the Spirit of liberation with us who pardons the sins of the oppressed and brokenhearted while working with them to forge a new humanity.

CONCLUSION

Jesus, the Spirit of total liberation with us, presents free grace to the least in society. Employing biblical accounts and ex-slave stories in this chapter, we have discovered that Jesus has a goal of liberation with us (that is, Jesus' purpose, location at the bar, and proclamation of his gospel). And the Spirit accompanies the oppressed along the road to the final goal (that is, through Jesus' gifts, power, and language). Along the way of this journey, the poor and marginalized gain fruit from their struggle (that is, Jesus' ongoing revelation with the poor, the act of living with Jesus, receiving him as a full time Savior and Liberator and One Master, and experiencing the event of being set free). The goal, the road to the goal, and the fruit of the journey, however, culminate in the establishment of the new self. This latter revelation and creation occur in the life and death event of conversion.

Perhaps the following Negro spiritual captures the multiple offerings of liberation and freedom for a full humanity that Jesus the Spirit with us bestows upon the bottom sectors of society.

> My God Is A Rock In A Weary Land
> Chorus: My God is a rock in a weary land
>   weary land
>   My God is a rock in a weary land
>   shelter in a time of storm. . . .
> Stop let me tell you 'bout the Chapter One
>   When the Lord God's work has jus' begun
> Stop and let me tell 'bout the Chapter Two
>   When the Lord God's written his Bible through
> Stop and let me tell you 'bout the Chapter Three

When the Lord God died on Calvary. . . .
Stop and let me tell you 'bout the Chapter Four
    Lord God visit 'mong the po'
Stop and let me tell you 'bout Chapter Five
    Lord God brought the dead alive
Stop and let me tell you 'bout the Chapter Six
    He went in Jerusalem and healed the sick. . . .
Stop and let me till you 'bout Chapter Seven
    Died and risen and went to Heaven
Stop and let me tell you 'bout Chapter Eight
    John see Him standin' at the Golden Gate
Stop and let me tell you 'bout Chapter Nine
    Lord God turned the water to wine
Stop and let me tell you 'bout the Chapter Ten
    John says He's comin' in the world again.[39]

Jesus has always been the Spirit with us. In the beginning, "when the Lord God's work has jus' begun," Jesus took part in the crafting of all of creation. He was with humanity before the fall into evil and sin. Prior to this downward turn away from God, the Spirit with us co-created all of the earth's resources for all of humanity. This paradise, utopia, or sacred vision provided every necessity of life for the first human creation. Ownership and control of resources and wealth belonged to all, and, therefore all shared equally in a Common Wealth. With the rise of selfishness, greed derived from private ownership and cutthroat competition, feelings of superiority, and institutional structures to undergird these demonic perspectives, humanity turned away from God's vision for full spiritual and material freedom of the self in community.

Yet, the Spirit of total liberation did not forsake humanity even in its most wicked hour. Instead, the word of God (that is, Jesus "written his Bible through") testified to the Spirit still being with oppressed humanity to work with them to re-turn back to the goal of a new Common Wealth. And this word (now in the sense of "in the beginning was the Word" John 1:1) assumed the paramount position of being with the poor. When those whom Jesus came for, as elaborated in Luke 4:18–19, could not on their own turn back the terrible tide of internal demons raging within the abused individual and victimized community, and when they likewise failed to overturn structures of oppression from wicked systems and sinister strata in society, the Spirit with us (e.g., Jesus the logos or word) took on the downtrodden's struggle to defeat evil. This is the fundamental reality experienced, identified, and accepted by the poor. That is to say, the death on Calvary by Jesus exemplified that he was truly Emmanuel (God with us).

In this sense, the crucifixion on Calvary denotes Jesus as the event that "visit 'mong the po'" (the poor in the above Negro spiritual). The spirit of total liberation dwells with and among the poor. Visitation imagery suggests conscious intent on the part of Jesus concerning where he chose and, today still, chooses to be. Visitation, moreover, not only symbolizes the Spirit deliberating with preordained providential purpose, but also illustrates coming to the home of relatives and family members. And in this poor community and family gathering, the Spirit activates its healing power for newness of life. "Lord God" Jesus becomes a doctor prescribing and administering medicinal remedies for the intangible soul and the visibly wounded among the community of the least. Indeed, the potent ingredient in this life producing and natural remedy consists of Jesus' own blood shed on Calvary in the victory over the many-layered masks of evil. On the cross, the Spirit goes to war with the old dead selves of the poor and the brokenhearted. And, consequently in triumph, the resurrection of the Spirit carries the poor along their journey to their new selves of a full humanity. Death of the many faces of evil no longer has dominion; therefore with the new humanity and into the new Common Wealth, Jesus has "risen and went to Heaven."

With an ascension and realization of the new person and new community, Jesus remains with us, but now as a gatekeeper. Having achieved the goal of liberation, the practice of ongoing freedom of the self and community must be ensured. As a result, the Spirit remains with those who have re-turned back to the divine space and place of democracy and equality (that is, the mapping of a geographic space and the construction of an architectural location for equal ownership of resources and equal affirmation of all God's people). This new heaven and revolutionized earth find the Spirit at the gate applying to the only biblical criteria for moving through this gate and embracing "heaven." Matt. 23:31-46 illustrates the narrative of Jesus dictating criteria for everlasting life: feeding the hungry, clothing the naked, visiting those in prison, giving water to the thirsty, providing shelter for the homeless, and healing for the sick. Only here in the word of God (that is, the word being Jesus found in the Gospel of John) does one discern the clearest mandate for obedient discipleship to enter the promised land of a new Common Wealth on earth as it is in heaven.

In what the spiritual calls Chapter Nine, in the persistent saga of the Spirit with us, Jesus reveals his abilities as culinary artist. On the one hand, he produces manna from heaven in the sense of the manna provided miraculously to the Hebrew people as they wandered forty years in the wilderness on their journey to their promised land of a new Common Wealth. Jesus' gift of transforming became apparent, in addition, in his spectacular feat of actually changing water into wine and multiplying a few fish and loaves of bread for the multitudes who pursued him on their journey to him. Today, the Spirit with us can perform similar miracles by giving sustenance to an individual hungry person as well as radically altering systems where one or two profit-driven families dominate the food industry at the expense of millions of poor people and babies starving for lack of owning a food company. Simultaneously, the culinary beauty of the Spirit provides intangible food for the soul by way of a folk interpretation of the Bible, embodied preaching, music-based worship, radical prayer, and the collective spirituality displayed in group struggles against exploitative systems.

Finally, in chapter ten in the above Negro spiritual, the book of John says Jesus "is comin' in the world again." It is this hope that there is something different and better than this world of pain, oppression, and mere survival that engenders a profound faith and expectation among the economically poor, those heavy laden with worry and pain, poor and working people seeking better lives for their children and their children's children, and victims of all types of cruel and domineering structures. In black folk wisdom, one hears the adage: what goes around, comes around. Restated, the rich, male supremacy, white supremacists, heterosexual privilege, and private owners of monopolized corporations will reap what they sow. Why? Because Jesus will return to radically overturn the old world and establish a new world for the least in society (Luke 4:18-19 and Matt. 25:31-46). Former black chattel, Tom Windham, confirms the return to earth of the Spirit with us on behalf of the bottom of society. "My idea of Heaven is that it is a holy place with God. We will walk in Heaven just as on earth. As in him we believe, so shall we see. The earth shall burn, and the old earth shall pass away and the new earth will be created. The saints will return and live on, that is the ones who go away now. The new earth is when Jesus will come to earth and reign."[40]

When Jesus returns to earth to persist as the Spirit of total liberation with us, we can expect with joy and experience with pleasure a new dispensation never crafted on earth before. The earth's wealth, capital, and technology will return to all folk for common ownership and usage. And all peoples from a multitude of diverse walks of life will discover their full material and spiritual humanity expressed in the conclusion of the struggle for liberation that is the practice of freedom.

Until that eventful epoch, however, the faithful adherents to Jesus, the Spirit with us, must strive to proclaim in word and construct in practice a foretaste of that second coming to earth in order to build that new earth. It is the vocation of the followers of that way, maintaining enduring hope, a grounded vision, and persistent trial and error, to cry out "thus says the Lord Jesus." In her conversion experience with Jesus, another ex-slave asserted:

> I thought I heard a voice saying, "Art thou willing to be saved?" I said, Yes Lord. . . . I stood speechless until he asked me again. . . . Then I heard a whispering voice say, "If thou art not saved in the Lord's way, thou canst not be saved at all;" at which I exclaimed, "Yes Lord, in thy own way." . . . I was shown the world lying in wickedness, and was told I must go there, and call the people to repentance, for the day of the Lord was at hand; and this message was as a heavy yoke upon me so that I wept bitterly at the thought of what I should have to pass through. While I wept, I heard a voice say, "weep not, some will laugh at thee, some will scoff at thee, and the dogs will bark at thee, but while thou doest my will, I will be with thee to the ends of the earth."[41]

Echoing the sacred charge given by Jesus (in Matt. 28:19, "Go therefore and make disciples of all nations . . ."), this great commission, to be followed in the between time of Jesus' spirit with us now and Jesus' return to be with us in the final dispensation of the new earth, at its root calls on all to struggle for the liberation of the poor and those undergoing discrimination. It is, in a word, to believe, feel, and act as if the Spirit of total liberation is not only *for* us and *with* us, but, fundamentally it is *in* us.

NOTES

1. Albert, ed., *House of Bondage*, 34.

2. James W. C. Pennington's "The Fugitive Blacksmith; or, Events in the History of James W. C. Pennington, Pastor of a Presbyterian Church, New York, Formerly a Slave in the State of Maryland, United States," in Katz, ed., *Five Slave Narratives*, 74–75.

3. Botkin, ed., *Lay My Burden Down*, 37.

4. *Narrative of the Life and Adventures of Henry Bibb,* 202–3.

5. Katz, ed., *Five Slave Narratives,* 82 and 83.

6. Browne, *Autobiography of a Female Slave,* 21–22.

7. Blassingame, ed., *Slave Testimony,* 115.

8. In Perdue, ed., *Weevils in the Wheat,* 201.

9. Katz, ed., *Five Slave Narratives,* 76.

10. In *The American Slave,* Florida, vol. 17, 182.

11. *Unwritten History of Slavery,* 9, no name.

12. Arna Bontemps, "Introduction," *Five Black Lives.*

13. *David Walker's Appeal* 42.

14. *Unwritten History of Slavery,* 20.

15. Alberts, ed., *House of Bondage,* 12.

16. In *Six Women's Slave Narratives,* 14.

17. Alberts, ed., *House of Bondage,* 43.

18. Blassingame, ed., *Slave Testimony,* 541, no name.

19. Kate Drumgoold, in *Six Women's Slave Narratives,* 18.

20. *David Walker's Appeal,* 11–12.

21. Alberts, ed., *House of Bondage,* 33.

22. Blassingame, ed., *Slave Testimony,* 114.

23. Blassingame, ed., *Slave Testimony,* 50.

24. *Unwritten History of Slavery,* 35, from an interview with Milton, an ex-slave.

25. Perdue, ed., *Weevils in the Wheat,* 322.

26. Perdue, ed., *Weevils in the Wheat,* 319–20.

27. *Six Women's Slave Narratives,* 17–18.

28. In *The American Slave,* Georgia, supplemental series 1, vol. 3, pt. 1, 9–10.

29. In *The American Slave,* Florida, vol. 17, 160–61.

30. In *The American Slave,* Georgia, supplemental series 1, vol. 3, pt. 1, 228.

31. *David Walker's Appeal,* 16.

32. In *The American Slave,* Georgia, vol.13, pt. 4, 146.

33. See Coleman's "'Coming Through 'Ligion.'"

34. *Unwritten History of Slavery,* 82–83.

35. For engaging primary sources on ex-slave conversion stories, see Johnson, ed. *God Struck Me Dead.*

36. *Unwritten History of Slavery,* 83.

37. Margaret Washington, ed., *Narrative of Sojourner Truth* (New York: Vintage Books, 1993), 50–51.

38. Katz, ed., *Five Slave Narratives,* 17.

39. Parrish, *Slave Songs of the Georgia Sea Islands,* 161.

40. *The American Slave,* Arkansas, vol. 11, pt. 7, 214.

41. *Six Women's Slave Narratives,* 6–7.

CHAPTER 6

Human Purpose—
The Spirit of Total Liberation in Us

The one doctrine of my mother's teaching which was branded upon my senses was that I should never let anyone abuse me. "I'll kill you, gal, if you don't stand up for yourself," she would say. "Fight, and if you can't fight, kick; if you can't kick, then bite." Ma was generally willing to work, but if she didn't feel like doing something, none could make her do it.

Unnamed ex-slave

To be changed from a chattel to a human being is no light matter, though the process with myself practically was very simple. And if I could reach the ears of every slave today, throughout the whole continent of America, I would teach the same lesson, I would sound it in the ears of every hereditary bondman, "break your chains and fly for freedom!"

Henry Bibb, ex-slave

During all my slave life I never lost sight of freedom. It was always on my heart; it came to me like a solemn thought, and often circumstances much stimulated the desire to be free and raised great expectation of it. . . . We always called "freedom" "possum," so as to keep the white people from knowing what we were talking about. We all understood it.

Ambrose Headen, ex-slave

I had a brother who got to the line of Canada. We all had freedom in our bones. "Give me liberty or give me death" was in my bones.

Unnamed ex-slave[1]

To CONTINUE the project of constructing a black theology, this final chapter concerns the purpose of humanity—what has God created and called oppressed people to be and do? We have reached this point in our conversation by beginning with our primary research question: What is the relation between the slave religion of Protestantism and American culture, on the one hand, and a theological statement about black faith, practice, and self for liberation, on the other hand? We have seen how the context for the question has been Protestantism and American culture and enslaved black folk's religious experiences. This context is developed in Part 1. Throughout the entire book, criteria to determine whether or not we have been consistent in the investigation of the question are (a) the Spirit's will of liberation and (b) a black faith and practice of liberation. To answer the primary research question, we have sought to elaborate a constructive black theology of liberation and the co-constitution of the self with the Spirit. We explain this black theology in Part 2.

The co-constitution of the self with the Spirit of liberation is being realized through (what we have called) disciplines of creativity—the macro (or political economic), the micro (or everyday and ordinary life), the language, and the racial cultural identity levels. These disciplines entail what we have also called methods of the self—that is, knowing oneself and taking care of oneself. In other words, implementing disciplines of creativity is to work with the Spirit to constitute the self through methods of the self. With the work of the Spirit in the least in society, the black poor, the brokenhearted, and the oppressed engage in these disciplines of creativity (or methods of the self) to struggle for liberation and to practice freedom. The final outcome is the revelation of a new self (that is, a full spiritual and material humanity) and a new Common Wealth.

In Part 2 of this book, we have seen so far that God is the Spirit of total liberation for us and Jesus is the Spirit of total liberation with us. In this final chapter, we explore the relation between the Spirit and humanity, especially the poor and the oppressed. The focus on the oppressed, the poor, and the brokenhearted flows from the revelation of God's will against poverty and oppression in the biblical story and in the experience of enslaved black folk. Through the liberation of the poor and working people (the majority of the world), God helps to remove humanmade structures favoring the rich and the oppressor. Consequently, the empowerment of the majority provides the conditions of possibility for the oppressor to become one with and equal to the status of all humanity.

To be a human is to work with the Spirit of liberation within us on behalf of the oppressed, in contrast to working with the legion of demonic spirits within us that would turn us away from God's new humanity and new Common Wealth and toward selfishness. To be free in oneself means that one is a human being who transforms macrosystems of inequality. Therefore, the fundamental purpose of the Spirit of liberation in us is to work in us to help constitute the new self and the new Common Wealth. Oppressed humanity's purpose is to think, speak, and practice freedom with the Spirit of liberation in them.

In this chapter, we examine theologically various ways in which the liberating Spirit calls us to be and act in this world in order to co-constitute a better self and new social relations. At the very end, we briefly engage the overall project of constructing a systematic black theology and how this book advances that project.

Created to Be Free

In the original creation of humanity, God breathed the Spirit of liberation, the Spirit to be free, into the very act of creation itself. ". . . Then the LORD God formed [a human being] from the dust of the ground, and breathed into [the] nostrils the breath of life; and the [human being] became a living being" (Gen. 2:7).

As an act of grace, God creates through divine freedom women and men by giving them the freedom and liberation inherent in God's own self. "Then God said, 'Let us make a human being—someone like ourselves, to be the master of all life upon the earth and in the skies and in the seas.' So God created humankind in [God's] image, in the image of God [God] created them; male and female [God] created them" (Gen. 1:26-27). "Someone like ourselves" denotes that the image of God's liberation and freedom resided in the original created woman and man (that is, the imago dei or image of God of liberation is embedded and cannot be erased completely). Because God was the Spirit of total liberation and freedom for humanity, God imparted this in humanity. The imago dei, therefore, is the Spirit of total liberation in all humanity.

The existence of this Spirit of liberation within human beings had definite implications for human beings' relation to the divinely created order or that which belonged to God. "The LORD God took the man and placed him in the garden of Eden to till it and keep it" (Gen. 2:15). Thus, creation belonged to God and was not the personal possession of human beings. Human beings had a vocation to be collective stewards of the divine creation. In a word, the most significant act of God was to create a new person (female and male) and to empower them to share equally in all of the divine creation without individual privilege or private and personal ownership of resources or wealth. Human beings were, by definition and by creation, free to enjoy all of God's work without the obstacles of internal demons or negative feelings and without external negative restraints of any kind. In sum, human beings were brought into existence to be in equal relationship at each stage of their interactions.

Consequently, this new creation valued equality on the level of political economy. All people enjoyed equal access to and control of God's wealth and resources. Likewise, all experienced equal decision making over the gifts of God found in creation. And all peoples enjoyed the power derived from equal co-ownership of divine wealth. In the vocational instructions to the first women and men, God defined the following: "'have dominion over the fish of the sea and over the birds of the air and over every living thing that moves upon the earth.' God said, 'See, I have given you every plant yielding seed that is upon the face of all the earth, and every tree with seed in its fruit; you shall have them for food" (Gen. 1:28-29). Politics, capital, resources, and wealth were given to the common "you" of all humanity and not to an individual or to a few families to own, control, and distribute.

Furthermore, the divine creation of women and men embraced the beauty of differences. God did not breathe the life of liberation into only one manifestation of the human being. In fact, creation celebrates and affirms the aesthetic difference between female and male as equal partners having equal value. Likewise, we can conclude that God created all skin colors and racial cultural identities as normative of beauty. Moreover, if all human beings reflect the image of God in them, then knowledge of the cultural identity created by God includes those marginalized in society, especially black people. To be marginalized, in a word, is to exist outside of or on the extreme bottom of the hierarchical margins of the norms of what the powerful races have defined as beautiful and clean.

The creation narrative, in addition, instructs us about the breath of God symbolizing a form of divine speaking the liberation image into created humanity. The breath of God comes from the sacred mouth and encodes the depths of liberation and freedom into women and men, and different races on earth. The norm of liberation dwells in all people. This reality or spark or sign bonds us all together. Though God's breath speaks the language of deliverance of the captives, the downfall of the monopolizers of wealth, and the exalting of the lowly, this language bursts forth in diverse sounds of discourse. Restated, the norm of language validity resides in which languages adhere to the norm. There is no such thing as a standard language or method of talking that privileges itself. But those in power use their power to define their language as normative. Likewise the powerful (the minority of the world) have the force to reward others who accept and imitate the language of the powerful. From the biblical perspective, however, all expressions of the norm of liberation in whatever language (including the speaking of the black poor) determine which languages are standard.

Finally, God implanted liberation in the created human beings not merely in the spheres of macropolitical economy, racial cultural identity, and language. God also infused liberation within people so that this liberation would be in and act out on the everyday and ordinary levels of existence. Creation leaves out no area of human thought, word, and witness; it floods all space, time, architecture, laughter, rhetoric, sensuality, the body, manners, mannerisms, rituals, etc.

The initial intent of creation by God was to provide a full spiritual and material self both individually and internally to the personal soul and collectively to the communal social relations with one's family, neighbors, animals, and nature. In this sense, human beings were created to be called to God, to be fully turned to God's liberation that is in them and calling out to them. Thus, to be a human being is to pursue continually a path of turning or a way of conversion emotionally, spiritually, politically, culturally, and ethically toward the divine way of liberation. We are human beings when we respond to the vocation of the Spirit of liberation and freedom within us, the sacred breath to be free and to do freedom on earth.

The Genesis story, however, does not end with the calling into full humanity the free self existing in a Common Wealth. A countervailing spirit desiring to turn away from God's internal spark of liberation raised its head like a poisonous serpent about to strike an unsuspecting victim. Indeed, the narrator of Genesis deploys the image of a snake to bring to bear the full metaphorical substance of the thought, speech, and act of turning away from the created nature for liberation. To sin, in a word, is to convert away from freedom. It is an active rebellion against God. The turn away from God's will results in devastating effects.

First, there is estrangement from God, the Spirit of total liberation for us, and a focus on one's self (that is, the beginning of hubris or self-centeredness). The creator of the Genesis narrative writes: "[Eve and Adam] heard the sound of the LORD God walking in the garden at the time of the evening breeze, and the man and his wife hid themselves from the presence of the LORD God among the trees of the garden. But the LORD God called to the man, and said to him, 'Where are you?'" (Gen. 3:8-9). The first sin brings about a breaking of relationship between humanity and God. God's plan entailed full freedom for humanity and a harmonious and balanced interaction between creator and the created in a Common Wealth. But severance of a healthy divine-human interchange yields (on the part of the sinning human being) fear, guilt, shame, hiding, anxiety, lying, excuses, blaming—all in response to God's question about whether or not human beings are pursuing their nature of freedom.

The second sin follows directly from the initial breach between the selfish knowledge and desires of human beings, on the one hand, and their opposition to their vocational calling to pursue liberation, on the other. When God confronts them, Eve and Adam then break their state of freedom that God had granted them in the divine creation. Adam and Eve begin to argue and fight between themselves and to blame each other for turning away from God. The initial sin against God causes them to commit the second sin of infighting among the family and loved ones. There can never be peace at home when the individual and the collective do not undergo a conversion toward their spiritual calling. Finally, severance from the drive toward liberation is replaced by a selfish turn to the self that is a form of learned behavior passed down to the next generations. For instance, jealousy, lying, and murder are attributes assumed by the children of Eve and Adam. Out of envy, Cain kills Abel because the latter pursued God's intentions: that is, a conversion to the Spirit of freedom in him (Gen. 4).

By creating us with a liberation nature, God evidenced the Spirit of liberation for us. Being for us prompted the divinity to be for our total emancipation spiritually and materially. The turn away from God and to a negative focus on the self brought about a derailment from the vocation toward freedom. Yet, the reality of Jesus, especially in the plight and heart of the poor and working-class people, reflected the Spirit of liberation working with oppressed humanity to return or convert toward the initial goal of struggling for liberation and practicing freedom. Consequently the purpose of humanity today is to build on the enabling power of the Spirit with us in order to respond to the vocation of the Spirit in us.

NATURAL FREEDOM

Enslaved African Americans believed in their natural state of freedom, despite the ever present danger of systemic and personal bondage and pain. Poor folk, in tune with their created reality, realize that they are made to be free from the beginning of time. Accordingly their duty is to return to or convert to the path of a full spiritual and material humanity. Escaped bondman James Curry pronounced this theological conclusion at an antislavery rally.

> Of course, no slave would dare to say, in the presence of a white man, that he wished for freedom. But among themselves, it is their constant theme. No slaves think they were made to be slaves. Let them keep them ever so ignorant, it is impossible to beat it into them that they were made to be slaves. I have heard some of the most ignorant I ever saw, say, "it will not always be so, God will bring them to an account."[2]

This feeling and faith in the liberation in them dovetailed with the biblical witness of creation which we encountered above. Having gained his freedom, Tom Robinson spoke forcefully about the created nature to be free as a natural desire. "Was I happy? Lord! You can take anything. No matter how good you treat it—it wants to be free. You can treat it good and feed it and give it everything it seems to want—but if you open the cage—it's happy!"[3] If one is made in freedom, an unquenchable thirst burning inside of one's soul compels a person to pursue liberation.

In spite of all the apparent power, monopolization of capital, and other resources that the minority powerful populations own in this world, the bottom of society, the majority, harbors a divine spark for freedom. The cage of various discriminations (racial, gender, class, sexual orientation) cannot forever contain the longing to be free. Once "you open the cage—[the oppressed are] happy!" It is precisely this longing deep within a person's being that believes in and holds on to liberation—"God will bring them to account." And no amount of food, good treatment, and benefits can soothe or anesthetize the aching toward freedom. When the time comes, the inner call of liberation will witness externally to the Spirit of liberation in us.

In her confessional writings, Lucy Delaney made it quite explicit. She recalled running away, suffering capture, and being locked into jail. But still she pictured defiantly her inner pursuit: "My only crime was seeking for the freedom which was my birthright!"[4] To be born on earth is to follow one's natural instinct to have liberty. At birth we receive the gift within us of longing to be free and to practice freedom. Similarly Harriet Robinson, former chattel, recalled slavery days and how a Mr. Isom ran away continually from his white slave master. Once he returned and "they give him three hundred lashes, and bless my soul, he run off again."[5] What is it that enabled and empowered this poor black worker to continually run away, suffer bodily violence from white owners of black flesh, and run away again? The subversive embedded freedom impulse permeated his identity and self. Restrictions of oppression cannot touch this dimension of instinctual reality because racialists cannot beat out what they did not put inside of the victims of white supremacy. At creation, black folk received a natural freedom reflex. Of course, whether or not the oppressed respond to this calling is another question. In this instance, Mr. Isom answered in the affirmative and obtained his freedom. Like Mr. Isom, our created purpose on earth is to give a resounding "yes" to God's questioning which way we will turn in this world.

A response to the question of what human beings are called to be and do, moreover, presents further sacred obligations. It demands one carry the self as divinely created humanity and not like a four-legged animal. Simultaneously, it requires that one seek respect from others about one's natural human state of liberty. Tom Windham rightly concluded the following: "Us folks was treated well. I think we should have our liberty cause us ain't hogs or horses—us is human flesh."[6] The fundamental divide demarcating God's two-legged animals as human flesh from the four-legged creature kingdom occupied by hogs and horses is the internal drive toward liberation deposited at creation as a birthright to humanity, especially oppressed humanity.

Human flesh, in addition, denotes the action of self-possession in divinely ordained freedom. The dynamic of running away or pursuing liberty cannot substitute for the final space and result of owning one's own self in relation to the sacred impulse to be free. Former chattel, Mingo White narrated this life embodiment exemplified in an epistle written from a runaway named Ned to his former master. White recalls: "After Old Ned got such a terrible beating for praying for freedom, he slipped off and went to the North to jine the Union army. After he got in the army he wrote to Master Tom. In his letter he had those words: 'I am laying down, Master, and gitting up, Master,' meaning that he went to bed when he felt like it and got up when he pleased to."[7] Praying for freedom becomes a necessary moment in the unfolding drama to be free. Likewise repeated attempts to attain the state of full spiritual and material existence are vital in the struggle for liberation. However, it is when one returns to the original Edenic space, time, and awareness where one actually owns one's own body, labor, rest, and rising that one can claim the arrival of a natural freedom. The practice of freedom suggests the non-necessity of one's body jerking awake to an alarm clock signifying time to work for oppressive structures. Thus, prayer and struggle culminate in ownership of one's desire to go to sleep and to rise awake, deciding voluntarily what will be the day's agenda of freedom.

A final aspect of natural freedom, following the practical ownership and control of one's rest and body, concerns a display of ecstasy. Once one locks into the wavelength of one's own natural free self, without concern for the powerful of this world but turned to the vocation of divine liberation, joy bubbles up from within one's bones. Ecstatic joy spills over into accepting that a human being is naturally free and into attempts to change the world to realize this freedom. Ms. Mary Anderson recounted the experience of enslaved African Americans once emancipation became real for them. "The [Civil] War was begun and there were stories of fights and freedom. The news went from plantation to plantation and while the slaves acted natural and some even more polite than usual, they prayed for freedom. . . . [The Yankees came eventually.] They called the slaves, saying 'You are free.' Slaves were whooping and laughing and acting like they were crazy."[8]

In this instance, Ms. Anderson offers a double meaning for the word "natural." On face value, the reader encounters a contradiction. The initial surface usage of "natural" connotes enslaved blacks acting in their normal way of subservience to white supremacist owners. Yet further unpacking of "natural" reveals this acting "natural" as a duplicitous state of ordinary and everyday way of being (on a micro level) in relation to oppressors. It was natural for enslaved folk to harbor plans for freedom under the camouflage of naturally being subservient. Yet with the proper circumstances favorable to unveiling their natural state, victims of discrimination will display the full panorama of their naturally free instinct. Most often this reflection or representation has some ecstatic manifestation signified as a crazy state. The natural joy of pulsating liberation erupts from the inside and spills over into the outside of oneself. Ecstasy of freedom becomes whooping, laughing, and another form of sanity. Here, the purpose of humanity is to heed the call of this reverberating pulsing and enter the ecstatic state of liberation.

TO BE FREE

The Spirit of liberation in us, particularly in people at the bottom of society, includes, as mentioned in the previous section, a call to accept one's natural freedom given as a birthright. In a similar manner, this translates into being free now. By nature the oppressed are free; they must, in turn, conduct themselves as if they were free.

To be free calls for the oppressed to think they are free. In order to pursue relentlessly the vocational necessities of the Spirit in us, part of preparing for this struggle and participating in it demands a radical *metanoia* (or conversion) of the thought processes of those at the bottom of society. One of the greatest chains with which oppressors enslave the oppressed is the chain around the minds of the marginalized. Therefore through intentional contemplation, the intellect has to come in tune with the pre-existing presence of the Spirit of liberation within. Reflecting this point, former chattel James Bradley reminisced about slavery in the following excerpt: "My master had kept me ignorant of everything he could. I was never told anything about God, or my own soul. Yet from the time I was fourteen years old, I used to think a great deal about freedom. It was my heart's desire; I could not keep it out of my mind."[9] The necessity of knowing about freedom or thinking consciously about it precedes formal catechism and the established instructions of doctrinal obligations of Christian denominations. (These are, of course, crucial when they follow the norm of the Spirit of liberation in us.) What Mr. Bradley teaches us is that we need to gain knowledge of the subterranean freedom Spirit that is already planted deeply in our being. Somehow, prior to a conventional introduction about God or his (that is, Mr. Bradley's) soul, he became aware of freedom in his thoughts and his mind. Once the least in society understand the power existing in them as a given to their natural creation, they can think like free people. Mr. Bradley attained this state during his early teen years. And this knowing sustained him through hardship after heartbreak until he achieved freedom. The poor must know that they have freedom in them and this awareness, in turn, spurs them on through sacrifice for the ultimate freedom. Knowing one has freedom inside of oneself helps to carry one on toward the actualization of freedom. And such knowledge derives from a direct and unmediated encounter with the Spirit of liberation.

Moreover, self-reflected consciousness of the power from within energizes one to allow this power to alter harmful external conditions that prevent one from pursuing a full humanity. A runaway slave expressed this reality in a cogent and concise manner:

> It is true, our condition as slaves was not by any means the worst; but the mere idea that we were held as chattels, and deprived of all legal rights—the thought that we had to give up our hard earnings to a tyrant to enable him to live in idleness and luxury—the thought that

we could not call the bones and sinews that God gave us our own; but above all, the fact that another man had the power to tear from our cradle the new-born babe and sell it in the shambles like a brute and then scourge us if we dared to lift a finger to save it from such a fate, haunted us for years.[10]

Engagement with the idea or thought of mistreatment coupled with wrestling with the already given gift of freedom within enlivens the will to alter difficulties in one's life. On the economic level, slavery that produces unjust profits for the personal benefit of an exploiting white family necessitates a radical transformation. Workers who suffer the shame and hardship of losing "hard earnings" to the owners of their labor need to organize and claim that which they produce and the machinery and technology they use to produce.

Similarly, politics is an additional arena of struggle and transformation which knowledge of the Spirit within compels the least in society to investigate. Any woman or man deprived of legal rights (for example, the power to decide for themselves how the poor want to conduct themselves on earth) is obligated by the Spirit to work for liberation in spite of the minority population who use money and wealth to hold the reins of political rights.

Furthermore, "the bones and sinews" given by God bring to the surface the concept of theological creation of human beings. If one person has power over the daily and ordinary way of life of another, then the person with power has turned away from God because only God has the authority of creating humanity. The thought that one could not call one's very body one's own—mannerisms, body language, and other very ordinary and perhaps mundane ways of being in the world—indicates loss of self.

Finally, the sacredness of the family, which God metaphorically and symbolically exemplifies with Eve and Adam, is torn asunder when minority populations hoard resources and make decisions that put the majority of the world's babies at risk. Hence, economics, politics, and, among other things, micro ways of being ordinary are areas that the Spirit of liberation in us causes the bottom of society to fight to reconstitute so that the poor might have the life of their humanity made real.

To be free also requires a consciousness that ultimately home as the final resting place resides "on the other side of Jordan" after death. Envisioning a final life after death becomes revolutionary on two accounts. (1) Freedom emboldens one with a hope that whatever happens in this world, the final victory of liberation is beyond this world. Because allegiance, in the final analysis, belongs not to the forces of this earth, then the poor and working people can fight even harder for a new self and new Common Wealth on earth. Home beyond this world breaks any subservience to this world and thereby inspires one to transform this world.

(2) Envisioning a final life after death becomes a subversive vision, moreover, because the poor and working people have faith in a long sought after reward and rest from all the toils of struggle against diverse forms of discrimination (whether racial, gender, class, or sexual orientation). Even the movement for the establishment of the new self and new Common Wealth on earth cannot resolve the full flowering of the internal Spirit of liberation. Why? Because human beings are broken vessels and the new human being and new space created will fall short of what God, the Spirit of liberation for us, has for us on the other side of Jordan. Even when humans struggle for the crafting of the new person and new social relations, we need to be aware that, no matter how perfect we might think we are, no one can realize the fullness of that which is the ultimate goal for all of humanity and all of creation—achieving the fullest potential of our spiritual and material selves. Only after death (that is, the complete defeat of human selfishness and private monopolization of God's wealth) will all people be equal in the state of complete liberation.

This consciousness of being free, moreover, impels us to be intentional about a journey home, home indicating both our place on earth and after death. One cannot be free totally if one limits home to the capabilities and powers of this earth. This would eliminate the transcendence of the Spirit for us. At the same time, one cannot limit home only to heaven because this would deny the Spirit in us that empowers us to struggle for liberation and practice freedom on earth even in our fallible state as broken human vessels. Home, as the object of conducting ourselves as free, embodies polyvalent dimensions. Enslaved black workers deployed song to suggest such a substance to their faith.

> I'm On My Way
> If a seeker gets to Heaven before I do,
> Look out for me, I'm on my way too.
> Shout, shout the Heaven-bound King!
> Shout, shout I'm on my way![11]

Seeking entails an awareness of a vision of something better than the state in which poor and working people find themselves. To be a human being is to voice this clear vision. When one takes the first conscious step toward liberation, when freedom of one's Spirit evolves from knowledge that one is already in the process of becoming, then one is on the way to the new self and new Common Wealth. The Spirit of liberation in us turns decisively, methodologically, and joyously to God, the Spirit of liberation for us. Conversion includes subversive thought.

Consciousness of the journey home, as one form of being free, means one is acutely aware of being a child of God, the Spirit of liberation for us. A slave religious song echoes these themes.

> My knee-bones achin',
> My body's rackin' with pain,
> I calls myself de child of God
> Heaven am my aim.
> If you don't believe I'se a child of God,
> Just meet me on dat other shore,
> Heaven is my home.
> I calls myself a child of God,
> I'se a long time on my way,
> But heaven am my home.[12]

The pain and turmoil of oppression on this side of Jordan wither in their debilitating effects on the brokenhearted and marginalized because they know in their minds and hearts that they are children of God. Yet this childlike state is not a paralyzed infantile posture. On the contrary, it is an active knowing and consciousness of a journey leading inevitably toward the new self and new Common Wealth both on earth and in heaven.

The proactive nature of this knowledge assumes further undergirding from the black workers (who created and sang these theological songs) when the pronoun "I" comes to the fore in their lyrics. The oppressed know they are children of God due to their self-consciousness about the journey home. And on this journey, which they pursue through song, they are emboldened through the repeated refrain "I calls myself de child of God." Through pain, "I calls myself"; if you don't believe me, "I calls myself"; and it may take a long time to get home, but "I calls myself." The assertion of "I" not only emboldens the oppressed to pursue the home journey, it also permits them to recreate themselves from the old self of relying only on themselves to the new self of turning to God, the Spirit of liberation for us. In a word, consciousness of the journey comes when those without power name themselves and decide for themselves to whom they belong on their way home to freedom.

To be free, a manifestation of the Spirit of liberation in us, requires a link between premeditated self-naming as a child of God, an instance of one's consciousness of the journey home, with a profound intuitive feeling of the end goal of heaven. We remember that heaven denotes and connotes the co-constituted new self by the Spirit in us for a full spiritual and material humanity. Heaven unfolds in its fullness when the old human being, relying on the self and selfishness, dies and the new self arises, turning to the Spirit for, with, and in the oppressed. Heaven includes both the attempt to create a foretaste on earth as it is in heaven; and it entails the fullest expression which the poor hope to experience on the other side of Jordan. To attain this goal, a feeling of the intuitive self complements the intentions of the knowing self. The coexistence of an intellectual passion and a compassionate intellect is another way to be free.

One former slave experienced this unprecedented feeling of absolute freedom and liberation when his bondage ended with the payment of money to his mistress. "When the money was paid to my mistress and the conveyance fairly made to Mr. Smith, I felt that I was free. And a queer and joyous feeling it is to one who has been a slave. I cannot describe it, only it seemed as though I was in heaven."[13] The radical contrast between "one who has been a slave" and one who is free resides on the feeling level. What exactly is the feeling? It is a sensation of the inner entrenchment of the Spirit of liberation in the oppressed. The body has to feel this sensation and experience it intuitively just as the mind consciously contemplates it. It is not merely a knowledgeable experience. To be called by the Spirit within is to undergo a complete and "queer and joyous feeling" of the entire body.

For instance, Ms. Lucy Delaney gained this sentiment from her mother who was a former free woman eventually falsely enslaved; consequently, the enslaved daughter "always had a feeling of independence" against her white female owner. Likewise, Mr. Solomon Bradley, an escapee from slavery, could "not feel right so long as" he was not taking up arms to fight for the overthrow of slavery.[14] Feeling freedom will lead the poor to dare to dream outlandish visions and perform acts of courage which oppressor populations will deem insane and suicidal.

Perhaps another former slave's testimony best sums up the vibrant interplay and complex but concise connectedness between sense and feeling. His clarity resides in his simplicity: "I had too much sense and feeling to be a slave."[15] The head and the body, the mind and the gut, and the contemplative and the intuitive respond to God's gift at creation of the spark or presence of liberation. We undergo the conversion toward overall freedom when all parts of our being cohabit in balance. One has to feel liberation and think freedom in the dynamic of struggling for liberation and practicing freedom.

Communalism

The vocational obligations which the Spirit within us, especially in the black poor, places upon us cover all spheres of life, including the communal.[16] Communal, in this instance, encompasses issues of rearranging ownership and control of God's wealth and resources. Communalism cuts directly against the self-centered grain of private ownership and monopolization of the divine gift of creation. Here the negative turn toward the self as an act of privatization and monopolization and the fatal turn away from God's gift of creation to all people indicate hubris and sin.

Specifically, in the initial creation story in Genesis, God creates human beings to be servants of and accountable only to God (who is the Spirit of liberation for humanity). In addition, all creation (plants, birds, animals, land, sea, air, etc.) are granted to every human being equally so that humans can act as guardians over God's wealth and resources. In the beginning, all held in common their responsible stewardship of wealth.

Accordingly, the early church imitated this theological paradigm in the realm of political economy. The group of female and male apostles who were left behind immediately after Jesus' death instituted a holistic implementation of politics and economics. "All who believed were together and had all things in common; they would sell their possessions and goods and distribute the proceeds to all, as any had need. Day by day, as they spent much time together in the temple, they broke bread at home and ate their food with glad and generous hearts, praising God and having the goodwill of all the people" (Acts 2:44-46). This integrated experience of political economy shows the multidimensional boundaries of wealth, money, and resources. It avoids two deviations. One is the vulgar Marxist understanding that capital, its monopoly usage and people's re-appropriation of it, is a one-dimensional, cold, and calculating phenomenon best left to career politicians and economic number crunchers. People and the spiritual, non-material aspects of life are absent. The second error perceives political economy in an extreme otherworldly, disembodied state. For this trajectory, matters of wealth and resources have nothing to do with the nitty gritty struggle on earth veen identifiable monopoly capitalists and poor and working people, especially black folk.

On the contrary, the book of Acts, like the original Genesis narrative, presents a layering and texturing of political economy. First, the apostles meet together, indicating a formal turn away from the isolation of the individual self-focus of a capitalist. Second, in their coming together, they present their full selves, suggesting an equal input of information, respect for and listening to others who might differ, and intimating mutual input about the fate of resources. Next, they share everything in common. No one person or family owns capital or the labor of another individual, race, gender, class, or group of people in society. Furthermore, on the economic front, they sell their private possessions, marking the submission of individual enterprises to the general economic welfare of the group.

Then profound acts of service ensue; the women and men disciples of Christ give wealth and resources directly to the bottom strata of society. Thus the vision of political economy offered in Acts (that is, how the Spirit of liberation in us calls us to be human) flows first of all from the well-being of the bottom of society. In other words, not the financial barons but the fallen brothers and sisters determine and decide the nature and health of a community, nation, or country. What is done against and for the least of these drives the heartbeat of society. At this juncture, we see political economy grounded in earthly interactions.

At the same time, political economy receives its oxygen and resuscitation from a sacred source. In the above Acts passage, political economic measures are defined and circumscribed by a relation to the holy. Lifting up the ritual of worship, the women and men disciples engage in fellowship and sorority in church; they attend church regularly, thereby exhibiting a structural and institutional visibility and accountability. Similar rituals occur in the home; they build up the family by sharing in Communion (that is, the Lord's Supper) and breaking bread with a meal. Finally, through intense prayer, great joy, and jubilant thanksgiving, political economy incorporates celebration of communal ownership and distribution as God's blessings.

Various former black workers in slavery verify similar perspectives on their political economic calling as human beings. After escaping from slavery, Jack Scott stated that he was "moved to leave simply because he had got tired of working for the 'white people for nothing.'" If a monopolizer of resources and wealth fails to turn over God's creation for communal ownership, then labor has the duty to stop working. Mattie Jackson not only departed illegally from her status as a black worker under the chattel system, her theological anthropology caused her to grasp some capital in her exiting to a new self and free life.

> When I made my escape from slavery I was in a query how I was to raise funds to bear my expenses. I finally came to the conclusion that as the laborer was worthy of his hire, I thought my wages should come from my master's pocket. Accordingly I took twenty-five dollars. After I was safe and had learned to write, I sent him a nice letter, thanking him for the kindness his pocket bestowed to me in time of need.[17]

The criteria for ownership in a land of plenty are: to each according to her or his need and all equally sharing. Capital and wealth belong to God and never to the private individual or a small group of ruling class families. Workers and those at the bottom of society cannot steal that which belongs to God and that which they have poured their own labor into. How can one steal that which is already given to them at creation and as a birthright?

Runaway Henry Bibb's experience and faith coincide with this theology. "I hold that a slave has a moral right to eat, drink and wear all that he needs." Morality underscores the presence of the sacred in the decision to "steal" or take all that is needed (that is, to each according to her need); and "it would be a sin on his part to suffer and starve in a country where there is a plenty to eat and wear within his reach."

Again, this worldview and vantage point originate from the bottom, from the majority of workers and working poor people who stand at the opposite end of the spectrum of the small minority of families gripping the reins of a country's capital. This is the perspective of communal ownership where whatever grows in the field belongs to those who walk by and need sustenance. "I consider that I had a just right to what I took, because it was the labor of my own hands," concludes Bibb.[18]

The African belief in and practice of communalism prior to the arrival of European whites shed further light. Mr. Johnson, an escaped slave originally born free in Africa, offers a model for collective work and responsibility and mutual accountability and service. "I was born in Africa, several hundred miles up the Gambia river." He elaborates how people are called to be in relation to one another. The villagers of his country are extremely kind; they see the other person not as a potential threat or competitor for profit making. People are perceived as human beings and, therefore, all their needs are secured freely, ıding food. "When you go into house, first question is, have you had any thing to eat?" As to hygiene: "Bring water, you wash, and den eat much you want and all you got to do is tank them for it—not one fip you pay." Health care: "If you are sick, nurse you, and make you well—not one fip you pay." Clothing: "If you want clothing, one woman put in two knots warp, one put in two knots filling, and so on; den men weave it, and you cut just such garment you like—not one fip you pay."[19] The forces of the capitalist market are replaced by viewing and interacting with people, first as people endowed by liberation within. Satisfying communal needs replaces the quest for individual profit.

MicroResistance and Self-Creation

The Spirit of total liberation in the poor expresses itself not only on the macro but also on the micro level. The macro level involves a direct engagement with the larger structures of political economic power. The micro trajectory comprises instances of the Spirit's presence revealed on smaller everyday experiences of liberation beliefs and practices that accompany the struggle for liberation in the systems of the political state and the economic wealth complexes. Micro ways of being in the world concern the everyday and ordinary lifestyles of the poor and the marginalized. In these often overlooked and undervalued crevices of life, how does the Spirit of liberation in those at the bottom of society challenge them to be fully human? Micro exigencies contrast and complement the broad macropicture of political economy. What welds them together, however, is the norm of the Spirit of liberation within the least in society. Micro comprises, but is not exhausted by, instances of humor, communication, space and time, and architecture.

Full spiritual and material humanity, in order to reflect the fullness of God's gift of liberation from creation and by nature, must include all aspects of what it means to be human. If one remains on the political economic plane (that is, the macroreach of resource and wealth redistribution), the new self and new Common Wealth would be incomplete. Political economy frames necessarily the larger systemic parameters, but it also requires the textured fluidity of the ordinary and the everyday. At this point, the notion of micro (for instance, the game of laughter) serves to round out the contributions derived from macrocreativities (for instance, a new political economy).

On the death of his master, ex-chattel Peter Randolph recounted the following joke.

Pompey, how do I look?
O, massa mighty.
What do you mean "mighty," Pompey?
Why, massa, you look noble.
What do you mean by "noble"?
Why, sar you just look like one lion.
Why, Pompey, where have yo ever seen a lion?
I see one down in yonder field the other day, massa.
Pompey, you foolish fellow, that was a jackass.
Was it, massa? Well you look just like him.[20]

Mr. Randolph deployed humor on an everyday level. Now that his master was dead, he could reveal the secret of laughter held within his heart. Laughter kept him sane and free to live without suicidal plans while a slave. Harboring humor here emboldens the enslaved both at the level of sheer survival amidst the absurdity of the idea that one is enslaved, and on the level of resistance. Inadequate data exist to substantiate any claim that Randolph participated in any organized act of self-defensive violence. Yet we can surmise that he identified with old Pompey in this act of verbal acrobatic resistance between fictional slave and master. The amount of glee this old slave exhibited each time he thought about and shared this joke secretly with his fellow bondwomen and men, one will never know. But no doubt he felt better about himself when he could imagine calling his own master a jackass.

The resistance operates on the spiritual, feeling, and wits levels. Spiritually, if his master represents a four-legged ass, then Reynolds is closer to the human imago dei of the Creator. Feeling wise, the stronger the sense of his spiritual and human self, the more Reynolds develops a positive self-identity; he literally feels good about himself. Feeling good about oneself is akin to feeling and knowing about the Spirit of liberation within. And on the wits level, Reynolds, vicariously embracing the intellect of Pompey, survives as the superior intelligence.

Part of being human, as an expression of the Spirit within, is to make fun of the oppressor. Joking fosters a leveling of the apparent omnipotence of the monopolizers of divine creation. When the exploiter is laughed at, he or she can be better seen as just another human being and not some type of demi-god to be feared sheepishly and automatically by the least in society. The very process of laughing and retelling the story helps to alleviate the insanity of being victimized by abuse. Thus one continues down the path of co-constituting the new self influenced by the Spirit.

Another ex-slave's memory substantiates further the importance of ongoing humor for the oppressed:

> I myself and three or four others, have received two hundred lashes in the day, and had our feet in fetters; yet, at night, we would sing and dance, and make others laugh at the rattling of our chains. Happy men we must have been! We did it to keep down trouble, and to keep our hearts from being completely broken: that is as true as the gospel! Just look at it,—must not we have been very happy? Yet I have done it myself—I have cut capers in chains.[21]

From sunup to sundown marks the time and space of pain on the part of the black oppressed and the sadistic sensuality of white masters administering blows against black bodies. At night, from sundown to sunup, African Americans worked with the Spirit of freedom within their own souls by employing laughter to declare a statement about the unbroken self. Whites with power cannot fathom the logic of laughter gushing forth from black bodies lame from injury. Indeed, black laughter, expressed in excruciating pain, creates and exhibits its own rhetoric of survival, resistance, and self-transformation for the black oppressed. Why is it that a person suffering two hundred lashes from a bullwhip, from sunup to sundown, would then, from sundown to sunup, participate in the spectacle of dancing and singing (that is, cutting capers)? From sundown to sunup is when victims and the least in society operate on their own turf and rhythm. Only in this context can pain imposed by whites with power be reconstructed into a radical type of laughter that helps engineer a new self.

Moreover, laughing does not exist as a solitary act of the isolated victim. On the contrary, it gains a great deal of its power of survival and resistance and draws on the liberating Spirit from within when it grows among family, friends, and allies. Laughter, of course, enhances the sanity and oppositional capabilities of the individual black poor and working woman or man. Yet, simultaneously, it nurtures its strength from within by drawing on the collective liberating Spirit which transcends (but glues together) one person to a community. That is why the ones enduring intense pain "would sing and dance, and make others laugh at the rattling of our chains." Restated, the notion of being fully human via laughter can only attain its fullness by interacting with community. The individual's humor reaches its sacred calling (as a vocational response from within) when it spreads to other poor and working people and solicits many laughing responses from them. The humorous "I" exists because of its impact on the "we" and the "we" receives nourishment from the "I."

Furthermore, laughter, in the above black worker's story, parallels and dovetails with the gospel's content. From the perspective of theological anthropology (that is, what God has called women and men to be and do), the good news of liberation heals the brokenhearted and makes sure that trouble does not last always. Fundamentally, this good news is the reality of God, as a result of creation, implanting the Spirit of liberation within each oppressed and marginalized person. Despite the layers of external structural abuse and internal emotional self-disdain, this sacred image of God remains among the poor. Laughter facilitates the connection of this Spirit back to the victims' own materialities and truths of conscious knowing and intentional feeling. Freedom pushes further toward actualization when a liberating laughter becomes a material force and a real truth for the least in society. Both by its role, its effect, and its definition, humor is the gospel of liberation.

In addition to laughter, people oppressed and struggling to survive are also called to communicate, to express their internal freedom impulse in practical stratagems for a better life. Ordinary, everyday technologies of communication offer a terrain of struggle and debate because an information flow and the control of such a flow impact greatly the degree to which oppressed folk think and decide for themselves in an independent fashion. Communication media are never neutral, yet daily they are taken for granted as objective means of sending and receiving information. In his comments on black workers' usual ways of talking to one another during worship rituals, one former chattel from the state of Virginia exemplifies the class and racial bases of communication: "An' when they was havin' a meetin' an' de patterollers come, Uncle Jackson wouldn' never let them slip up an' break up a meetin'. Used to station niggers in relays from the trail to the meetin' place an' when the patterollers would show up Uncle Jackson who was always the one farthest out, would whistle like a bob-cat to warn the others."[22] For the oppressed, communication is a dynamic of establishing alternative methods of secret truths. This creative process involves a collective effort of those who assemble for a liberation worship of the sacred. In fact, the affirmation of the sacred suggests, in this story, clandestine worship and praise of the desire (and plan?) for emancipation. The emancipation discourse in this underground holy meeting is the hidden truth held by black workers. It becomes a live truth in the context of a communal gathering and praise. Here too, like the flow of humor in the resisting society, communication of the secret truths of an individual's knowledge and feel of freedom materializes within the communal institution. Thus creative imagination, clandestine gatherings, and collective faith mark compelling indicators of forging novel communication networks on an ordinary, daily basis. In addition, such a web of transferring information enables the oppressed to declare their voice and faith in the medium and belief indigenous to them while being hemmed in by the macro political economic structure.

The importance of communication expressing the liberation Spirit within the oppressed individual and among the collective least in society looms large in its significance. Throughout slavery and across regions, enslaved black workers crafted consistent communication devices. This universal application of the liberation impulse in the realm of transferring and receiving information signals the crucial role of communication for authentic liberation. The marginalized and the abused need to seize resources to forge their own types of talking.

> References to a secret slave communication system appear in many narratives. Some, like Douglass, talk of double meanings in songs, but most just mention the fact that the system existed. Andrew Jackson wrote that slaves "have a means of communication with each other, altogether unknown to their masters, or to the people of the free states." . . . The fugitive blacksmith who became one of the most influential black clergymen in the North, J. W. C. Pennington, wrote: "The telegraph, which by the speed of lightning carries news from one end of this land to another, does not more certainly report news than the slaves do one to another."[23]

Effective communication ensures a transference of information that fulfills a need of rapidity and familiarity in deliverance. The marginalized do not simply create an alternative route of discussion and news. The replacement of the oppressor's system with a parallel system of talking must be of a quality standard. It necessitates a speedy back and forth between sender(s) and receiver(s). In crisis and critical instances, the quickness of delivery can make the difference between successful or aborted plans, and life and death efforts.

Black working folk historically have created "the grapevine" or "the telegraph," which has operated at "the speed of lightning." It served and serves as a mechanism for updating, warning, fundraising, gossiping, disciplining, prophesying, organizing, ventilating, mentoring, fighting, praying, and creating the individual and collective self. Because the mainstream means and media remain in the hands of other racial and ethnic groups—hands that have attacked or distorted and, at times, supported the black community—black folk utilize their own tools of talking back and forth to persevere in maneuvering through a mass of racial abuse, neglect, and taken-for-grantedness.

Linked to humor and communication, space and time, a third grouping of a micro-illustration of liberation, evolves from the following Negro spiritual composed by enslaved black workers. This unique form of lyrical communication was sung by chattel on their way to and thereafter during the intense pain of plantation life in the deep southern United States.

> See those poor souls from Africa
> Transported to America;
> We are stolen, and sold to Georgia,
> Will you go along with me?
> We are stolen, and sold to Georgia,
> Come sound the Jubilee![24]

In this stanza, the identity of the self of the enslaved resides in awareness of space and time on at least two layers. On one level, the wailing song of this individual or group (departing for a new plantation) calls out to fellow comrades remaining in chains (at the original plantation) to go along with them in the memory of time and space. Here, the self of the ones transported physically survives with an identity maintained by those who remember the self of the stolen ones. As long as those remaining in chains recall the departing wail and vibrant lives of the black chattel sent to the Georgia deep south, the longer will the reality of those departed chattel live in memory.

Therefore the enslaved black workers who remain respond to the plaintive cry for memory by re-imaging and re-visioning how those departed occupied the spaces before their departure and used their former time with those now remembering them. By "rememory" of space and time, a community fractured by abuse and discrimination can refashion and recreate continually the self of those departed. The oppressor segment of society that uses its wicked power to destroy community through forced disruption succeeds only if one assumes just the physical aspect of life's dimensions. With the case at hand, space and time serve in the process of both maintaining and constituting the self.

Furthermore, this stanza reveals that the composer of this spiritual acknowledges awareness of historical spacial and time identity. Enslaved blacks were ripped from the Continent; yet they held on to a historical time of origin in Africa. For oppressed black working people, the process of heeding the liberation call requires forever revisiting the space and time of Africa as historical self.

But this spiritual is not a mandate to return to Africa in some idealistic, precolonial state—as if modernity and monopolistic capitalistic culture from the United States had not already had an impact on "traditional" Africa. The return to the source acts as identity formation because it provides a time and space of historical continuity for black folk today. African Americans came originally from the Continent (and not Europe). Though the souls may be poor (in the sense of suffering enslavement), these souls have a space and time of origin, freedom, and independence in the past that contradicts their minority status facing racial discrimination today. The positive space and time of history can undergird a re-framing of the self-creation and its self-perception in the present.[25]

An architecture of liberation, the final example of practicing freedom in the microrealm, flows from the need to avoid or lessen further the intensity of discrimination. Architecture involves how the oppressed, against the grain and threats of the powerful, constitute their lives as well as how they build their homes. The least in society are called to construct alternative means of ordinary living, even in the midst of danger and the threat of discovery. The risk-laden vocation is for the poor to assemble the necessary resources to build an ordinary way of living on a daily basis that endures even within the geography of the oppressor.

No matter how confining the rituals of repression or how enticing the seduction of rewards, the poor and working people must craft an ordinary way of living each day that allows them some control over who they are and what they do. To break away from the formal constructions of life deemed normative by the dominant, a defiant reorganization of lifestyle on the part of the oppressed facilitates the undermining of the prescribed space, directions, and movement allocated to the oppressed.

Moreover, architecture not only includes building a new way of being, but also affects the vocational response of constructing new and, if needed, secret living quarters that the least in society can name as their own. The point is to answer the call of liberation from within. And this summons, at times, will lead to waging a struggle on the architectural front—what type of structure should the marginalized erect in order to have a place they can call home?

The story of the following enslaved black family presents a paradigm of resistance both in the architecture of life and physical living quarters. These ordinary and daily ways of being in the world of oppression and poverty, but not defined or completely confined by them, point to the need to use all types of resources. Simultaneously, this narrative challenges the black poor today to respond to the call for freedom by being more conscious of the relative ease of access to assets for rebuilding some safe dwellings for rest and resistance.

> We had one slave dat runned away an' he had a vault in th' woods fixed jes like dis room an' he had a wife an' two boys dat he raised under dar. . . . Dar wuz a hole cut in de groun'. . . . Den dirt wuz piled on top of dis plank so dat hit won't rain in dar. Den he has him some piping—trough-like—made of wood dat runned so many feet in de groun'. Dis carried smoke way away form dis cave. . . . He had him a hole to come up on lan'. [26]

The ingenuity of this created housing permitted this family to carry on a new life literally right under the feet of the structures of racial oppression. Because this family used sticks, pines, and trash to cover the hole and because the underground pipe took the smoke away from this house, many patrollers, slave hunters, and white masters probably walked over this hole. Consequently, the architecture was fortified against outside detection and attacks.

Inside this architectural structure, the family constructed a daily living space to arrange their freedom from slavery. They built a bed made of rails with a mattress produced from the mother's old dresses. A fireplace consisted of rocks and bricks; and sawed-off wood blocks served as chairs. Cooking utensils came from broken pots and pans found at the Big House. Each scrap of the ingredients signaled a declaration of independence from the architectural imposition of systems of white supremacy, labor exploitation, and gender vulnerability. The master's designated slave shack lifestyle became a thing of the oppressive past.

The family removed itself from the backbreaking labor of plantation drudgery. They no longer experienced the danger of being whipped just because of their skin color. And the mother transplanted herself from unpredictable sexual lusts of white men to a safe space and environment fabricated with her own hands. The runaway slave occupants crafted their framework for living from nature (dirt, trash, and trees), from recycling their own clothes, and from appropriating implements from the oppressor's own home. What is at hand in nature, the mundane belongings of the oppressed, and the resources of the ruling sectors of a society can all be employed for the foundation of a new everyday design and mood of resistance.

Racial Cultural Identity

The Spirit of liberation within oppressed people, particularly black poor and working people, calls them to liberate themselves from the chains of self-hatred, misinformation, and subservience to whiteness as normative.[27] A renaissance of affirming blackness is mandatory as a means of grasping the theological significance of black culture and black racial identity. Many blacks, the majority of whom are at the bottom of American society, still suffer from a longing to be white, either in skin color, hair texture, or some other phenotype form. Likewise, even though it is affected by black culture, white culture reigns as classic and standard in visual, aural, and written formats. To be black in the United States is to be the negative opposite of white texts.

But the theological dimension of black racial cultural identity formation lies not in some movement to bring God to the side of a narrow nationalist cultural self-glorification. Nor is it the hubris of privileging one branch of human kind (that is, the black race) over another (the white race). God has a special word for black folk because God abhors the oppression of African American people who suffer from the heresy of white racism. The color line, the line that whites with power have drawn to establish the "fact" that white is normative, was the problem of the twentieth century and is the continuing problematic of the twenty-first century. Now, however, it accents its effects on black working and poor women and men.

Does the Spirit of liberation within poor black folk call them to be black (that is, to accept the beauty of their own color and phenotype) and "do" black (to affirm their unique contributions to North America and the world)? The answer is a resounding "yes," for no people can turn toward God if they cannot perceive, think, and feel God already in them. Even the appreciation of "whiteness" derives from a healthy, sacred love of the black self. The more strongly African Americans open themselves to love of themselves as a reflection of God's love of them, the more they can appreciate the difference of others.

Theologically, poor and working black folk are the image of God or the imago dei. But, in the United States, to be either poor, working class, or black is to reside outside of the mainstream. Furthermore, to be a poor, working, black person (and even more so a woman) at the same time, means one is classified by the dominant discourse as languishing on society's designated dump heap. Yet it is precisely for the least in society that God the Spirit of liberation has come and Jesus the Spirit of liberation is with. However, the "for" and the "with" connect with the Spirit of liberation already living "in" the black self. The image of God in the black poor is the deeply entrenched Spirit that God's grace gave black folk at creation and that, now through generation after generation, exists by nature.

In addition, this Spirit within summons the black marginalized sectors of society to further liberate their captivity to false white normativity by claiming biblical indicators and pointers of black presence in the Bible itself. Biblical passages refer to Jesus with hair like wool and skin of a bronze color. In fact, the only white people in the Christian Scriptures during the time of Jesus' birth are the European Roman exploiters and colonizers. Not only was Jesus not white, Jesus was from African and Asian ancestry.

Moreover, prior to debates about Jesus' ancestry, arguments continue to surface about the Garden of Eden being located in northeast Africa. The implication suggests that even in the mythos of the creation narrative, Eve and Adam were Africans. Though the Spirit of liberation dwells in all people, no matter how much it might be submerged and surrounded by one's effort to turn away from it and thereby from God, God, in one sense, projected God's African-Asian image into the first human creation. When God said let us make human beings in our own image and created the first human beings in Africa, on a logical level, God was an African who reflected the divine self into human beings on the African continent.[28]

Consensus on God's and Jesus' blackness will, nevertheless, probably be one of the hardest (if not the hardest) theological realities for black folk to embrace. Black people continue consciously or subconsciously to image God as an old white man with a white beard and a white robe. Likewise, Jesus is a clean, fresh pink baby in a manger or a triumphant or bloodstained Italian man on a cross. Perhaps when the liberation Spirit within sweeps through black people with a dethroning of the false theological white portrayals and replaces within black consciousness the true blackness of God and Jesus, the new self will be much closer to fruition.

Still there were enslaved blacks who offer us a glimpse of where the liberation Spirit within can lead the black oppressed today. In certain slave religious traditions, the connection between racial cultural identity and theology is definitely not neutral. For instance, Ms. Charity Moore deployed her own biblical hermeneutic based on faith, a rereading of Hebrew Scripture, and her own direct experiences with black colors and hair textures. She argues and clarifies the creation account's relation to racial cultural identity: "de fust man, Adam, was a black man. Eve was ginger cake color, wid long black hair down to her ankles. Dat Adam had just one worriment in de garden and dat was his kinky hair."[29]

In this tradition, the textual exegesis and contemporary life experiences of the black reader coincide at the point of divine racial cultural affirmation. Again, Adam and Eve, the initial and prototypical human beings, are black and thereby substantiate a claim for Africa as the site of the Garden of Eden. Likewise, it underscores the argument that God or Yahweh was black or an African because the first human image created was an ebony hue. God chose to position the Spirit of liberation in an ebony phenotype, including the "worriment" about kinky hair.

Furthermore, in contrast to the illogic of Eve and Adam being white and thereby only one color, the existence of the rainbow-like nature of color gradation among the black race could account for the eventual diversification and color differentiation produced from the two primal parents. If Eve and Adam were white, it would be difficult to increase color shades in the human race. However, because they were black, Eve's ginger cake and Adam's black colors contained a variety of genetic information capable of giving birth to a variety of colors and characteristics in the overall human family. God called forth the human race out of the dust and breathed the life of liberation into it. That freedom impulse first resided in a black person. And from the logic of some enslaved narratives, this dark body then spawned the kaleidoscopic variety to the entire human population.

Similarly, one interviewer of ex-slave Ms. Mary Minus recorded Ms Minus' recollections about an elderly slave whom Ms. Minus had encountered during bondage: "An old Christian slave who perceived things differently could sometimes be heard to mumble, 'Yeah, wese jest as good as deys is only deys white and we's black, huh.'"[30] In retelling this account to an interviewer, Ms. Minus felt it important to identify the enslaved person who mumbled as an old Christian. Either in the thought of Ms. Minus or in the thought of the old enslaved person, Christianity or faith matters had something to do with the substance of the mumbling.

Restated, the mumbling about racial supremacy of white folk and the affirmation about the humanity of black folk are linked to God and Jesus. In the faith of this unnamed old Christian, racial equality exists because Christianity tells her or him so. This is what is meant by "just as good as dey is." And this "just as good" theological proclamation cuts across what white supremacist culture declares. The latter exposes itself in the phrase "only deys" (that is, "only they are"), which draws us into white-imposed cultural definitional distinctions between white and black. Theologically blacks and whites are equal before God; nevertheless, white culture attacks this norm by creating and sustaining a racial hierarchical structure. Yet there is something that her or his Christianity has given this unnamed slave that empowers her or him to voice theological racial equality. Though living in the world controlled by whites, faith in freedom sustains this enslaved person's knowledge and feeling about racial equality.

Even the actual details of turning away from individualism and use of people as profit-making objects to the liberation in oneself for oppressed humanity touch on racial cultural affirmation. Because of so many years of bombardment of pictures and statues of white European models posing as Jesus, many black folk today, including the poor, worship a white man for their savior, lord, and liberator. To use Bibles with a white Jesus, God, and Mary, to worship at the feet of white pictures and icons of the same in their homes and churches for four hundred years, has an apparent conscious and insidious unconscious impact on blackness, whiteness, and God issues.

As a result, in the process of being "struck dead" by God's Spirit (a popular phrase for religious conversion), many such converts describe a crisis in their lives and the appearance of a white intermediary (Jesus) between the pitfalls of hell and fresh oasis of God's care.[31] The white sacred intermediary leads them to the Eden of divine healing. These most intimate feelings and knowledge of religious experiences have been damaged by consistently imaging God and the intermediary, Jesus, as white men, the same phenotype and color of those who claim earthly lordship and authority over black poor and working women and men.[32]

But one tradition of enslaved faith and witness about the Spirit of freedom in oppressed blacks refutes the white supremacy descriptions of conversion. An unnamed former chattel professes: "When people 'fess religion in these days all you have to do is answer a few questions. Do you believe that Jesus Christ is the Son of God, and if so give me your hand."[33] The speaker who sets out this conversion dynamic establishes the direct democratic and simplistic profession of faith and reception of salvation and liberation. Then she or he contrasts this good news with the white supremacy arguments of others: "I don't believe in all that what the people say about having to

see a little white man. That is all fogieism. What was it for them to
see? Always a little white man." Instead of "comin' through 'ligion"[34]
by way of a white man, poor African Americans converts need only
accept the liberation within themselves to enjoy the new life of salvation and freedom.

The crucial point here is the argument that it is "always" a white
man who bridges between sin and liberation. In contrast, her or his
hermeneutical insights and direct experiences lead this critic to hoist
the antennae of suspicion. If the conversion stories fluctuated
between the visitation of a black and white Jesus and God or if most
of the tales imaged and described mainly black divinities, then the
occasional possibilities of salvation through a white male image would
be less an instance of subservience to white supremacist authority.
In fact, marginalized black folk need only confess their black selves,
with all their warts and brokenness, accept themselves as black, and
through the event of self-acceptance, they can better work with the
Spirit within in the co-constitution of the new self.

Language

The use of language to resist obstacles to freedom and to craft new
possibilities for the oppressed self adds to the revelation of liberating
Spirit in macro, micro, and racial cultural identity formations. The
power and urgency of the linguistic realm is better grasped when one
confronts the stumbling blocks preventing one's response to the
Spirit within. For instance, the language of submission fostered by
oppressive structures and individuals comes as demonic claws from
outside of a person that work to smother the freedom impulse within.
An unnamed former chattel recalls the upside down, racial hierarchy
pressed against her when she was forced to confront her new over-
lord in the form of a baby. "When we got to the house, my mistress
came out with a baby in her arms and said, 'Well, here's my little nigger. Shake hands with me.' Then he come up and said, 'Speak to your
young mistress,' and I said, 'Where she at?' He said, 'Right there' and
pointed to the baby in my mistress' arms. I said, 'No, I don't see no
young mistress, that's a baby.'"[35] Blacks in American culture were
perceived as subservient to whites, including babies. To establish and
confirm this "fact," oppressors deployed a language of submission.
Note that the language is not merely transparent. If this black worker
had consented to the discourse of slavery accountability to a baby,
then this demeaning rhetoric would have also confirmed the racial
political economy. For instance, to hail the baby as a master or lord

over an adult black person would denote and support white folk's right to own blacks as private wealth. Furthermore, such a threatening conversation attempted to ritualize black servility by forcing this black worker to participate unwillingly in a catechism of capitulation. Fortunately, this chattel followed the liberating Spirit within and her common sense, and refused to engage in a greeting that would have required self-degradation.

Mrs. Annie Young, a former slave in Tennessee, models alternative methods to a language of submission when she recounts tales in harmony with the Spirit of liberation within the least in society. Mrs. Young narrates the comical but combative interchange between an enslaved worker and a master. The enslaved black person takes a shoat (that is, a pig) from the master to eat, is caught, and tells the white plantation owner that actually it is a possum, not a swine. The master examines the animal closely and says it is a shoat. "The master said, 'Let me see.' He looked and seen it was a shoat. The nigger said, 'Master, it may be a shoat now, but it sure was a possum while ago when I put 'im in this sack.'"[36]

In addition to the joy, relief, and sense of triumph this humorous black vernacular provides for different black hearers down through the years, it opens up multilayered potential for African American discourse. Mrs. Young's anecdote displays the art of survival in the midst of a close, hand-to-hand combat of diverse intellectual cataloging. The story exemplifies two different worldviews. From the perspective and cosmology of those looking up from the bottom of a racial, gender, and social hierarchy, the criterion of survival serves one's hunger needs. Thus the black worker does not steal but takes, and when it comes to resisting the descriptions of the oppressor, the marginalized perceive phenomena in such a way that they enhance their liberation.

Also, we see the power of naming one's own reality. Language has the revolutionary or counterrevolutionary force to reflect, create, transform, and interpret reality. Similarly, words, paragraphs, and sentences can facilitate participation in the ownership of wealth. The reconfiguration of the shoat into a possum signified the black worker's fight over resources and capital. Accordingly, language offers an important front of struggle between a liberation Spirit and a self-defeating turn to submissive talk of the powerful.

In the case of Harriet Tubman, black bodies as wealth escaped successfully to Canada. The designated Moses of the Underground Railroad smuggling blacks north to freedom, Tubman helped compose the following triumphant song while standing on the threshold of Canada.

> Glory to God and Jesus, too,
> One more soul got safe;
> Oh, go and carry the news
> One more soul got safe.
> Joe, come and look at the falls!
> Glory to God and Jesus, too.
> One more soul got safe . . .[37]

Tubman and her band of escapees not only responded to the Spirit within by recreating themselves as new free people, they teach us the importance of declaring our achievements through ritual. We find them involved in the ritualization of recognizing, acknowledging, naming, and claiming each victory. Ritualization initiates a new tradition that the poor desperately need in order to counteract the oppressive traditions forced upon them. Tradition comprises regularized and expected ways of professing one's triumph over hardship and acceptance of deliverance. It is in the communal act of voluntary participation and joyful anticipation that the self of the marginalized undergoes a dynamic of transformation. Ritual produces signs and symbols to exhibit how a people craft ceremonies to prolong and pass on new ways of being in the world. When poor and working people institutionalize and recognize the small and big victories, they facilitate memory, history, lessons learned, and communicate the necessity of enjoying life. These mechanisms serve to enhance the quality of life and struggle for new ways of being a fuller self.

However, sometimes it is not a question of ritualizing the language of victory, but simply developing a rhetoric for survival. Survival falls short of triumph, but it nonetheless enables the victim to move from victimization to become a survivor who lives and fights another day. Note the difference between only existing in life as an object of negative attacks either outside of or inside of one's being. A victim suffers such an existence. In contrast, oppressed people travel the path from the negative implications of victimization when they become proactive in their thinking and feeling and, thereby, chart some action language for eventual personal and social change. Accordingly, sustaining oneself through duplicitous and subversive language can prove to be one vital dimension of one's long-term durability. Not all of one's life consists of indulging in the glory and heady acts of ritualizing the achievement of goals. Indeed for the poor and the oppressed, most times will entail choosing their battles. To decide which path and to distinguish between options requires a language of survival. Mrs. Bird Walton recalled hearing such a language game played between her mother and another enslaved worker.

> One time de slaves was plannin' a big dance over to de folkes' [Follkes'] place, an' mother was aimin' to go. But dat ev'nin' Jerry de footman come in fum court wid Marsa, an' he say to mother right in front of Missus, "Howdy, Mary, did you know dey was bugs in de wheat?" "What you talkin' 'bout, Jerry?" Missus ast. "Nothin'. Nothin' 'tall, Missus," explained Jerry. . . . But mother knew what he meant. De bugs was de ole patterollers, and dey was comin' roun' to de quarters dat night.[38]

Such conversations created by the oppressed ensure the room needed to plan future acts of maneuver for more healthy spaces and times of freedom.

Another important aspect of responding to the call of liberation from within is linking language formation with healing. God the Spirit of liberation for us serves as the premier doctor for the oppressed. The "medicine" that oppressed people receive cures both physical as well as spiritual ailments. Those at the bottom of society symbolically carry on their shoulders the small group of powerful and rich families that monopolize the nation's wealth. Unlike the latter, oppressed people cannot afford the most up to date advancements in medicine. Hence, they rely on their faith in God's healing powers and the natural gifts that God puts at their disposal. Spiritual recovery and physical healing become successful only in conversation with God. George White became a master at this God-talk regarding medicine. "Dere's a root for ev'y disease an' I can cure most anything, but you have got to talk wid God an' ask him to help out. . . . We is got to talk wid God an' ask Him to do His will, an' He will show us what to do. . . . Dey call us fogy, but I tell you if you don't talk to God, you ain' gonna git far."[39]

Again, for the oppressed, access to medicine is not a given. In certain urban areas, working and poor people are victims of crimes committed by those desperate for income. Even in some rural places, wages do not adequately cover the needs of families. Without health insurance or appropriate protection, many folk are denied treatment by multibillion dollar health corporations. Other oppressed suffer maltreatment or shoddy long-term care. But the rich and the upper classes perceive no need to talk to God about medical affairs because they have monopolized access to these sources. Because they do not own the health monopoly corporations and they do not define

themselves by how much profit they make from these capitalist busi-
nesses, the poor, in contrast, have no material stake in this world and
are more suited for turning to the Spirit of liberation as their final
doctor. Therefore, a language of prayer to the Spirit of liberation
within aids the well-being of the injured.

Finally, a language of sacred healing and reliance on the medicinal
clarity and power of the liberating Spirit not only can make the
oppressed feel better and help them discover relief from ailment. In
addition, hearing about what the Spirit of liberation has done can
produce miracles of freedom. Listening to the word of liberation can
foster actual physical liberation. An ex-slave relayed the following in
an interview after emancipation. "I heard them tell the slaves they
were free. . . . Old colored folks, old as I am now, that was on sticks,
throwed them sticks away and shouted."[40] The power of the word of
emancipation induces a radical transformation in the physical infir-
mities of the oppressed. The point, however, is to rely on the language of liberation in all that poor and working folk think, say, and
do. To think in affirming imagery (to formulate discourse), to talk in
a language of faith (to verbalize imagined texts), and to act on sacred
speech (to witness to language in practice), all signify responding to
the Spirit on the discursive level.

Spiritual Inspiration

The Spirit of liberation implanted in humanity at creation and fostered by nature in each generation can enable the oppressed to
achieve unimagined feats if the oppressed will take the risk and allow
the fullness of the inspiration to blossom forth. To be human is to
heed the benefits and blessings of spiritual intuition and sacred stim-
ulation. Too often marginalized folk plod along amidst the doldrums
of daily drudgery. The excruciating pressures of mundane daily life
(that is, worries about income for food, clothing, shelter, transporta-
tion, safety, etc.) and the more direct and obvious forms of dehumanization (that is, racial, gender, class, and sexual orientation discriminations) can inundate one's capability to have vision beyond the
immediate. With these burdens to bear, pausing to see oneself differently in the future could seem a foolish form of idealism and an irre-
sponsibility to survive financially in the immediate here and now.

Yet precisely by opening oneself to and delighting in the grace of
the Spirit of liberation, poor and working people can, indeed, undertake the frightening but rewarding path to a newness of life. The
sheer willpower of the oppressed proves insufficient, as do good

intentions and thinking one way into changing lifestyles. The force of habit of daily dodging painful demands, sidestepping varied attacks upon oneself, and reacting to powers greater than oneself prevent those at the bottom of society from marshaling adequate power, let alone energy, to change the world and themselves. The vision of what the new self and new Common Wealth can be like derives from the Spirit of liberation within working with the oppressed to co-constitute a new reality. Fredrick Douglass received his powerful inspiration from the Spirit in the process of self-defensive risk taking. "I was a changed being after that fight [with the Negro breaker]. I was nothing before; I was a man now. It recalled to life my crushed self-respect and my self-confidence, and inspired me with a renewed determination to be a FREEMAN. . . . I had reached the point, at which I was not afraid to die. This Spirit made me a freeman in fact, while I remained a slave in form."[41]

Once Douglass opens himself to novel possibilities of acting differently against the slavery structure and its hired torturers, he receives the empowering inspiration of the Spirit. He becomes a new self with respect and confidence. He becomes a "changed being" who attains an adult maturity. Prior to this Spirit-induced transformation, he had the age of a man but was treated like a child and accepted an infantile status in society.

In a word, the Spirit works with poor and working people to compel them to fight against exploitative systems. The resulting effect is an experience of a fuller spiritual and material humanity. The oppressed have no benchmark to judge what it means to feel and be free. Regardless of their age, they still work jobs belonging to others, purchase products made by others, and experience diverse dimensions of society owned and controlled by others. Such a state of existing in a world owned by others provides no option for the least in society to sense a new reality. That is why, restricted by harmful systems and dulled by their own lack of vision to imagine, they hover in a limbo zone between child and adult. But the Spirit inspires and makes them to be free women and men—liberated in substance while structurally dominated in form. ("This Spirit made me a freeman in fact.")

At times spiritual inspiration takes the form of a thought. In another instance it operates as an itching and guiding "impelling" which translates thought into unplanned action. For instance, George Brooks "once left a chore he was doing for his second 'Marster's' wife, 'stepped' to a nearby well to get a drink of water, and impelled by some strange irresistible 'power,' 'jes kep on walkin 'til he run slap-dab inter de Yankees.'"[42] Hence the Spirit has the authority and vitality to possess the oppressed and guide not only their thought but also their feet to a fuller spiritual and material humanity.

Moreover, once the least in society open up to the Spirit within, it will become impossible any longer to turn away from one's call to do God's will of liberation in whatever form it assumes. Old Elizabeth, though free at age thirty in 1796, felt called by God to remain in the slave state of Maryland in order to preach the good news of a new life. At first when "I rose upon my feet I felt ashamed," she reminisces. But "I could not quench the Spirit." Despite overcoming her internal demons of shame, she still faced inevitably the patriarchal and racist dismissals claiming the impossibility of God calling a woman to preach. The elders and the rulers in church, government, and society expressed violent "indignation for my holding meetings contrary to discipline—being a woman."[43] Yet she persevered under physical harm and emotional torture because the Spirit impelled her to minister to both enslaved and free blacks, the downtrodden least in society. On her own, she would have sunk beneath the weight of internal shame and external danger. But one cannot quench the Spirit of freedom.

Inspiration produces and is accompanied by certainty in one becoming a new self when one risks opening the old self to the Spirit's inspiration. Thus the oppressed must dare to allow the emancipatory sacred presence to work with and on them. A definite result is acquiring rock-like confidence that this Spirit will make a way out of no way. One can only benefit from firmness of belief when one releases the fears of the self's weaknesses and of sinful structures to enable the Spirit to do its job. After that, confidence goes with the oppressed on their journey toward a full humanity. Mrs. Mattie Jackson exclaimed "her trust and confidence was in Him who rescued his faithful followers from the fiery furnace and the lion's den and led Moses through the Red Sea."[44]

Speaking of her search for her son sold in slavery, Sojourner Truth confessed fervently: "Oh my God! I kno'd I'd have him agin. I was sure God would help me to get him. Why, I felt so tall within—I felt as if the power of a nation was with me!"[45] Inspired certainty enhances the self-perceived stature of the oppressed. Before opening up to the Spirit, the least in society feel like victimized objects. But a vitalized confidence causes the feeling of growth in one's height and one's power. Moreover, it surrounds one with a cloud of witnesses who serve as an army. Indeed, as in Truth's case, unexpected armies of friends and physical protectors appear where the oppressed previously lacked a feeling or thought that they had anyone on their side in life. Benefiting from this new way of viewing, being, and acting in the world, William Cornish achieved freedom because he "always had sufficient confidence for" attaining liberation.[46]

Ultimately inspiration leads to acting on God's word to change the self and the world. This remains the basic vocational imperative to the query: What has God created and called humanity to be and to do? Even mouthing passages from the Bible and praying do not substitute for struggling for liberation and practicing freedom. For example, Anthony Loney was a Baptist and his white master was a Presbyterian who held family prayers with his slaves. But Mr. Loney felt that the master "was no more than a 'whitened sepulchre,' who was fond of saying, 'Lord, Lord,' but did not do what the Lord bade him." Furthermore, Mr. Loney did not believe that the many prayers of his master would stand up before "the Great Judge," so he fought and reached his freedom.[47] Pious words without direct planning, meticulous organizing, and accountable execution are not only empty, they are like the bloodless face of a sickly hypocrite. God requires us to do justice and not simply utter scriptural texts and hollow prayers.

To act on God's word harnesses the Spirit and resources of the individual and the collective among the least in society. Personal salvation dovetails with and gains its substance from remembering and working toward communal freedom. The individual call by the Spirit of liberation within achieves complete fruition when it turns toward encouraging and enhancing the liberation Spirit within other oppressed people. Individual salvation, in and of itself, is impossible without a commitment to the struggle for the new self and the new Common Wealth. A former chattel's religious experiences verify this theological anthropology claim.

> I was a lost sinner and a slave to Satan; and soon I saw that I must make another escape from another tyrant. I did not by any means forget my fellow-bondmen, of whom I had been sorrowing so deeply, and travailing in spirit so earnestly; but I now saw that while man had been injuring me, I had been offending God; and that unless I ceased to offend him, I could not expect to have his sympathy in my wrongs; and moreover, that I could not be instrumental in eliciting his powerful aid in behalf of those for whom I mourned so deeply.[48]

Conclusion

This book, *Down, Up, and Over: Slave Religion and Black Theology,* is part of my ongoing journey to develop and produce a constructive and systematic black theology of liberation. In my first book, *Black Theology U.S.A. and South Africa: Politics, Culture, and Liberation,*[49] I pursue and present an appreciative affirmation and a trenchant critique of some of the leading black theologians in the world. That text interpreted two major global as well as domestic theological trends: cultural and political thrusts. At the end of that work, I called for a meticulous elaboration of five sources indigenous to the black religious, cultural, and political realities in the United States.

In my *Shoes That Fit Our Feet: Sources for a Constructive Black Theology,* I answered that call by elaborating theologically and systematizing constructively the five sources: slave religion, black women's experiences, politics, folk culture, and social analysis and social vision. At the end of that work, I called for in-depth theological construction of each of the five sources. *Down, Up, and Over* concerns the first source, slave religion.

Along the journey of constructing a systematic black theology, I authored a basic book called *Introducing Black Theology of Liberation.* Its purpose was to take stock of black theology, where had it come from, where is it now, and where might it go in the future. It examined critically the overall movement, trends, schools of thought, and personalities in black theology in the United States. Moreover, an additional purpose for writing that text was to help put my ongoing project in perspective. One does not do theology in a vacuum. Diverse interlocutors and discursive communities always exist.

My basic belief and thought is that the Spirit of liberation is incarnational, manifesting in various realms of human interaction. According to my read of African American experiences, I have chosen to add my voice by building theology based on the aforementioned five sources. Out of these five sources, this Spirit operates on at least the following four levels—macro, micro, language, and racial cultural identity. These four levels are not arbitrary selections, but flow directly from the substance of the five sources themselves. The foundational process of the incarnation of this Spirit is to work with us to co-constitute the new self and the new Common Wealth. The four levels, when working with the Spirit, become disciplines of creativity for the new individual and community. However, along that way, various obstacles are to be confronted, such as internal negative demons that weaken our ability to work with the Spirit of liberation already in us, and disparate systemic exploitations (that is, racism, male patriarchy, class, and heterosexism).

Based on the biblical witness, African American church tradition, and the black community's ongoing efforts toward a full spiritual and material humanity, I firmly believe that the good news for all humanity begins when those at the bottom of society, the majority of humankind, work with the Spirit of liberation to overcome internal demons and participate communally in the wealth that God created and still gives to all humankind equally today.

NOTES

1. The first quote is found in *Unwritten History of Slavery*, 143; the second in Henry Bibb, *Narrative of the Life and Adventures of Henry Bibb*, xi; the third in Blassingame, ed., *Slave Testimony*, 744-45; and the fourth in *Unwritten History of Slavery*, 148.

2. Blassingame, ed., *Slave Testimony*, p. 135.

3. Yetman, ed., *Life Under the "Peculiar Institution,"* 255.

4. Lucy A. Delaney's "From the Darkness Cometh the Light or Struggles for Freedom," in *Six Slave Women's Narratives*, 35.

5. Botkin, ed., *Lay My Burden Down*, 180.

6. In *The American Slave*, Arkansas, vol. 11, pt. 7, 211.

7. Botkin, ed., *Lay My Burden Down*, 8.

8. Yetman, ed., *Life Under the "Peculiar Institution,"* 17.

9. Blassingame, ed., *Slave Testimony*, 688.

10. Craft, *Running a Thousand Miles for Freedom*, 1–2.

11. Estella Jones, *The American Slave*, Georgia, vol. 12, pt. 2, 350.

12. Henry Lewis quoted in Yetman, ed., *Life Under*, 205. Ellen Lindsay also recalled two Negro spirituals which pursued the theme of awareness of the journey home. (1) "I'm bound fer the promise Land, I'm bound fer the promise Land, Thars a better day acoming by and by." (2) "Im' gwine ter tell the Lord all about it, Im' gwine ter tell the Lord all about it, When I reach the promise Land." See *The American Slave*, Georgia, supplemental series 1, vol. 3, pt. 1, 134.

13. Lunsford Lane's "Narrative of Lunsford Lane," in Katz, ed., *Five Slave Narratives*, 17.

14. Lucy Delaney, "From the Darkness Cometh the Light or Struggles for Freedom," in *Six Slave Women's Narratives*, 26. Her mother was kidnapped as a child and made a slave. Solomon Bradley's quote is found in Blassingame, ed., *Slave Testimony*, 372.

15. William Grimes's "Life of William Grimes, the Runaway Slave, Brought Down to the Present Time," in *Five Black Lives*, 76. Mr. James

Bradley confirms this point. "I do not believe there ever was a slave who did not long for liberty. I was never acquainted with a slave, however well he was treated, who did not long to be free. There is one thing about this that people in the free states do not understand. When they ask slaves whether they wish for their liberty, they answer, 'No,' and very likely they would say they would not leave their masters for the world. But, at the same time, they desire liberty more than anything else. The truth is, if a slave shows any discontent, he is sure to be treated worse, and worked the harder for it; and every slave knows this. When they are alone, all their talk is about liberty—liberty! It is the great thought and feeling that fills the mind full all the time." Mr. Bradley purchased his freedom in 1832. "Testimony of James Bradley an Emancipated Slave," found in *The American Anti-Slavery Almanac for 1839*, vol. 1, no. 4, 44.

16. For analysis, statistics, and trends relative to the racial monopolization of wealth in the United States, issues of racial discrimination against African Americans, and perspectives on all areas of black life, see Cornel West, *Race Matters* (Boston: Beacon Press, 1993) and the annual reports of the National Urban League (based in New York City), titled *The State of Black America*.

17. *Six Women's Slave Narratives*, 38; Mr. Scott's reference comes from Still, *The Underground Railroad*, 94.

18. *Narrative of the Life and Adventures of Henry Bibb*, 194–95.

19. Blassingame, ed., *Slave Testimony*, 125.

20. Osofsky, ed., *Puttin' On Ole Massa*, 22.

21. Osofsky, ed., *Puttin' On Ole Massa*, 39–40.

22. Perdue, ed., *Weevils in the Wheat*, 182.

23. Osofsky, ed., *Puttin' On Ole Massa*, 26.

24. Osofsky, ed., *Puttin' On Ole Massa*, 197.

25. Stanzas two and three of this Negro spiritual pour out hope in a future time and space. Hence, part of reformulating a new liberating identity involves faith in the "not yet" of the future based on a belief in the role of God, the Spirit of liberation for us. "O, gracious Lord! When shall it be, That we poor souls shall all be free; Lord, break them slavery powers."

26. Perdue, ed., *Weevils in the Wheat*, 209–10. Martha Showvely, ex-chattel, also tells a similar story of her uncle running away and constructing an alternative to the dwelling provided by his master. In his new way of being, he sustained himself for two years in a house in the ground well stocked with food. See *Weevils in the Wheat*, 265.

27. One of the largest multibillion dollar industries in the black community in North America is the industry catering to blacks attempting to change their racial cultural identity by imitating whites: beauty salons, barber shops, facial and hair products, and, for the black bourgeois class, plastic surgery of noses.

28. See the following black biblical scholars' writings on these topics: Cain Hope Felder, *Troubling Biblical Waters: Race, Class, and Family*

(Maryknoll, N.Y.: Orbis, 1989); Cain Hope Felder, ed., *Stony the Road We Trod: African American Biblical Interpretation* (Minneapolis: Fortress, 1991); William Mosley, *What Color Was Jesus?* (Chicago: African American Images, 1987); and Randall C. Bailey and Jacquelyn Grant, eds., *The Recovery of Black Presence: An Interdisciplinary Exploration* (Nashville, Tenn.: Abingdon, 1995).

29. *The American Slave,* South Carolina, vol. 3, pt. 3, 206.

30. *The American Slave,* Florida., vol. 17, 35.

31. Johnson's *God Struck Me Dead* contains interviews with ex-slaves who recount their conversion experiences. A "little man" as intermediary appears consistently throughout the narratives. The testimony of many blacks today about the role of a white or colorless Jesus in their conversion process has antecedents as far back as slavery.

32. The question of whether or not a white male image of God and Jesus can deliver poor black folk into the realm of the new self and the new Common Wealth has to be situated within the definite historical context and contemporary hierarchy of race, class, and gender configurations in North America. And it has to answer the question of why the scholarship claiming the blackness or African origin of Jesus and God is not taken seriously.

33. *Unwritten History of Slavery,* no name, 22.

34. This phrase is what many enslaved blacks used to describe their conversion experiences. See Will Coleman's "'Coming Through 'Ligion.'"

35. *Unwritten History of Slavery,* 133.

36. Botkin, ed., *Lay My Burden Down,* 4.

37. Nichols, *Many Thousand Gone,* 102.

38. Perdue, ed., *Weevils In the Wheat,* 299.

39. Perdue, ed., *Weevils in the Wheat,* 310–11.

40. Yetman, ed., *Life Under the "Peculiar Institution,"* 14.

41. Nichols, *Many Thousand Gone,* 107–8.

42. In *The American Slave,* Georgia, vol. 12, pt. 1, 133. Likewise, Henry Bibb wrote: "and inspired by an elevated thought that I was fleeing from a land of slavery and oppression, bidding farewell to handcuffs, whips, thumbscrews and chains" *Narrative of the Life and Adventures of Henry Bibb,* 51.

43. *Six Women's Slave Narratives,* 12–15.

44. *Six Slave Women's Narratives,* 7. For other examples of how black chattel deployed a liberation biblical hermeneutic see: *The Anti-Slavery Advocate,* London, March 1857, 22–23; Washington, ed., *Narrative of Sojourner Truth,* 87–88; and Craft, *Running a Thousand Miles for Freedom,* 98. This certainty does not imply naiveté. For instance, John Bates remembered: "Man, Niggers had a hard time. But de Lord brought us thru. Chile, sometime de white fokes done us so bo, I wondered if de Lord heared us pray or not." Here oppression is so bad that it tried his faith, à la Job who questioned God. So there is certainty in God's liberation, but not a naive certainty (John Bates interview, Cade Library Archives, no page).

45. Washington, ed., *Narrative of Sojourner Truth,* 31.

46. Blassingame, ed., *Slave Testimony*, 423.

47. Still, *Underground Railroad*, 114.

48. Katz, ed., *Five Slave Narratives*, 52. Other references to being inspired to do God's word are found in *The American Slave,* Florida, vol. 17, 76; Yetman, ed., *Life Under the "Peculiar Institution,"* 13–14 and 146; and *The American Slave,* Georgia, supplemental series, vol. 3, pt. 1, 4–5.

49. Maryknoll, N.Y.: Orbis Books, 1989.

BIBLIOGRAPHY

Abrahams, Roger D. *Singing the Master: The Emergence of African American Culture in the Plantation South.* New York: Pantheon Books, 1992.

Abrahams, Roger D., ed. *Afro-American Folktales: Stories from Black Traditions in the New World.* New York: Pantheon Books, 1985.

Ahlstrom, Sydney E. *A Religious History of the American People.* Vol. 1. Garden City, N.Y.: Image Books, 1975.

Albert, Octavia V. Rogers, ed. *The House of Bondage or Charlotte Brooks and Other Slaves.* 1890. Reprint, New York: Oxford University Press, 1988.

Allen, Theodore W. *The Invention of the White Race.* Vol. 1, *Racial Oppression and Social Control.* New York: Verso Press, 1994. Vol. 2, *Class Struggle and Social Control: A Pattern Established.* New York: Verso Press, 1995.

Anderson, Daisy. *From Slavery to Affluence, Memoirs of Robert Anderson, Ex-Slave.* 1927. Reprint, Steamboat Springs, Colo.: Steamboat Springs Pilot, 1986.

Aptheker, Herbert. *To Be Free: Studies in American Negro History.* New York: International Publishers, 1948.

Bailey, Randall C., and Jacquelyn Grant, eds. *The Recovery of Black Presence: An Interdisciplinary Exploration.* Nashville, Tenn.: Abingdon Press, 1995.

Baker, Lee D. *From Savage to Negro: Anthropology and the Construction of Race, 1896–1954.* Berkeley: University of California Press, 1998.

Balme, Rev. J. R. *American States, Churches, and Slavery.* 1862. Reprint, New York: Negro Universities Press, 1969.

Barndt, Joseph. *Dismantling Racism: The Continuing Challenge to White America.* Minneapolis: Fortress Press, 1991.

Bennett, Lerone, Jr. *Before the Mayflower: A History of the Negro in America, 1619–1964.* Baltimore, Md.: Penguin Books, 1973.

Bibb, Henry. *Narrative of the Life and Adventures of Henry Bibb, An American Slave, Written by Himself.* 1850. Reprint, Philadelphia, Pa.: Rhistoric Publications, n.d.

Birney, James Gillespie. *The American Churches: The Bulwarks of American Slavery.* 1842. Reprint, New York: Arno Press and The New York Times, 1969.

Blakely, Thomas D., Walter E. A. van Beek, and Dennis L. Thomson, eds. *Religion in Africa: Experience and Expression.* Portsmouth, N.H.: Heinemann, 1994.

Blassingame, John W., ed. *Slave Testimony: Two Centuries of Letters, Speeches, Interviews, and Autobiographies.* Baton Rouge: Louisiana State University Press, 1977.

Botkin, B. A., ed. *Lay My Burden Down: A Folk History of Slavery.* Chicago: University of Chicago Press, 1945.

Bradford, Sarah. *Harriet Tubman: The Moses of Her People.* Secaucus, N.J.: The Citadel Press, 1961.

Browne, Martha Griffith. *Autobiography of a Female Slave.* 1857. Reprint, New York: Negro Universities Press, 1969.

Cade, John. "Out of the Mouths of Ex-Slaves," *Journal of Negro History*, 20 (1935): 294–337.

Coleman, Will. "'Coming Through 'Ligion': Metaphor in Non-Christian and Christian Experiences with the Spirit(s) in African American Slave Narratives." In *Cut Loose Your Stammering Tongue: Black Theology in the Slave Narratives,* edited by Dwight N. Hopkins and George Cummings. Maryknoll, N.Y.: Orbis Books, 1991.

Commanger, H. S., ed. *Documents of American History to 1898.* Vol. 1. New York: Appleton-Century-Crofts, 1968.

Craft, William, and Ellen Craft, *Running a Thousand Miles for Freedom; or the Escape of William and Ellen Craft from Slavery.* 1860. Reprint, Salem, N.H.: Ayer Company, 1991.

Creel, Margaret Washington. *A Peculiar People: Slave Religion and Community-Culture Among the Gullahs.* New York: New York University Press, 1988.

Curtin, Philip D. *Africa Remembered: Narratives by West Africans from the Era of the Slave Trade.* Madison: University of Wisconsin Press, 1968.

Davis, Brion David. *The Problem of Slavery in Western Culture.* Ithaca, N.Y.: Cornell University Press, 1970.

Davis, Cyprian, O.S.B. *The History of Black Catholics in the United States.* New York: Crossroad, 1990.

Didron, Adolphe. *Christian Iconography: The History of Christian Art in the Middle Ages.* 2 vols. New York: Frederick Unger, 1965.

Dillard, J. L. *Black English: Its History and Usage in the United States.* New York: Random House, 1972.

Douglass, Frederick. *Life and Times of Frederick Douglass.* Rev. ed. 1892. Reprint, New York: Crowell-Collier Publishing Company, 1962.

Du Bois, W. E. B. *The Suppression of the African Slave Trade to the United States of America, 1638–1870.* New York: Longmans, Green, and Co., 1896.

Emerson, William C., M.D., *Stories and Spirituals of the Negro Slave.* Boston: Gorham Press, 1930.

Everett, Gwen. *John Brown: One Man Against Slavery.* New York: Rizzoli International Publications, 1993.

Faulkner, William J. *The Days When the Animals Talked.* Chicago: Follett Publishing Co., 1977.

Felder, Cain Hope. *Troubling Biblical Waters: Race, Class, and Family.* Maryknoll, N.Y.: Orbis Books, 1989.

Felder, Cain Hope, ed. *Stony the Road We Trod: African American Biblical Interpretation.* Minneapolis, Minn.: Fortress Press, 1991.

Fisk University Social Science Institute. *Unwritten History of Slavery.* Nashville, Tenn.: Fisk University Social Science Institute, 1945.

Five Black Lives. Introduction by Arna Bontemps. Middletown, Conn.: Wesleyan University Press, 1971.

Foner, Eric, ed. *Nat Turner.* Englewood Cliffs, N.J.: Prentice Hall, 1971.

Foster, William Z. *The Negro People in American History.* New York: International Publishers, 1970.

Frankenbery, Ruth. *White Women, Race Matters: The Social Construction of Whiteness.* Minneapolis: University of Minnesota Press, 1993.

Fredrickson, George M. *White Supremacy: A Comparative Study in American and South African History.* Oxford: Oxford University Press, 1982.

Georgia's Writers' Project. *Drums and Shadows.* Athens: University of Georgia, 1940.

Goldberg, David Theo. *Racist Culture: Philosophy and the Politics of Meaning.* Cambridge, Mass.: Blackwell, 1993.

Gregory, Steven, and Roger Sinjuku, eds. *Race.* New Brunswick, N.J.: Rutgers University Press, 1994.

Harding, Vincent. *There Is a River: The Black Struggle for Freedom in America.* New York: Harcourt Brace Jovanovich, 1981.

Hodges, Graham Russell, ed. *Black Itinerants of the Gospel: The Narratives of John Jea and George White.* Madison, Wis.: Madison House, 1993.

Holloway, Joseph E., ed. *Africanisms in American Culture.* Bloomington and Indianapolis: Indiana University Press, 1990.

Hopkins, Dwight N. *Black Theology U.S.A. and South Africa: Politics, Culture, and Liberation.* Maryknoll, N.Y.: Orbis Books, 1989.

——. *Shoes That Fit Our Feet: Sources for a Constructive Black Theology.* Maryknoll, N.Y.: Orbis Books, 1993.

——. *Introducing Black Theology of Liberation.* Maryknoll, N.Y.: Orbis, 1999.

Ignatiev, Noel. *How the Irish Became White.* New York: Routledge, 1995.

Jacobs, Harriet A. *Incidents in the Life of a Slave Girl Written by Herself.* 1861. Reprint, Cambridge, Mass.: Harvard University Press, 1987.

Jacobson, Matthew Frye. *Whiteness of a Different Color: European Immigrants and the Alchemy of Race.* Cambridge, Mass.: Harvard University Press, 1998.

Jefferson, Thomas. "Notes on Virginia." In *American Catholics and Slavery: 1789–1866,* edited by Kenneth J. Zanca. Lanham, Md.: University Press of America, 1994.

Jones, Thomas H. *The Experience of Thomas H. Jones, Who Was a Slave for Forty-Three Years.* Boston: Bazin & Chandler, 1862.

Johnson, Clifton H., ed. *God Struck Me Dead: Religious Conversion Experiences and Autobiographies of Ex-slaves.* 1945. Reprint, Philadelphia, Penn.: Pilgrim Press, 1969.

Jordan, Winthrop D. *White Over Black: American Attitudes Toward the Negro, 1550–1812.* New York: W.W. Norton, 1977.

Katz, William Loren, ed. *Five Slave Narratives*. New York: Arno Press, 1968.

Labor, John J., ed. *Cyclopaedia Political Science, Political Economy, and of the Political History of the United States*. Vol. 3. Chicago: Melbert B. Cary, 1884.

Magesa, Laurenti. *African Religion: The Moral Traditions of Abundant Life*. Maryknoll, N.Y.: Orbis Books, 1997.

Malice, Kenyan. *The Meaning of Race: Race, History and Culture in Western Society*. Washington Square, N.Y.: New York University Press, 1996.

Mbiti, John S. *Introduction to African Religion*. 2d ed. Portsmouth, N.H.: Heinemann, 1991.

——. *African Religions and Philosophy*. New York: Anchor Books, 1970.

McColley, Robert. *Slavery in Jeffersonian Virginia*. Urbana: University of Illinois Press, 1973.

Meier, August, and Elliott Rudwick. *From Plantation to Ghetto*. New York: Hill and Wang, 1970.

Mills, Charles W. *The Racial Contract*. Ithaca, N.Y.: Cornell University Press, 1997.

Morrison, Toni. *Playing in the Dark: Whiteness and the Literary Imagination*. Cambridge, Mass.: Harvard University Press, 1992.

Mosley, William. *What Color Was Jesus?* Chicago: African American Images, 1987.

Mugambi, J. N. K., and Laurenti Magesa, eds. *Jesus in African Christianity*. Nairobi, Kenya: Initiatives Ltd., 1989.

Nelson, Dana D. *The Word in Black and White: Reading "Race" in American Literature 1638–1867*. New York: Oxford University Press, 1993.

Nichols, Charles H. *Many Thousand Gone: The Ex-slaves' Account of Their Bondage and Freedom*. Leiden, Netherlands: E. J. Brill, 1963.

Northup, Solomon. *Twelve Years a Slave*. 1854. Reprint, New York: Dover Publications, 1970.

Olupona, Jacob K., ed. *African Traditional Religions in Contemporary Society*. New York: Paragon House, 1991.

Opoku, Kofi Asare. *West African Traditional Religion*. Accra, Ghana: FEP International Private Limited, 1978.

——. "Aspects of Akan Worship," 286–99. In *The Black Experience in Religion,* edited by C. Eric Lincoln. Garden City, N.Y.: Anchor Books, 1974.

Osofsky, Gilbert, ed. *Puttin' On Ole Massa: The Slave Narratives of Henry Bibb, William Wells Brown, and Solomon Northup.* Reprint, San Francisco: Harper and Row, 1969.

Owens, Leslie Howard. *This Species of Property: Slave Life and Culture in the Old South.* Oxford: Oxford University Press, 1977.

Painter, Nell Irvin. *Sojourner Truth: A Life, A Symbol.* New York: W.W. Norton, 1997.

Paris, Peter J. *The Spirituality of African Peoples: The Search for a Common Moral Discourse.* Minneapolis: Fortress Press, 1995.

Parrish, Lydia. *Slave Songs of the Georgia Sea Islands.* Athens: University of Georgia Press, 1992.

Pearson, Michael Parker, and Colin Richards, eds. *Architecture and Order: Approaches to Social Space.* New York: Routledge, 1994.

Perdue, Charles L., Jr., ed. *Weevils in the Wheat: Interviews with Virginia Ex-Slaves.* Bloomington: Indiana University Press, 1980.

Piersen, William D. *Black Legacy: America's Hidden Heritage.* Amherst: University of Massachusetts Press, 1993.

Pobee, John S. *Toward an African Theology.* Nashville, Tenn.: Abingdon Press, 1979.

Pope-Hennessy, James. *Sins of the Fathers: A Study of the Atlantic Slave Trade 1441–1807.* London: Cassell Publishers, 1967.

Quarles, Benjamin. *The Negro in the Making of America.* London: Collier Books, 1969.

Rawick, George P., ed. *The American Slave: A Composite Autobiography.* Westport, Conn.: Greenwood Publishers, 1972–1979.

Reedier, David R. *Towards the Abolition of Whiteness: Essays on Race, Politics, and Working Class History.* New York: Verso Press, 1994.

Reinhart, Cornel, ed. *Slavery Days in Old Kentucky by Isaac Johnson, a Former Slave.* 1901. Reprint, Canton, N.Y.: Friends of the Owen D. Young Library and the St. Lawrence County Historical Association, 1994.

Rives, John C. *The Congressional Globe: The Official Proceedings of Congress, U.S. 35th Congress. 1st Sess.* Washington: Rives, 1858.

Schomburg Library of Nineteenth-Century Black Women Writers, ed. *Six Women's Slave Narratives*. Reprint, New York: Oxford University Press, 1988.

Smedley, Audrey. *Race in North America: Origin and Evolution of a Worldview*. Boulder, Colo.: Westview Press, 1993.

Smith, James L. *Autobiography of James L. Smith*. Norwich, Conn.: Press of the Bulletin Company, 1881.

Smitherman, Geneva. *Talkin and Testifyin: The Language of Black America*. Detroit: Wayne State University Press, 1977.

Sobel, Mechal. *Trabelin' On: The Slave Journey to an Afro-Baptist Faith*. Westport, Conn.: Greenwood Press, 1979.

Southern, Eileen. *The Music of Black Americans: A History*. New York: W.W. Norton, 1983.

Steward, Austin. *Twenty-Two Years a Slave and Forty Years a Freeman, Embracing a Correspondence of Several Years While President of Wilberforce Colony, London, Canada West*. 2d ed. Rochester, N.Y.: Allings and Cory, 1859.

Stewart, Charles, and Rosalind Shaw, eds. *Syncretism/Anti-Syncretism: The Politics of Religious Synthesis*. New York: Routledge, 1994.

Stewart, Maria W. "Productions of Mrs. Maria W. Stewart, Presented to the First African Baptist Church & Society of the City of Boston." In *Spiritual Narratives*, edited by The Schomburg Library of Nineteenth-Century Black Women Writers. 1835. Reprint, New York: Oxford University Press, 1988.

Still, Peter and Vina Still, *The Kidnapped and the Ransomed: The Narrative of Peter and Vina Still After Forty Years of Slavery*. 1856. Reprint, Philadelphia, Penn.: The Jewish Publication Society of America, 1970.

Still, William. *The Underground Railroad: A Record of Facts, Authentic Narratives. Letters, Etc., Narrating the Hardships, Hairbreadth Escapes and Death Struggles of the Slaves in their Efforts for Freedom As Related by Themselves and Others, or Witnessed by the Author; Together with Sketches of Some of the Largest Stockholders, and Most Liberal Aiders and Advisers, of the Road*. 1872. Reprint, Chicago: Johnson Publishing Company, 1970.

Stuckey, Sterling Stuckey. *Slave Culture: Nationalist Theory and the Foundations of Black America.* New York: Oxford University Press, 1987.

Trefz, Edward K. "Satan as the Prince of Evil: The Preaching of New England Puritans," *The Boston Public Quarterly* (January 1955): 3–22; (April 1956): 71–84; (July 1956): 148–59.

Turner, Victor W. *The Ritual Process.* London: Routledge and Kegan Paul, 1969.

Vass, Winifred Kellersberger. *The Bantu Speaking Heritage of the United States.* Los Angeles: The Center for Afro-American Studies, University of California at Los Angeles, 1979.

Vlach, John Michael. *Back of the Big House: The Architecture of Plantation Slavery.* Chapel Hill: University of North Carolina, 1993.

Walker, David. *David Walker's Appeal to the Coloured Citizens of the World, but in Particular and Very Expressly, to Those of the United States of America.* Edited by Charles M. Wiltse. 1829. Reprint, New York: Hill and Wang, 1965.

Walker, Williston. *A History of the Christian Church.* 3d ed. New York: Charles Scribner's Sons, 1970.

Washington, James Melvin. *Frustrated Fellowship: the Black Baptist Quest for Social Power.* Macon, Ga.: Mercer University Press, 1986.

Washington, Joseph R. *Anti-Blackness in English Religion.* New York: Mellen Press, 1984.

Washington, Margaret, ed. *Narrative of Sojourner Truth.* New York: Vintage Books, 1993.

Watkins, Mel. *On the Real Side: Laughing, Lying, and Signifying— The Underground Tradition of African-American Humor That Transformed American Culture, from Slavery to Richard Pryor.* New York: Simon & Schuster, 1994.

Watson, Sophie, and Katherine Gibson, eds. *Postmodern Cities and Spaces.* Cambridge, Mass.: Blackwell, 1995.

West, Cornel. *Race Matters.* Boston: Beacon Press, 1993.

Williams, George W. *A History of the Negro Race in America, 1619– 1880.* New York: Arno Press, 1968.

Williams, Isaac. *Sunshine and Shadow of Slave Life. Reminiscences as Told by Isaac D. Williams.* East Saginaw, Mich.: Evening News Printing and Binding Company, 1885.

Wilmore, Gayraud S. *Black Religion and Black Radicalism.* Maryknoll, N.Y.: Orbis Books, 1986.

Wood, Forrest G. *The Arrogance of Faith: Christianity and Race in America from the Colonial Era to the Twentieth Century.* New York: Alfred A. Knopf, 1990.

Wright, Donald R. *African Americans in the Colonial Era: From African Origins Through the American Revolution.* Arlington Heights, Ill.: Harlan Davidson, 1990.

Yetman, Norman R., ed., *Life Under the "Peculiar Institution": Selections from the Slave Narrative Collection.* New York: Holt, Rinehart and Winston Inc., 1970.

INDEX

abolitionist movement: early American Protestantism and emergence of, 32, 42; glory and unity of God as inspiration for, 173–74

Acts, Book of, 196, 251–52

acts of God, black theology of liberation and, 158–62

Adams, Rachel, 78, 119

Adams, William, 190n.15, 195

aesthetics: black redefinition of, 126–28; in creation, 240; of white privilege, 27–28, 48n.48

Africa, as historical source, 259–60

African-American religion. *See also* liberation, black theology of; religious practices of slaves; West African religion: affiliation with Israelites, 159–62; conversion experience in, 227–31; demons within, 227; independent nondenominational in-stitutions in, 105n.71; role of Bible in, 6–7; spirit of liberation in, 157–89

African-Americans, discrimination against, 226

African religion. *See also* religious practices of slaves; West African religion: African self-constitution and elements of, 108; communalism in, 253–54; European characterization of, 18; as source of revelation, 7, 10n.3; theology of, 109–16

Akan of Ghana, 124

Alexander VI (Pope), 43n.6

Allen, W. B. (Rev.), 162

American Colonization Society, 29

American Free Baptist Mission Society, 42

American Revolution, institutionalization of slavery following, 23–26

American Slave: A Composite Autobiography, The, 96n.11

Anderson, Mary, 245

Anglican theology: institutionalization of slavery and, 17–18; justification of castration by, 66; religious justification of slavery and, 30–31, 41, 48n.52, 93–94

anonymity of slaves, fugitive slave notices as reinforcement of, 79–83

antislavery legislation, growth of, in Northern states, 22–23

architecture: of liberation, 260–61; slave redefinition of, 126–28

ascension imagery, in black liberation theology, 233

atonement, meaning of, in black liberation theology, 198–99

attributes of God: constancy and eternity, 177–81; glory and unity, 171–74; grace and holiness, 181–85; righteousness and omnipresence, 174–77; wisdom and patience, 185–89

auction block owners, 102n.59

Bailey, Florence, 98n.33, 100n.44, 116

baptismal rights: legal status of slaves following, 22; segregation of, in slavery churches, 69, 87–89, 104nn.67

Baptists, justification of castration by, 66

Bates, John, 54, 277n.44

bed checks of slaves, 77

behavior patterns, slaves' imitation of white owners, 60–62

being of God, in African-American religion, 162–66

belief systems, of West African religion, 110–16

Berkeley, Dean George, 30–31, 48n.52

Bibb, Henry, 21, 62, 121, 163, 197, 210, 237, 253, 277n.42

Bible: former slaves' interpretation of, 170–71; rebellion scenarios based on, 133–34; sacred word power of slave religion and, 120–24; sermons and catechism of slavery churches based on, 89–94; as source of liberation, 3–6; theological justification of castration and, 66–67

biology: misuse of, by white culture, 2–3; as scientific body of knowledge, 1–2; slavery and aesthetics of white superiority and, 39

black aristocracy, in slave culture, 60–62, 97n.19

blackness, as religious metaphor for evil, 90–93

blacksmiths, torture devices designed by, 69

black theology. *See* liberation, black theology of

Black Theology U.S.A. and South Africa: Politics, Culture, and Liberation, 274

black-white relationships, colonial legislation against, 19–21, 45n.28

bodies of knowledge, creativity and liberation and, 2–10

bodies of slaves: maiming of, as control mechanism, 66–72; recategorization of, as denial of self-identity, 81–83

Bolton, James, 118–19

bondspeople, resource redistribution through, 125–28

Bostwich, Alec, 89

Bradford, Sarah, 129

Bradford, William (Governor), 14, 43n.8

Bradley, James, 246, 275n.15

branding of slaves, 67

breeder-stud configuration, of masters and slave women, 63–66

Brooke, Samuel, 104n.65

Brooks, Charlotte, 137–38, 193, 205, 208

Brooks, George, 271–72

Brown, Easter, 70

Brown, John, 16, 44n.12, 46n.38, 50n.62, 68

Brown, Julia, 191n.28

Brown, Simon, 107

Brown, William Wells, 69, 77, 139–40, 153n.72

Bunts, Queen Elizabeth, 88

burial ceremonies of slaves, white owners' prohibition of, 65–66

Burns, Jennie, 97n.21

bush arbor gatherings, 138

business practices of slaves, resource redistribution through, 125–28

Byrd, Sara, 86

Cain and Abel narrative, 242

Calhoun, John C., 28, 58

Calhoun, Mary, 58

capital accumulation: communalism of liberation and, 251–54; concentration of wealth and, 251–54, 276n.16; slavery as key to, 24–25, 38–39, 53–54, 95n.8

cartography, epistemology of God and, 169–70

caste system for slaves: division of black labor and, 56–59; segregation in slavery churches and, 88–89; whipping as reinforcement of, 71–72

Castle, Susan, 57

castration, legal statutes for, 66–67

Charleston African Church, 134

children of slaves: clothing of, 75; diet of, 74, 100n.45; legal status of, 21, 45n.28; separation parents, 65–66; whites as fathers of, 62–64

Christianity: African self-constitution and elements of, 108; discipline of slaves institutionalized by, 70–72, 99n.41; in Maroon communities, 131–32; prohibition of black-white relationships and, 19–20; reclassification of slaves and suspension of, 81–83; religious justification of slavery under, 22–26, 31–37; slavery churches and, 83–93; syncretized religion theology of slaves and, 135–45; West African religion blended with, 109–16

Citizens Bank of Louisiana, slaves listed as chattel in, 55

Civil War, slavery and, 29

Claibourn, Ellen, 57

class structure among whites, 102n.59

clothing of slaves: caste system of slave culture and, 59–62; as control mechanism for whites, 74–75

co-constitution of self: black theology of liberation and, 158–62, 165–66, 238; Jesus as salvation and liberation and, 221–23; spirit of Jesus and, 193–94

Cody, Pierce, 138

Coleman, Eli, 74

Collins, Bill, 139

Columbus, Christopher, 43n.6

communalism: black liberation theology and, 251–54; in West African religion, 111–16

communication media, micro-resistance and self-creation through, 257–59

consciousness of freedom, 245–51

constancy, eternity and, 177–79

Constitutional Convention, institutionalization of slavery continued

under, 23, 45n.36

conversion to Christianity: legal status of slaves following, 22; missionary efforts involving, 48n.52; racial cultural identity and, 265–66; spirit of liberation in, 226–31, 235; as subversion of black humanity, 83–87

Cornish, William, 273

corn-shucking ritual, theology of pleasure and, 118–20

cotton production, slave labor as key to, 98n.31

courage, as gift of Jesus, 201–5

Craft, William and Ellen, 25, 33

creation, epistemology of, 166–71

creation narrative, 239–51; communalism in, 251; racial cultural identity in, 263–64

creativity: disciplines of, 2–3; as source of liberation, 3–6, 238

Creator, in West African religion, 111–16

criminalization of slaves, by fugitive slave notices, 80–83

Crocker, Sara, 222–23

Crowell, William (Rev.), 33

crucifixion, as symbol of liberation, 232–33

culture: institutionalization of slavery in colonial America, 19–26; religious justification of slavery and, 26–37; white superiority as

basic tenet, 39–40

Curry, James, 166, 243

daily rituals of slaves, 77–78

dancing: ring shout dance, 142–43, 154n.82; theology of pleasure and, 118–20, 149n.17

Daughters of the Dust, 151n.46

Davidson, Elija, 137

Davidson (Rev. Dr.), 33–34

Davis, Cyprian, 44n.13

Davis, Hugh, 19

Delaney, Lucy, 177, 243, 250

demonic spirits, Jesus' liberation of man from, 221–23, 227

Disciples of Christ, religious justification of slavery and, 37

discipline of slaves, white legalization of, 66–72

divine-human interaction: black liberation theology and, 7–10, 10n.3; in creation narrative, 241–42; early black theology and, 1

divine power, omnipotence and mercy in, 179–81

divine revelation: epistemology of, 167–71; of the poor, 215–17; wisdom and patience in, 185–89

Douglass, Frederick, 59–60; on disciplining of slaves, 71; on food rationing for slaves, 73; on runaway slaves,

130, 151n.50; on sacred word power, 121–24; on spirit of inspiration, 271

Drumgoold, Kate, 163–64, 206

drums, syncretization of religion and, 142–43

ecstasy, freedom displayed through, 245

education of slaves. *See also* literacy of slaves: Protestant concern over, after hegemony, 53–54; in slavery churches, 105n.69

elderly slaves, white owners' mistreatment of, 64–65

Emancipation Proclamation, 29

Ephesians, Letter to: eternity and constancy in, 178–79; holiness and grace in, 183–85

Episcopal catechism, use of, in slavery churches, 89–93

epistemology, knowledge of God as, 166–71

Equiano, Olaudah, 17, 44n.14

eternity, constancy and, 177–79

ethics, black theology of liberation and, 158–62

Ethiopia paradigm, black theology of liberation and, 170–71

Euro-American culture: anonymity of slaves reinforced in, 80–83; class structure in white control of slavery, 102n.59; control of

slave life and, 72–78, 238; institution of slavery by, 18, 44n.20; language standards of, 8, 60–62; racial cultural identity and norm of, 262–66, 276n.27; reconstruction of African Americans through, 80–83; sermon and catechism of slavery churches based on, 89–93; West African religion blended with, 113–16, 149n.14

evangelicalism of Jesus, 221–23

Exodus, Book of: black theology of liberation and, 158–62; theological justification of castration and, 66–67

faith: as gift of Jesus, 201–5; Jesus as spirit of, 195–200; in West African religion, 111–16

family structure of slave families, 62–66; fragmentation of, 65–66

fear, conversion dynamic and, 228–31

Ferdinand (King of Spain), 43n.6

Fergus, Mary, 136

Finger, Orleans, 187

folk wisdom: African self-constitution and elements of, 108; black liberation theology and, 234–35; West African religion blended with, 110–16

food: control of slave life through, 72–74, 100n.44; transforma-

tion of, by Jesus, 234

Fox, George, 32–33

Franckean Evangelical Lutheran Synod, 42

Franklin, Benjamin, 27

Fredrickson, George M., 18

freedom. *See also* liberation, black theology of: coded language for, 129–35; consciousness of, 245–51; content of syncretized religion and theme of, 140; conversion as path to, 227–31; creation of humanity for, 239–51; as gift of Jesus, 201–5; glory and unity in, 172–74; God as divine face of, 158–62; holiness and grace in, 182–85; Invisible Institution and, 136–38; Jesus as spirit of, 194–200; as natural state, 242–45; ontology of divine freedom, 165–66; spirit of, among the poor, 215–17; supremacy of Jesus as way to, 223–26

freed slaves, reclassification system as denial of, 80–83

Free Presbyterians, 42

fugitive slaves: newspaper notices of, 79–83; post-Revolutionary legislation concerning, 23

funeral rituals of slaves: right of resistance through, 133; white owners' denial of, 65–66

Gandling, Clayborn, 187–88

Garrett, Leah, 180

gay people, discrimination against, 226

"gelding laws," 66

gender: being of God and, 165–66; humanity and, 210; righteousness and omnipresence and, 176–77

Genesis, Book of: communalism in, 251–52; creation described in, 239–42; holiness and grace in, 183–84; knowledge of God in, 166–71; omnipotence and mercy in, 179–80; theological justification of castration and, 66–67

gifts, of Jesus Christ, 200–205

Gladdy, Mary, 154n.77

glory, unity and, 171–74, 190n.15

God Struck Me Dead, 277n.31

grace: creation of freedom through, 239–51; holiness and, 181–85; syncretism of slave religion and, 145

grammar, as scientific body of knowledge, 1–2

Grandy, Moses, 65

Great I AM concept, being of God as, 163–66

Green, Rev., 76, 82–83

Gresham, Harriet, 218

Grimes, William, 45n.28, 250–51, 275n.15

Gullah society, 134–35, 154n.82

Gullins, David, 87

Hagens, Jennie, 100n.44

hair of slaves, shaving of, as control mechanism, 81–82

Hale (Rev.), 205

Hanson, Francis (Rev.), 104n.69

Hawkins, Tom, 77

Headen, Ambrose, 237

healing: Jesus as spirit of, 196–97, 206, 209; language of, 269–70

Hebrews, Book of, gift of Jesus in, 202

Henderson, Julia, 55

Henry, Elmina, 104n.65

Henry, Jefferson F., 70

Henry, Robert, 88

hired whippers, control slavery using, 102n.59

holiness. *See also* sacred domains: African-American concept of, 165–66; grace and, 181–85

Holy Spirit: theology of African religion and, 110–16; wisdom and patience of, 188–89

Hopkins, (Rt. Rev. Bishop), 33

house slaves, at top of slave hierarchy, 59–62

housing for slaves, 75–78, 260–61, 276n.26

Houston, Rufus, 100n.44

humanity: at bar of judgment, 197–99; in black theology of liberation, 237–75; creation of, for freedom, 239–51; as gift of Jesus, 201–5; Jesus as spirit of, 194–95, 210–15; relationship with God in creation myth, 241–42; in West African religion, 111–16

humor, microresistance through, 254–57

Hurley, Emma, 75

Hyde, Patsy, 145, 154n.86

Ibo culture: ring dances in, 143; suicide within, 129

indentured servants, legal distinction between slaves and, 19

Indiana Yearly Meeting of Anti-Slavery Friends, 42

inspiration, spirit of, in black liberation theology, 270–73

intermediary divinities, of West African religion, 110–16

Introducing Black Theology of Liberation, 274

Invisible Institution: content of, 140; syncretized religion created with, 135–38

Isabella (Queen of Spain), 43n.6

Isaiah, 194; holiness and grace in, 185

Jackson, Andrew, 27

Jackson, Martha, 100n.44

Jackson, Mattie, 253, 272

Jackson, Squires (Rev.), 201

Jacobs, Harriet, 27, 65, 97nn.23

Jagsch, Alama, 32–33, 49n.61

James, Book of, 203–4

James I (King of England), 13

Jamestown, Virginia, slave

culture in, 17–18, 44n.14, 45n.23, 93, 146, 157

Jay, John, 37

Jea, John, 51

Jefferson, Thomas, 27, 48n.48, 68

Jesus Christ: at bar of judgment, 197–99; black theology of liberation and, 158; conversion to, 227–31; gifts of, 200–205; good news gospel of, 200; justification of disciplining and control of slaves through, 72, 84–87; living with, 217–20; message of, in Protestant sermons and catechism, 89–93; power of name of, 205–7; purpose of, 194–97; racial cultural identity of, 263; role of, in slavery churches, 83–93; as savior and liberator, 220–23; self-constitution through, 226–31; as spirit of liberation, 193–235; as spirit of the poor, 215–17; suprem-acy as one master, 223–26; theology of African religion and, 110–16; whites as slaves' intermediary to, 86–87

John, Gospel of, 232; holiness and grace in, 183

Jordon, Stephen, 63–64

jubilant continuous testimony, as form of worship, 141–42

judgment bar, Jesus at, 197–99

justice: being of God and, 165; discipline of slaves and African American vision of, 70; righteousness and omnipresence of, 174–77

kinship networks, in West African religion, 111–16

knowledge of God, in African-American religion, 166–71

Krebs (Rev. Dr.), 34

labor as capital: discipline of slaves and, 66–72; division of black labor for white privilege, 55–59; division of white labor in control slavery, 102n.59; slavery as key to, 24–25, 38–39, 53–55, 95n.8; slavery church as tool for ensuring, 85–87

Lacy, Ned, 57, 100n.44

landscaping, African-American redefinition of, 125–28

language: caste system of slave culture and, 60–62; epistemology of God and, 170–71; Eurocentric norms and standards of, 8; games with, during slavery, 269; homeness metaphor in Jesus Christ, 218–20; institutionalization of slavery and codification of, 40–42; of Jesus Christ, 209–15; of liberation, 129–35, 209–15, 238; misuse of, by white culture, 3; norm of liberation in, 240–41;

origins of black theology and, 2, 7; sacred word power and, 121–24; theology of pleasure and, 117–20; use of, in theology of black liberation, 266–70; of white theology, institutionalization of oppression through, 85–87

Lewis, Henry, 275n.12

Lewis, Isham, 67

Lewis, Lilburn, 67

liberation, black theology of: acts of God as, 159–62; African American faith and, 6–7; in African-American religion, 160–89; attributes of God and, 171–89; being of God as, 162–66; black theology of, 8–10, 158; communalism in, 251–54; content of syncretized religion and theme of, 140; epistemology of, 166–71; eternity and constancy in, 178–79; glory and unity of God and, 171–74; goal of, for African-Americans, 194–215, 231–35; holiness and grace in, 181–85; humanity ex-pressed in, 237–75; Jesus as instrument of, 220–23; Jesus Christ as spirit of, 193–235; language of, 129–35, 209–15; language use in, 266–70; living with Jesus as, 217–20; in Maroon communities, 131–32; micro-resistance and self-creation through, 254–61; omnipotence and mercy in, 179–81;

for the poor, 215–17; racial cultural identity and, 262–66; righteousness and omnipresence in, 174–77; scriptures as source of, 3–6; self-constitution as means of, 108; spirit of, 155; spiritual inspiration and, 270–73; summary and future issues in, 274–75; syncretized theology and, 138–40; as theme of constructive theology, 1–3; theological presuppositions for, 8–10, 157; white control of message of, 86–87; wisdom and patience and, 185–89

Lincoln, Abraham, 29–30, 186–87

Lindsay, Ellen, 275n.12

literacy of slaves, sacred word power of slave religion and, 120–24

Loney, Anthony, 273

love: epistemology of God and, 168–70; as gift of Jesus, 201–5

Luke, Gospel of, 226, 232; Jesus' sermons in, 194, 208, 210; omnipotence and mercy in, 179

macrostructures: epistemology of God and, 167–71, 238; in slave religion, 113–16

Madison, James, 27

Mark, Gospel of, omnipotence and mercy in, 181

Maroon communities, right of resistance in, 130–35

marriage rituals, of masters and slave women, 63–66, 97n.25

mathematics, as scientific body of knowledge, 1–2

Mather, Cotton, 31–32

Matthew, Gospel of: gifts of Jesus in, 201–5; Jesus' healing in, 209–10; judgment of Jesus in, 197, 199; obedience to Jesus in, 233

Mayflower: Pilgrim's voyage in, 14–15, 146; as slave ship, 15

Mayflower Compact, implications for Protestantism in, 13, 85, 93, 155

McCoy, Lizy, 199

McMillan, Bell, 57

McWhorter, William, 70, 184

mercy, omnipotence and, 179–81

metanoia, to freedom, 246–51

Methodist church, split over slavery doctrine in, 36, 49n.62

microstructures: consciousness of freedom and, 247–51; micromechanisms of recreation, 2; microresistance and self-creation, 254–61; in slave religion, 113–16; as source of revelation, 7, 238

Minus, Mary, 264

Missouri Democrat, 132–33

Mobile Com. Register and Patriot, The, 26

Mobile Register and Journal, 79

Monroe, James, 27

Moore, Charity, 263–64

music, theology of pleasure and, 118–20

naming rituals: power of Jesus' names, 205–8; renaming of slaves, control of identity through, 82–83; sacred word power through, 124; syncretized religion and, 139–40, 153n.72; in West African religion, 112–16; white renaming as control mechanism, 82–83

naturalness of freedom, 242–45

Negro pen owners, 102n.59

New England Great Awakening, 32

newspapers, reclassification of slaves in, 79–83

nigger hunters, control of slavery using, 102n.59

norms: of racial cultural identity, 262, 276n.27; as source of revelation, 7–8

Northup, Samuel, 176

obedience, slavery churches as tool for establishing, 84–87

obligation, in West African religion, 111–16

Offley, G. W. (Rev.), 177

omnipotence, mercy and, 179–81

omnipresence, righteousness and, 174–77

"On the Duties of Christians Owning Slaves," 34

ontology, of divine freedom, 162–66

oppression: black theology of liberation and, 159–62, 238–75; freedom from, as gift of Jesus, 204–5, 216–17; holiness and grace and, 183–85; slavery church as tool for institutionalization of, 83–87

ordinary living, micromechanisms of, origins of black theology and, 2–3

Other, Christians' perceptions of black as, 38–39

overseers, control of slavery using, 102n.59

overturned pot ritual, 116, 144–45, 149n.15, 154n.86

ownership, *vs.* communalism, 253–54

pain, expression of, through humor, 256

parenting habits of slaves, white owners' denial of, 65

patience, wisdom and, 185–89

patrollers, control of slavery using, 102n.59

Penn, William, 22

Pennington, J. W. C., 83–84, 194, 198

Philip, John, 45n.23

Pilgrims: origins of American Protestantism and, 14–15, 146, 157; origins of white superiority and, 15, 29, 37–38, 41; theology of, 16

"pilot" as name of Jesus, 207–8

planned reproduction, by slave masters, 63–66

plantation system: impact on black family of, 64–65; resource redistribution within, 126–28; right of resistance in, 132–35; slave housing in, 75–78; slave production of food on, 100n.44; slavery churches in, 88–89, 93–94

pleasure, theology of, 116–20

political economy: communalism and, 251–54; in creation, 240; origins of black theology and, 2–3, 238; slavery as cornerstone of, 38–42; as source of revelation, 7

political structure: consciousness of freedom and engagement in, 247; Jesus' liberation of man from, 222–23, 230–31; justification of slavery in, 26–37; syncretized religion and, 139–40

power, white monopolization of, black theology of liberation and, 159–62

prayer: as gift of Jesus, 202–4; holiness and grace in, 182–85; Invisible Institution and, 136–38; sacred word power and, 121–24; by slaves, white desire to control, 86

Presbyterian Church, split over slavery doctrine in, 36, 49n.62

Progressive Friends, 42

property image of slaves: reclassification system as reinforcement of, 79–83; slavery churches as display of black property, 86–87

property ownership: communalism of liberation and, 253–54; resource redistribution by slaves through, 126–28

Prosser, Gabriel, 133–34

Protestantism: branding of slaves justified by, 67; castration justified by, 66–67; concerns for slave welfare after hegemony, 53–54; control of slave life through, 72–78, 83–93, 238; culture of slavery and, 17–18; daily rituals imposed on slaves by, 77–78; discipline of slaves justified by, 66–72, 99n.41; institutionalization of racism in, 16, 60–62; origins of black theology and, 1–2, 6; reclassification system as enforcement of, 78–83; religious justification for slavery in, 30–37, 52–55; segregated worship conditions imposed by, 87–89; sermon and catechism of slavery churches and, 89–93; split over slavery in, 13–42, 37–38, 83–84; West African religion blended with, 113–16; whipping of slaves justified by, 69–72

Proverbs, Book of, 191n.35; wisdom and patience in, 186

Psalms, Book of: eternity and constancy in, 178–79; omnipotence and mercy in, 179–80; righteousness and omnipresence in, 174–77; voice of the spirit in, 214; wisdom and patience in, 185–86
Punch, John, 20–21
Puritans: institutionalization of slavery and, 18; origins of American Protestantism and, 14–15; theology of, 15–16; view of blacks by, 15, 38

Quakers, split concerning slavery among, 32–33, 37, 49nn.61–62
quill band ritual, theology of pleasure and, 118–20
quilting parties, theology of pleasure and, 149n.17

racial cultural identity: aesthetics of beauty in, 240–41, 262, 276n.27; black theology liberation and, 2–3, 7, 169–70, 238, 262–66; Eurocentric norms of, 8; righteousness and omnipresence and, 176–77
racial hierarchy: internalization of self-disdain and, 59–62; master-slave housing system and enforcement of, 76–78; origins of, in white Christian culture, 18–20; reclassification system as enforcement of, 78–83; slave caste system and, 55–59

Randolph, Peter, 254–55
rebellion scenarios, right of resistance and, 133–35
reclassification system for slavery, 78–83
re-creation process, self-constitution as means of, 108–47
Reed, Reverend, 1–6, 124
Refield, Roy, 69
religious persecution, origins of American Protestantism in, 13–14
religious practices of slaves. *See also* African-American religion: divine right to resist, 128–35; marriage and funeral rituals, 65–66; plantation rebellions and, 132–33, 152n.58; pleasure theology of, 116–20; re-source redistribution, 124–28; sacred word power, 120–24; segregated worship conditions, 87–89; seizure of sacred domain in, 116–28; self-constitution through, 108–47; sermons and catechism of slavery churches and, 89–93; slavery churches and, 83–93; syncretism within, 135–45; whipping as deterrent to, 71–72, 99n.41; white-imposed daily rituals, 77–78
resistance: divine right to, in black theology, 128–35; micro-resistance and self-creation, 254–61

resource redistribution. *See also* communalism: theology of, 124–28
resurrection, consciousness of freedom and, 247–51
Richard, Shade, 87
righteousness, omnipresence and, 174–77
ring shout dance, syncretization of religion and, 142–45, 154n.82
ritualization, liberation expressed through, 267–70
Roberts, Dora, 117
Robinson, Harriet, 243
Robinson, Harry, 124
Robinson, Tom, 243
Rogers, Ferebe, 120–21
Rogers, W. M. (Rev.), 33
Rolfe, John (Sir), 17
roll calls of slaves, 77
Roman Catholicism: American colonial exploration and, 43n.6; early black slave migration to America and, 44n.13
Romans, Letter to, 181, 229
routinization of slave life, as control mechanism, 77–78
"runaway's irons" for fugitive slaves, 68–69
running away: impetus for freedom and, 243–44; right to resist and, 129–35

sacred domains: epistemology of God and, 170–71; of glory and unity, 172–74; Invisible Institutions as, 135–38; pleasure theology, 116–

20; of righteousness and omnipresence, 174–77; sacred word power, 120–24; secular domains intermingled with in slave religion, 114–16; seizure of, in slave religion, 116–28; of wisdom and patience, 186–89

Saltbacks (stolen slaves), 23–24, 46n.38, 47n.40, 131

salvation: Jesus as instrument of, 220–23; sermons and catechism of slavery churches based on, 92–93

Samuel I, Book of, holiness and grace in, 185

Scott, Jack, 252–53

secular signs: of glory and unity, 172–74; sacred domain in slave religion and, 114–16

self-constitution: consciousness of freedom and, 247; divine right to resist, 128–35; Invisible Institution as, 137–38; Jesus as key to, 226–31; micro-resistance and, 254–61; pleasure theology and, 116–20; religion as means of, 108; resource redistribution and, 124–28; sacred word power and, 120–24; syncretized religion and, 139–40; as theme of constructive theology, 1; through freedom, 244–45

self-disdain, internalization of, in slave culture, 59–62

self-identity of African Americans: black theology of liberation and, 159–62; reclassification system as weapon against, 78–83

Sewell, Alice, 142, 154n.77

sexuality. *See also* children of slaves; marriage rituals: castration of slaves as subduing of, 66–67; epistemology of God and, 168–70; of slaves

Shepherd, Virginia Hayes, 190n.15

Shoes That Fit Our Feet: Sources for a Constructive Black Theology, 274

Showvely, Martha, 276n.76

Sibbes, Richard, 18

Siebert, W. H., 4962

singing. *See also* spirituals: jubilant continuous testimony as form of, 141–42, 154n.77; right of resistance through, 130; sacred word power through, 122–24

Sister Kelly, 59

slavery: biological determination of, 21; capital accumulation as result of, 24–25; churches of, 83–93; clothing as control mechanism for, 74–75; consciousness of freedom during, 250–51, 275n.15; continuation of, after banning of, 23–26; control of slave life, 72–78; daily rituals for enforcement of, 77–78; disciplining by whites, legalization of, 66–72; division of labor and caste system in, 55–59; division of white labor in control of, 102n.59; European culture of, 18, 44n.20; family structure of Africans controlled by, 62–66; food as control mechanism for, 72–74, 100n.44; housing system as control mechanism, 75–78; inspiration as survival tool during, 272–73; institutionalization of, in colonial American culture, 17–26; legislative acts establishing, 19–26; migrations in early colonial America, 14–17, 44n.14; origins of black theology and, 1–2; political establishment's support for, 27–28; post-Revolutionary persistence of, 23–26; racial cultural identity during, 264–66, 277n.31; reclassification as control mechanism, 78–83; religious conversion and legal status of, 22; religious justification of, 26–37; renaming of slaves, control of identity through, 82–83; "sandwiching" of Africans during, 23–24, 46n.40; West African religion continued with, 114–16

"Slavery and the Slaveholder's Religion: As Opposed to Christianity," 104n.65

slavery churches: catechism and sermons in, 89–93; confessional gatherings in, 84; as display of white wealth, 86–87; institutional arrangements within, 87–89; as Invisible Institutions, 152n.63; sermons and catechism in, 89–93; white preachers in, 88–89, 104n.69

slave traders, 102n.59

Smalls, Robert, 136

Smith, James L., 46n.37, 186

Smith, Venture, 44n.14

snake imagery, in creation narrative, 241–42

socialization of slaves, slavery church as tool for, 84–87

Society for the Propagation of Gospel in Foreign Lands (SPG), 48n.52

Song of Songs, epistemology of God in, 168–69

"soul sweetener," Jesus as, 208

Southern Baptist Convention, split over slavery doctrine in, 36–37

speculators, in slave trade, 102n.59

spirituals: "Chapter" spiritual, 231–35; consciousness of freedom in, 248–51, 275n.12; evangelicalism in, 221; gift of Jesus in, 202; liberation expressed through, 169–70; living with Jesus expressed in, 217–20; micro-resistance and self-creation through, 259–61, 276n.25; sacred word power through, 122–24; spirit of Jesus in, 211–14; Underground Railroad ex-

pressed through, 268

Spring, Gardiner, (Rev. Dr.), 33

Stanly, Levi, 80

"stealin' the meetin'," syncretized religion created with, 135–38, 152n.63

Steward, Austin, 60–61

Stewart, Maria, 188

stocks, torture of slaves with, 68, 98n.35

Stuart, Moses (Rev. Dr.), 33

"studious silence" over slavery, 34–35

suicide, divine right to resist as, 128–29

Sullivan, Ben, 127, 151n.44

Summerson, William, 185

Supreme Being, in West African religion, 110–16

syncretized religion: content of, 138–40; forms of worship in, 141–45; Invisible Institutions of, 135–45, 152n.63

Taylor, (Rev. Dr.), 33

"technologies of re-created power," slavery churches as tool for, 94

telos, as source of revelation, 7–8

Times, The (Charleston), 81

tithing practices, in slavery churches, 87–88, 104n.67

torture of slaves, 67–72, 81, 83, 98n.35

Truth, Sojourner, 230, 272–73

Tubman, Harriet, 129–30, 267–68

Turner, Nat (Rev.), 133, 135

Underground Railroad: history of, 49n.62; origins of black theology and, 42, 267–68

unity, glory and, 171–74

Unwritten History of Slavery, The, 96n.11

U.S. Constitution: slavery institutionalized in, 149n.14; white privilege institutionalized in, 85, 93–94

vernacular language, liberation expressed through, 267–70

Vesey, Denmark, 133–34

Vinson, Addie, 57

violence, as metaphor in slavery church, 89, 105n.71

Virginia General Assembly, right bear arms denied to black by, 20

visitation imagery, in black liberation theology, 233

voice, language of Jesus and, 210–15

Walker, David, 54, 165, 179–80, 188–89, 204, 207, 224

walking: jubilant continuous testimony and, 142; theology of pleasure and, 117–20

Walton, Bird, 269

Walton, Rhodus, 78

Ward, Samuel Riggold, 13, 34–60

Ward, William, 63

Washington, George, 27

Washington, Lula, 61

wealth: concentration *vs.* communalism, 251–54, 276n.16; slave redistribution of, 124–28

Wesleyan Methodists, 42, 49n.62

West African religion: divine right to resist in, 128–35; drums and dancing in, 142–45; in Maroon communities, 131–32; sacred word power and, 124; theology of, 109–16

whipping of slaves, justification for, 69–72, 102n.59

White, John W., 100n.44

White, Mamie, 107

White, Mingo, 244

Whitefield, George, 32

white privilege: biological and cultural institutionalization of, 39–40, 52; black labor divisions and, 55–59; branding of slaves as enhancement of, 67; clothing of slaves as code for, 74–75; daily rituals for reinforcement of, 77–78; fear of, by blacks, religion as means of conditioning, 85–87; Jefferson's assertion of, 27, 48n.48; Jesus' con-demnation of, 204–5; legal institutionalization of, 24–26; master-slave housing system and enforcement of, 76–78; Protestantism as means of establishing, 88–89; Puritan origins of, 15; racial cultural identity and norm of, 262–66, 276n.27, 277n.32; reclassification system as enforcement of, 78–83; siring of slave children and, 62–66; whipping of slaves as enhancement of, 70–72

Whitney, Jackson, 199, 209

Wiley, Calvin H., 35

Wilkers, Dora, 95n.8

Wilkins, Dora, 81

Willbanks, Green, 225

Williams, Isaac, 141

Williams, Mack, 68, 98n.35

Williams, Nancy, 213–14

Windham, Tom, 244

Winthrop, John (Governor), 15–16

wisdom: as gift of Jesus, 205; patience and, 185–89

women: creation of, 240; discrimination against, 226; glory and unity of God as inspiration for, 173–74; reproduction by, 62–66; tripartite pain of, 174

Wood, Forrest G., 43n.8

woods gatherings: as Invisible Institutions, 137–38; theology of pleasure and, 117–20

worship, forms of, in syncretized religion, 141–45

Yahweh, promise of, in African-American religion, 159–62

Yoruba culture: proverbs of, 111–12; ring dances in, 143

Young, Annie, 267

Printed in the United States
138595LV00007B/5/A